The Collected Courses of the Academy of European Law
Series Editors: Professor Marise Cremona,
Professor Bruno de Witte, and
Professor Francesco Francioni,
European University Institute, Florence
Assistant Editor: Anny Bremner, *European University Institute, Florence*

VOLUME XIX/2

Market Integration and Public Services in the European Union

The Collected Courses of the Academy of European Law
Edited by Professor Marise Cremona,
Professor Bruno de Witte, and Professor Francesco Francioni
Assistant Editor: Anny Bremner

This series brings together the Collected Courses of the Academy of European Law in Florence. The Academy's mission is to produce scholarly analyses which are at the cutting edge of the two fields in which it works: European Union law and human rights law. A 'general course' is given each year in each field, by a distinguished scholar and/or practitioner, who either examines the field as a whole through a particular thematic, conceptual, or philosophical lens, or who looks at a particular theme in the context of the overall body of law in the field. The Academy also publishes each year a volume of collected essays with a specific theme in each of the two fields.

Market Integration and Public Services in the European Union

Edited by

MARISE CREMONA

OXFORD
UNIVERSITY PRESS

OXFORD
UNIVERSITY PRESS

Great Clarendon Street, Oxford OX2 6DP

Oxford University Press is a department of the University of Oxford.
It furthers the University's objective of excellence in research, scholarship,
and education by publishing worldwide in

Oxford New York

Auckland Cape Town Dar es Salaam Hong Kong Karachi
Kuala Lumpur Madrid Melbourne Mexico City Nairobi
New Delhi Shanghai Taipei Toronto

With offices in

Argentina Austria Brazil Chile Czech Republic France Greece
Guatemala Hungary Italy Japan Poland Portugal Singapore
South Korea Switzerland Thailand Turkey Ukraine Vietnam

Oxford is a registered trade mark of Oxford University Press
in the UK and in certain other countries

Published in the United States
by Oxford University Press Inc., New York

First published 2011

British Library Cataloguing in Publication Data
Data available

Library of Congress Cataloging in Publication Data
Data available

Typeset by SPI Publisher Services, Pondicherry, India
Printed in Great Britain
on acid-free paper by
CPI Antony Rowe, Chippenham, Wiltshire

ISBN 978–0–19–960773–0

1 3 5 7 9 10 8 6 4 2

Contents

List of Contributors

Thomas von Danwitz has been a Judge at the European Court of Justice since 2006, and was President of the eighth chamber from October 2008 to October 2009. He received his Doctor of Laws from the University of Bonn in 1988, the international diploma in public administration from the École nationale d'administration in 1990, and his teaching authorization at the University of Bonn in 1996. Von Danwitz was Professor of German Public Law and European Law from 1996 to 2003, Dean of the Faculty of Law of the Ruhr University, Bochum from 2000 to 2001, has been Professor of German Public law and European Law at the University of Cologne since 2003, and was Director of the Institute of Public Law and Administrative Science since 2006. He has been a Visiting Professor at the Fletcher School of Law and Diplomacy, the François Rabelais University, Tours, and the University of Paris I, Panthéon-Sorbonne.

Tamara K Hervey is Jean Monnet Professor of European Union Law at the University of Sheffield, UK. She previously held Lectureships at the Universities of Durham and Manchester, and a Readership and subsequently Chair at the University of Nottingham. She received her PhD from the University of Sheffield. She has written on European social and constitutional law, in particular its application in health fields, social security and welfare, and non-discrimination. She is interested in the phenomenon of 'new governance' in the EU, in particular as an alternative or supplement to 'command and control' means of regulation in social fields. She is co-author (with Professor Cryer, Dr Sokhi-Bulley, and Alexandra Bohm) of *Research Methods in EU and International Law* (Hart, 2010); co-author (with Professor McHale, University of Leicester) of *Health Law and the European Union* (Cambridge University Press, 2004); and author of *European Social Law and Policy* (Longman, 1998).

Roberto Mastroianni is Professor of European Union Law at the University 'Federico II' in Naples, Italy, where he also teaches Media Law. He holds a PhD in European Law from the University of Bologna, as well as an LLM from the Penn State Dickinson School of Law in Carlisle (PA), USA. He was a Researcher of International Law at the University of Florence from 1992 to 1997, and served as *Référendaire* at the European Court of Justice in Luxembourg, in the Cabinets of Advocate General Giuseppe Tesauro and Antonio Saggio from 1997 to 2000. He also researched International Copyright Law and in European Media Law at the Universities of Geneva, Amsterdam, and New York (NYLS). Among his publications are a treatise on International Copyright Law (Giuffré, 1997), a book on the recent reform of Italian Broadcasting Law (Giappichelli, 2004), and a book on the Audiovisual Services Directive (Giappichelli, 2009), as well as several articles and notes on EU law, international law, and media law.

Christopher McCrudden received his legal education in Belfast (LLB), Yale University (LLM), and Oxford (D Phil). He has been a fellow of Lincoln College, Oxford since 1980. He is currently also a Professor in Human Rights Law at the University of Oxford, the William W Cook Global Law Professor at the University of Michigan, and a barrister at Blackstone Chambers, London. One of his main interests is in the field of public procurement law, with a particular specialization in the relationship between public procurement and social policies. He combines this academic research with an interest in making connections between theory and practice. He has served on several governmental committees, including the (Northern Ireland) Procurement Board. He has also advised the European Commission, the United Nations, and the ILO on the linkage between procurement and social policies in the past. He has published extensively on these issues, in particular *Buying Social Justice* (Oxford University Press, 2007), which won the Certificate of Merit from the American Society of International Law in 2008.

Hans-W Micklitz is Professor of Economic Law at the European University Institute, on leave from the Jean Monnet Chair of Private Law and European Economic Law at the University of Bamberg, Germany. He is also head of the Institute of European and Consumer Law (VIEW) in Bamberg. He has undertaken consultancies for OECD in Paris, UNEP in Geneva/Nairobi, and CI (Consumers International) in The Hague/Penang Malaysia. He has been a Visiting Professor at the University of Michigan and at Somerville College at the University of Oxford, and was a Jean Monnet Fellow at the European University Institute. He was co-founder of the Centre of Excellence at the University of Helsinki. His main fields of research interest include European Law, European Private Law, and Consumer Law.

Heike Schweitzer is Professor for Private Law, European Economic Law, and Competition Law at the University of Mannheim, Germany. She previously held the chair for competition law at the European University Institute and was an assistant professor at Hamburg University from 2004 to 2006. Heike Schweitzer studied law at the University of Freiburg, Germany and at the Yale Law School (USA) where she received her LLM degree in 2000. She was a researcher, and then a senior researcher at the Max-Planck-Institute for Comparative and International Private Law from 1996 to 2004, and did research at the Université Paris I Panthéon-Sorbonne and at Columbia University from 2005 to 2006. Her main research interests lie in the area of European, German, and comparative competition law and regulation; European, German, and US corporate law; and comparative private law. She has published widely on issues of competition law and on 'services of general economic interest'.

Table of Cases

CASES OF THE EUROPEAN COURT

ALPHABETICAL TABLE OF CASES OF THE EUROPEAN COURT

EFTA CASES

EUROPEAN COURT OF HUMAN RIGHTS CASES

NATIONAL CASES

France

United Kingdom

DECISIONS OF NATIONAL COMPETITION AUTHORITIES

Table of Legislation

TREATIES

INTERNATIONAL LABOUR ORGANIZATION INSTRUMENTS

EU LEGISLATION

Regulations

Directives

Decisions

NATIONAL LEGISLATION

Belgium

France

Hungary

Ireland

Finland

Germany

1

Introduction

Marise Cremona

On 9 May 2010 Mario Monti published a report commissioned by the President of the European Commission called 'A New Strategy for the Single Market: At the Service of Europe's Economy and Society'. As its title suggests, a theme of the report is the challenge posed to the single market—which is 'less popular than ever, more needed than ever'[1]—by social concerns. Monti argues:

> the Lisbon Treaty has introduced, even formally, the objective of achieving a 'highly competitive social market economy' [Art 3(3) TFEU]. If the *market* and the *social* components do not find an appropriate reconciliation, something has to give in. Following the [2009 financial] crisis, with the declining appetite for the market and the increasing concern about inequalities, it is by no means clear that it would be the market, i.e. the single market, to prevail. A distinct category of social concerns has to do with services of general economic interest and the real or perceived threats posed to them by the single market.[2]

As Monti recognizes, this concern is not a new phenomenon: 'Since the nineties, the place of public services within the single market has been a persistent irritant in the European public debate.'[3] The drafters of the original Treaty of Rome had seen the need to include provision for state monopolies, public undertakings, and services of general economic interest,[4] but it was indeed during the late 1980s and 1990s that the impact of market integration on public services became really visible, as a result both of decisions of the Court of Justice (for example relating to broadcasting and health), and of the legislative programme for the liberalization of key public services, including postal and telecommunication services. Controversies arose over the application of the free movement rules,[5] the role of state aid in relation to public service obligations,[6] and the use of competition policy and the powers of the Commission

[1] 'A New Strategy for the Single Market: At the Service of Europe's Economy and Society,' report to the President of European Commission José Manuel Barroso by Mario Monti, 9 May 2010, 20.
[2] Ibid 26.
[3] Ibid 73.
[4] Arts 37 and 106 TFEU (ex Arts 31 and 86 EC).
[5] Case C–260/89 *Elliniki Radiophonia Tiléorassi AE v Dimotiki Etairia Pliroforissis* [1991] ECR I–02925.
[6] Case C–280/00 *Altmark Trans GmbH* [2003] ECR I–7747.

under Article 106(3) TFEU (ex Article 86 EC).[7] The increased activism of the Commission in the wake of the '1992' single market programme, followed by the Council's willingness to use its legislative competence to open up public services to competition, produced a response: the introduction by the Treaty of Amsterdam of Article 16 EC (now Article 14 TFEU) which reaffirmed the importance of services of general economic interest, their link to the Union's 'shared values' and 'their role in promoting social and territorial cohesion'. The Treaty of Lisbon amends this provision in two ways: it includes a specific decision-making power which operates alongside the provision for single market legislation in Article 114 TFEU and for Commission action under Article 106 TFEU; and it adds an express recognition of 'the competence of Member States, in compliance with the Treaties, to provide, to commission and to fund such services'.[8] Access to services of general economic interest 'as provided for in national laws and practices, in accordance with the Treaties' is to be recognized and respected by the Union, according to the Charter of Fundamental Rights.[9] In addition, a new Protocol on services of general interest sets out what the Union's 'shared values' mean in this context:

— the essential role and the wide discretion of national, regional and local authorities in providing, commissioning and organizing services of general economic interest as closely as possible to the needs of the users;
— the diversity between various services of general economic interest and the differences in the needs and preferences of users that may result from different geographical, social or cultural situations;
— a high level of quality, safety and affordability, equal treatment and the promotion of universal access and of user rights.[10]

Thus public services in the European Union challenge the roles of state and market, and raise complex questions about the relationship between the rules governing free movement and competition policy.[11] They have also raised questions, only partly answered by Article 106 TFEU, of the intersection between national and EU regulation, and the space remaining for the Member States' policy

[7] Cases 188–190/80 *France, Italy, UK v Commission* [1982] ECR 2545; Case C–202/88 *France v Commission* [1991] ECR I–1223; Cases C–271, 281, 289/90 *Spain, Belgium, Italy v Commission* [1992] ECR I–5833.

[8] Art 14 TFEU provides:

> 'Without prejudice to Article 4 of the Treaty on European Union or to Articles 93, 106 and 107 of this Treaty, and given the place occupied by services of general economic interest in the shared values of the Union as well as their role in promoting social and territorial cohesion, the Union and the Member States, each within their respective powers and within the scope of application of the Treaties, shall take care that such services operate on the basis of principles and conditions, particularly economic and financial conditions, which enable them to fulfil their missions. The European Parliament and the Council, acting by means of regulations in accordance with the ordinary legislative procedure, shall establish these principles and set these conditions without prejudice to the competence of Member States, in compliance with the Treaties, to provide, to commission and to fund such services.'

Cf also with respect to healthcare, Art 168(7) TFEU.

[9] Charter of Fundamental Rights, Art 36.

[10] Protocol No 26 on Services of General Interest, Art 1.

[11] J Baquero Cruz, 'Beyond Competition: Services of General Interest and European Community Law' in G de Búrca (ed), *EU Law and the Welfare State: In Search of Solidarity* (OUP 2005).

choices in a context of market integration. Within the EU, then, we see a debate not only over the balance between state control and market freedom, but also over the relationship between EU regulation and national policy choices; the Commission has referred to the 'joint responsibility' of Union and Member States recognized by the Protocol.[12]

This collection of essays is intended to contribute to this ongoing debate. But before going further in introducing the individual chapters, we should first pause for a moment over terminology. The title of this book uses the more generally used term, public services, and this is also the term used by Monti in the relevant section of his recent report, although the term 'social services' has also been used,[13] and EU documents increasingly use the term 'services of general interest'. Public services are not necessarily publicly owned, or operated by public undertakings; they may be privately owned but subjected to regulation in the public interest. Member States may decide on the extent to which services of general interest should be publicly owned,[14] but the degree of public ownership does not determine the application of EU rules. As the Commission puts it:

> Services of general interest . . . can be defined as the services, both economic and non-economic, which the public authorities classify as being of general interest and subject to specific public service obligations. This means that it is essentially the responsibility of public authorities, at the relevant level, to decide on the nature and scope of a service of general interest. Public authorities can decide to carry out the services themselves or they can decide to entrust them to other entities, which can be public or private, and can act either for-profit or not for-profit.[15]

Articles 14 and 106 TFEU refer to 'services of general economic interest' (SGEI). Protocol 26 introduces for the first time at the level of primary law the concept of 'services of general interest', while containing two articles, one relating to services of general economic interest (Article 1) and the other to 'non-economic services of general interest' (Article 2). The difference between them is not defined. According to the Commission,[16] the latter involve 'traditional state prerogatives' and include police, justice, and statutory social security schemes, while SGEI include telecommunications, electricity, gas, transport, postal services, public service broadcasting,

[12] Commission Communication 'Services of General Interest, including social services of general interest: a new European commitment', COM (2007) 725 final, 3. Earlier Commission policy papers include Communication on Services of general interest in Europe, [1996] OJ C 281/3; Commission Communication on Services of general interest in Europe, COM (2000) 580 final, of 20 September 2000; Report to the Laeken European Council on services of general interest, COM (2001) 598 of 17 October 2001; Communication on Services of general interest in Europe, [2001] OJ C 17/4; Green Paper on services of general interest COM (2003) 270 of 21 May 2003; White Paper on services of general interest COM (2004) 374 of 12 May 2004; Communication on Implementing the Community Lisbon programme: social services of general interest in the European Union, COM (2006) 177.

[13] See n 1 above. Although section 3.3 is headed 'Social Services', it refers in the text to 'public services'.

[14] Art 345 TFEU (ex Art 295 EC) provides that 'The Treaties shall in no way prejudice the rules in Member States governing the system of property ownership.'

[15] COM (2007) 725 final; see n 12 above, 3.

[16] Ibid 4–5.

waste management, and water supply. The key to the distinction, however, is not sectoral, nor based on the status of the provider or the method of funding, but rather the nature of the activity and the conditions under which the service operates—a functional approach—and we will return at the end of this introduction to some of the implications of this.

A service will be economic if it is normally provided for remuneration, although it is not necessarily the recipient that pays for the services received. Consequently the same undertaking may provide both economic and non-economic services,[17] and the distinction is highly relevant for the operation of EU rules. SGEI are subject to internal market, public procurement, consumer protection, competition, and state aids rules, subject to the possibility of derogations under Article 106(2) TFEU. In the case of some SGEI, such as telecommunications, gas and electricity, postal services, and (partially) broadcasting, a specific EU regulatory regime applies. Non-economic services of general interest, on the other hand, are not subject to internal market or competition rules, precisely because they are non-economic; they are, however, subject to general Treaty rules such as non-discrimination. These categorizations and different terminologies are confusing (and have not been helped by the differentiated sector-based exclusions from the Services Directive[18]), and Ross has pointed to the need to escape 'the unproductive search for resolution by hard definitional boundaries'.[19] In Chapter 3, Micklitz traces the debate over the meaning of these terms and indeed argues that neither the EU institutions nor the Member States have seriously attempted a clear delimitation between the categories of public service.

The fragmented nature of EU rules on services of general interest is probably inevitable given the diverse nature of these services in themselves and their regulation in different Member States. In practice this means considerable scope for Commission and Court discretion in applying the rules to specific issues, for example to financial compensation for public service obligations.[20] The Monti report took the view that the added value of a horizontal framework regulation on SGEI would be small; it would be more useful to identify clear gaps and instances where greater clarity and/or flexibility is required. In the application of competition (including state aid) rules a key concern has been the scope and implementation of public service and especially universal service obligations. The application of internal market rules to public services funded by the state (such as health services) has created challenges to national systems as both recipients and service providers seek to rely on rights of free movement.

[17] See, eg, Case C–82/01P *Aéroports de Paris v Commission* [2002] ECR I–09297, paras 68–82.

[18] Directive 2006/123/EC on services in the internal market [2006] OJ L 376/36.

[19] M Ross, 'Promoting Solidarity: From public services to a European model of competition?' (2007) 44 CML Rev 1057, 1059. On the classification of social services, see Commission Communication COM (2007) 725, n 12 above, and Schweitzer in ch 2 of this volume.

[20] See, eg, Commission Decision 2005/842/EC on the application of Article 86(2) of the EC Treaty to State aid in the form of public service compensation granted to certain undertakings entrusted with the operation of services of general economic interest, [2005] OJ L 312/67; Community framework for State aid in the form of public service compensation [2005] OJ C 297/4.

This collection of essays, which is based on a series of specialized courses given as part of the Academy of European Law's summer course on the Law of the European Union at the European University Institute in July 2008, attempts to present a picture of the most important current issues relating to market integration and public services in the EU, while addressing some of the more underlying systemic questions. The first two chapters consider public services and markets (Schweitzer), and public services and the consumer (Micklitz) respectively. We then turn to the application to public services of two specific branches of EU law, relating first to competition: state aids (Von Danwitz), and then to the internal market: procurement law (McCrudden). The final two chapters examine two public service sectors where the mix of Treaty rules, case law, and legislation has operated in rather different ways: public service media (Mastroianni) and health services (Hervey).

Schweitzer's initial chapter argues that 'the persistent friction' between EU law and the Member States' public service traditions is the result of 'fundamentally different conceptions of the role of markets and the role of states'. Although, she argues, accommodations may be possible case by case, the different underlying visions account for the persistence of the debate. These different visions are explored here, both in terms of different conceptions within Member States of public service, *service public* and *Daseinsvorsorge*, and of the evolution within EU law of the principles and concepts designed to mediate between national public service regimes and free movement, competition and state aid rules. The chapter provides an overall assessment of the approach of the Court of Justice to the issues that will be explored in subsequent chapters, ranging from special and exclusive rights, the 'solidarity exception' for national social security schemes, the 'Altmark package', the application of free movement and public procurement rules where SGEIs are outsourced, to the ability of the Member States to define an SGEI and the concept of 'entrustment', and the application of the proportionality test under Article 106(2) TFEU.

In considering the role of secondary legislation, Schweitzer points out that while liberalization of the network industries such as energy and postal services has—since the earlier Telecommunications Directives adopted by the Commission under what is now Article 106(3) TFEU—been based on the internal market legal base (Article 114 TFEU), negotiations within the Council and Parliament have nonetheless been conducted 'in the shadow' of the EU Treaty rules and in particular Article 106(2) TFEU. She identifies three patterns of approach in the legislated sectors: the 'universal service' model (typical in telecommunications, postal services, and to some extent energy) 'based on the presumption that the protection of well-defined consumer interests and full competition can be made compatible by an adequate set of framework rules'; the 'regulated competition' model, used for public passenger transport which accepts exclusive rights to provide a specific SGEI but requires periodic competition *for* the market; and cases where even competition *for* the market seems incompatible with the values attached to the service (as, for example, public broadcasting).

A number of uncertainties still remain but, since a conclusion to be drawn from this analysis is that 'EU law has not taken a radical stance towards national public service regimes', it is not so obvious why the apparent tension Monti refers to is still so acute. Where exactly does the tension lie? It is not, Schweitzer argues, simply between public service and competition; nor is it simply a matter of inroads into traditional preserves of state sovereignty—although Schweitzer recognizes the 'culture shock' to the Member States of having to subject their policy choices to transparency and external (legal) scrutiny. Instead Schweitzer points to a 'fundamental contrast in philosophy' between the traditional Member State opposition between the market and the public interest on the one hand, and the EU's underlying reliance on the link between individual economic rights and the European 'general interest' on the other. It is this that explains the attempts at different times to engage in adjustments to the Treaty: the introduction in the Amsterdam Treaty of Article 16 EC, its amendment in Article 14 TFEU, and the adoption of the Protocol on services of general interest. Nevertheless, the social-market approach is so deeply engrained in the EU's structure that Article 16 EC, though by no means irrelevant, did not lead to a significant shift in approach and neither, Schweitzer predicts, will Article 14 TFEU. Considering the more promising avenues for the future development of EU law on SGEIs, the concept of the universal service is one of its most important achievements, demonstrating the possibility of combining public interest and open markets, European and national policy choices, and public monopoly providers with user/consumer interests.

Schweitzer's conclusion on universal service is that it is 'essentially consumer protection. It provides a safety net for those consumers whom, due to geographical or social disadvantages, the market might exclude'. In the next chapter Micklitz follows through this link between universal service and consumer protection: 'EC law on universal services has and is yielding a new social policy-oriented consumer *leitbild*—the protection of the vulnerable consumer'. It is even conceivable that the developing concept of universal service might fill the gap left by the move within EU consumer law away from the vulnerable citizen-consumer and towards the 'circumspect' consumer-shopper. Having traced the debate on economic and non-economic services of general interest through to the Treaty of Lisbon, he shows how the concept of universal service has migrated from the network industries such as telecommunications to SGEI more generally, services of general interest, even possibly including non-economic services. He then goes on to analyse the universal service in terms of the contractual relationship: the move from a bilateral relationship between customer and the state monopoly governed by public law, to a triangular relationship between the citizen-consumer, the supplier, and the regulatory agency, on the boundary of private and public law.

This relationship, in the context of universal services, is increasingly seen in rights-based, constitutional terms; the inclusion of Article 36 in the Charter of Fundamental Rights, with its emphasis on access to SGEI and social and territorial cohesion, is one example of this process,[21] as is the extension of the concept of

[21] See n 9 above.

universal service in the *BUPA-Ireland* case. Micklitz agrees with the conclusion of Hervey in Chapter 7, that the main contribution of that case is the Court's wide view of what constitutes a service of general economic interest, and indeed would go further in seeing the case as of potentially 'overwhelming importance' in defining the scope and content of universal service obligations. The Protocol on services of general interest is another example of the constitutionalization process: as Micklitz points out, SGEIs are 'upgraded from a mere defence in Article 106(2)' to a value shared by the Union as a whole, and among these shared values are universal access and user rights; indeed the Protocol may be said to provide an indication of the content of the universal service obligation, including affordability and equal treatment. Towards the end of this chapter, the potential for the expansion of the universal service is tested in the context of financial services, and in particular banking. Could, or should, the private banking sector be obliged to grant all citizens access to a private bank account? The Monti report indeed recommends that the Commission should consider proposing a regulation that would entitle all citizens to a number of basic banking services.[22] Proposals relating to broadband internet access could also be made.[23]

One of the ways in which states ensure the supply of a universal service is by compensating suppliers, and here the EU's state aids rules have played a crucial part. This is the theme of Von Danwitz's chapter on the concept of state aid in liberalized sectors. The starting point is the specific mandate of state aid control, to eliminate selective distortions of competition resulting from specific state intervention, as opposed to what Von Danwitz calls the 'general, far-reaching regulatory mandate to maintain a level playing field' for all undertakings in the single market, the province of general competition, and indeed free movement law. Cross-subsidization has been recognized as falling within Article 106(2) TFEU (ex Article 86(2) EC) at least since the *Corbeau* case,[24] in the context of postal services; the development of principles for the application of state aid controls is more recent.[25] As Von Danwitz points out, it may be that the new legal basis provided by Article 14 TFEU will to some extent replace the instruments hitherto used to address the status and operation of public services in the single market; however, state aid has been and is likely to remain of fundamental importance. From the perspective of this author, the issues raised concern not only the technicalities of cross-subsidization, but also the powers of the European Commission in assessing state aids and the role of the courts (in particular the Court of Justice), and the extent and nature of judicial review of Commission decisions.

In Chapter 5 we turn to the implementation of rights of free movement in the application of EU rules on public sector procurement. Through the lens of the

[22] Monti report, see n 1 above, 74.

[23] Monti report, see n 1 above, 75. In fact since 1 July 2010 all telecommunications companies in Finland are obliged to provide all customers with broadband internet access of a minimum 1 Mbps.

[24] Case C–320/91 *Corbeau* [1993] ECR I–2533.

[25] Case C–280/00 *Altmark Trans*, see n 6 above and subsequent Commission Decision, n 20 above.

Rüffert case,[26] in which conditions designed to protect collective wage agreements were attached to public procurement contracts, McCrudden discusses the interaction of municipal, state, and federal procurement laws in Germany, and their compatibility with EU law on freedom to provide services. Here, the debate on the relationship between open markets and social objectives takes place at a national as well as a European level and involves different levels of government. In *Rüffert* the fact that the contested measure applied only to public contracts called into question, for the Court of Justice, its effectiveness as a means to ensure the protection of workers. McCrudden argues that the Court could and should have taken more seriously the use of procurement contracts to achieve social objectives, as indeed it has done in a series of procurement cases—a line of reasoning that the *Rüffert* judgment appears to ignore.[27] The Procurement Directives themselves address this issue, and would have provided firmer ground from which to consider the application of Article 56 TFEU (ex Article 49 EC) to the balance between market opening and social concerns.

McCrudden also points to the distinction between equal treatment of economic operators, as envisaged in the Procurement Directives, and non-discrimination on grounds of nationality. Whereas reverse discrimination may be permissible under Article 56 TFEU,[28] it is by no means clear that it is allowed by the Procurement Directives, which insist on equal treatment in balancing the market opening and social dimensions of procurement regulation.[29] Here, then, we see the Court failing to recognize the salience of legislation—and indeed its own line of judgments—which have always accepted the specific role played by public procurement in promoting social policies and public values.

The two final chapters in this volume are directed at contrasting examples of public services: public health services and public service broadcasting. Public service broadcasting has its own Protocol, dating from the Amsterdam Treaty and affirming its public service remit 'as conferred, defined and organised by each Member State',[30] but the first cases involving broadcasting date from the early 1970s,[31] laying down some of the fundamental principles on the freedom to provide services, and there is a plentiful case law on the application of the free movement rules, state aids, and Article 106 TFEU to broadcasting, as well as the Television Without Frontiers Directive and now the Audiovisual Media Services Directive. The key

[26] Case C–346/06, *Rüffert v Land Niedersachsen* [2008] IRLR 467 (ECJ).

[27] See Commission Communication on Community Law Applicable to Public Procurement and the Possibilities for Integrating Social Considerations into Public Procurement [2001] OJ C 333/27.

[28] See, eg, Case C–76/90 *Manfred Säger v Dennemeyer & Co Ltd* [1991] ECR I–04221. As a result of the decision in *Rüffert* locally based contractors may be under a disadvantage since they are required to comply with the domestic law on minimum wages, whereas out-of-state contractors cannot be required to do so.

[29] In this respect the Procurement Directives are very different from 'minimum harmonization' Directives such as, in a different field, the Audiovisual Media Services Directive which permits Member States to impose stricter rules on media service providers within their jurisdiction: Directive 2010/13/EU OJ L 95/1, Art 4; see ch 6 in this volume.

[30] Protocol 29 annexed to the TEU and TFEU.

[31] Case 155/73 *Sacchi* [1974] ECR 409.

issues have been the principle of home state control (or in other words, the extent to which, if at all, the host state may impose its own regulatory controls on out-of-state broadcast(er)s) and state-resourced financing of public service broadcasting). Mastroianni traces the relation between EU free movement law and broadcasting, from the early cases in which the Court, while insisting that broadcasting companies were 'undertakings' for the purposes of free movement and competition law, accepted a large degree of freedom on the part of Member States to run state monopolies and grant special or exclusive broadcasting rights, to the influential 1984 Green Paper on TV Without Frontiers and then the Directive itself. The Directive notably makes no distinction between public and other broadcasting, so that on the one hand public broadcasters are subject to the same market integration measures as commercial providers; and on the other hand both public and commercial suppliers are subject to the same Directive-defined public interest objectives, including consumer protection and promotion of (European) culture.

With the financing of public service broadcasting we return to state aid controls, and Mastroianni analyses the application of three distinct but connected rules: the *Altmark* rule of reason determining when the state aids rules will apply; the grounds for compatibility of aid in Article 107(3)(d) TFEU (ex Article 87(3)(d) EC); and the application of Article 106(2) TFEU (ex Article 86(2) EC). Given the limited possibility of applying *Altmark* to broadcasting and the narrowness of Article 107(3)(d) TFEU, the focus falls on the application of Article 106(2) in the light of the public broadcasting Protocol. Mastroianni identifies a 'remarkable deference' to public broadcasting organizations on the part of legislature, Commission, and courts, which he links to the existence of the Broadcasting Protocol. It will be interesting to assess, in this light, the effects of the new Protocol on services of general interest.

Public health services make an appropriate subject for the final chapter. They illustrate very clearly the complex relationship between the market and the state, the 'economic' and the 'social', and between national solidarity and integrated markets, explored by Heike Schweitzer in Chapter 2. It is not putting words into Tamara Hervey's mouth—since she makes the point herself—to say that her conclusions are relevant not only to public health services but to welfare services more generally and thus also to the debate about the place of EU law in the provision and regulation of services of general interest.

Public health services, as Hervey says, have an almost iconic status for EU Member States (old and new), and symbolize many of the EU's values as well as being central to the 'European Social Model'. And yet it is hard to think of a public service where the Member States have so jealously guarded their autonomy: Article 168 TFEU (ex Article 152 EC) speaks in terms of the complementary nature of EU action, cooperation, and coordination between the Member States, explicitly prohibits any harmonization of national law, and requires the Union to 'respect the responsibilities of the Member States for the definition of their health policy and for the organisation and delivery of health services and medical care', including management of health services and the allocation of resources. Despite this, the application of state aid and procurement rules to public health services is increasingly relevant, the Treaty's free movement rules have had a great impact on public health provision in the Member States, and at the time of writing the Council had recently reached political agreement on a proposed Directive on patients' rights in cross-border healthcare. Hervey's conclusion is that the application of both competition and free movement law implies a movement in public healthcare, away from national integrated public healthcare *systems* and towards a set of individual public *services*, which may or may not be categorized as services of general interest, and away from an exclusion of the system as a whole from EU law towards a case-by-case examination of specific services. The Treaty of Lisbon offers the Court of Justice a number of possible opportunities for restructuring its approach to public health services, and indeed to services of general interest, including an increased emphasis on social solidarity, and the new Protocol. If the Court takes up this challenge, it will need at least to recognize, if not reconcile, the different visions of the relationship between state and market which, as the next chapter demonstrates, is at the heart of the dilemma.

Note on Treaty numbering

In this book, the abbreviation 'TEU' used after a Treaty article refers to the Treaty on European Union in the version in force after 1 December 2009, while 'TFEU' refers to the Treaty on the Functioning of the European Union. The abbreviation 'EC' after a Treaty article refers to a provision of the European Community Treaty in the version in force until 30 November 2009; similarly 'EU' refers to an article of the Treaty on European Union in the version in force until that date.

2

Services of General Economic Interest: European Law's Impact on the Role of Markets and of Member States

Heike Schweitzer

1. Introduction

For more than 20 years now, services of general economic interest have been a focal point of European discourse.[1] Conflict and debate have been sparked by the EU Commission's attempt to apply the TFEU's free movement rules and competition rules more consistently and forcefully in those sectors that the Member States have traditionally considered to be reservations of national sovereignty. The Member States have reacted strongly to these attempts: not only have they frequently challenged the application of TFEU rules to allegedly 'reserved' sectors in the European courts. The political pungency of the conflicts is illustrated most vividly by the Member States' repeated initiatives to change the Treaty rules themselves.

Despite the undisputed importance of the conflict, and the significant attention it has received in communications by the EU Commission[2] as well as in

[1] For excellent and comprehensive recent overviews see B Cruz, 'Beyond Competition: Services of General Interest and European Community Law' in de Búrca (ed), *EU Law and the Welfare State. In Search of Solidarity* (2005) 169 et seq; B Sierra, *Exclusive rights and state monopolies under EC law* (1999); B Sierra, 'Article 86—Exclusive Rights and Other Anti-Competitive State Measures' in Faull and Nikpay, *The EC Law of Competition* (2nd edn 2007) ch 6; Holmes, 'The Control of State Action under EC Competition Law' in Korah (ed), *Competition Law of the European Community* (2nd edn 2005); Sauter, 'Services of general economic interest and universal service in EU law' (2008) 33 EL Rev 167 et seq; E Szyszczak, *The Regulation of the State in Competitive Markets in the EU* (2007). See also: Mestmäcker and Schweitzer in Immenga and Mestmäcker (eds), *Wettbewerbsrecht EG / Teil 1* (4th edn 2007) Art 31, 86 EGV, Parts B–D; Schweitzer, *Daseinsvorsorge, 'service public', Universaldienst* (2001/2002).

[2] A series of communications by the Commission only faintly reflects the fierceness of these debates: the Commission's most recent communication is a communication on 'Services of general interest, including social services of general interest: a new European commitment', 20 November 2007, COM (2007) 725 final. The following communications have preceded the most recent package: EU Commission, 'Services of General Economic Interest in Europe', 11.9.1996, COM (1996) 443 final; EU Commission, 'Services of General Economic Interest in Europe', 20.9.2000, COM (2000)

academia,[3] its nature and causes remain controversial. According to some, the real battle is about the primacy of social goals versus economic freedoms and competition rules.[4] More obviously, a fight about the division of competences between the EU and the Member States is being fought, with the latter defending what they consider to be the last hard reserves of state sovereignty.[5] This chapter will illuminate yet another dimension to the debate: the persistent friction between EU law and the Member States' public service traditions is ultimately caused by fundamentally different conceptions of the role of markets and the role of states. While well-defined social guarantees and public interest missions can frequently be reconciled case by case with the Union's interest in the protection of free movement and competition rules, the underlying visions remain at odds and are ultimately irreconcilable. This explains the remarkable persistence and fierceness of the debate.

In order to show the different conceptions, the chapter will start with a look at the national 'public service' traditions, notably the French '*service public*' conception and the German concept of '*Daseinsvorsorge*' (Part 2), and contrast them with the principles according to which EU law tries to reconcile the protection of national public interest conceptions with the Union's interest to implement the free movement, competition, and state aid rules. Part 3 and Part 4 delimit the scope of typical tensions between national public service regimes and EU law by looking at exclusive rights (Part 3) and state subsidies (Part 4) consecutively. Part 5 will briefly review the evolution of the case law on Article 106(2) TFEU (ex Article 86(2) EC) which is meant to mediate the tensions. Part 6 shall highlight some models of SGEI provision as developed in sector-specific secondary law. Part 7

580 final; EU Commission, 'Report on Services of General Economic Interest to the Laeken European Council', 17.10.2001, COM (2001) 598 final; EU Commission, 'Communication: A Methodological Note for the Horizontal Evaluation of Services of General Economic Interest', 18.6.2002, COM (2002) 331 final; EU Commission, 'Green Paper on Services of General Interest', 21.5.2003, COM (2003) 270 final; EU Commission, 'White Paper on Services of General Interest', 12.5.2004, COM (2004) 374 final. For a summary and discussion of these communications see Mestmäcker and Schweitzer in Immenga and Mestmäcker (eds), n 1 above, Art 31, 86 EGV, Part D, paras 25–30.

[3] From the vast body of literature see, eg, Mestmäcker, 'Daseinsvorsorge und Universaldienst im europäischen Kontext: Ein Beitrag zur Funktion von Art 89 Abs. 2 EGV' in Ruland, Baron von Maydell, and Papier (eds), *Festschrift für Hans F Zacher zum 70. Geburtstag* (1998) 635; Behrens, 'Public Services and the Internal Market—An Analysis of the Commission's Communications on Services of General Interest in Europe' (2001) 2 EBOR 469 et seq; von Danwitz, 'Dienste von allgemeinem wirtschaftlichem Interesse in der europäischen Wettbewerbsordnung' in *Bitburger Gespräche*, Jahrbuch 2002/I, 2003, 73–89; Koenig and Kühling, 'Totgesagte Vorschriften leben länger'. Bedeutung und Auslegung der Ausnahmeklausel des Art 86 Abs. 2 EG', (2002) ZHR 166, 656 et seq; Krajewski, *Öffentliche Dienstleistungen im europäischen Verfassungsrecht* (2005) 665; Boeger, 'Solidarity and EC competition law' (2007) 32 EL Rev 319 et seq.

[4] For a general claim that EU law gives priority to economic over social policy see Scharpf, 'The European Social Model' (2002) 40 JCMS, 645, 647 and 665. For the claim that the 'priority problem' is key in the interpretation of Art 106(2) TFEU (ex Art 86(2) EC) see Baquero Cruz, n 1 above, 174 et seq, claiming that Art 106(2) TFEU (ex Art 86(2) EC) gives 'relative priority' to competition over services of general economic interest, but that this understanding of Art 86(2) should be replaced by an interpretation which regards this provision as a 'switch-rule that establishes the conditions for the application or non-application of the Treaty'.

[5] See Jacobs, 'The State of International Economic Law: Re-Thinking Sovereignty in Europe' (2008) 11 Journal of Int'l Econ L 5, 6 et seq for more general discussion on how EU law has replaced state sovereignty with the rule of law.

draws together the various threads, explicating the conception of the role of the market and the role of the state underlying EU law and contrasting it with traditional national conceptions. Part 8 will take a look at some open questions, discussing in which direction European law on SGEIs may evolve.

2. National 'Public Service' Traditions and EU Law: Conceptual Tensions

The legal and political conflicts surrounding the organization, financing, and provision of what EU lawyers today call 'services of general economic interest' are of an intensity that is puzzling for anyone freshly entering the debate. This is all the more true since there is full agreement that infringements of EU law are justified where this is necessary to ensure the fulfilment of a public interest mission an undertaking has been entrusted with. A key to understanding the conflicts is the different public service conceptions as they have evolved in Continental Europe over the last century, in reaction to the practical importance of state-driven infrastructure development.[6]

A. The Evolution of the '*Service public*' Conception in France

As a legal and political concept, public services have gained the greatest relevance in France.[7] It was Léon Duguit, a French public law scholar strongly influenced by the evolving field of legal sociology who, in the early years of the 20th century, first started reflecting the implications of the state's engagement in infrastructure building and service provision for the legal conception of the nature and role of the state. In opposition to the then established view that the state's particular nature was embodied in the public power it possessed vis-à-vis its citizens—the '*puissance publique*'—Duguit claimed that the state must be conceptualized by reference to its '*fonction*' as the basis of its legitimacy:[8] Any type of state action and state intervention into society could only be legitimized by its function to serve the needs of society ('*service public*'), or, as Duguit put it, 'to protect the necessary preconditions for social interdependence and interaction'.[9]

The reconceptualization of the state around its legitimizing principle of action—the unifying idea of what has come to be known as the '*École de service public*'—has had enormous influence on French legal theory and public law. The focus and practical implications of the '*service public*'-approach have, however, shifted over time. Duguit himself was convinced that the 'preconditions for social interdependence

[6] For a comparison of the concepts of *Daseinsvorsorge* and *service public* see also Mestmäcker, n 3 above, 635 et seq; Bullinger, 'Französischer Service Public und deutsche Daseinsvorsorge' (2003) JZ 874 et seq.

[7] For an overview see Schweitzer, *Daseinsvorsorge, 'service public', Universaldienst* (2001/2002) 61–73.

[8] Duguit, *Traité de droit constitutionnel* (1927) 673–4.

[9] Duguit, *Traité de droit constitutionnel, tome II* (1928) § 8, 61 and 70–1.

and interaction' could be observed and defined objectively. The state should furthermore only be legitimated to act and intervene where these preconditions could not be guaranteed by society itself. In this perspective, the '*service public*' was not only the basis of the state's legitimacy; it was also its limit.[10] However, this conception was quickly contested within the '*École de service public*'. According to Gaston Jèze—less attracted to sociological approaches than his academic teacher Duguit and an avowed legal positivist—an objective delimitation of the public interest or of inherently legitimate public service tasks was neither possible nor desirable. The function of the '*service public*' concept was not to delimit state activity, but rather to make the public interest its binding goal.[11]

It has ultimately been this broader '*service public*' conception that has gained influence on French public law and politics. The state is defined by its task to represent the public interest; but defining the public interest is within the free discretion of the state. Wherever the state attaches a particular public interest to a given activity and takes responsibility for its provision, it becomes part of the '*service public*'. Contrary to Duguit's intentions, this has led to an expansion, rather than a delimitation, of the state's activities. Generally, the '*service public*' continues to represent the state's commitment to the value of solidarity in the form of territorial unity and cohesion.[12] In conceptually somewhat weaker forms, '*service public*'-like notions have been adopted also by Italy and Spain.

B. The German Concept of '*Daseinsvorsorge*'

A close equivalent to the French '*service public*' conception is notably absent in German public law. Under the dominant influence of Hegel's legal philosophy, characterized by an idealistic conception of the state as the objective expression of freedom and morality and a goal in and of itself, German public law scholars of the early 20th century did not question the state's legitimacy with similar insistence as Duguit had done in France, nor did they consider the state's concrete efforts in serving the public interest as a new and primary source of legitimacy. When Ernst Forsthoff, in the late 1930s, introduced the concept of '*Daseinsvorsorge*' into German law,[13] the impetus was not so much to justify the state as such, but to

[10] Duguit, *Traité de droit constitutionnel, tome II* (1928) § 8, 59; and Duguit, *Traité de droit constitutionnel, tome III* (1930) 589: '[...] il faut affirmer énergiquement et inlassablement que l'activité de l'État dans toutes ses manifestations est limitée par un droit supérieur à lui qu'il y a des choses qu'il ne peut pas faire, qu'il y en a qu'il doit faire, que cette limitation ne s'impose pas seulement à tel ou tel organe, qu'elle s'impose à l'État lui-même'.

[11] In France, Gaston Jèze is famous for saying that '[s]ont uniquement exclusivement services publics, les besoins d'intéret général que les gouvernants, dans un pays donné, à une époque donné, ont décidé de satisfaire par le procédé du service public. L'intention des gouvernants est seule à considerer'—cited after Kondilis, *Service public et intéret général*, DEA Paris I (1986) 9. For a broader overview and discussion see Schweitzer, n 7 above, 64–6 with further references.

[12] See also the Preamble of the French Constitution of 1958, which refers to the 1946 Constitution, which in turn states: 'La Nation proclame la solidarité et l'égalité de tous les Français devant les charges qui résultent des calamités nationales.'

[13] Forsthoff, *Die Verwaltung als Leistungsträger* (1938). For a discussion of the concept of Daseinsvorsorge in the work of Forsthoff see Kersten, 'Die Entwicklung des Konzepts der Daseinsvorsorge im

assert its primacy vis-à-vis civil society and the market sphere. Forsthoff found that the modern individual was increasingly incapable of producing the goods and services needed for survival himself or herself. Instead, the modern individual had grown dependent on the abstract forces of society and the market for the provision of even the most essential goods. These forces left him or her exposed to uncontrollable risks and to 'market' rationality driven by private interests instead of public interests. In such a situation, the state was to defend the primacy of human values vis-à-vis 'the world of things' and to take responsibility and control: the state was to ensure that all individuals were provided with the essential goods and services that a modern individual depended on. For that purpose, the state was legitimized to intervene into the market whenever it believed such intervention to be opportune. On a doctrinal level, this translated into the primacy of public law vis-à-vis private law: the fact of the state's engagement in the provision of goods and services implied that all relevant relations should be governed by public law.

Forsthoff's theory of '*Daseinsvorsorge*' had substantial impact on post-war German public law as far as the provision of 'public services' to the citizens was concerned. One of the more implicit, but far-reaching consequences was that the state's intervention into the economy undertaken under the heading of '*Daseinsvorsorge*' was subjected only to a weak degree of control under the fundamental economic rights as guaranteed in the German constitution.

C. Parallels of the French '*service public*' and the German '*Daseinsvorsorge*' in Conceptualizing the Role of the Market and the Role of the State

The brief comparison of the intellectual roots of the French '*service public*' and the German '*Daseinsvorsorge*' has highlighted important differences. Notable commonalities come into focus if we consider these conceptions from the perspective of EU law: both the French '*service public*' and the German '*Daseinsvorsorge*' approach 'services of general economic interest' from the perspective of the state. Whether it is the legitimizing function of public services or the proposition that the state is inherently responsible for the provision of all essential services: the underlying idea is that of a natural antagonism between the public interest and the market regime. Quite contrary to the idea of a process of decentralized coordination of private interests that, within a framework of rules, will normally tend to work to the benefit of all—an idea captured in Adam Smith's famous metaphor of the invisible hand of the market—both the French '*service public*' conception and the German '*Daseinsvorsorge*' have tended to presume that the realization of the public interest requires a planning rationality and a steering institution to implement such plans.

Werk von Ernst Forsthoff' (2005) Der Staat 543 et seq. For a more recent discussion of the concept of 'Daseinsvorsorge' see Bull, 'Daseinsvorsorge im Wandel der Staatsformen' (2008) Der Staat 1 et seq; Ronellenfitsch, 'Daseinsvorsorge als Rechtsbegriff' in Blümel (ed), *Ernst Forsthoff. Kolloquium aus Anlaß des 100. Geburtstags von Ernst Forsthoff* (2003) 53 et seq. For a critical discussion of the concept of 'Daseinsvorsorge' from the perspective of EU law see Schweitzer, n 7 above, 74–80.

The market, by contrast, has been regarded as an anarchic process producing arbitrary results.[14]

Where the provision of goods or services has a strong public interest dimension, the state has therefore tended to exclude competition. Exclusive rights have ensured the viability of central planning as well as the direct influence of the state. Economic freedoms were not considered to constrain this choice: the public interest was considered to carry greater weight. The definition of the public interest was regarded as a prerogative of the state, as was the identification of the appropriate means for its implementation. In the Continental European tradition, a state's decision to treat a given service as a public service has thus justified state intervention of any kind.[15] The states' delineation of the sphere of the market and the sphere of the state was not subjected to meaningful legal controls. The conceptions of '*service public*' and '*Daseinsvorsorge*' have empowered the state; they have not delimited it.

3. The National Organization of 'Services of General Economic Interest' in the Light of Free Movement and Competition Rules

A. Compatibility of Special and Exclusive Rights with the TFEU

The TFEU rules are based on a fundamentally different conception regarding the delineation of the sphere of the market and the sphere of the state. During the first 25 years or so of the European Community's existence, the tensions between the Member States' public service traditions and EU law were, however, not systematically explored. It was only in the mid-1980s and in the context of the renewed momentum created by the White Paper on Completing the Internal Market[16] that the Commission took up the task. The extent to which the Treaty's fundamental freedoms and competition rules mandate a liberalization of national public service sectors has, however, not been obvious.[17] In 1995, Judge David Edward has distinguished four possible approaches to judicial control of the existence of legal monopolies:[18] an 'Absolute Sovereignty approach', according to which Member States have exclusive competence in relation to the grant of legal monopolies; an

[14] See eg Broß, 'Daseinsvorsorge–Wettbewerb–Gemeinschaftsrecht', (2003) JZ 874 et seq.

[15] See Mestmäcker, 'Zur Anwendung der Wettbewerbsregeln auf die Mitgliedstaaten und die Europäischen Gemeinschaften', reprinted in Mestmäcker, *Recht in der offenen Gesellschaft* (1993) 242, 243.

[16] EU Commission, 'White Paper: Completing the Internal Market', 14 June 1985, COM (85) 310 final.

[17] For a review of the earlier case law see Mestmäcker, 'Gemeinschaftsrechtliche Schranken für die Begründung und Ausübung besonderer oder ausschließlicher Rechte nach Art 90 Abs. 1 EWG-Vertrag' reprinted in Mestmäcker, n 15 above, 254 et seq; and later Mestmäcker, 'Grenzen staatlicher Monopole im EG-Vertrag', reprinted in Mestmäcker, *Wirtschaft und Verfassung in der Europäischen Union* (2nd edn 2006) 275 et seq.

[18] See David AO Edward, *Article 90 EC Treaty and the deregulation, liberalisation and privatisation of public enterprises and public monopolies* (1996) 8 et seq. See also Edward and Hoskins, 'Article 90: Deregulation and EC Law. Reflections arising from the XVI FIDE Conference' (1995) 32 CMLR 157 et seq.

'Absolute Competition approach', according to which the mere grant of a legal monopoly would be a 'per se violation' of Article 106(1) TFEU (ex Article 86(1) EC), since the Member State necessarily places the relevant undertaking in a dominant position free of the normal market constraints, so that it is able to pursue abusive practices; a 'Limited Sovereignty approach', according to which Member States are free to grant legal monopolies provided that the operation of the monopoly does not have the *necessary* consequence of contravening the rules of the TFEU; and a 'Limited Competition' approach, according to which Member States may create legal monopolies only where this is justified by a legitimate national objective and where the consequent restriction of competition is limited to what is necessary to achieve this objective. Edward found that the European Court of Justice (ECJ) had clearly rejected an 'Absolute Sovereignty approach':[19] it follows from the terms of the TFEU that the Member States have not retained complete sovereignty in relation to the creation of legal monopolies. Edward also dismissed an 'Absolute Competition' approach: the very existence of Article 106(1) TFEU (ex Article 86(1) EC) would deny an approach under which the mere creation of special or exclusive rights is in per se conflict with the competition rules. Even from an economic perspective, an approach which would prevent Member States from granting legal monopolies under any circumstances, including the conditions of a 'natural monopoly', would appear to be nonsensical. As to the remaining choice between a 'Limited Sovereignty' and a 'Limited Competition' approach, ie to the question whether Member States, with some restrictions, should be presumed to have the freedom to create legal monopolies, or whether the restrictions of competition inherent in legal monopolies should presumed to be illegal unless justified and necessary, Edward found the case law to be divided.[20] The ambiguities contained in the Treaty remained to be resolved.

Fifteen years later, the ambiguities remain. As regards the assessment whether special and/or exclusive rights are compatible with Article 106(1) TFEU (ex Article 86(1) EC) and with Article 102 TFEU (ex Article 82 EC), the test most frequently applied in recent case law has been the one that Edward has associated with the 'Limited Sovereignty approach': the ECJ has frequently restated that

> the mere creation of a dominant position through the grant of special or exclusive rights within the meaning of Article 86(1) EC is not in itself incompatible with Article 82 EC. A Member State will be in breach of the prohibitions laid down by those two provisions only if the undertaking in question, merely by exercising the special or exclusive rights conferred upon it, is led to abuse its dominant position or where such rights are liable to create a situation in which that undertaking is led to commit such abuses . . .[21]

[19] Citing Case C–202/88 *France v Commission (Telecoms Terminal Equipment)* [1991] ECR I–1223 para 22.

[20] Cases cited in support of the 'Limited Sovereignty approach' are: Case C–41/90 *Höfner v Macrotron* [1991] ECR I–1979 para 29; Case C–323/93 *La Crespelle* [1994] ECR I–5077 para 18; and Case C–387/93 *Banchero* [1995] I–4663 para 51. Among the cases cited in favour of the 'Limited Competition' approach is, most importantly, Case C–230/91 *Corbeau* [1993] ECR I–2533 para 13.

[21] Case C–451/03 *Servizi Ausiliari Dottori Commercialisti Srl* [2006] ECR I–2941 para 23. See also Case C–163/96 *Raso* [1998] ECR I 533 paras 27–29; Case C–475/99 *Ambulanz Glöckner* [2001] ECR

No finding is required that any abuse has actually occurred.[22] It suffices that a measure imputable to a Member State, and in particular a measure by which a Member State confers special or exclusive rights within the meaning of Article 106 (1) TFEU (ex Article 86(1) EC), gives rise to a risk of an abuse of a dominant position.[23] Generally, '[i]f inequality of opportunity between economic operators, and therefore distorted competition, results from a State measure, such a measure constitutes an infringement of Article 86(1) EC in conjunction with Article 82 EC'.[24] According to a well-established line of case law, inequality of opportunity, and thus a risk of an abuse, will be found where a dominant undertaking which itself operates in the relevant market is entrusted with the task to decide upon, or consent to, applications by other undertakings to engage in the same type of activity: such rights place the dominant undertaking at an obvious advantage over its competitors and are incompatible with a system of undistorted competition which must secure equal opportunities for all economic operators in the market.[25] They create incentives to deny other operators access to the relevant market, or to distort competition by favouring its own activity.[26] In a recent Article 106(3) TFEU (ex Article 86(3) EC) decision the EU Commission has found that by granting quasi-monopolistic rights for lignite exploration and exploitation to the public undertaking PPC, which thus enjoyed privileged access to the cheapest source of electricity generation, Greece has placed competitors in the electricity wholesale market at a competitive disadvantage. The resulting distortion of competition in favour of PPC has substantially increased barriers to entry and has reinforced PPC's dominance.[27]

I–8089 para 39; Case C–49/07 *MOTOE v Elliniko Dimosio* [2008] ECR I–4863 paras 48–49. See, furthermore, Case C–462/99 *Connect Austria* [2003] ECR I–5197 para 84, different formula: 'A Member State breaches the prohibitions laid down by Article 86(1) EC in conjunction with Article 82 EC if it adopts any law, regulation or administrative provision that creates a situation in which a public undertaking or an undertaking on which it has conferred special or exclusive rights cannot avoid abusing its dominant position.'

[22] Case C–55/96 *Job Centre* [1997] ECR I–7119 para 36; Case C–49/07 *MOTOE v Elliniko Dimosio* [2008] ECR I–4863 para 49.

[23] Case C–49/07 *MOTOE v Elliniko Dimosio* [2008] ECR I–4863 para 50; *ERT* para 37; Case C–179/90 *Merci convenzinali porto di Genova* [1991] ECR I–5889 para 17; and Case C–380/05 *Centro Europa 7* [2008] ECR I–349 para 60.

[24] Case C–462/99 *Connect Austria* [2003] ECR I–5197 para 84. See also Case C–202/88 *France v Commission* [1991] ECR I–1223 para 51; and Case C–18/88 *GB-Inno-BM* [1991] ECR I–5941 para 25, where the ECJ has held that a system of undistorted competition as laid down by the EC Treaty can only be guaranteed if equality of opportunity is secured between the various economic operators.

[25] Case C–49/07 *MOTOE v Elliniko Dimosio* [2008] ECR I–4863 para 51:

> A system of undistorted competition, such as that provided for by the Treaty, can be guaranteed only if equality of opportunity is secured as between the various economic operators. To entrust a legal person such as ELPA, which itself organises and commercially exploits motorcycling events, the task of giving the competent administration its consent to applications for authorisation to organise such events, is tantamount *de facto* to conferring upon it the power to designate the persons authorised to organise those events and to set the conditions in which those events are organised, thereby placing that entity at an obvious advantage over its competitors.

[26] Case C–49/07 *MOTOE v Elliniko Dimosio* [2008] ECR I–4863 paras 51, 52.

[27] EU Commission, 5 March 2008, Art 86(3) decision on the granting or maintaining in force by the Hellenic Republic of rights in favour of Public Power Corporation SA for extraction of lignite, para 190.

The inequality of competitive opportunities, and the resulting risk of an abusive exploitation of such competitive advantages which special or exclusive rights may confer, must be established with a view to the specific facts of each case. There is no general *presumption* that special or exclusive rights will always invite abuse. Thus, in *Servizi Ausiliari Dottori Commercialisti Srl* the ECJ found itself unable to give a useful answer to the question whether the conferral of the exclusive right to provide certain kinds of tax advice upon so-called 'Tax Advice Centres' (CAF) infringed Article 102 TFEU (ex Article 82 EC) with Article 106(1) TFEU (ex Article 86(1) EC) because it lacked 'the factual and legal information which would enable it to determine whether the requirements as to the existence of a dominant position or of abusive conduct, for the purposes of Article 82 EC, are met'.[28]

In some cases, the ECJ cites the test first developed in *Corbeau*,[29] recalling that

> Article 86(2) EC allows Member States to confer, on undertakings to which they entrust the operation of services of general economic interest, exclusive rights which may hinder the application of the rules of the Treaty on competition in so far as restrictions on competition, or even the exclusion of all competition, by other economic operators are necessary to ensure the performance of the particular tasks assigned to the undertakings holding the exclusive rights . . . '[30]

Contrary to Edward's interpretation, who has associated this test with the 'Limited Competition approach', the ECJ does not appear to link this test to a presumption that competition rules will be violated unless the exclusive right is justified by a legitimate national objective and under a proportionality test. Rather, the test merely seems to *exclude* an infringement of competition rules where the requirements of Article 106(2) TFEU (ex Article 86(2) EC) are met.

On the other hand, the ECJ has apparently tightened the control of special and exclusive rights under the free movement rules. In *Servizi Ausiliari Dottori Commercialisti Srl*, the ECJ has found that the exclusive rights conferred upon the so-called Tax Advice Centres (CAF) to provide certain types of tax advice and assistance, although they may have been compatible with Article 106(1) TFEU (ex Article 86(1) EC) and with Article 102 TFEU (ex Article 82 EC), constituted an unjustified restriction on the freedom of establishment and the freedom to provide services (Article 49 TFEU (ex Article 39 EC) and Article 56 TFEU (ex Article 49 EC)).[31] Article 49 TFEU and Article 56 TFEU require the elimination of restrictions on the freedom of establishment and the freedom to provide services. All measures which prohibit, impede or render less attractive the exercise of such freedoms must be abolished unless justified.[32] According to the ECJ, conferring the exclusive power to provide taxpayers with certain kinds of tax advice and assistance to CAF—despite being non-discriminatory—completely prevents access to the

[28] C–451/03 *Servizi Ausiliari Dottori Commercialisti Srl* [2006] ECR I–2941 para 25.
[29] Case C–320/91 *Corbeau* [1993] ECR I–2533 para 14.
[30] Case C–49/07 *MOTOE v Elliniko Dimosio* [2008] ECR I–4863 para 44.
[31] C–451/03 *Servizi Ausiliari Dottori Commercialisti Srl* [2006] ECR I–2941 para 50.
[32] C–451/03 *Servizi Ausiliari Dottori Commercialisti Srl* [2006] ECR I–2941 para 31; with reference to Case C–439/99 *Commission v Italy* [2002] ECR I–305 para 22.

market for these services by economic operators established in other Member States, and is liable to make it more difficult, or completely prevent, the exercise by these economic operators of their right of establishment (at paras 33–4). A justification based on overriding requirements relating to the public interest failed in this case since the exclusive right went beyond what was necessary in order to attain the objectives pursued.[33]

Whereas the application of Article 106(1) TFEU (ex Article 86(1) EC), together with EU competition rules, thus appears to follow more a 'Limited Sovereignty approach', the application of the free movement rules seems to go a long way into the direction of a 'Limited Competition approach'. A justification for the stricter application of the free movement rules may lie in the availability of a broader set of public interest justifications available.

B. Limits to the Application of Competition Rules: The Concept of an 'Undertaking' and the Solidarity Exception

Another indication of the ECJ's ambiguity in mediating between the Member States' claim of unrestrained sovereignty in the organization of those sectors that have traditionally been closely associated to the state and the Union's claim to a 'horizontal' application of the competition rules is the case law on the concept of an 'undertaking'. Under EU competition law, the qualification of economic actors as 'undertakings' is the precondition for the applicability of the competition rules. Where the competition rules apply, any infringement must be justified and is subject to control by the courts.

1. *The Functional Concept of an 'Undertaking' under EU Competition Rules*

The development of the concept of 'an undertaking' in the ECJ's case law was driven by the aim to ensure an equal and fully effective application of the EU competition rules in all Member States, irrespective of the different organizational choices and the differences in legal forms.[34] The ECJ has therefore chosen a 'functional approach': according to settled case law, the concept of an 'undertaking' covers any entity engaged in an economic activity,[35] the latter being defined as any

[33] The same test has recently been applied by the Commission in its Art 86(3) decision on the special rights granted to La Banque Postale, Caisses d'Epargne and Crédit Mutuel for the distribution of the livret A and livret bleu—see *EU Commission*, 10 May 2007, C (2007) 2110 final, paras 28–29. The Commission doesn't appear to be completely sure about this approach, however, and therefore adds an analysis of the concrete effects of the special rights on the possibility of foreign banks to enter the French market for liquid banking savings products, finding that the special rights make such market entry less attractive and constitute a serious obstacle.

[34] See Mestmäcker, n 15 above, 243–244.

[35] Case C–49/07 *MOTOE v Elliniko Dimosio* [2008] ECR I–4863, para 21; C–41/90 *Hoefner and Elser* [1991] ECR I–1979, para 21; Joined cases C–264/01, C–306/01, C–354/01 and C–355/01 *AOK Bundesverband* [2004] ECR I–2493, para 46; Case C–222/04 *Cassa die Risparmio di Firenze* [2006] ECR I–289, para 107; Case C–237/04 *Enirisorse* [2006] ECR I–2843, para 28; Case C–280/06 *Ente Tabacchi Italiani* [2007] ECR I–10893, para 38.

activity consisting in offering goods and services on a market.[36] The legal form of the undertaking is irrelevant, as is the way an entity is financed,[37] the question whether it intends to make profits or not,[38] the social objectives associated with it,[39] or any regulatory arrangements it is subject to in a particular Member State.[40]

While the functional approach towards the concept of 'undertaking' ensures a wide application of the competition rules, not all providers of public services will qualify as 'undertakings' under these criteria. Outside the scope of the competition rules lie those activities that fall within the exercise of public power.[41] Examples include national defence or police services, air navigation safety or air traffic control.[42]

[36] Case C–49/07 *MOTOE v Elliniko Dimosio* [2008] ECR I–4863 para 22; Case T–155/04, *Selex v Commission* [2006] ECR II–4797, para 50; Case C–41/90 *Höfner and Elser* [1991] ECR I–1979, para 21; Case C–244/94 *Fédération française des sociétés d'assurances* [1995] ECR I–4013, para 14; Case C–55/96 *Job Centre* [1997] ECR I–7119, para 21; Case C–35/96 *Commission v Italy* [1998] ECR I–3851, para 36; and Joined Cases C–180/98 to C–184/98 *Pavlov* [2000] ECR I–6451, para 74; Case C–222/04 *Cassa di Risparmio di Firenze* [2006] ECR I–289, para 108; Case C–280/06 *Ente Tabacchi Italiani* [2007] ECR I–10893, para 29. See also: *EU Commission*, 'Staff Working Document: Frequently asked questions in relation with Commission Decision of 28 November 2005 on the application of Article 86(2) of the EC Treaty to State aid in the form of public service compensation . . . ', SEC (2007) 1516 fin, 7–8, with examples. Normally, the offering of goods and services on a market will involve remuneration—which does not necessarily have to be paid by those benefiting from the service—see *EU Commission*, 'Services of general interest, including social services of general interest: a new European commitment', 20.11.2007, COM (2007) 725 final, 5. Healthcare services, paid by a healthcare insurance, are an example for this. But the absence of remuneration does not exclude the possibility that an activity is economic in nature—it is merely an indication in this respect—see CFI, 12.12.2006, Case T–155/04 *Selex v Commission* [2006] ECR II–4797, para 77.

[37] Case C–49/07 *MOTOE v Elliniko Dimosio* [2008] ECR I–4863, para 21; Case C–237/04 *Enirisorse* [2006] ECR I–2843, paras 28 and 33.

[38] Case C–49/07 *MOTOE v Elliniko Dimosio* [2008] ECR I–4863, para 27; Case C–244/94 *FFSA* [1995] ECR I–4013, paras 17–18; ECJ, Case C–67/96 *Albany* [1999] ECR I–5751, paras 84–87; Case C–222/04 *Cassa di Risparmio di Firenze* [2006] ECR I–289, paras 122–123: the fact that the offer of goods or services is made without profit motive does not prevent the entity which carries out those operations on the market from being considered an undertaking, since that offer exists in competition with that of other operators which do seek to make a profit.

[39] Case C–237/04 *Enirisorse* [2006] ECR I–2843, para 34; Case C–475/99 *Ambulanz Glöckner* [2001] ECR I–8089, para 21.

[40] See AG Jacobs, Conclusions, in *AOK*, para 26. See also EU Commission, Film Purchases by German Television Stations, OJ [1989] L 284/36. See also EU Commission, Services of general interest, including social services of general interest: a new European commitment, 20.11.2007, COM (2007) 725 final, 5. Based on these criteria, the ECJ has, for example, qualified a public employment agency engaged in the business of employment procurement as an 'undertaking' within the meaning of the EC competition rules, despite the fact that this activity was normally entrusted to public agencies—see ECJ, Case C–41/90 *Höfner and Elser* [1991] ECR I–1979, paras 21–22.

[41] Case C–49/07 *MOTOE v Elliniko Dimosio* [2008] ECR I–4863, para 24; Case C–364/92 *SAT Fluggesellschaft* [1994] ECR I–43, paras 31–32; Case C–343/95 *Diego Cali & Figli* [1997] I–1547, para 15 et seq. For a review of the case law see Schröter, 'Zur Einschränkung des wettbewerbsrechtlichen Unternehmensbegriffs' in Monti, Liechtenstein, Vesterdorf, Wetbrook, and Wildhaber (eds), *Economic Law and Justice in Times of Globalisation. Festschrift für Carl Baudenbacher* (2007) 593, 599–600; Mestmäcker and Schweitzer, in Immenga and Mestmäcker (eds), n 1 above, Art 31, 86 EGV, Part C, paras 15–20. See also Baquero Cruz, n 1 above, 181 et seq.

[42] Case C–364/92 *SAT Fluggesellschaft* [1994] ECR I–43, para 30: 'Eurocontrol's activities, by their nature, their aim and the rules to which they are subject, are connected with the exercise of powers relating to the control and supervision of air space which are typically those of a public authority. They are not of an economic nature justifying the application of the Treaty rules of competition.' See also

2. *The 'Solidarity-exception': Compulsory Social Insurance Schemes*

Beyond the well-accepted exception for activities directly related to the exercise of state prerogatives, some uncertainty existed regarding the right test for qualifying an activity as 'economic' in nature. In *Höfner*, the ECJ found that the fact that employment procurement activities are normally entrusted to public agencies could not affect the economic nature of such activity, because '[e]mployment procurement has not always been, and is not necessarily, carried out by public entities'.[43] In *Ambulanz Glöckner*, the economic nature of the provision of emergency transport services and patient transport services was established on similar grounds.[44] According to AG Jacobs' conclusions in *AOK*, the economic character of an activity should be determined by asking 'whether it could, at least in principle, be carried on by a private undertaking in order to make profits'.[45] In line with the purpose of a functional approach, these tests appeared to make the *potential* marketability of a given activity the relevant benchmark. The *actual* organization of the activity, on the other hand, and the corresponding policy choices by the Member States should be irrelevant.

This approach has remained controversial, however.[46] With a view to national social security schemes, including compulsory sickness or pension funds—but so far also limited to this field—the ECJ has abandoned this pro-competition approach and has replaced it with what one may again call a 'Limited Sovereignty approach', according to which EU competition rules will not be applied to a Member State's social insurance regime if this regime is, on its own terms, incompatible with competition. In contrast to its general approach to the concept of an 'undertaking', where the ECJ asks for the *potential* marketability of a given type of activity, defined abstractly, the ECJ will, in the context of compulsory social security schemes, apply the marketability test based on a Member State's concrete choices regarding the modalities of service provision. On this basis, the ECJ has, in an important line of case law starting with *Poucet et Pistre*, developed a list of criteria under which to exempt compulsory social insurance schemes from the scope of application of the EU competition rules.[47]

Case T–155/04 *SELEX* [2006] ECR II–4797, para 50 et seq, for a discussion whether Eurocontrol's activities in the field of standardization, research and development, and assistance to national administrations qualify as 'economic' activities. The case is currently pending before the ECJ—see Case C–113/07 P. The concept of an 'undertaking' will be one of the points to be addressed. See also AG Trstenjak's conclusion in this case, 3 July 2008, para 60 et seq.

43 Case C–41/90 *Höfner and Elser* [1991] ECR I–1979, para 22.

44 Case C–475/99 *Ambulanz Glöckner* [2001] ECR I–8089, para 20.

45 AG Jacobs, conclusions, in Joined Cases C–264/01, C–306/01, C–354/01, and C–355/01 *AOK Bundesverband*, [2004] ECR I–2493, para 28.

46 For a critical view on the 'hypothetical competition' test see, eg, Baquero Cruz, n 1 above, 180: 'The decision of the Member States about the limits of the market would play no role whatsoever . . . This would amount to an excessively strong presumption in favour of the applicability of the economic rules of the Treaty'. For a discussion of the different approaches see also AG Maduro, conclusions, para 11 et seq, in Case C–205/03 P *FENIN* [2006] ECR I–6295.

47 For a review and discussion of the relevant case law see Schröter, n 41 above, 600 et seq; Mestmäcker and Schweitzer, in Immenga and Mestmäcker (eds), n 1 above, Art 31, 86 EGV Part C, paras 21–28.

The providers of such schemes will not be qualified as 'undertakings' if they pursue an exclusively social objective and, based on tight framework of state regulation, are functioning under a strict principle of solidarity which would leave little or no room for private pension or insurance providers offering for-profit services.[48] The (in)compatibility with private for-profit activity depends on the degree of redistribution provided for, and on whether the benefits provided still bear some relation to the amount of contributions to be made.[49] Where state regulation left the social security institutions no meaningful influence on the extent of the services to be provided or the amount of the contributions that it received, the ECJ has found against the applicability of the competition rules.[50] It is characteristic for this line of case law that the ECJ, in testing the marketability of social security services, fully respects the Member States' policy choices not only regarding redistributive goals, but also regarding the organization of the sector—choices which might otherwise be reviewed under a proportionality principle. The non-application of the EU competition rules and the concomitant proportionality test governing exceptions under Article 106(2) TFEU (ex Article 86(2) EC) implies that the Treaty rules lose some of their de-regulatory potential. The ECJ has implicitly justified the 'solidarity exception' with its special respect for the Member States' competences in the social policy field.[51]

Some recent judgments have arguably expanded the scope of the exemption beyond what can be justified on 'division of competences' grounds. In *AOK*, the ECJ found that German statutory sickness funds were not engaged in an economic activity when offering their health insurance services, since they were compelled by law to offer their members essentially identical obligatory benefits which did not depend on the amount of contributions paid, and since the legislator had provided for a risk equalization scheme between the various sickness funds. According to the ECJ, the German statutory sickness funds fulfilled an exclusively social function, were founded on the principle of national solidarity and therefore exempt from the scope of the EU competition rules.[52] This was so despite the fact that the German legislator had deliberately opened some scope for competition between the sickness

[48] AG Jacobs, conclusions, paras 33–35, in Joined Cases C–264/01, C–306/01, C–354/01, and C–355/01, *AOK Bundesverband*, [2004] ECR I–2493.

[49] In *Poucet et Pistre*, for example, the management of an entirely non-profit-making sickness fund was classified as a 'non-economic activity', because the amount of the contributions, the use of assets and the level of benefits were fixed by law, and the benefits paid bore no relation to the amount of the contributions paid—see Joined Cases C–159/91 and C–160/91 *Poucet et Pistre* [1993] ECR I–637, paras 15 and 18. See also Case C–218/00, *Cisal and INAIL*, [2002] ECR I–691, paras 43–48; Joined Cases C–264/01, C–306/01, C–354/01, and C–355/01, *AOK Bundesverband*, [2004] ECR I–2493, paras 47 and 51–55; and Case C–355/00, *Freskot* [2003] ECR I–5263, para 78–79. For a review of the relevant cases see AG Jacobs, Conclusions, paras 31 et seq, in Joined Cases C–264/01, C–306/01, C–354/01, and C–355/01 *AOK Bundesverband* [2004] ECR I–2493.

[50] Joined Cases C–159/91 and C–160/91 *Poucet and Pistre* [1993] ECR I–637, paras 18–19; Case C–218/00, *Cisal* [2002] ECR I–691, para 45; Joined Cases C–264/01, C–306/01, C–354/01, and C–355/01 *AOK Bundesverband* [2004] ECR I–2493, paras 47 and 49.

[51] See Schweitzer, 'Öffentliche Unternehmen im Binnenmarkt—Rechtfertigen mitgliedstaatliche Regulierungsinteressen die Beschneidung des Geltungsbereichs von Gemeinschaftsrechtsnormen?' in Behrens, Braun, and Nowak (eds), *Europäisches Wettbewerbsrecht nach der Reform* (2006) 81, 94–95.

[52] Joined Cases C–264/01, C–306/01, C–354/01, and C–355/01, *AOK Bundesverband*, [2004] ECR I–2493, paras 51–56.

funds—namely competition for members and price competition with regard to the contributions to be paid. In the eyes of the ECJ, these elements of competition were introduced only to encourage the sickness funds to operate in accordance with principles of sound management, ie in the most effective and least costly manner possible, in the interests of the proper functioning of the German social security system, and did not in any way change the non-economic nature of the sickness funds' activity.[53] The introduction of such a concept of unprotected 'managed' or 'instrumental' competition that a legislator can open, restrict or close at any time outside the realm of judicial control is in clear conflict with a long-standing jurisprudence according to which all types of actual or potential competition, including 'residual' competition, are protected by the EU competition rules.[54] In his conclusions, AG Jacobs had therefore argued in favour of the application of the competition rules, with an exemption available under Article 106(2) TFEU (ex Article 86(2) EC).[55] The ECJ's judgment, by contrast, appears to be driven by a rather unprincipled desire not to interfere with the Member State's organizational sovereignty in a complex sector which is generally considered to be of great political sensitivity.

Even more problematic is the *FENIN* judgment.[56] In *FENIN v Commission*, the Court of First Instance (CFI) held that an organization which purchases goods solely for its use in the context of an activity which is qualified as non-economic due to the exclusively social objectives pursued and its functioning according to the principle of solidarity, cannot be considered an 'undertaking' even in its purchasing activity.[57] This finding was approved by the ECJ.[58] From a competition policy perspective this decision is difficult to understand, let alone justify. The aim of EU competition law to ensure undistorted competition and protect the competitive process against abuses of market power should have guided the CFI and the ECJ to determine the economic character of such purchasing activity on the basis of a general assessment whether the relevant entity was acting like an undertaking on the buyer's side. This test is well accepted in many national competition law orders.[59] Neither the need to protect the well-functioning of compulsory social security schemes nor the protection of Member States' organizational policy choices can explain the decision to generally exclude potential abuses of buyer power from the scope of the EU competition rules, and thereby leave unprotected the seller's side.[60]

[53] Joined Cases C–264/01, C–306/01, C–354/01, and C–355/01, *AOK Bundesverband*, [2004] ECR I–2493, para 56.

[54] For a more thorough discussion see Schweitzer, n 51 above, 96–98. See also Krajewski and Farley, 'Limited Competition in National Health Systems and the Application of Competition Law: The AOK Bundesverband Case' (2004) 29 EL Rev 842, 848 et seq.

[55] See AG Jacobs, conclusions, para 22 et seq, in Joined Cases C–264/01, C–306/01, C–354/01, and C–355/01, *AOK Bundesverband*, [2004] ECR I–2493.

[56] For a critical review see also Schröter, n 41 above, 607–610; Boeger, n 3 above, 330–332; Schweitzer, n 51 above, 98–100.

[57] Case T–319/99 *FENIN* [2003] ECR II–357, para 37.

[58] Case C–205/03 P *FENIN* [2006] ECR I–6295.

[59] For an overview see van den Gronden, 'Purchasing Care: Economic Activity or Service of General (Economic) Interest' (2004) ECLR 87, 91.

[60] See Schweitzer, n 51 above, 98–100. Boeger, n 3 above, 337–338, tries to explain *FENIN* with the need to protect 'public ethos'. The alleged abuse in *FENIN* was, however, in no way related to

More recently, new uncertainties in the delineation of economic and non-economic services have arisen in the area of social services. The Commission has dealt with this issue in some detail in its Communication of 20 November 2007 on Services of General Interest,[61] and has suggested a distinction between two main groups of social services of general interest:[62] on the one hand the statutory and complementary schemes for social protection, and on the other hand other essential services provided directly to the individual (assistance to persons in need, assistance with insertion and training, the inclusion of the handicapped and the sick, and subsidized housing). It proposes the following criteria to delineate *non-economic* social services of general interest: operation on the basis of the principle of solidarity; the multidisciplinary and personalized nature of the service, including the guarantee of fundamental human rights, absence of a profit-making intent, participation of volunteers and unpaid workers, and great proximity and an asymmetrical relationship between the providers and the beneficiaries of the service that cannot be assimilated to a 'normal' supplier/consumer relationship and thereby requires the participation of a third party to provide funding. This proposal shows that the Commission is aware of the complex and varied missions associated with social services, frequently reflecting different collective preferences at the national, regional, or local level. At the same time it demonstrates that in the qualification of social services as economic or non-economic, many issues remain unresolved.[63] The uncertainties extend to fields as important as public education which has so far generally been treated as a non-economic activity.[64] As the traditional financing out of the public budget is replaced or complemented by private financing schemes, this qualification may, however, become a matter of dispute.

The remaining uncertainties give relevance to a broader debate about the meaning and implications of the 'solidarity exception' for the development and future orientation of EU law in mediating between European economic law and social goals. Some have hailed the 'solidarity exception' as signalling an increasing importance of non-economic values in EU law, and as a new willingness to respect democratic choices.[65] It is important to recall, however, that the 'solidarity exception' says little about the value of solidarity at the level of the EU. In EU law, ideas

public ethos, and it is difficult to argue that the legal control of abuses of buyer power would stand in the way of 'public ethos' in such cases.

[61] EU Commission, Communication of 20 November 2007 on services of general interest, including social services of general interest—a new European commitment, n 40 above.

[62] See ch 2.3 of COM (2007) 725.

[63] See Conseil Economique et Social, Analysis of the implications of the Lisbon treaty on Services of General Interest and proposals for implementation, Discussion paper drawn up by European experts, March 2008, para 27.

[64] Case C-263/86 *Humbel* [1988] ECR 5365 para 18; ECJ, Case C-318/05 *Commission v Germany* [2007] ECR I-6957, paras 74–75. See also EU Commission, Staff Working Document: Frequently asked questions in relation with Commission Decision of 28 November 2005 on the application of Article 86(2) of the EC Treaty to State aid in the form of public service compensation . . . , SEC (2007) 1516 fin, 10, with further references.

[65] Boeger, n 3 above, 338–340. More cautious in particular with respect to the 'solidarity exception' in EU competition law: Ross, 'Promoting Solidarity: From Public Services to a European Model of Competition' (2007) 44 CMLR 1057, in particular 1067 et seq.

of 'solidarity' are partially enshrined in the free movement rules and the open market access that competition rules protect, as well as in the concept of EU citizenship. The 'solidarity exception' defines the boundaries within which the Member States' competences to decide and organize *national* solidarity schemes shall enjoy full primacy over the European interest in open markets and equal opportunities, and in maintaining a degree of judicial control. From the perspective of European conceptions of solidarity, the 'solidarity exception' is thus ambivalent.

C. The Increased Emphasis on 'Effects on Trade between Member States'

A less controversial way to mediate between the protection of the Member States' sovereignty and the need to secure the preconditions for an effective and well-functioning internal market with undistorted competition is to place greater weight on the analysis of the 'effects on trade between Member States'. In the past, the 'effects on trade' have been interpreted widely,[66] and they were frequently established based on a rather cursory analysis. More recently, the ECJ tends to ask for a greater degree of substantiation of foreseeable and sufficiently likely effects on trade which, in addition, must be 'appreciable'. In *MOTOE*, the ECJ found that an effect on trade between Member States within the meaning of Article 102 TFEU (ex Article 82 EC)

> can be assumed only if it is possible to foresee with a sufficient degree of probability, on the basis of a set of objective legal and factual elements, that the behaviour in question may have an influence, direct or indirect, actual or potential, on trade between Member States in such a way as might hinder the attainment of a single market between Member States [...]. Purely hypothetical or speculative effects that the conduct of an undertaking in a dominant position may have do not satisfy that criterion. Similarly, the impact on intra-community trade must not be insignificant...[67]

With regard to the free movement rules as applied to the award of public contracts that fall outside the scope of the Procurement Directives, the ECJ has held that it is, in principle, for the contracting authority concerned to assess whether there may be a cross-border interest in a contract, although this assessment may be subject to judicial review; and that legislation may lay down some objective criteria, at the national or local level, indicating under what preconditions there is a certain cross-border interest (eg the value of the contract, the place where the work is carried out).[68]

[66] See Eilmansberger in Streinz (ed), *EUV/EGV* (2003), Art 81, para 29 et al.

[67] Case C–49/07 *MOTOE v Elliniko Dimosio* [2008] ECR I–4863, para 39.

[68] See Case C–507/03, *Commission v Ireland* [2007] ECR I–9777, para 29; Joined Cases C–147/06 and C–148/06, *SECAP* [2008] ECR I–3565, para 21 and paras 30–31. See also Case C–231/03 *Coname* [2005] ECR I–7287, para 20. For a discussion on what exactly the Commission needs to show in an infringement procedure in order to prove an effect on cross-border trade see AG Stix-Hackl, conclusions of 14 September 2006, paras 78–81, in Case C–532/03 *Commission v Ireland* [2007] ECR I–11353.

4. Financing 'Services of General Economic Interest' in the Light of State Aid Rules

Article 101 TFEU (ex Article 81 EC) and 102 TFEU (ex Article 82 EC) have the potential to severely restrict Member States' choices in organizing public interest sectors and the provision of public interest tasks. In comparison, the application of the EU state aid rules appears uncontroversial at first sight. State subsidies are, under most circumstances, the least intrusive instrument to ensure the provision of SGEIs, and are thus easily defended under a proportionality principle, as long as no over-compensation occurs. Difficulties may, however, arise in exactly determining the net costs incurred in the provision of SGEIs. New transparency and accounting requirements had to be imposed upon the Member States,[69] which in the past frequently had not kept track of the actual costs. The monopoly regimes had allowed for a cross-subsidization between profitable and unprofitable segments on a broad scale, where the actual flows of money were frequently intransparent even to the monopolist itself. The liberalization of some sectors, and even more so the partial liberalization of others,[70] called for a new degree of transparency and financial control so as to avoid the distortions of competition that subsidies and cross-subsidization can bring about.

Article 107 TFEU (ex Article 87 EC) provides the legal framework for assessing the compatibility of state financing of SGEIs with EU law. According to Article 107(1) TFEU (ex Article 87(1) EC), 'any aid granted by a Member State or through State resources in any form whatsoever which distorts or threatens to distort competition by favouring certain undertakings or the production of certain goods shall, in so far as it affects trade between Member States, be incompatible with the internal market'. This broad prohibition of all forms of state aid is softened by the possibility of granting exceptions provided in Article 107(2) TFEU (ex Article 87(2) EC) and (3), as well as in Article 106(2) TFEU (ex Article 86(2) EC). Under Article 108(3) TFEU (ex Article 88 (3) EC), Member States are, however, required to notify any measure classified as 'state aid' under Article 107(1) TFEU (ex Article 87(1) EC).

This procedural duty of notification, combined with a standstill obligation until the Commission has issued its final decision, raised concerns among the Member States as to its compatibility with the requirement to ensure the continuous provision of SGEIs. In particular authorities at the regional and local level claimed

[69] See EU Commission Directive 2006/111/EC of 16 November 2006 on the transparency between Member States and public undertakings as well as on financial transparency within certain public undertakings, OJ [2006] L 318/17, which has replaced earlier versions of the Transparency Directive.

[70] In partially liberalized sectors, the calculation of the net costs of the provision of SGEIs by an undertaking that is active both in the liberalized and the reserved parts of the market involves the complex and difficult task to allocate costs, ie costs of the use of established infrastructures. For the litigation which has ensued in this regard before the ECJ see most recently T–266/02 *Deutsche Post AG v Commission* [2008] ECR II–1233. For a summary of the case law see von Danwitz, ch 4 in this volume. See also Hancher and Buendia Sierra, 'Cross-Subsidization and EC Law' (1998) CML Rev 35, 901 et seq.

that the bureaucratic burdens were indefensibly high and could impede an efficient and speedy state financing of the net costs associated with SGEIs. Against this background, a lively controversy ensued whether financial transfers of resources by the state that are meant to merely compensate an entrusted undertaking for the net costs incurred in providing SGEIs should nonetheless be qualified as state aid, because an administrative control for possible overcompensation is needed where the compensation is not determined in the marketplace; or whether such compensation should fall outside the scope of Article 107(1) TFEU (ex Article 87(1) EC) because in effect no economic advantage is conferred upon the recipient.[71] Both sides could point to ECJ judgments in support of their view.[72]

The conflict was ultimately resolved in *Altmark Trans*[73]—one of the ECJ's most-cited and most debated state aid decisions of recent years. The ECJ held that, where a state measure must be regarded as compensation for the services provided by the recipient undertaking in order to discharge public service obligations, and where the recipient undertaking thus does not enjoy a real financial advantage and is not put in a more favourable competitive position than its competitors, such measure is not caught by Article 107(1) TFEU (ex Article 87(1) EC).[74] However, four cumulative conditions must be met for a public service compensation to escape classification as state aid: (1) The recipient undertaking must actually have public service obligations to discharge, and the obligations must be clearly defined; (2) the parameters on the basis of which the compensation will be calculated must be established in advance in an objective and transparent manner; (3) the compensation must not exceed what is necessary to cover all or part of the costs incurred in the discharge of public service obligations, taking into account the relevant receipts and a reasonable profit; and (4) either the undertaking which is to discharge public service obligations has been chosen pursuant to a public procurement procedure which would allow for the selection of the undertaking capable of providing those services at the least cost to the community; or the level of compensation needed must be determined on the basis of an analysis of the costs which a typical undertaking, well run and adequately provided with means of transport, would have incurred.[75] These four criteria are objective criteria, and their presence will be

[71] For the central importance of this criterion for the qualification of a measure as 'state aid' within the meaning of Art 107 TFEU (ex Art 87 EC) see most recently Case T–266/02 *Deutsche Post AG v Commission* [2008] ECR II–1233 para 71. See also Case T–67/94 *Ladbroke Racing v Commission* [1998] ECR II–1, para 52.

[72] For a comprehensive discussion of the relevant case law see AG Jacobs, conclusions, paras 93 et seq, in Case C–126/01 *GEMO* [2003] ECR I–13769.

[73] Case C–280/00 *Altmark* [2003] ECR I–7747.

[74] Case C–280/00 *Altmark* [2003] ECR I–7747, para 87; ECJ, Joined Cases C–34/01 to 38/01 *Enirisorse* [2003] ECR I–14245, para 31.

[75] Case C–280/00, *Altmark* [2003] ECR I–7747, paras 89–93. For a review of the Commission's decision practice under the *Altmark* criteria see EU Commission, Staff Working Document, Frequently asked questions in relation with Commission Decision of 28 November 2005 on the application of Article 86(2) of the EC Treaty to State aid in the form of public service compensation granted to certain undertakings entrusted with the operation of services of general economic interest, and of the Community Framework for State aid in the form of public service compensation, Brussels, 20.11.2007, SEC (2007) 1516 fin, 14–15.

reviewed by the courts. The Commission does not enjoy discretion in establishing whether these criteria are satisfied.[76] Public service compensation which does not fulfil all four of the *Altmark* criteria cumulatively constitutes state aid. It may, however, be justified under Article 106(2) TFEU (ex Article 86(2) EC)[77] as long as it does not exceed all net costs incurred by the entrusted undertaking in carrying out the public service tasks, including where appropriate a reasonable profit.

The judgment is to be welcomed.[78] For the Member States, it has opened a possibility to avoid the bureaucratic constraints of the state aid notification procedure by designing procedural guarantees against overcompensation for the provision of SGEIs.[79] From an EU law perspective, the principles according to which the protection of undistorted competition and the guarantee of the financial viability of SGEIs as contained in Article 106(2) TFEU (ex Article 86(2) EC) and Article 14 TFEU (ex Article 16 EC) are generally reconciled are fully upheld. The relevant criteria for assessing whether compensation payments constitute state aid within the meaning of Article 107(1) TFEU (ex Article 87(1) EC) are in fact modelled upon the criteria of Article 106(2) TFEU (ex Article 86(2) EC)—partially tightened so as to make sure that no ex-ante control procedure before the Commission is needed to ensure the absence of competitive distortions. Contrary to the 'solidarity exception', the *Altmark* jurisprudence does not expand the scope of protection for the Member States' sovereignty.[80] It merely alleviates the administrative burdens that can go along with the exercise of control. In its practical implementation, the *Altmark* test has nonetheless posed difficulties. This is in particular true for the fourth *Altmark* criterion: there is broad recognition that it will not always be appropriate to select the undertaking to be entrusted with a public interest task through competitive tendering.[81] The alternative route accepted by the ECJ in *Altmark*, namely comparing the level of compensation with the costs of a 'typical

[76] Case T–266/02 *Deutsche Post AG v Commission* [2008] ECR II–1233, para 90.

[77] For a clear statement to this effect see T–354/05 *TF1* [2009] ECR II–471, para 135 et seq.

[78] See EAGCP, Services of General Economic Interest, Opinion prepared by the State Aid Group of EAGCP, 29 June 2006, 6; Schweitzer, n 51 above, 101–102. See also Knaul and Pérez Flores, 'State Aid' in Faull and Nikpay (eds), *The EC Law of Competition* (2007), para 16.243 et seq and Bartosch, 'Die Kommissionspraxis nach dem Urteil des EuGH in der Rechtssache Altmark—Worin liegt das Neue?' (2004) EuZW 295, 300–301. For a more critical account see, eg, Ehricke, in Immenga and Mestmäcker, n 1 above, Art 87(1), para 51: *Altmark* has reduced the Commission's state aid control to an abuse control and has weakened the Commission's possibilities for an effective review. Similar: Möschel, (2003) JZ 1021, 1026; v Wallenberg, in Grabitz and Hilf, *Kommentar zur Europäischen Union—EUV/EGV* (2005), Art 87, para 23.

[79] With a view to the 'proceduralization' of the concept of state aid through *Altmark Trans* see Pöcker, 'Der EuGH, das Beihilfenrecht und die Prozeduralisierung' (2007) EuZW 167 et seq; Gromnicka, 'Services of General Economic Interest in the State Aids Regime: Proceduralisation of Political Choices?' (2005) 11 EPL 429 et seq.

[80] This is confirmed by the finding in Hancher, Ottervanger, and Slot, *EC State Aids* (3rd edn, 2006), paras 8–026 to 8–028, that there are relatively few examples of decisions in which the *Altmark* criteria have been held to have been fulfilled.

[81] See EAGCP, Services of General Economic Interest, Opinion prepared by the State Aid Group of EAGCP, 29 June 2006, 5–6 and 6–7; Prosser, 'Competition Law and Public Services: From Single Market to Citizenship Rights?' (2005) 11 EPL 543, 562.

well-run undertaking', is, however, a complex task,[82] and the EU Commission has apparently not been strict in reviewing this criterion.[83] In other cases, the *Altmark* criteria may be too narrow: in its recent *BUPA* judgment, the CFI has therefore rejected the application of Article 107(1) TFEU (ex Article 87(1) EC) to a compensation mechanism although, technically speaking, the *Altmark* criteria were not met.[84] The necessity for such adjustments notwithstanding, the main objective of the *Altmark* jurisprudence is uncontested: pragmatically, it searches for criteria to distinguish between those cases where a risk of over-compensation is minimal and those cases in which financing schemes for SGEIs require a closer look.

In its so-called '*Altmark* package', adopted in July 2005, the Commission has extended this approach to the application of Article 106(2) TFEU (ex Article 86(2) EC).[85] The 'Decision on the application of Article 86(2) to State aid in the form of public service compensation granted to certain undertakings entrusted with the operation of SGEIs'[86] exempts public service compensation that qualifies as 'state aid' from the notification requirement if it does not exceed €30 million per year and is granted to an undertaking with an annual turnover before tax of less than €100 million during the two financial years preceding that in which the SGEI was assigned. Furthermore, the notification requirement is abandoned for public service compensation granted to hospitals or social housing undertakings carrying out activities qualified as SGEIs, irrespective of the amount. The notification requirement will, however, only be dropped if an act of entrustment clearly specifies the nature and duration of the public service obligations, the entrusted undertaking, the territory concerned, the nature of any exclusive or special rights assigned to the undertaking, the parameters of calculating, controlling, and reviewing the compensation, as well as the arrangements for avoiding and repaying any overcompensation. The compensation must not exceed what is necessary to cover the cost incurred in discharging the public service obligation; and the Member State must ensure a mechanism of control, so that overcompensation can be detected. Where these conditions are not met, the public service compensation must be notified in accordance with Article 108(3) TFEU (ex Article 88(3) EC). A 'Community

[82] EAGCP, Services of General Economic Interest, Opinion prepared by the State Aid Group of EAGCP, 29 June 2006, 6–7, warning that the Commission should not become a price regulator through the back door: 'There should be a presumption that the compensation for an SGEI is reasonable unless it can be demonstrated to be otherwise.'

[83] See Case T–388/03 *Deutsche Post and DHL v Commission* [2009] ECR II–199, para 115, reprimanding the Commission for not verifying that the services of general interest which La Poste provided were at a cost which would have been borne by a typical undertaking which was well run, in accordance with the principle laid down by *Altmark*. For the problems raised by the practical application of the 4th criterion see Bartosch, n 77 above, 300; Sinnaeve, 'State Financing of Public Services: The Court's Dilemma in the Altmark Case' (2003) European State Aid Law Quarterly 351, 358 et seq.

[84] Case T–289/03 *BUPA v Commission* [2008] ECR II–81, paras 160 et seq.

[85] For the interaction between Art 107(1) TFEU (ex Art 87(1) EC) and Art 106(2) TFEU (ex Art 86(2) EC) after *Altmark Trans* see Bauer, 'Rechtssicherheit bei der Finanzierung gemeinwirtschaftlicher Leistungen?' (2006) EuZW, 7 et seq.

[86] EU Commission, Decision on the application of Article 86(2) of the Treaty to State aid in the form of public service compensation granted to certain undertakings entrusted with the operation of services of general economic interest, OJ [2005] L 312/67–73.

framework for State aid in the form of public service compensation'[87] specifies the criteria it will apply when assessing a justification under Article 106(2) TFEU (ex Article 86(2) EC).[88]

5. Article 106(2) TFEU (Ex Article 86(2) EC): (How) Does It Resolve the Remaining Tension?

Although the 'solidarity' exception and the *Altmark* jurisprudence have received a lot of attention, the central provision to reconcile the tensions between EU economic law and national 'public service' traditions remains Article 106(2) TFEU (ex Article 86(2) EC). According to this provision,

> [u]ndertakings entrusted with the operation of services of general economic interest . . . shall be subject to the rules contained in this Treaty, in particular to the rules on competition, in so far as the application of such rules does not obstruct the performance, in law or in fact, of the particular tasks assigned to them. The development of trade must not be affected to such an extent as would be contrary to the interests of the Community.

The provision was inserted into the Treaty so as to find a compromise between those Member States who insisted that their public service sectors should be excluded from the scope of the then EC Treaty (now, after amendment, TFEU) rules and other Member States with a more liberal tradition who feared that such sector exemptions would endanger the equal application of the Treaty rules in all Member States. The principles according to which Article 106(2) TFEU (ex Article 86(2) EC) would be interpreted and applied were left open. The ECJ's early judgments were written on a blank slate, and their tentativeness was palpable.[89] Since the mid-1980s, the experience with the provision has grown considerably, and today the case law has stabilized in many respects.[90] Significant uncertainties remain nonetheless. They start with the concept of 'services of general economic

[87] OJ [2005] C 297/4–7.

[88] More recently, the EU Commission has published a Staff Working Document which answers frequently asked questions in relation to the application of Art 106(2) TFEU (ex Art 86(2) EC) to state aid in the form of public service compensation—see EU Commission, Staff Working Document, Frequently asked questions in relation with Commission Decision of 28 November 2005 on the application of Article 86(2) of the EC Treaty to State aid in the form of public service compensation granted to certain undertakings entrusted with the operation of services of general economic interest, and of the Community Framework for State aid in the form of public service compensation, Brussels, 20.11.2007, SEC (2007) 1516 fin.

[89] See, eg, the shift in the ECJ's early jurisprudence regarding the question whether Art 106(2) TFEU (ex Art 86(2) EC) is directly applicable: in Case C–10/71 *Hafen von Mertert* [1971] ECR 723, para 8–12 the ECJ rejected the direct applicability of Art 106(2) TFEU (ex Art 86(2) EC). Since Case C–66/86 *Ahmed Saeed* [1989] ECR 803 paras 55–57, Art 86(2) is considered to be directly applicable.

[90] The current state of the law on Art 106(2) TFEU (ex Art 86(2) EC) has been summarized repeatedly by the Commission in its more recent communications (EU Commission, 'Communication on "Services of general interest in Europe"', COM (2001) 598, 17.10.2001, OJ [2001] C 17; EU Commission, Communication on 'Services of general interest in Europe', OJ [1996] 281; EU Commission, Green Paper, COM (2003) 270, 21.5.2003 and EU Commission, White Paper, COM (2004) 374, 12.5.2004).

interest' itself, extend to the concept of 'entrustment', and are particularly pronounced with regard to the application of the proportionality principle.

A. The Concept of 'Services of General Economic Interest'

The term 'services of general economic interest' is an 'artificial' term of EU law with no direct equivalents in the national legal orders of the Member States. It was deliberately chosen by the drafters of the EC Treaty to underline the autonomy of this concept of EU law vis-à-vis the national traditions of '*service public*', '*Daseinsvorsorge*' or similar concepts in other Member States. While no explicit definition exists in the Treaty,[91] it results from the case law that 'services of general economic interest' are services of an economic nature which the Member States (and sometimes the Union) subject to specific and clearly defined public service obligations by virtue of a general or public interest[92] criterion.[93] The public service obligations' core is the duty to contract on consistent conditions with any user requesting it even if the provision of goods or services on this basis is unprofitable for the undertaking entrusted with the task.[94] It is this feature which distinguishes SGEIs from other goods and services offered in the marketplace, and the reason why intrusions into the market mechanism may be justified.[95]

In the early years of the evolution of the law on Article 106(2) TFEU (ex Article 86 (2) EC), one of the controversial questions was to what extent Member States are free in specifying the services they consider to be of general economic interest, and in defining the public interest tasks attached.[96] This question goes to the heart of the function and force of Article 106(2) TFEU (ex Article 86(2) EC). Does this provision subject the Member States' fundamental choices of public policy goals to judicial review? Or is the judicial review primarily limited to the choice of instruments and their compatibility with EU law? Once again, the ECJ has opted neither for an 'Absolute sovereignty approach' nor for an 'Absolute Competition approach' but for an intermediate solution. According to the ECJ, Article 86(2) EC (now Article 106(2) TFEU)

> seeks to reconcile the Member States' interest in using certain undertakings, in particular in the public sector, as an instrument of economic or fiscal policy with the Community's interest in ensuring compliance with the rules on competition and the preservation of the unity of the common market.[97]

[91] Emphasized by T–289/03 *BUPA* [2008] ECR II–81, 165.

[92] SGEIs must be distinguished from services provided in the private interest, even though that interest may be more or less collective or be recognized by the State as legitimate or beneficial—see T–289/03 *BUPA* [2008] ECR II–81, para 178; and Case C–7/82 *GVL v Commission* [1983] ECR 483, paras 31–32.

[93] See, eg, *EU Commission*, 'White Paper on Services of General Interest', n 1 above, 7.

[94] T–289/03 *BUPA* [2008] ECR II–81, para 190. See also Case C–320/91 *Corbeau* [1993] ECR I–2533, para 15.

[95] Case T–289/03 *BUPA* [2008] ECR II–81, para 190; Case C–242/95 *GT Link* [1997] ECR I–4449, para 53; Case C–170/90 *Merci Convenzionali Porto di Genova* [1991] ECR I–5889, para 27.

[96] The debate has been revived in Case T–289/03 *BUPA* [2008] ECR II–81, para 163 et seq.

[97] Case C–159/94 *Commission v France ('import and export monopolies in gas and electricity')* [1997] ECR I–5815, para 55.

On this basis, Article 106(2) TFEU acknowledges in principle the Member States' right to define those services they want to link to public service obligations, which will then qualify as SGEIs.[98] Also, when specifying the public interests, Member States may take account of objectives pertaining to their national policy.[99] In doing so, Member States enjoy a wide discretion, subject only to control for manifest error.[100] According to the CFI's recent *BUPA* judgment, the discretion is particularly broad in those spheres of action which remain, in principle, within the competence of the Member States.[101] The principles according to which the EU Commission, and ultimately the European courts, will exercise control are less clear. Some case law has indicated that services, in order to be legitimately declared 'services of general economic interest' by a Member State, must exhibit some 'special characteristics' as compared with the general economic interest of other economic activities.[102] In *RTT* the ECJ refused to qualify the production and sale of telecommunication terminals, in particular telephones, as a service of general economic interest, holding that this is an activity that should be open to any undertaking.[103] In *Corbeau*, the ECJ distinguished between services of general economic interest—the collection, carrying, and distribution of mail on behalf of all users throughout the territory of the Member State at a uniform tariff—from 'specific services dissociable from the service of general interest which

[98] See Case T–106/95 *FFSA and others v Commission* [1997] ECR II–229, para 99; Case T–442/03 *SIC v Commission* [2008] ECR II–1161 para 195; and recently Joined Cases T–309/04, T–317/04, and T–336/04 *TV2/Danmark A/S v Commission* [2008] ECR II–2935 para 101 et seq. See also EU Commission, 'Communication on services of general interest in Europe', COM (2000) 580 final, para 22; and EU Commission, 'Services of general interest, including social services of general interest: a new European commitment', n 9 above, 4.

[99] Case C–159/94 *Commission v France ('import and export monopolies in gas and electricity')* [1997] ECR I–5815, para 56.

[100] EU Commission, 'Communication on Services of General Economic Interest' OJ [2001] C17/4 para 22. See also Case T–442/03 *SIC v Commission* [2008] ECR II–1161 para 195; Case T–289/03 *BUPA* [2008] ECR II–81, para 166; Case T–17/02 *Fred Olsen v Commission* [2005] ECR II–2031, para 216. According to Sauter, n 1 above, 175, the 'Member States' freedom to designate SGEI is almost absolute up until the moment that pre-emption occurs, ie the point where the relevant services are defined by Community legislation'. According to the point of view of the author of this paper, this claim goes too far.

[101] Case T–289/03 *BUPA* [2008] ECR II–81, para 167:

> The determination of the nature and scope of an SGEI mission in specific spheres of action which either do not fall within the powers of the Community, within the meaning of the first paragraph of Article 5 EC, or are based on only limited or shared Community competence, within the meaning of the second paragraph of that article, remains, in principle, within the competence of the Member States. As the defendant and Ireland maintain, the health sector falls almost exclusively within the competence of the Member States. In that sector, the Community can engage, under Article 152(1) and (5) EC, only in action which is not legally binding, while fully respecting the responsibilities of the Member States for the organisation and provision of health services and medical care. It follows that the determination of SGEI obligations in this context also falls primarily within the competence of the Member States. That division of powers is also reflected, generally, in Article 16 EC [. . .].

[102] Case C–179/90 *Merci Convenzionali Porto di Genova* [1991] ECR I–5889, para 27; and Case C–242/95 *GT Link* [1997] ECR I–4449, para 53. See also Case 41/83 *Italy v Commission* [1985] ECR 873, para 30, rejecting the Member States' discretion in applying Art 106(2) TFEU (ex Art 86(2) EC).

[103] Case C–18/88 *RTT* [1991] ECR I–5941, para 22.

meet special needs of economic operators' and could therefore not be reserved.[104] AG Van Gerven and AG Darmon have, on different occasions, suggested that services of general economic interest must directly benefit the public, or consumers, in order to be recognized as such.[105]

Against this background, the most common and essentially uncontroversial type of 'services of general economic interest' is what has come to be called a 'universal service', ie an obligation imposed on one or more undertakings to provide a defined set of services to all users throughout the territory of a Member State at a specified quality, irrespective of the specific situations or the degree of economic profitability of each individual operation, and at an affordable price.[106] 'Universal service obligations' of this kind are characteristic for the big infrastructure sectors such as telecommunications, postal services or electricity. Universality thus defined is, however, not a precondition for qualifying a service as an SGEI. SGEIs need not necessarily correspond to a need common to the whole population or be supplied throughout the territory.[107] Rather, SGEI obligations can also have a limited territorial reach or cover a relatively limited group of users.[108] Many SGEIs, like, for example, some social services or waste management, are of a more local kind. The defining feature of SGEIs is thus not their universal coverage, but the public-interest-driven compulsory nature of the service provision to any user of a defined group, regardless of the existence of commercial incentives to provide the service in any given case (see above), and the corresponding uncoupling of the service provision from the 'natural laws' of the marketplace.

Recent judgments, in particular judgments by the CFI, have not pursued the idea of searching for an objective delimitation of legitimate public service missions, and have advocated a mere abuse control. In its recent *BUPA* judgment, the CFI finds that:

> the Member State's power to take action under Article 86(2) EC and, accordingly, its power to define SGEIs is not unlimited and cannot be exercised arbitrarily for the sole purpose of removing a particular sector, such as telecommunications, from the application of the competition rules.[109]

Therefore, any Member State relying on Article 106(2) TFEU (ex Article 86(2) EC) is required to 'indicate the reasons why it considers that the service in question, because of its specific nature, deserves to be characterised as an SGEI and to be distinguished from other economic activities'.[110] The concept of a mere abuse control signals the CFI's readiness to preserve the broad discretion of the Member

[104] Case C–320/91 *Corbeau* ECR I–2533, para 19.

[105] AG Darmon, conclusions, para 137 in Case C–393/92 *Almelo* [1994] ECR I–1477; *AG Van Gerven*, conclusions, para 27, in Case C–170/90 *Merci Convenzionali Porto di Genova* [1991] ECR I–5889.

[106] See for this definition Art 3(1) of Directive 2002/22/EC of 7 March 2002, OJ [2002] L 108/51; and Case C–320/91 *Corbeau* [1993] ECR I–2533, para 15.

[107] Case T–289/03 *BUPA* [2008] ECR II–81, para 186; Case C–66/86 *Ahmed Saeed Flugreisen* [1989] ECR 803, para 55; Case C–266/96 *Corsica Ferries* [1998] ECR I–3949, para 45; Case T–17/02 *Olsen v Commission* [2005] ECR II–2031, para 186 et seq.

[108] Case T–289/03 *BUPA* [2008] ECR II–81, para 187.

[109] Case T–289/03 *BUPA* [2008] ECR II–81, para 168.

[110] Case T–289/03 *BUPA* [2008] ECR II–81, para 172.

States and to protect their policy competences. Article 14 TFEU (ex Article 16 EC) may provide additional arguments in favour of such a reading of Article 106(2) TFEU (ex Article 86(2) EC).[111] The ECJ has, however, not subscribed to this concept so far. Its case law is better understood as a search for an objective delimitation of what can constitute an SGEI.

B. The Concept of 'Entrustment'

Article 106(2) TFEU (ex Article 86(2) EC) will only apply if the relevant undertaking has been entrusted with the provision of SGEIs by an official act carrying legal force under national law.[112] An entrustment must be distinguished from general rules that set the general framework for all commercial activity in a given sector:[113] Article 106(2) TFEU (ex Article 86(2) EC) is only at issue where some risk of distortion of competition exists between those fulfilling the task and those not fulfilling it, or fulfilling it to a lesser degree.[114]

The act of entrustment must clearly define the general interest mission, its scope, and the general conditions of the functioning of the SGEI,[115] and it must oblige the entrusted undertaking to provide the services concerned, irrespective of their profitability. This ensures that the relevant decision about the content and scope of a public service is taken by the public authority[116] and not by the undertaking itself—a necessary precondition for the granting of an exception under Article 106(2) TFEU (ex Article 86(2) EC). Furthermore, only a transparent and

[111] Case T–289/03 *BUPA* [2008] ECR II–81, para 167 explicitly cites Art 14 TFEU (ex Art 16 EC) in this regard.

[112] While EU law does not prescribe a specific form of the act, an approval given by a public authority to a service provider, authorizing him to provide some services, will not suffice. This is because it does not create an obligation for the operator to provide the services concerned, but just allows him to exercise an economic activity by offering some services in a market. For examples of acts of entrustment see EU Commission, Staff Working Document, 'Frequently asked questions in relation with Commission Decision of 28 November 2005 on the application of Article 86(2) of the EC Treaty to State aid in the form of public service compensation granted to certain undertakings entrusted with the operation of services of general economic interest, and of the Community Framework for State aid in the form of public service compensation', Brussels, 20.11.2007, SEC (2007) 1516 fin, 21–22.

[113] Case T–289/03 *BUPA* [2008] ECR II–81, para 178; Case 7/82, *GVL v Commission* [1983] ECR 483, para 32.

[114] Such a risk may also exist in a case where an SGEI mission is imposed on a large number of, or indeed all the operators active on the same market, if possibilities exist for some to commercially avoid or lessen the burden associated with the fulfilment of the task—see for such a case T–289/03 *BUPA* [2008] ECR II–81, para 179.

[115] Case T–289/03 *BUPA* [2008] ECR II–81, paras 181–182. For the limits of this requirement see EU Commission, Staff Working Document, 'Frequently asked questions in relation with Commission Decision of 28 November 2005 on the application of Article 86(2) of the EC Treaty to State aid in the form of public service compensation granted to certain undertakings entrusted with the operation of services of general economic interest, and of the Community Framework for State aid in the form of public service compensation, Brussels', 20.11.2007, SEC (2007) 1516 fin, 22: 'Where it is not possible to define more specifically the services concerned, broad definitions of the public service mission can be accepted, as long as the scope of the mission is clearly set out. . . . '.

[116] For the relevance of this aspect see also EU Commission, White Paper on Services of General Interest, n 1 above, 5.

clear definition of the public service task will render possible a meaningful proportionality control.[117]

The question whether Union law limits the Member States' freedom to choose which undertaking(s) to entrust with public service obligations has received attention only more recently. For a long time, this question appeared to be outside the reach of Union law. The evolving jurisprudence on public procurement law and on the free movement rules as applied to the award of contracts or concessions that fall outside the scope of these Procurement Directives has significantly modified this picture: while public authorities continue to be free to carry out SGEIs themselves, they have to observe all rules of EU primary and secondary law once they decide to outsource.[118] The Public Procurement Directives impose strict procedural requirements. For those public contracts or concessions that are not covered by them, the Member States must nonetheless select their contracting partner in a fair and transparent procedure[119] in order to comply with Article 49 TFEU (ex Article 43 EC) and Article 56 TFEU (ex Article 49 EC), and the principles of non-discrimination, equality of treatment, transparency, and proportionality.

These rules appeared to have far-reaching consequences for the application of Article 106(2) TFEU (ex Article 86(2) EC): whenever a public authority would not

[117] EU Commission, Communication OJ [2001] C 17/4 para 22: 'the public service mission needs to be clearly defined and must be explicitly entrusted through an act of public authority (including contracts) (5). This obligation is necessary to ensure legal certainty as well as transparency vis-à-vis the citizens and is indispensable for the Commission to carry out its proportionality assessment'.

[118] EU Commission, Staff Working Document, 'Frequently asked questions concerning the application of public procurement rules to social services of general interest', 20.11.2007, SEC (2007) 1514; EU Commission, 'Interpretative Communication on the application of Community law on Public Procurement and Concessions to Institutionalised Public-Private Partnerships (IPPP)', 5.2.2008, COM (2007) 6661. Only within the narrow confines of the so-called 'in-house exception' will the public authority be exempt from the rules on open, fair, and transparent tendering. The 'in-house exception' covers situations where a public authority decides to provide a service through a legally independent entity, but the legally independent entity and the public authority are effectively to be regarded as one. This is the case where the following conditions apply: (1) the public authority exercises over the legally independent entity a control which is similar to that which it exercises over its own departments; and (2) the legally independent entity carries out the essential part of its activities with the controlling public authority—see for this 'in-house exception' Case C–107/98 *Teckal* [1999] ECR I–8121, para 50. The in-house exception will not apply with regard to so-called 'institutionalised public-private partnerships' (IPPPs) (for a definition see EU Commission, 'Communication on Institutionalised Public-Private Partnerships', COM (2007) 6661, 2: IPPPs are defined as 'a cooperation between public and private parties involving the establishment of a mixed capital entity which performs public contracts or concessions. The private input to the IPPP consists—apart from the contribution of capital or other assets—in the active participation in the operation of the contracts awarded to the public-private entity and/or the management of the public-private entity'). For a more detailed description of the rules that apply when an IPPP shall be entrusted with the provision of a SGEI see EU Commission, Communication on Institutionalised Public-Private Partnerships, COM (2007) 6661, 4 et seq. The participation—even as a minority—of a private undertaking in the capital of a company in which the contracting entity in question is also a participant excludes the possibility of an in-house relationship (Case C–26/03 *Stadt Halle* [2005] ECR I–1, para 49. According to Case C–410/04 *ANAV* [2006] ECR I–3303 paras 30 et seq, the contracting entity's intent to open up the capital of its daughter company to private third parties in the future will in fact suffice to exclude the in-house status of a publicly owned company).

[119] See ECJ Case C–507/03 *Commission v Ireland* [2007] ECR I–9777. See also the EU Commission's 'Interpretative Communication on the Community law applicable to contract awards not or not fully subject to the provision of the Public Procurement Directives', OJ [2006] C 179/2.

want to carry out the SGEI itself, it would have to create an open market for the SGEI if it wished to rely on an exception from the competition rules. However, the CFI has been hesitant to subscribe to such a rule. In *Olsen v Commission* it found that Article 106(2) TFEU (ex Article 86(2) EC) does not generally require Member States to follow a competitive tendering procedure for the award of the SGEI.[120] It remained unclear whether Article 106(2) TFEU (ex Article 86(2) EC) should exempt the Member States from such a requirement, or whether *Olsen* was simply meant to emphasize that the need for a competitive tendering procedure did not follow directly from Article 106(2) TFEU (ex Article 86(2)). In *SIC v Commission*, the CFI has clarified its view. In reaction to a private commercial television company's complaint that Portugal had entrusted RTP, the Portuguese public television service provider, with the provision of public service television without conducting a competitive tendering procedure, the CFI did not only reject the claim that Portugal was required to have recourse to competitive tendering.[121] In an obiter dictum it elaborated that Article 106(2) TFEU (ex Article 86(2) EC) should be applied irrespective of whether the undertaking to be entrusted should have been selected on the basis of a competitive tendering procedure under primary or secondary Union law. Infringements of the Public Procurement Directives or of Article 49 TFEU (ex Article 43 EC) or Article 56 TFEU (ex Article 49 EC) should be enforced pursuant to Article 258 TFEU (ex Article 226 EC). The absence of competitive tendering 'cannot, by contrast, have the result that State funding of the SGEI holder's public service obligations must, even though the requirements concerning the definition of the SGEI, the remit and proportionality are fulfilled, be considered to be State aid incompatible with the common market' (para 147).

From the perspective of the effective enforcement of Union law, this is a setback. Withdrawing the availability of the exception in Article 106(2) TFEU (ex Article 86(2) EC) in those cases in which Member States don't fully comply with Union law would act as a powerful threat. On the other hand, the purpose of Article 106 (2) TFEU (ex Article 86(2) EC) is to protect the fulfilment of legitimate public interest tasks, and ultimately the general public or the consumers who stand to benefit. It would raise serious concerns to endanger this goal where a Member State has violated procedural obligations under procurement rules or free movement rules. In a different case, *AG Stix-Hackl* has suggested that Article 106(2) TFEU (ex Article 86(2) EC) itself applies to the violation of public procurement rules: where compliance with the stipulated procedures would obstruct the fulfilment of the entrusted task, in particular with a view to the time that such a procedure can take, an infringement of those rules should be justified.[122] A similar reasoning should arguably apply in cases where a Member State failed to follow an open tendering procedure although it could and should have complied: the aim to ensure the

[120] Case T–17/02 *Olsen v Commission* [2005] ECR II–2031, para 239. Confirmed in Case T–442/03 *SIC v Commission* [2008] ECR II–1161, para 145.

[121] Case T–442/03 *SIC v Commission* [2008] ECR II–1161, paras 151, 153–154, 156.

[122] AG Stick-Hackl, conclusions of 14 September 2006, para 103, in Case C–532/03 *Commission v Ireland* [2007] ECR I–11353.

continuous provision of public service obligations takes priority over the effective sanctioning of the Member State by way of a withdrawal of the Article 106(2) TFEU (ex Article 86(2) EC) privilege.

C. The Application of the Proportionality Principle in Article 106(2) TFEU (Ex Article 86(2) EC)

According to Article 106(2) TFEU (ex Article 86(2) EC), violations of the Treaty rules, including competition rules, can only be justified 'in so far as' their application would obstruct the performance of the protected public service task. Article 106(2) TFEU (ex Article 86(2) EC) thus incorporates a proportionality principle. Its application has been one of the politically most sensitive and legally controversial issues in the context of Article 106(2) TFEU (ex Article 86(2) EC). The balance struck between the Member States' sovereignty and the European rule of law depends to a significant degree on whether the proportionality principle is strictly or loosely applied. In either case, the court will ask whether the infringement of Union law is necessary and appropriate in order to achieve the objectives legitimately pursued, and it will analyse whether there is a causal link between the infringement and the public service objective pursued. Under a strict form of the proportionality test, the court will furthermore ask whether the same legitimate objective could be achieved by less restrictive means. A loose interpretation of the proportionality test, on the other hand, would replace this test with the inquiry whether the measure in question is manifestly inappropriate by reference to the objective pursued.[123] Such a review partially coincides with the requirement under Article 106(2) TFEU (ex Article 86(2) EC) that 'the development of trade must not be affected to such an extent as would be contrary to the interests of the Community'. In the terminology of former Judge Edwards, a strict proportionality test could be associated with a 'Limited Competition approach'. The 'manifestly inappropriate' test could be linked to a 'Limited Sovereignty approach'. The difference between the two versions is apparent where the justification of special or exclusive rights is concerned: a strict proportionality review will ask whether the special or exclusive rights can be replaced by more pro-competitive forms of regulation and/or financing. A review for manifest inappropriateness will normally respect a Member State's organizational choice and not challenge such rights where a clear causal link with the achievement of public service objectives can be shown.

While the distinction seems clear in principle, a conspicuous uncertainty exists as to which approach is actually followed by the European courts. A widespread view holds that a loose version of the proportionality test has prevailed.[124] The picture

[123] For such an inquiry see Case T–289/03 *BUPA*, [2008] ECR II–81, para 222. For the two possible versions of proportionality test in the application of Art 106(2) TFEU (ex Art 86(2) EC) see also Sauter, n 1 above, 186 et seq.

[124] Sauter, ibid. See also EU Commission, 'Services of general interest, including social services of general interest: a new European commitment', 20.11.2007, COM (2007) 725 final, 9 et seq. According to the Commission, Member States not only enjoy broad discretion in determining what services are to be regarded as SGEIs, and to define the scope of the public service obligations attached.

that emerges from a perusal of the case law is, however, less clear. In *Corbeau*,[125] the ECJ found that an exclusive right for the provision of a core set of essential universal postal services would be justified to avoid cream-skimming:

> to authorize individual undertakings to compete with the holder of the exclusive rights in the sectors of their choice corresponding to those rights would make it possible for them to concentrate on the economically profitable operations and to offer more advantageous tariffs than those adopted by the holders of the exclusive rights since, unlike the latter, they are not bound for economic reasons to offset losses in the unprofitable sectors against profits in the more profitable sectors.[126]

Therefore, restrictions of competition in the economically profitable sectors can be justified so as to ensure that the undertaking entrusted can provide the services of general economic interest in conditions of economic equilibrium.[127] It seems to follow from *Corbeau* that the ECJ is not willing to analyse possible means less restrictive than exclusive rights to ensure the provision of SGEIs. Clearly, a Member State cannot be forced to finance the provision of universal services through direct state subsidies.[128] But neither does the ECJ review other possible means of financing losses, like, for example, a 'universal service fund'. In *Corbeau*, the ECJ limits itself to an analysis of whether the scope of the exclusive right does not exceed what is necessary to cross-subsidize unprofitable services, and establishes the principle that exclusive rights should normally not extend to value-added services that are not themselves SGEIs.

These principles are implicitly called into question, however, by the ECJ's reasoning in three parallel judgments issued in 1997.[129] The Commission had brought cases against, inter alia, France, the Netherlands, and Italy arguing that the national import and export monopolies for gas and electricity violated Article 37 TFEU (ex Article 31 EC) and requesting their abolition. According to the Commission's opinion, Article 106(2)

They also enjoy broad discretion to decide how to organize, regulate, and finance SGEIs. This seems to be in line with a mere 'manifestly inappropriate' test. However, the EU Commission never forgets to add that Member States, in exercising their discretion, must comply with EU law. It usually remains open what this means more specifically.

[125] Case C–320/91 *Corbeau* [1993] ECR I–2533, paras 14–16.

[126] Case C–320/91 *Corbeau* [1993] ECR I–2533, para 18.

[127] Case C–320/91 *Corbeau* [1993] ECR I–2533, para 17. In para 16, the ECJ emphasizes that Art 106(2) TFEU (ex Art 86(2) EC) is to ensure that the undertaking entrusted benefits from 'economically acceptable conditions'.

[128] The Commission regularly emphasizes the Member States' autonomy to choose the financing mechanism to be applied to SGEIs—see EU Commission, 'White Paper on Services of General Interest', n 1 above, 13:

> The principle of the Member States' autonomy to make policy choices regarding services of general economic interest equally applies with regard to financing the latter. Indeed, Member States enjoy a wide margin of discretion when deciding whether and in what way to finance the provision of services of general economic interest. The financing mechanisms applied by Member States include direct financial support through the State budget, special or exclusive rights, contributions by market participants, tariff averaging and solidarity-based financing. As a general rule, Member States can choose which financing mechanism is used. In the absence of Community harmonisation, the main limit to this discretion is the requirement that such financing mechanism must not distort competition within the common market. It is for the Commission, as the guardian of the Treaty, to ensure that this rule is respected to the benefit of taxpayers and the economy at large.

[129] See Case C–159/94 *Commission v France* [1997] ECR I–5815; Case C–157/94 *Commission v Netherlands* [1997] ECR I–5699; Case C–158/94 *Commission v Italy* [1997] ECR I–5789.

TFEU (ex Article 86(2) EC) was generally not applicable to infringements of Article 37 TFEU (ex Article 31 EC). Should the ECJ find otherwise, a justification under Article 106(2) TFEU (ex Article 86(2) EC) would fail because alternative, less restrictive means would be available to ensure the fulfilment of the public interest tasks that the relevant undertakings were entrusted with. The ECJ, holding that Article 106(2) TFEU (ex Article 86(2) EC) was generally applicable in the context of Article 37 TFEU (ex Article 31 EC), found in favour of the Member States. Interestingly, the ECJ did not, however, refuse to look at the availability of less restrictive means in principle. Rather, it criticized the Commission for not being specific enough in its suggestions for alternative means:

> Whilst it is true that it is incumbent upon a Member State which invokes Article 90(2) [now Article 106(2) TFEU] to demonstrate that the conditions laid down in that provision are met, that burden of proof cannot be so extensive as to require the Member State, when setting out in detail the reasons for which, in the event of elimination of the contested measures, the performance of the tasks of general economic interest under economically acceptable conditions would, in its view, be jeopardized, to go even further and prove, positively, that no other conceivable measure, which by definition would be hypothetical, could enable those tasks to be performed under the same conditions. In proceedings under Article 169 [now Article 258 TFEU] of the Treaty for failure to fulfil an obligation, it is incumbent upon the Commission to prove the allegation that the obligation has not been fulfilled and to place before the Court the information needed to enable it to determine whether the obligation has not been fulfilled.[130]

Implicitly, this judgment thus suggests that in an infringement proceeding brought by the EU Commission, the ECJ might be willing to assess the availability of less restrictive alternatives to the maintenance of exclusive rights, in particular regulatory models, if the Commission's suggestions in this regard would only be specific enough. In particular, it keeps open the possibility for the Commission to specify less restrictive means on the basis of Article 106(3) TFEU (ex Article 86(3) EC). At the same time, the *energy monopoly* decisions provide an explanation why the ECJ did not inquire into the availability of less restrictive alternatives in *Corbeau*—a preliminary ruling proceeding in which neither the Commission nor the relevant Member State participated, and in which an abolition of the exclusive rights would have required re-regulation on a broad scale. However, in *Dusseldorp*, a much less complex preliminary ruling proceeding concerning the legality of an exclusive right conferred upon AVR Chemie to process dangerous waste, the ECJ rejected a justification based on Article 106(2) TFEU (ex Article 86(2)) because

> it is for the Netherlands Government . . . to show to the satisfaction of the national court that that objective [to enable the undertaking entrusted to be economically viable] cannot be achieved equally well by other means. Article 90(2) [now Article 106(2) TFEU] of the Treaty can thus apply only if it is shown that, without the contested measure, the undertaking in question would be unable to carry out the task assigned to it.[131]

130 Case C–159/94 *Commission v France* [1997] ECR I–5815, paras 101–102.
131 Case C–203/96 *Dusseldorp* [1998] ECR I–4075, para 67.

Against the background of this case law, the claim that the ECJ is generally unwilling to perform a 'less restrictive means' test under Article 106(2) TFEU (ex Article 86(2) EC) cannot be upheld.[132] Also, the entrusting Member State or the undertaking entrusted with a specific public service task continues to bear the burden of proof for the necessity of an exception under Article 106(2) TFEU (ex Article 86(2) EC).[133] Nonetheless, the ECJ proceeds with notable caution and considerable attention to the specific circumstances of each case when applying that norm. Whereas the ECJ normally refrains from considering the difficulties a Member State may encounter in complying with the Treaty when it examines the availability of an exception to the free movement rules, the ECJ pays close attention to such arguments in the context of Article 106(2) TFEU (ex Article 86(2) EC) as long as secondary law has not provided harmonized solutions for the relevant concerns. There is a general presumption in favour of the legitimacy and value of the social and policy choices protected by Article 106(2) TFEU (ex Article 86(2) EC)—a presumption possibly strengthened by Article 14 TFEU (ex Article 16 EC)—and a supposition that they don't primarily pursue protectionist aims. These principles may explain the palpable differences in the application of the proportionality principle in the context of the exceptions to the free movement rules and in the context of Article 106(2) TFEU (ex Article 86(2) EC).[134] Nonetheless, the ECJ continues to state that Article 106(2) TFEU (ex Article 86(2) EC), being a provision that permits derogations from the Treaty rules, must be interpreted strictly.[135]

6. Sector-specific Attempts to Reconcile the Provision of SGEIs and the Application of EU Competition Rules: Between Telecoms and Broadcasting

In the *energy monopoly* cases, the ECJ has emphasized the limits of a purely judicial application of Article 106(2) TFEU (ex Article 86(2) EC). According to the Court,

> [i]t is certainly not for the Court, on the basis of observations of a general nature . . . , to undertake an assessment, necessarily extending to economic, financial and social matters, of the means which a Member State might adopt in order to ensure the supply of electricity and gas in its national territory, continuity of supply and equal treatment for all customers and consumers.[136]

[132] Against Baquero Cruz, n 1 above, 193.

[133] ECJ, 15 November 2007, C–162/06—*International Mail Spain SL v Administracion del Estado*, para 49, with reference to Case C–340/99 *TNT Traco* [2001] ECR I–4109, para 59.

[134] Against the claim by Buendia Sierra, *Exclusive Rights and State Monopolies under EC Law: Article 86 of the EC Treaty* (1999), 300–306, according to whom the proportionality test contained in Art 106 (2) TFEU (ex Art 86(2) EC) is no different from those existing in other areas of EU law.

[135] See, eg, Case C–157/94 *Commission v Netherlands* [1997] ECR I–5699, para 37. For discussion see Baquero Cruz, n 1 above, 176.

[136] Case C–159/94 *Commission v France* [1997] ECR I–5815, para 106.

Indeed, a liberalization of whole infrastructure sectors of the economy solely on the basis of EU primary law remains unrealistic. A legislative framework is needed to ensure the continuous provision of services of general economic interest. In the telecommunications sector, the liberalization based on Commission Directives under Article 106(3) TFEU (ex Article 86(3) EC)[137] has therefore been accompanied by re-regulation contained in harmonization Directives based on Article 95 EC (now, after amendment Article 114 TFEU).[138] Due to the Member States' strong opposition against the Commission acting alone in specifying the Member States' duties to liberalize,[139] the Commission has refrained from relying on Article 106(3) TFEU (ex Article 86(3) EC) in liberalizing the other large network industries, in particular energy, postal services, railways and public passenger transport. The liberalization process in these sectors has been based on Article 95 EC (now, after amendment, Article 114 TFEU) Directives instead, and thus fully involved the Council and the European Parliament. Nonetheless, negotiations have proceeded in the shadow of the Treaty rules, including the limited exception available under Article 106(2) TFEU (ex Article 86(2) EC).[140] EU secondary law has thus become an important reservoir of experience on how Member States' public interest goals can be reconciled with EU law.

A cursory survey reveals that the EU legislator has clearly rejected a 'one size fits all' model of pro-competitive SGEI provision and financing. Rather, a plurality of approaches exist, each fine-tuned to the specificities of the sector and the nature of the public interest concerns.

However, some typical patterns emerge.

In telecommunications, postal services, and to some extent energy, SGEI legislation has focused on consumer rights. From this, the 'universal service' model has

[137] Commission Directive 2002/77 of 16 September 2002 on competition in the markets for electronic communications networks and services, OJ [2002] L 249/21, has now replaced all previous Art 86(3) Directives which had, step by step, abolished the special and exclusive rights conferred upon the former state monopolies.

[138] Of particular interest here is Directive 2002/22/EC of the European Parliament and of the Council of 7 March 2002 on universal service and users' rights relating to electronic communications networks and services (Universal Service Directive), OJ [2002] L 108/51.

[139] The intense litigation following each Art 86 Directive is evidence of this—see in particular Case C-188–190/80, *Transparency Directive I* [1982] ECR 2545; ECJ, Case C-118/85 *Transparency Directive II* [1987] ECR 2599; Case C-202/88 *France v Commission* [1991] ECR I-1223; Case C-271/90, 281/90, and 289/90 *Telecommunications Services* [1992] ECR I-5833.

[140] Art 106(2) TFEU (ex Art 86(2) EC) also remains relevant for the interpretation of the scope of 'public service' exceptions available under the relevant internal market Directives. This has been confirmed recently by the ECJ in *International Mail Spain SL*. According to this judgment, Art 7(2) of Directive 97/67/EC of the European Parliament and of the Council of 15 December 1997 on common rules for the development of the internal market of Community postal services (OJ [1997] L 15/14, as amended by Directive 2002/39 of the European Parliament and of the Council of 10 June 2002, OJ [2002] L 176/21) which allows Member States to continue to reserve cross-border mail to the universal service provider, within certain price and weight limits, '[t]o the extent necessary to ensure the maintenance of universal service', must be interpreted by reference to Art 106(2) TFEU (ex Art 86 (2) EC); see Case C-162/06 *International Mail Spain SL v Administracion del Estado* [2007] ECR I-9911, paras 31–37. A Member State which makes use of the option to reserve cross-border mail to the provider of the universal postal service will bear the burden of proof that the reservation of cross-border mail is in fact necessary to ensure the maintenance of universal service (para 49).

emerged. In its pure form, it is based on the presumption that the protection of well-defined consumer interests and full competition can be made compatible by an adequate set of framework rules (A.).

EU legislation shows that this model is not adequate in all sectors. A different approach, termed 'regulated competition', has, for instance, been chosen in public passenger transport:[141] it acknowledges that a political choice to ensure a level of services that significantly exceeds the level the market would provide may imply a need to uphold exclusive rights, but it introduces competition *for* the market at regular intervals (B.).

In some cases, the public service mission is of such a kind that it completely defies a 'marketization', so that even competition *for* the market is not viable. This is in particular true where the fulfilment of the public service task is inherently tied to some form of 'public ethos' or 'value rationality',[142] and would thus change in character where it were provided privately and according to a market rationality. Public service broadcasting may be representative. For EU law, this remains the most difficult category (C.).

A. The Universal Service Model—The Example of Telecommunications

The European 'universal service' model has evolved as a corollary to the full liberalization of telecommunications. In the early phases of liberalization, the Commission had, step by step, cut back the scope of the exclusive rights conferred upon national telecommunications organizations, but had respected a core of monopoly rights that it assumed to be necessary in order to finance the provision of essential services to all users throughout the territory at a specified quality and at a uniform price determined by the Member States. The decision in favour of full liberalization implied that the traditional model of cross-subsidizing unprofitable services would no longer work. A new mode of financing unprofitable services was needed that should be compatible with open markets and a competitive environment. The 'universal service' model as set out today in the Universal Service Directive[143] has come to stand for such a regime.[144] First, it imposes upon all Member States the obligation to ensure that all end-users have access to a specified set of services[145] of defined quality

[141] Regulation (EC) No 1370/2007 of 23 October 2007 on public passenger transport services by rail and by road and repealing Council Regulations Nos 1191/69 and 1107/70, OJ [2007] L 315/1.

[142] The term is taken from Max Weber, *Wirtschaft und Gesellschaft* (1922), Kap 1 § 2.

[143] Universal Service Directive, OJ [2002] L 108/51. See also Proposal for a Directive amending the Universal Service Directive and the Privacy Directive, 13.11.2007, COM (2007) 698 final. The proposal leaves the main content, namely the scope and concept of universal service, untouched.

[144] For a thorough description and discussion of the Universal Service Directive see De Streel, 'The Protection of the European Citizen in a Competitive E-Society: The new EU Universal Service Directive' (2003) 4 (2) Journal of Network Industries 189 et seq.

[145] Currently, 'universal service' in telecommunications encompasses a connection to the public telephone network at fixed location and access to publicly available telephone services at fixed location (Art 4), together with a number of additional services (directories, public payphones, certain services for disabled users—see Arts 5–7).

throughout the territory at an affordable price[146] (Article 3(1)). Secondly, a mechanism is developed which shall ensure the provision and financing of universal service within an environment of open and competitive markets such that market distortions are minimized. Member States may designate one or more undertakings as having universal service obligations, but shall do so based on an efficient, objective, transparent, and non-discriminatory designation mechanism (Article 8(1) and (2)). Where the provision of universal service becomes an unfair burden on the designated undertaking(s), the undertaking(s) shall be compensated for the net costs incurred. Compensation may occur via direct state subsidies, or through a sharing mechanism so that all providers of electronic communications networks and services contribute to the costs proportionately (Article 13). It is for the Member States to determine the most efficient approach in this respect, but again they are bound by the principles of objectivity, transparency, non-discrimination, and proportionality, and shall seek to minimize market distortions (Article 13(3)).

The 'universal service' model in telecommunications is remarkable for its forceful attempt to make competition and universal service complementary concepts and to minimize the scope for friction between the two.[147] This aim is visible in the framework for financing unprofitable services. But it is also underlying the definition of universal service itself. Annex V of the Universal Service Directive sets out the principles on which the periodical review of the scope of universal service is to be based: in particular, the Commission has to take into consideration which specific services are available to and used by a majority of consumers, whether the lack of availability or non-use by a minority would result in social exclusion, and whether the availability and use of specific services conveys a general net benefit to all consumers such that public intervention is warranted. The starting point for the definition of universal service in telecommunications is thus consumer demand: only those services can become part of a universal service obligation which an average consumer expects to receive and needs in order to be a full member of society. Member States as well as the Commission are thus prevented from instrumentalizing the concept of universal service for industrial policy purposes.[148]

[146] What constitutes an affordable price has to be determined by each Member State in the light of specific national conditions—Art 9. The Directive emphasizes that affordability can be increased by differentiation, eg by providing specific options for consumers with particular needs, like for low-income users. These mechanisms may help to minimize market distortions. Nonetheless, geographical averaging remains a legitimate instrument.

[147] This does not mean that the imposition of universal service obligations will have no effects on the markets and competition—a point made by EAGCP, Services of General Economic Interest, Opinion prepared by the State Aid Group of EAGCP, 29 June 2006, 3–5.

[148] The Commission has therefore so far consistently rejected proposals to extend the 'universal service' to broadband internet access, which is currently only used by a minority of users, although a growing one. The underlying assumption is that mandating certain new technologies in a changing technological landscape is troublesome, and that any extension of the scope of universal service to such technologies and their financing would deter competition, hinder investment, and stifle the innovation which has made the new technologies possible in the first place. This does not prevent Member States from supporting the rollout of broadband infrastructures in conformity with the EU state aid rules—see EU Commission, Report regarding the outcome of the Review of the Scope of Universal Service, 7.4.2006, COM (2006) 163 final, 5.

'Universal service' in telecommunications is essentially consumer protection. It provides a safety net for those consumers which, due to geographical or social disadvantages, the market might exclude.[149] With these clear constraints on the reach of the public interest mission and on the instruments used to finance it, 'universal service' has become a model of how the friction between competition and public service provision can be minimized where the public interest can be reduced to guaranteeing disadvantaged consumers access to a core of essential services that the market typically provides.[150]

B. 'Regulated Competition'—Competition for the Market in Public Passenger Transport

In the field of public passenger transport, the belief that open markets with undistorted competition will generally produce results that coincide with the public interest and lead to high-quality services, low price, innovation, and consumer choice is much less pronounced. The aim of Regulation (EC) No. 1370/2007 on public passenger transport services,[151] which has replaced the previous Community framework[152] since December 2009, is therefore not to provide a safety net for minor gaps in the provision of generally adequate market services to certain disadvantaged consumers. Rather, it is 'to define how, in accordance with the rules of Community law, competent authorities may act [...] to guarantee the provision of services of general interest which are among other things more numerous, safer, of a higher quality or provided at lower cost than those that market forces alone would have allowed' (Article 1(1)). In these cases, the public interest calls for a level of services which the market would generally not provide.[153]

This is clearly reflected in the Public Passenger Transport Regulation: the level and quality of public passenger transport services to be guaranteed is not to be

[149] Explicitly so in *EU Commission*, 'Report regarding the outcome of the Review of the Scope of Universal Service, 7.4.2006', COM (2006) 163 final, 2.

[150] See EU Commission, White Paper on Services of General Interest', n 1 above, 8:

> [...] universal service is a key concept the Community has developed in order to ensure effective accessibility of essential services. It establishes the right of everyone to access certain services considered as essential and imposes obligations on service providers to offer defined services according to specified conditions, including complete territorial coverage and at an affordable price. Universal service is a dynamic and flexible concept and has proven to be an effective safety net provision for those who could otherwise not buy essential services for themselves. It can be redefined periodically in order to be adapted to the social, economic and technological environment. The concept allows common principles to be defined at Community level and the implementation of these principles to be left to the Member States, thus making it possible to take account of specific situations in each country, in line with the principle of subsidiarity.

[151] Regulation (EC) No 1370/2007 of 23 October 2007 on public passenger transport services by rail and by road and repealing Council Regulations Nos 1191/69 and 1107/70, OJ [2007] L 315/1.

[152] Council Regulations (EEC) No 1191/69 and (EEC) No. 1107/70.

[153] See also Recital 5 of Reg 1370/2007, explaining that '[a]t the present time, many inland passenger transport services which are required in the general economic interest cannot be operated on a commercial basis. The competent authorities of the Member States must be able to act to ensure that such services are provided'.

determined with a view to average market realities, but it is to be defined by the competent authorities with a view to public interest criteria.[154] The Regulation thus opts for a supply-driven, not a demand-driven approach. This increased divergence between public interest and market realities then translates into a greater discretion of the Member States in how to finance such policy choices: according to the Regulation, the award of exclusive rights to public service operators, and thus the exclusion of competition, is found to be a legitimate instrument for guaranteeing and financing SGEIs.[155] The commitment to competition and open markets is upheld in a different manner: where competition *in* the market is not feasible, it must be replaced by competition *for* the market. Whenever a Member State's competent authority decides to outsource a public service contract for public passenger transport services to a third party, it must do so on the basis of an open, fair, transparent, and non-discriminatory competitive tendering procedure (Article 5(3)), and this procedure must be repeated periodically (see Article 4 for the maximum length of public service contracts). Where a public authority chooses to provide public passenger transport in-house, it is prohibited from taking part in competitive tenders concerning the provision of public passenger transport services elsewhere. The introduction of such 'regulated competition' between operators is expected to lead to 'more attractive and innovative services at lower cost and is not likely to obstruct the performance of the specific tasks assigned to public service operators' (Recital 7).

C. 'Value Rationality' in Public Service Provision: 'Fencing In' Public Interest Tasks—The Example of Public Service Broadcasting

Public passenger transport stands for a public interest task that can, in principle, be provided by public or private undertakings, but where the market is believed not to provide that level, quality, and frequency of services that is optimal from a public interest point of view. In other cases, the market is regarded to be per se incapable of providing a public interest task. This is particularly so where the public interest is directly linked to a certain ethos and value orientation that is inherently foreign to any form of market rationality. Public service broadcasting provides an example for this: in a recent judgment, the CFI pointed, inter alia, to the 'specific nature' of public broadcasting, namely its direct relation to 'the democratic, social and cultural needs of society', and its 'specific status' under the Amsterdam Protocol, in support of its finding that 'a Member State cannot be required to have recourse to competitive tendering for the award of such an SGEI, at least where it decides to ensure that public service itself through a public company'.[156] In such circumstances, a balance between the fulfilment of the public service mission and competition can only be found by ensuring that competition *in* the market is distorted as little as possible. In the case of public broadcasting, this implies requesting the Member States to define the public service mission as precisely as possible so that

[154] See Recital 17 of Reg 1370/2007.
[155] See Art 3 and Recital 5 of Reg 1370/2007.
[156] Case T–442/03 *SIC v Commission* [2008] ECR II–1161, paras 151, 153, 154.

the Commission can police its limits and so as to provide a basis for an effective state aid control.[157] At the same time, the Commission has to respect the Member States' fundamental policy choices, and it has to examine seriously the actual conditions under which any form of compensation for public service broadcasting is determined. Where a Member State determines the amount of compensation to be paid for public service broadcasting within the framework of a procedure which involves a serious economic analysis drawn up with relevant input from the competitors of the public service broadcasters, the European courts are likely to conclude that the *Altmark* conditions are fulfilled, and thus to reject the application of Article 107(1) TFEU (ex Article 87(1) EC).[158]

D. Conclusions

The approaches discussed above are not exhaustive. They are just examples for how the nature of the public interest mission and different market characteristics determine the balance between public interest protection and the Union's interest in ensuring compliance with Union rules.[159]

What we observe in secondary law is a process of experimentation. In different contexts, EU law has recognized the legitimacy of very different types of public interest missions, and has been able to accommodate their specificities within the framework of Article 106(2) TFEU (ex Article 86(2) EC).

Some uncertainty remains about the relevant principles. When exactly can the Member States prevail with the argument that public services would change in character if they were submitted to a 'market logic',[160] and therefore require the state itself to act as a service provider? What types of public service mission defy a contractual specification, and would necessarily be so incomplete as to invite opportunism on a systematic scale where there is no 'public interest ethos' to counter such tendencies? And is 'public-mindedness' indeed a sufficient safeguard against abuses, considering the vast negative experiences with state monopolies that EU law has helped to uncover over the last 20 years? Overall, EU law has been

[157] EU Commission, Communication on the application of state aid rules to public service broadcasting, [2001] OJ C 320/5. See also EU Commission, Communication on the application of State aid rules to public service broadcasting [2009] OJ C 257/1.

[158] Joined Cases T–309/04, 317/04, 329/04, and 336/04 *TV2/Denmark A/S v Commission*, [2008] ECR II–2935 paras 232–233.

[159] The aspect of diversity has recently been stressed by the Commission—see EU Commission, 'Services of general interest, including social services of general interest: a new European commitment', n 9 above, 3.

[160] For a potentially very broad version of this claim see Freedland, 'The Marketization of Public Services, in Crouch, Eder, and Tambini (eds), *Citizenship, Markets, and the State* (2001), 90 et seq, observing that the marketization of public services and the resulting triangular relationship between the state, the public service provider, and the citizen as such fundamentally change the character of public service provision and subvert the idea of public or social citizenship. Freedland observes the following three effects: the citizen–public service provider relationship is consumerized—each consumer has a bilateral relationship with the service provider which is conceptualized in market terms; the citizen–state relationship becomes an indirect one and is marginalized—as a regulator, government is only indirectly accountable; the public service provider–state relationship is economized, and public service professionalism is consequently humbled.

cautious in accepting arguments about the limits of contractualization.[161] Article 106(2) TFEU (ex Article 86(2) EC) calls for a clear definition of the public interest task to be protected, typically in forms of precisely circumscribed outputs to be produced. In the area of public service broadcasting—the most notable exception in this regard—EU law at least requires intense monitoring and control of an output that cannot be measured quantitatively.[162] Under Article 106(2) TFEU (ex Article 86(2) EC), Member States are no longer free to rely on arguments of 'value rationality' at will.

The boundaries of the scope of Article 106(2) TFEU (ex Article 86(2)) of protection have remained unclear also with regard to 'strategic' public interest goals. The question of which state interventions into energy markets can be justified with a view to ensuring security of supply in the provision of electricity and gas remains essentially unresolved.[163]

7. EU Law versus National Public Service Conceptions: Conflicting Conceptions of the Role of Markets and of Member States

In the light of this survey on recent evolutions in EU law, the acuity of the tensions between the EU and the Member States in the area of SGEIs remains somewhat puzzling. EU law has not taken a radical stance towards national public service regimes. It fully respects the protection of social and general interest goals.[164] The 'solidarity exception' for national social security schemes stands for the willingness to qualify as 'non-economic', and thus completely exempt from the application of EU law, those regimes that, based on the goals and structural choices of a Member State, are incompatible with the logic of private for-profit provision. The Commission has recently proposed to extend it to the field of social services.[165] The 'solidarity exception' is based on a particular respect for the Member States' competences for some policy fields which has led the ECJ to shift, within narrow confines, from an 'abstract' functional approach towards the concept of an 'undertaking' to a 'concrete' functional approach which takes the Member States' organizational choices as a given.

[161] Eg, arguments of the type that have been brought forward by Freedland, n 159 above, 90 et seq would not suffice for applying Art 106(2) (ex Art 86(2) EC). An example for the much more narrow conception of Art 86(2) is the rejection of French arguments that the state provision of postal service should be protected as such because of the direct link they created between the citizen and the French government all over the territory.

[162] See for further limits to be imposed on the state aid financing of public service broadcasting EU Commission, Draft Communication on the application of state aid rules to public service broadcasting of 4.11.2008, available at: <http://ec.europa.eu/competition/state_aid/reform/broadcasting_communication_en.pdf>.

[163] See in this context Directive 2005/89/EC concerning measures to safeguard security of electricity supply and infrastructure investment, OJ [2006] L 33/22.

[164] Jacobs has characterized the European model as a 'balanced compromise, accommodating both a market economy and a developed welfare state'—see Jacobs, 'The State of International Economic Law: Re-Thinking Sovereignty in Europe' (2008) 11 Journal of Int'l Economic L, 5, 27.

[165] EU Commission, 'Communication of 20 November 2007 on Services of General Interest', COM (2007) 725, ch 2.3.

Within the broader field of those activities that are qualified as 'economic activities' and are therefore governed by EU law, Article 106(2) TFEU (ex Article 86(2) EC) has been applied with great respect for the aim to ensure the fulfilment of public service missions. Both the ECJ and the EU Commission have acknowledged the Member States' broad discretion in deciding which services to qualify as 'services of general economic interest' and in defining the public interest missions. In applying the proportionality test, the ECJ has taken into account the difficulties Member States may encounter in adjusting to the standards of EU law, and has granted an exception where alternative and more pro-competitive solutions were not sufficiently specified. In this regard, the application of Article 106(2) TFEU (ex Article 86(2) EC) differs significantly from the application of the public interest exceptions to the free movement rules. Overall, the ECJ has thus taken a cautious and pragmatic approach towards the interpretation of Article 106(2) TFEU (ex Article 86(2) EC) and has paid close attention to the specific circumstances of each sector, including the market conditions, possible liberalization experiences in other Member States, and the division of competences between Member States and the EU under the Treaty rules. Most liberalization processes have been based on politically negotiated harmonization Directives. Hence, the allegation that the conflict between the Member States and EU law in the area of SGEIs is about whether or not the guarantee of public service missions enjoys primacy over competition rules and free movement rules[166] is difficult to maintain. Implicit in the exception provided for by Article 106(2) TFEU (ex Article 86(2) EC) is the acknowledgment that in case of conflict, the need to ensure the fulfilment of the relevant public interest mission prevails. This has been fully respected by the EU Commission and the European courts.

More obvious is the conflict about the limits of the Member States' sovereignty. The Member States have continued to regard the prerogatives of intervention traditionally associated with the concepts of '*service public*' or '*Daseinsvorsorge*' as a hard core of state sovereignty that EU law must not touch. EU law, on the other hand, is generally applied 'horizontally' to all activities that qualify as economic. The application of the free movement and competition rules to the provision of public services implies that it is no longer the sovereign will of a single Member State alone which determines where the lines between the state and the market are to be drawn. For the Member States, this has been a culture shock. Despite the ECJ's caution and pragmatism in the application of the Treaty rules, the Member States' activity in these sectors has for the first time been removed from the 'laws of politics' and subjected to the rule of law.[167] Member States have been required to clearly define SGEIs and the concomitant public interest missions, and thus to

[166] See, eg, Baquero Cruz, n 1 above, 207, who criticizes Community legislation for giving 'relative priority to competition over services of general interest'.

[167] For the general importance of this fundamental change brought about by EU law see Jacobs, n 163 above, 7. For a discussion of the subjection of the market–state intersection to the rule of law as a central element of the European economic constitution see also Schweitzer, 'Die Daseinsvorsorge im Verfassungsentwurf des Europäischen Konvents—Ein europäischer Service Public?' in Schwarze (ed), *Der Verfassungsentwurf des Europäischen Konvents* (2004), 269, 309.

ensure transparency.[168] For the first time, they had to implement transparent accounting systems that would reflect the net costs and profits of the entrusted undertakings' various activities, and monitoring systems that would help to show that the public interest mission was indeed fulfilled. This has obstructed the formerly pervasive flexible ad hoc instrumentalization of state monopolies for changing political goals. At the same time, it has revealed how much the state monopolies had become independent from their original goals. In many cases, it has, for example, been impossible to demonstrate the exact public interest effects of entrenched cross-subsidization schemes. Nonetheless, EU law has generally shown great respect for the Member States' competences. The 'solidarity exception' and the recognition of the Member States' broad discretion in defining SGEIs and in providing an organizational and financial framework for them reflect the ECJ's sensitivity in this regard.

The tension between the Member States and EU law thus appears to reach beyond a battle of competences.[169] Ultimately, the Member States' traditional conceptions of '*service public*', '*Daseinsvorsorge*', and similar concepts display a fundamentally different vision of the role of the state and the role of the market than the one inherent in EU law. According to the traditionally prevalent view in the Member States, direct state intervention into the economic process for public interest purposes was essentially self-legitimizing. The identity between the state, or public undertakings, and the public interest went essentially unquestioned.[170] Economic freedoms were considered 'selfish' freedoms and therefore freedoms of a second rank[171] that would always have to cede to a Member State's finding that the public interest required a public regime. The delineation between the state and the market, the sphere of planning and the sphere of decentralized coordination was thus essentially a political decision, unconstrained by law. The Member States did not have to justify their decision on the basis of empirical data showing that a public regime was indeed superior to the market regime. The presumption was that by definition a public regime would better serve the public interest and human needs, since this—and not profit making—was the logic of public service. Theories of government failure were disregarded. The market was inherently suspect where public interests were involved. Against this background, all that was required was a general political decision to withdraw a certain sector from the sphere of competition and private for-profit activity, and to subject it to a public interest logic by entrusting the relevant activity to a public entity. A precise public interest mission

[168] EU Commission, White Paper on Services of General Interest, n 1 above, 10–11; EU Commission, Communication [2001] OJ C17/4 Recital 9.

[169] Franz Mayer, 'Competences—Reloaded: The vertical division of powers in the EU and the new European Constitution' (2005) 3 J Int'l J Const L 493, 514–515 for the frequent interaction of the competences debate with broader questions about the purpose of integration.

[170] McGowan, 'State Monopoly Liberalization and the Consumer' in Geradin (ed), *The Liberalization of State Monopolies in the European Union and Beyond* (2000), 214–215.

[171] See, eg, Habermas, *Die postnationale Konstellation* (1998), 142. For a somewhat different version of this claim see Freedland, n 159 above, 107–108. For a critical account of Habermas' view see Mestmäcker, 'Economic and Legal Foundations of Constitutional Liberty', November 2007, Working Paper [unpublished; on file with the author].

was not required.[172] The monitoring of economic outcomes was replaced with general political accountability.

EU law stands for a fundamentally different conception of the role of the market and the role of the state. Where the Member States have traditionally presumed an antagonism between the market and the public interest, the TFEU is based on a strong belief in the link between individual economic rights and the European 'general interest'. Establishing an internal market as a driver of European integration, economic growth, and prosperity is one of the TFEU's fundamental aims, and the free movement rules and a system of undistorted competition are its constitutive elements. The traditional state prerogative to exclude competition where public interests are of particular concern is therefore replaced with a system in which the Member States are expected to demonstrate that infringements of free movement and competition rules are in fact necessary to protect a legitimate public interest and proportionate with regard to the aims pursued. The proportionality principle encapsulates the conviction that the 'general interest' is not necessarily best defended through an exclusion of the market and competition regime, and by relying on the 'public-mindedness' of a state monopoly. Generally, EU law places faith in the beneficial effects of open markets with undistorted competition, which are expected to constrain market power, foster innovation, orient the supply towards consumer demand, increase choice, bring about improvements in quality, and put pressure on price. Member States relying on an exception must demonstrate that competition is nonetheless incompatible with the fulfilment of an important public interest mission pursued. They are no longer sovereign to delineate the sphere of the market and the sphere of the state based on their political preferences and presumptions. The economic sphere is constituted as a sphere in its own right vis-à-vis the sphere of the state.

The pragmatism and caution which has characterized the application of EU law to SGEIs cannot cover up this fundamental contrast in philosophy. It is reflected in each single element of Article 106(2) TFEU (ex Article 86(2) EC): the Member States enjoy broad discretion in specifying what services constitute SGEIs and what public interest missions shall be attached—but there are limits to this discretion, however vaguely conceptualized currently. By requiring a clear specification of the public interest mission in an 'act of entrustment', EU law negates the identity of public interest with public provision and replaces it with a concept of 'output legitimacy'. General political accountability is replaced with a monitoring whether the public interest mission is indeed fulfilled.[173] In case of non-fulfilment, the exception is not available. The idea of an identity of public interest and public

[172] See McGowan, 'State Monopoly Liberalization and the Consumer' in Geradin (ed), *The Liberalization of State Monopolies in the European Union and Beyond* (2000) 207, 215.

[173] For the relevance attached to such 'output control' under EU law see EU Commission, 'White Paper on Services of General Interest', n 1 above, 9–10; EU Commission, 'Services of general interest, including social services of general interest: a new European commitment', n 40 above, 11. Evidence of this are also the evaluation reports on the performance of network industries (telecommunications, electricity, gas, transport, and postal services) published yearly by the Commission since 2001—for the latest edition see SEC (2007) 1024, 12.7.2007. For the assessment methodology used see EU Commission, Communication, COM (2002) 331, 18.6.2002. A particular focus of these reports is the compatibility of market outcomes with the social and economic objectives of the EU.

organization is replaced by the principle of neutrality between public and private entities as a fundamental principle of EU law. It is the mission, not the form of organization which counts. Finally, the proportionality review under Article 106(2) TFEU (ex Article 86(2) EC)—however strictly or weakly performed—clearly puts an end to the idea that individual economic rights must always cede to political choice. All in all, EU law has brought about a fundamental shift from a state-centred philosophy towards a market-based approach—though clearly a 'social market' approach: while acknowledging the Member State's role in determining the social framework and structure that must always remain guaranteed, it accords to the state a more residual role as far as the direct provision of goods and services is concerned, and puts greater faith in the beneficial role and in the capabilities of a private law society.

The fundamental character of the shift explains the intensity of the Member States' opposition, and in particular their repeated attempts to change the rules of the EC Treaty themselves: with the Amsterdam Treaty of 1996, a new Article 16 (now, after amendment, Article 14 TFEU) was introduced into the EC Treaty,[174] as a reaction to insistent and far-reaching calls by France to make public services a *domaine réservée*. During the debates on the Constitutional Treaty, and later on the Treaty of Lisbon, the issue was raised again. Ultimately, then Article 16 EC (now, after amendment, Article 14 TFEU) was slightly revised. Furthermore, a Protocol on Services of General Interest has been added to the Treaty of Lisbon. Interestingly, then Article 16 EC (now, after amendment, Article 14 TFEU) has not led to major changes in the EU law's approach towards SGEIs, and in particular in the interpretation of Article 106(2) TFEU (ex Article 86(2) EC).[175] With due caution, the same may be predicted for Article 14 TFEU and the Protocol on Services of General Interest.[176] The market-based approach is deeply engrained in the structure of the TFEU as a whole. All Treaty rules are ultimately to be interpreted in the light of the free movement and competition rules which are among the pillars of EU law, and constitutive for the internal market as one of the aims and greatest achievements of the EU.

This does not mean that Article 14 TFEU (ex Article 16 EC) is devoid of legal relevance.[177] In the light of Article 14 TFEU (ex Article 16 EC), the Commission

174

> Without prejudice to Articles 73, 86 and 87, and given the place occupied by services of general economic interest in the shared values of the Union as well as their role in promoting social and territorial cohesion, the Community and the Member States, each within their respective powers and within the scope of application of this Treaty, shall take care that such services operate on the basis of principles and conditions which enable them to fulfil their missions.

175 See Mestmäcker, n 3 above, 651; Buendia Sierra, 'Article 86: Exclusive Rights and Other Anti-competitive State Measures' in Faull and Nikpay (eds), *The EC Law of Competition* (2nd edn, 2007), para 6.214; Sauter, n 1 above, 171.

176 See Sauter, n 1 above, 173: '. . . the Protocol appears to add little of substance as regards SGEI themselves'. For an in-depth analysis of the change to Art 16 EC that was contained in the proposed European Constitutional Treaty—a change similar to, but not identical with, the change proposed in Art 14 of the Treaty on the Functioning of the EU, see Schweitzer, 'Der Verfassungsentwurf des Europäischen Konvents' in Schwarze (ed), *Der Verfassungsentwurf des Europäischen Konvents* (2004) 269, 293 et seq.

177 Art 14 TFEU (ex Art 16 EC) is rather frequently cited in CFI judgments—see, eg, T–442/03 *SIC v Commission*, [2008] ECR II–1161, para 196; Order of the President of the CFI in Case T–153/01 R,

has been careful to underline the Member States' wide margin of discretion in shaping their SGEI policies, subject only to control for manifest error.[178] Both the Commission and the CFI have emphasized the relevance of the Member States' policy competences in the field of SGEIs,[179] which may contribute to an attenuation of the proportionality test. It is still an open question whether the frequently cited principle that provisions permitting derogations from the fundamental Treaty rules must be interpreted strictly can still be applied to Article 106(2) TFEU (ex Article 86(2) EC) after the entry into force of Article 16 EC (now, after amendment, Article 14 TFEU).[180] The Union's commitment to well-functioning high-quality 'services of general economic interest' as established in Article 16 EC (now, after amendment, Article 14 TFEU) may provide an argument that the protection of SGEIs in Article 106(2) TFEU (ex Article 86(2) EC) is more than a mere derogation from TFEU rules: it is itself a fundamental principle. In the balancing between a Member State's interest in protecting the fulfilment of a public service mission versus the Union's interest in the development of trade under Article 106 (2) TFEU (ex Article 86(2) EC), Article 14 TFEU (ex Article 16 EC) increases the weight to be given to Member States' concerns.

Poste Italiane v Commission [2006] ECR II–1479, para 132; Case T–289/03 *BUPA* [2008] ECR II–81, para 167; and also in the conclusions of the AGs—see, eg, AG Alber, para 94, in Case C–340/99 *TNT Traco* [2001] ECR I–4109, I–4112; AG Jacobs, para 175, in Case C–475/99 *Ambulanz Glöckner* [2001] ECR I–8089, I–8094; AG Jacobs, para 124, in Case C–126/01 *GEMO* [2003] ECR I–13769, I–13772; AG Poiares Maduro in Case C–205/03 P *FENIN* [2006] ECR I–6295, I–6297, footnote 35, para 26; AG Stix-Hackl, conclusions of 14 September 2006, in Case C–532/03, *Commission v Ireland* [2007] ECR I–11353, para 108. For different readings of the legal meaning of Art 14 TFEU (ex Art 16 EC) in the literature see, eg, Bull, (2008) Der Staat 1, 17 (an interpretation principle that can be determinative in case of conflict); similar: Baquero Cruz, n 1 above, 177; Koenig, 'Daseinsvorsorge durch Wettbewerb: Wider der (sic) Trübung des scharfen Blicks gegen soziale oder kulturelle Misswirtschaft durch das Wettbewerbsopiat von Ausnahmebereichen', in *Festschrift für Isensee* (2007) 375, 387 (a guarantee of the 'Prinzip Daseinsvorsorge'); Reiner Schmidt, 'Die Liberalisierung der Daseinsvorsorge', (2003) 42 Der Staat 225, 238–239 (a 'Bestandsgarantie', ie a guarantee of existing SGEIs); Ross, n 65 above, 1072 (highlights the 'signpost value' of Art 14 TFEU (ex Art 16 EC) and the 'Court's apparently renewed propensity to adopt flexible interpretative approaches in the name of securing the effectiveness of essential elements in the European Social Order'); Prosser, n 80 above, 553–554 (Art 16 as the basis of a constitutionalization of SGEIs in the EU). For a discussion of various ways in which Art 14 TFEU (ex Art 16 EC) could impact the interpretation of TFEU rules: Schweitzer, n 7 above, 394 et seq. For the claim that Art 14 TFEU (ex Art 16 EC) has involved no substantive changes to Art 86: Sauter, n 1 above, 171.

[178] See, eg, EU Commission, 'Communication on Services of general interest in Europe', COM (2001) 598, 17.10.2001, OJ [2001] C 17, para 22: 'In areas that are not specifically covered by Community regulation Member States enjoy a wide margin for shaping their policies, which can only be subject to control for manifest error'.

[179] See, eg, EU Commission, 'Services of general interest, including social services of general interest: a new European commitment', 20.11.2007, COM (2007) 725 final, 8: 'All Community action must respect the responsibilities of the Member States to organize, finance and ensure the delivery of health services and medical care, as it follows from Art 152 EC'. See also Case T–289/03 *BUPA* [2008] ECR II–81, para 167: where the EC Treaty has clearly assigned the relevant competences to the Member States, as for example in the field of public health (Art 152 EC), this may call for a particular respect for the Member States' organizational choices in the application of Art 86(2).

[180] Case C–157/94 *Commission v Netherlands* [1997] ECR I–5699, para 37 et al. AG Stix-Hackl has recently confirmed this principle in her conclusions of 14 September 2006, para 108, in Case C–532/03, *Commission v Ireland* [2007] ECR I–11353.

The changes resulting from the Lisbon Treaty are equally limited:[181] the second sentence which has been added to then Article 16 EC (now, after amendment, Article 14 TFEU) provides a legal basis for the EU to pass regulations regarding the principles and conditions upon which SGEIs shall be provided, commissioned, and funded.[182] It is surprising that only regulations and no Directives are foreseen which would leave more leeway to the Member States. Since Article 14 TFEU again emphasizes the respect for the competences of the Member States, its legal relevance would probably be limited to those large infrastructure sectors where a 'European' universal service already exists. It is unlikely that Article 14, second sentence would free the European legislator from its commitment to an internal market with undistorted competition. Whatever the intentions of the Member States may have been, Article 14 requires full compliance with the European Treaties, and does not free either the Member States or the European legislator from existing constraints. Clearly, Article 14, second sentence is meant to provide a counterpoise to the Commission's competence under Article 106(3) TFEU (ex Article 86(3) EC): apart from the Commission, the European legislator can now act to specify the requirements for the structuring of SGEIs resulting from EU law. The Member States and the European Council can be expected to argue that the ordinary legislative procedure shall generally be preferred to the use of Article 106 (3) TFEU (ex Article 86(3) EC), since it provides the greater degree of democratic legitimacy.[183] The Commission's special competences under Article 106(3) TFEU (ex Article 86(3) EC), by contrast, have been justified as a necessary counterweight to the Member States' strong self-interests in this field.[184] To some extent, the balance may thus shift from law to politics—but only marginally so. Even under the ordinary legislative procedure, the initiative stays with the Commission, and the

[181] For an analysis of the legal potential of Art 14 TFEU and of the Protocol on Services of General Interest see *Conseil Economique et Social*, Analysis of the implications of the Lisbon Treaty on Services of General Interest and proposals for implementation, Discussion Paper, March 2008. See also Krajewski, 'Dienstleistungen von allgemeinem Interesse im Vertrag von Lissabon' (2010) 33 ZögU 75 et seq; Wuermeling, 'Auswirkungen des Lissaboner Vertrages auf die Daseinsvorsorge' (2008) WiVerw 247 et seq; Schorkopf, 'Das Protokoll über die Dienste von allgemeinem Interesse und seine Auswirkungen auf das öffentliche Wettbewerbsrecht' (2008) WiVerw 253 et seq.; Ruge, 'Kommentar zu den Auswirkungen des Protokolls über Dienste von allgemeinem Interesse auf Daseinsvorsorge und Vergaberecht' (2008) WiVerw 263 et seq.

[182] The second sentence of Art 14 of the TFEU reads: 'The European Parliament and the Council, acting by means of regulations in accordance with the ordinary legislative procedure, shall establish these principles and set these conditions without prejudice to the competence of Member States, in compliance with the Treaties, to provide, to commission and to fund such services.' Another slight change introduced into the first sentence of then Art 16 EC (now, after amendment, Art 14 TFEU), is the reference to Art 4 of the Treaty on the European Union ('Without prejudice to Article 4 of the Treaty on European Union or to Articles 93, 106 and 107 of this Treaty . . . '). In particular, Art 4(2) may be of relevance, which reads: 'The Union shall respect the equality of Member States before the Treaties as well as their national identities, inherent in their fundamental structures, political and constitutional, inclusive of regional and local self-government. It shall respect their essential State functions, including ensuring the territorial integrity of the State, maintaining law and order and safeguarding national security. . . . '.

[183] See also Sauter, n 1 above, 170.

[184] Mestmäcker and Schweitzer, in Immenga and Mestmäcker (eds), n 1 above, Art 31, 86 EGV, Part E, para 1.

fundamental commitment to a market approach as required by the internal market rules remains in place.

The same is true for the new Protocol No 26 on Services of General Interest,[185] which is to be considered in interpreting the European Treaties. It introduces the notion of 'services of general interest' into EU primary law,[186] but in conformity with well-established principles it emphasizes that TFEU rules do not affect the Member States' competence to provide, commission, and organize *non-economic* services of general interest at will (Article 2 of the Protocol). The legal relevance of the Protocol therefore lies in its treatment of those services that qualify as *economic*. In this regard, the Protocol summarizes the 'shared values' of the Union that shall provide guidance for the interpretation of Article 14 TFEU (ex Article 16 EC) and Article 106(2) TFEU (ex Article 86(2) EC). The list included in Article 1 of the Protocol is remarkable both for those principles included and for those left out. The Protocol highlights the 'role and wide discretion of national, regional and local authorities' in operating SGEIs 'as closely as possible to the needs of the users'; the diversity between various services of general economic interest and the differences in the needs and preferences of users that may result from different geographical, social or cultural situations; and the high level of quality, safety, and affordability, equal treatment, and the promotion of universal access and of user rights. It thereby emphasizes the competences of the Member States, as well as the principle of subsidiarity;[187] but also the interests of the users. This is an integral part of the European approach towards SGEIs, and differs from the more state-centred, supply-side-oriented approach which was inherent to the traditional national public service policies. Not mentioned among the 'shared values' are the undistorted competition, the free movement rules, and the principle of proportionality.[188] Nonetheless, it is unlikely that the Protocol will effectuate sharp changes in the

[185] The Protocol No 26 on services of general interest [2010] OJ C 83/201 reads: 'The High Contracting Parties, wishing to emphasise the importance of services of general interest, have agreed upon the following interpretative provisions, which shall be annexed to the Treaty on European Union and to the Treaty on the Functioning of the Union:

Art 1: The shared values of the Union in respect of services of general economic interest within the meaning of Article 14 Treaty on the Functioning of the European Union include in particular:
– the essential role and the wide discretion of national, regional and local authorities in providing, commissioning and organising services of general economic interest as closely as possible to the needs of the users; – the diversity between various services of general economic interest and the differences in the needs and preferences of users that may result from different geographical, social or cultural situations; – a high level of quality, safety and affordability, equal treatment and the promotion of universal access of user rights.

Art 2: The provisions of the Treaties do not affect in any way the competence of Member States to provide, commission and organise non-economic services of general interest.'

[186] Art 106(2) TFEU (ex Art 86(2) EC) and Art 14 TFEU (ex Art 16 EC) only refer to 'services of general *economic* interest'.

[187] For the principle of subsidiarity see also EU Commission, 'Services of general interest, including social services of general interest: a new European commitment', 20.11.2007, COM (2007) 725 final, 9.

[188] These principles are regularly mentioned by the EU Commission in its communications; see, eg, EU Commission, Services of general interest, including social services of general interest: a new European commitment, n 40 above, 9 (emphasis on the principle of proportionality).

interpretation of Article 106(2) TFEU (ex Article 86(2) EC).[189] The principles mentioned in the Protocol were already part of the EU's SGEI policy[190] before the entry into force of the Lisbon Treaty. Once again, the Protocol has signalled to the Commission and the European courts the high political sensitivity of the issues involved. It will thus provide further arguments to those who favour a broad discretion of the Member States not only in defining SGEIs and public interest missions, but also in their organizational choices, and a weak application of the proportionality principle. But it will arguably not change the legal balance between the Member States' public interest commitments and the Union's interest in enforcing the internal market rules as such.

All in all, the Treaty changes which have resulted from the Member States' vigorous attempts to protect their traditional state-centred model of public service provision against the intrusion of EU law paradoxically underline how strongly the EU's 'social market' approach is engrained in the structure of EU law as a whole. The Member State's opposition has certainly raised awareness of how politically sensitive the application of EU law to the provision of national services of general economic interest remains. The Treaty changes may furthermore have contributed, and continue to contribute, to a very cautious application of EU law in this field. But ultimately, the balance provided for in the TFEU rules, namely the free movement and competition rules, together with Article 106(2) TFEU (ex Article 86(2) EC), has withstood the test of time and of political attack. The Treaty changes have not fundamentally altered it. Rather, the Member States have slowly adjusted to the requirements of EU law. Over the last 20 years, EU law has had a tremendous impact on the structure of the national welfare systems, and has contributed to their rationalization and reform in line with economic requirements. In many cases, the new requirement of justification and accountability structure imposed by Article 106(2) TFEU (ex Article 86(2) EC) has been an important impetus for beneficial change: it has helped to identify and curb formerly widespread inefficiencies and abuses of monopoly power inherent in entrenched structures which were justified by nothing but tradition and the Member States' interest to secure their political influence over strategic parts of the economy, and it has resulted in a greater focus on user and/or consumer rights. At times, the insight that competition can frequently better protect consumer interests than the alleged

[189] See also EU Commission, 'Services of general interest, including social services of general interest: a new European commitment', n 40 above, 3, finding that no changes are to be expected, and that the new Protocol will consolidate rather than disrupt the current state of the law:

> These new provisions build on a decade of debate about the responsibilities of the EU and about whether or not the EU should adopt an overarching framework for services of general interest. . . . A broad agreement has emerged on the need to ensure legal certainty and consistency across EU policies, while respecting the diversity of sectors and situations. There is also broad recognition of the need to improve general awareness and understanding of EU rules. By spelling out the role of the Union, the Protocol brings the necessary clarity and certainty to EU rules.

[190] See, eg, EU Commission, Services of general interest, including social services of general interest: a new European commitment', n 40 above, 10, stressing its respect for the diversity of services, situations, and needs and preferences of users.

public-mindedness of state monopolies[191] and that markets and social guarantees can frequently be reconciled has led to a shift from the traditional state-centred model to a more market-based approach also in national policies.[192] Under the influence of EU law, the traditional Continental European welfare state has fundamentally changed.[193] Against this background, a return to the traditional purely state-centred approach is today difficult to conceive.

8. Moving Beyond the Tension: The Future Issues for a European Law on SGEIs

The fact that the European 'social market approach' is here to stay does not mean that the law on SGEIs has reached 'the end of history'. Recent contributions[194] show that there is an intense search for new orientations and for a new conceptual basis for the European law on SGEIs. It is part of the broader discussion on whether Europe, in order to regain attraction, needs to rebalance economic freedoms and social goals or otherwise develop its 'social soul',[195] based inter alia on values like solidarity or a more substantive concept of citizenship. According to some, SGEIs, being placed directly at the junction between internal market rules and social goals, could be an opportunity for the EU to step beyond its 'structural' role and take on a more active part as a promoter of European SGEIs. In the light of a growing scepticism vis-à-vis Europe, these are particularly important debates.

Not all of the conceptions currently discussed are likely to open promising roads, however. The previous look at the evolution of the concept of SGEI and at the limitations inherent in European law may help us to avoid some impasses in the debate—and at the same time to identify the more promising paths.

The first observation is that the sensitivity for the need to protect the Member States' competences in relevant fields—in particular in the area of social policy and health—has grown over time.[196] It is already fully integrated into the European

[191] Fundamentally opposed to this position is Freedland, n 159 above, 90 et seq, speaking of the 'false objectivity of economic rationalism' (at 108).

[192] See, eg, the broad discussion in German public law on the concept of a 'Gewährleistungsstaat': Schuppert, 'Vom produzierenden zum gewährleistenden Staat' in König and Benz (eds), *Privatisierung und staatliche Regulierung* (1997), 539 et seq; Eifert, *Grundversorgung mit Telekommunikationsdienstleistungen im Gewährleistungsstaat* (1998); Knauff, *Der Gewährleistungsstaat: Reform der Daseinsvorsorge* (2004) et al.

[193] See, eg, Bull, 'Daseinsvorsorge im Wandel der Staatsformen' (2008) Der Staat 1, 10 who observes the emergence of a new type of state—the state of an economic society with social and cultural responsibility.

[194] Ross, n 65 above; Barnard, 'EU Citizenship and the Principle of Solidarity' in Dougan and Spaventa (eds), *Social Welfare and EU Law* (2005), 157 et seq. See also the contributions in Freedland and Sciarra (eds), *Public Services and Citizenship in European Law* (1998).

[195] See, eg, Hatzopoulos, 'A (More) Social Europe: A Political Crossroad or a Legal One-way? Dialogues between Luxembourg and Lisbon' (2005) 42 CML Rev 1599 et seq. For a critical view on the debate see Mestmäcker, 'Soziale Marktwirtschaft und Europäisierung des Rechts' reprinted in Mestmäcker, *Wirtschaft und Verfassung in der Europäischen Union* (2nd edn 2006), 288 et seq.

[196] See Schweitzer, n 51 above, 81 et seq, and 102 et seq.

approach towards SGEIs. The 'solidarity exception'—the reference to concepts of 'solidarity' at the national level and their use as a 'shield' against the applicability of EU law—may be slightly expanded, for example to cover some social services beyond the social insurance schemes for which it was originally developed. In particular with regard to more local social services, the 'effects on trade between Member States' will probably be scrutinized more carefully in the future. But no major evolutions are to be expected that would modify the current EU approach more fundamentally based on aspects of divisions of policy competences between the EU and the Member States.

It is sometimes suggested that SGEIs could be an occasion to develop a positive concept of solidarity at the European level,[197] as a counterpart to the notion of solidarity as a 'shield' against the application of EU law. Proposals as to how this could be done have remained notably vague. In fact, the current European law on SGEIs has little to offer in this regard. It is certainly remarkable that 'European universal services' have been established in some of the large infrastructure sectors—in particular telecommunications and postal services. It shows the EU's willingness to engage in a more proactive SGEI policy and to make use of its potential to promote territorial cohesion at the level of the EU.[198] But while this policy stands for an attempt to approximate the conditions of living and working in the European internal market, it does not stand for European solidarity: the redistributive schemes that may be required to finance non-profitable services are to be organized on a national scale.

Implicit in the discussion on SGEIs as a potential core for a new concept of European solidarity may be an expectation that, as EU law challenges national welfare state conceptions for their foreclosure effect, a European welfare state may ultimately emerge. This hope is likely to be disappointed: neither the structure of the EU nor the structure of European law lend themselves to the evolution of a 'strong' concept of redistributive solidarity within the EU. First, the hypothesis that a core of the state-centred welfare approach could be saved by shifting it from the national to the European level and thus freeing it from its discriminatory and foreclosure effect relies on the presumption that the core aim of EU primary law is the prohibition of discrimination and foreclosure, but not the guarantee of individual economic rights. This interpretation is to be rejected, however: in EU law, the protection of individual economic rights and the prohibition of discrimination are inherently linked. A specifically European dimension of solidarity results from the protection of individual economic rights: the principle that economic opportunities shall be open to all. Secondly, one of the legal principles that has consistently been strengthened over time is the principle of subsidiarity.[199] It advocates strongly

[197] Ross, n 65 above, 1057: '. . . the concept of solidarity is identified as the pre-eminent core value possessing the capacity to direct and delineate the relationships between providers, regulators and users of public services in a European civil society'; and also at 1080 which calls for a 'translation of public service responsibility discourse from a closed local or national setting into the European space'.

[198] EU Commission, 'White Paper on Services of General Interest', n 1 above, 3.

[199] See Art 5(2) TEU. For a general commentary to this provision see, eg, Calliess in Calliess and Ruffert (eds), *EUV/EGV* (3rd edn 2007), Art 5. For the expected future evolution of the concept see Craig, 'Competence: Clarity, conferral, containment and consideration' (2004) EL Rev 332 et seq.

against a broader transfer of competences for redistributive policies to the EU level—all the more since the political will for such transfer can safely be presumed to be minimal.[200]

European SGEI policy is thus bound to remain a cooperative or a framework policy: it relies on the close interaction of Member States' policies and European law, and thus on a system of 'multilevel governance'. EU law defines the framework within which the Member States can pursue social and redistributive policies—and will provide an impulse for pro-market reforms where they are compatible with the Member States' goals. Despite the high degree of refinement that the European framework for national SGEI policies has already achieved—in particular based on the evolution of the law on Article 106(2) TFEU (ex Article 86(2) EC)—some aspects require further clarification. Against some more recent claims[201] it follows clearly from the case law that Article 106(2) TFEU (ex Article 86(2) EC) acknowledges that a political choice to intervene into the market may be legitimate irrespective of a finding of a 'market failure' in a narrow economic sense.[202] The underlying aim of Article 106(2) TFEU (ex Article 86(2) EC) is not only to allow governments to fight information asymmetries and externalities or to deal with natural monopolies and realize public goods, but to implement social choices. It respects the Member States' political decision to pursue redistributive policies in the provision of essential services[203] and to pursue citizenship values over and beyond the mere protection of user rights.[204] Contrary to national traditions, limits are, however, inherent in Article 106(2) TFEU (ex Article 86(2) EC). Not all services are recognized as being sufficiently essential to justify their recognition as SGEIs. As regards the public interest missions attached, Article 106(2) TFEU (ex Article 86(2) EC) requires that it must be linked to the subject-matter of the SGEI and directly contribute to satisfying the relevant interest.[205] Furthermore, it must be clearly circumscribed. Article 106(2) TFEU (ex Article 86(2) EC) has thus favoured a 'contractualization' approach. While well-defined rights to access a universal service can be easily brought under Article 106(2) TFEU (ex Article 86 (2) EC), the extension of the privilege to those policy interests that are inherently

[200] For a very cautious view of the potential of a new, 'thick' concept of 'European Solidarity' see also Giubboni, 'Free Movement of Persons and European Solidarity' (2007) 13 ELJ 360 et seq.

[201] See Sauter, n 1 above, 179 et seq: '. . . the concept of market failure (and/or government failure) is a logical starting point when defining the scope of SGEI and universal service obligations'.

[202] See EAGCP, Services of General Economic Interest, Opinion prepared by the State Aid Group of EAGCP, 29 June 2006, 1 and 2–3; Prosser, 'Regulation and Social Solidarity' (2006) 33 Journal of Law and Society 364, 365, who distinguishes three different rationales for regulation: economic principles, individual rights, and social solidarity. In principle, all three grounds of market intervention are covered by Art 106(2) TFEU (ex Art 86(2) EC), as Prosser himself rightly suggests.

[203] Against the concern brought forward by McGowan, 'State Monopoly Liberalization and the Consumer' in Geradin (ed), *The Liberalization of State Monopolies in the European Union and Beyond* (2000) 207, 209.

[204] For the relevance of citizenship values in the protection of public service broadcasting see OFCOM, Review of Public Service Television Broadcasting: Phase 3—Competition for Quality, 2005, para 2.3.2.

[205] Case C–159/4 *Commission v French Republic (import and export monopolies for gas and electricity)* [1997] ECR I–5815, para 68.

vague, can only be specified ad hoc, and/or are inherently intertwined with the exercise of sovereignty has remained uncertain. EU law does accept such extensions in some cases, but only within narrow confines and where Member States can explain why the nature of the public interest mission resists further specification. Contrary to national traditions, EU law relies on objective criteria to delimit the state's power vis-à-vis the sphere of the market—although it is not yet fully clear what these criteria are.

Meanwhile, the prototypical SGEI is a 'universal service', that guarantees access at specified terms and at an affordable price to all users throughout the territory. The development of the 'universal service' concept is one of the important achievements of the European law on SGEIs. It exemplifies how the guarantee of a public interest mission and the protection of an open market with undistorted competition can be combined. The universal service conception is important in two other respects. First, it stands for a selective 'Europeanization' of SGEIs. In the large infrastructure sectors of European relevance, European SGEIs can promote market integration, but also territorial cohesion and social inclusion throughout the EU.[206] The EU Commission's occasional allusion to the promotion of European enterprises' competitiveness shows that even at the European level, SGEI policies are never free from the risk to include elements of industrial policy.

Secondly, 'universal service' shows how, in core areas, the public service conception can be reshaped from the perspective of ensuring user and/or consumer rights.[207] The requirement inherent in Article 106(2) TFEU (ex Article 86(2) EC) to clearly specify the public service mission and to demonstrate that and how it is indeed fulfilled has revealed the degree to which public service monopolies had become detached from their original purposes and ultimately pursued self-interests and ad hoc political interests, losing user interests out of sight.[208] By flatly presuming the identity between public provision and public interest, the state-centred approach towards public services essentially ignored the user/consumer: users/consumers had a right to access to whatever level of services the public provider offered, but were at the mercy of the public monopolist as far as slack and non-discriminatory abuses of monopoly power were concerned. EU law has helped to refocus public service missions in this regard, and to shift the perspective from the state's interest in flexible market intervention towards the consumer/citizen, or from supply to demand. In the Protocol on Services of General Interest, the Member States have acknowledged that 'a high level of quality, safety and affordability, equal treatment and the promotion of universal access of users' is one of the 'shared values of the Union' in respect to SGEIs.

[206] EU Commission, 'White Paper on Services of General Interest', n 1 above, 3.

[207] This does not mean, of course, that 'universal service' regulation can be identified with general consumer law—see for this point Rott, 'Consumers and Services of General Interest' (2007) 30 J Consumer Policy 49 et seq. For a differentiated account on the role of consumers in the liberalization processes in the UK see McGowan, 'State Monopoly Liberalization and the Consumer' in Geradin (ed), *The Liberalization of State Monopolies in the European Union and Beyond* (2000), 207 et seq.

[208] For a differentiated view in this regard see McGowan, ibid, 213–214.

European citizenship may provide another, or an additional angle on SGEIs. According to the EU Commission, 'services of general economic interest' have become an essential element of European citizenship.[209] Parts of the academic community believe that the concept of citizenship could become a cornerstone of a richer, positive European concept of SGEIs.[210] It is, however, not obvious what exactly follows from the concept of European citizenship[211] as far as SGEIs are concerned. At its current state of development, the Member States must guarantee to all EU citizens non-discriminatory access to their SGEIs.[212] The Member States remain free, however, in defining SGEIs and the relevant access conditions. European citizenship ensures rights of participation, and thereby extends user/consumer rights defined at the national level to all EU citizens. It is an important complement to Article 106(2) TFEU (ex Article 86(2) EC) and its focus on consumer rights at the national or local level in that it provides that these rights must be available to all. But it does not affect the decision how to delineate the role of the market and the role of the state.

These are only some of the many strands that today shape the debate on SGEIs. It continues to be the fascination of this area of law that it marks the junction between European economic law and the social goals that the Member States may legitimately pursue. Historically, the increasing willingness of the state to declare itself responsible not only for the guarantee of minimum services but for the provision of those services itself has been the basis of the development of the Continental European welfare states. It has partly been economic necessity to reverse this tendency and to question the identification of public interest goals and social guarantees with state provision; but this process has certainly been

[209] EU Commission, White Paper on Services of General Interest, n 1 above, 4.

[210] Ross, n 65 above, 1065 et seq argues that out of the concept of European citizenship, a new framework for European solidarity may emerge with regard to SGEIs. See furthermore Ross, 'The Europeanization of Public Services Supervision: Harnessing Competition and Citizenship?' (2004) 23 *Yearbook of European Law* 303, 318:

> For example, recognition that the social elements of public service delivery may trump the normal Treaty rules on competition is matched by an increasing acknowledgement that citizens' rights and protections under EU law extend beyond market freedoms. By designating citizenship as the fundamental status of EU nationals, the Court has endowed it with an instrumental capacity for interpreting the Treaty as a whole. In particular, citizenship can be used to redefine and re-prioritize existing Treaty provisions without apparently expanding their scope. When further harnessed to Article 16 EC, [...] citizenship holds a huge catalytic and directional potential and substantive expansion of content may of course ensue.

Barnard, n 193 above, 157 et seq. For the hypothesis that we need to distinguish between the traditional concept of 'community citizenship' and 'market citizenship' and that the latter may be destructive of what we have traditionally valued in 'community citizenship' see Freedland, n 159 above, 90 et seq.

[211] For a general review of the ECJ's citizenship jurisprudence see Jacobs, 'Citizenship of the European Union—A Legal Analysis' (2007) 13 ELJ 591 et seq; Elsmore and Starup, 'Union Citizenship—Background, Jurisprudence, and Perspective: The Past, Present and Future of Law and Policy' (2006) 26 *Yearbook of European Law* 57 et seq; and Spaventa, 'Seeing the Wood despite the Trees? On the Scope of Union Citizenship and its Constitutional Effects' (2008) 45 CML Rev 13 et seq.

[212] See also Art 36 of the Charter on Fundamental Rights, which reads, under the heading of 'solidarity': 'The Union recognizes and respects access to services of general economic interest as provided for in national laws and practices, in accordance with the Treaty establishing the European Community, in order to promote the social and territorial cohesion of the Union.'

supported and structured by EU law. Slowly, we see the contours of a genuinely European legal approach towards the role of the markets and the role of the state taking shape. Interestingly, it takes us back in many respects to the initial project of Léon Duguit: the search for a clearer delimitation of those 'preconditions for social interdependence and interaction' that the market alone cannot provide. *Duguit* believed in the possibility of an objective delimitation. EU law has taken a more modest approach: while it is willing to accept the relevance of political choices, it rejects an identification of the general interest with state sovereignty and is looking for a mix of criteria like the nature and economic characteristics of the relevant services, consumer demand, and inter-cultural experiences to define the balance between political accountability and respect for a market-based private law society.

3

Universal Services: Nucleus for a Social European Private Law

*Hans-W Micklitz**

1. The Hypothesis

I would like to develop the hypothesis in this chapter that the EC rules on universal services contain the nucleus of an emerging social European private law. The rise of universal services is strongly connected to the fall of consumer protection. The European Community has deprived and will increasingly deprive consumer law of its former protective elements. It is worth recalling that consumer law in the 1970s was predominantly understood as protection of the weaker party in the market.[1] The '*leitbild*' of early consumer policy was certainly not the circumspect, well-informed, and responsible consumer as developed by the ECJ in unfair commercial practices law.[2] Consumer law, at least in Europe, contained a strong social dimension with a view to protecting those consumers who were not well informed and lacked orientation in the market. When the EC took over consumer law in the 1980s it gradually changed its position.[3] The high-water mark of this development may be seen in the fight over whether EC secondary legislation should aim at full harmonization, which would preclude Member States from taking measures going beyond the EC-defined level of protection, or whether Member States should retain those precise powers.[4] The European Commission has already won half the battle and it might well be that full harmonization will become the rule in the core areas of EC consumer law—internet sales and services. I have elaborated elsewhere the rapidly changing paradigm

* This chapter contains a number of references to terms used in EC documents. I have italicized those of prime importance for the context of the analysis throughout the text. In my research I benefited from a seminar organized by Fabrizio Cafaggi and myself at the European University Institute in 2008/2009. I am grateful to the participants of the seminar. I would equally like to thank N Reich and W Sauter for helpful comments. The usual disclaimer applies.

1 See E von Hippel, *Verbraucherschutz*, 3. Auflage (1986) and N Reich, K Tonner, and H Wegener, *Verbraucher und Recht* (1976).

2 See S Weatherill, 'The Evolution of European Consumer Law and Policy: From Well Informed to Confident consumer' in H-W Micklitz (ed), *Rechtseinheit oder Rechtsvielfalt* (1996) 423.

3 See for an analysis H Rösler, *Europäisches Konsumentenvertragsrecht* (2004).

4 See H-W Micklitz and N Reich, 'Cronica de una muerte anunciada, The Commission proposal for a "Directive on Consumer Rights"' (2009) 46 CMLR 471.

of consumer law—from protection of the weaker party to the circumspect and well-informed consumer and on to the internet consumer-shopper.[5]

Whilst EC consumer law has reduced the consumer to his or her buying activities, EC law on universal services has and is yielding a new social policy-oriented consumer *leitbild*—protection of the vulnerable consumer. This development derives from the privatization policy of former state monopolies as initiated by the European Commission in the wake of its policy to complete the Internal Market. The setting up of markets for energy supply, for telecommunication and postal services, for transport and waste disposal, perhaps even for health care, education, and social security, cannot be done without fully recognizing that these services must meet the basic needs of *citizens*.[6] Being cut off from the market of these services could be equated with social exclusion. It is exactly in this context that the concept of universal services arose. It is intended to guarantee the supply of these services to those who lack the resources to buy them at the market price. The consumer turns into a citizen and the former citizen becomes a consumer. The result is the *citizen-consumer*. There is an abundant literature on public services, and on the extent to which the European Commission can privatize former state monopolies.[7] Much of the debate turns around the demarcation line between EU and Member State competences, as enshrined in the relationship between Article 106(2) TFEU and Article 14 TFEU, and the distinction between services of general interest, services of non-economic interest and services of economic interest. In this vein, the European Commission tends to expand the notion of economic services, which come under its competences, against the Member States, which remain competent for all non-economic services. Much less attention has been given to the impact of the privatization of state monopolies via primary and secondary EU law on private law matters.[8]

[5] H-W Micklitz, 'The Targeted Full Harmonisation Approach: Looking Behind the Curtain' in G Howells and R Schulze (eds), *Modernising and Harmonising Consumer Contract Law* (2009) 47; even more outspoken H-W Micklitz, 'Jack is out of the Box—The efficient Consumer-Shopper' in Festschrift T Wilhelmsson (ed) J Bärlund et, JFT 3–4/2009, 417; on the link between consumer and environmental protection, L Krämer, 'The European Union, Consumption and Consumer Law' in *Liber Amicorum Bernd Stauder* (2006) 177.

[6] See for a chronological analysis D Damjanovic and B de Witte, 'Welfare Integration through EU law: The Overall Picture in the Light of the Lisbon Treaty' in U Neergaard, R Nielsen, and LM Roseberry (eds), *Integrating Welfare Functions into EU Law—From Rome to Lisbon* (2009) 53.

[7] U Neergaard, 'Services of General (Economic) Interest and the Services Directive—What Is Left Out, Why and Where to Go?' in U Neergaard, R Nielsen, and RM Roseberg (eds), *The Services Directive, Consequences for the Welfare State in the European Social Model* (2008) 65.

[8] With a few exceptions, T Wilhelmsson, 'Services of General Interests and European Private law' in CEE Rickett and TGW Telfer (eds), *International Perspectives on Consumers' Access* (2003) 149; P Rott, 'A New Social Contract Law for Public Services?—Consequences from Regulation of Services of General Economic Interest in the EC' (2005) 3 European Review of Contract Law 323; P Rott, 'Consumers and Services of General Interest? Is EC Consumer Law the Future?' (2007) JCP 8; P Rott, 'The User-Provider Relationship: Informed Choice and User Protection through Private Law' in M Krajewski, U Neergaard, and J van de Gronden (eds), *The Changing Legal Framework for Services of General Interest in Europe—Between Competition and Solidarity* (2009) 215; C Willett, 'General Clauses on Fairness and the Promotion of Values Important in Services of General Interests' in C Twigg-Flesner, D Parry, G Howells, A Nordhausen (eds), *Yearbook of Consumer Law* (2008) 67; N Reich, 'Crisis or Future of European Consumer Law' in D Parry, A Nordhausen, G Howells, and C Twigg-Flesner, *Yearbook of Consumer Law* (2009) 1.

It is here that the following analysis must be located. I deliberately take a private law perspective. Therefore, I will examine the rules governing the contractual relationship between the user of privatized public services and the company providing the service.

My intention in this chapter is to demonstrate that the existing EU law, primary Community law as well as the numerous pieces of secondary Community law, meant to privatize former state monopolies, produce elements of a new European private law, which is designed to protect the economically and socially disadvantaged citizen. Understood in this way, universal services may be seen to form an integral part of the European Social Model.[9] I will develop my argument in three steps. Legal distinctions as conceptual differences are analysed in Part 2. Translated into a private law perspective, this part deals with the possible scope of the law on universal services.[10] Part 3 examines the hybridization of the public/private law divide in universal services. The traditional bilateral concept of private law relations does not work in universal services. It is much more a triangular relationship, where national and European regulatory agencies/networks intervene as intermediaries in the former citizen-state relationship and yield the citizen-consumer as a new social actor. Part 4 looks at the constitutionalization process of universal rights via the economic freedoms and fundamental basic rights enshrined in the Treaty. It is suggested that constitutionalization allows for the development of constitutive principles of the law on universal services. The fifth and final part of the chapter formulates possible perspectives on the law on universal services, the possibility of its generalization in the field of regulated markets as well as in the non-economic sector of public services where the impact of privatization is still strongly felt.

2. Legal Distinctions as Conceptual Differences or the Bumpy Road to a European Concept of Universal Services

The underlying perspective against which conceptual differences are characterized stems from the EU law on regulated markets, particularly EU secondary law on electricity, gas, telecommunications, postal services, railway, air passenger, ship, and bus transport. The law of the regulated market can largely be equated with services of general *economic* interest. Setting aside transport, for which Article 91 TFEU applies, all other Directives are based on Article 114 TFEU. Competence conflicts emerge when and where the European Commission claims regulatory power in the grey zone[11] of education, health care, research, and social security. Private law comes in only as far as the Member States have privatized or intend to

[9] F Scharpf, 'The European Social Model: Coping with the Challenges of Diversity' (2002) JCMS 645; same author, 'Legitimacy in the Multilevel European polity' (2009) European Political Science Review 173; Damjanovic and de Witte, n 6 above.

[10] See G Teubner, 'After Privatisation?—The Many Autonomies of Private Law' in T Wilhelmsson and S Hurri (eds), *From Dissonance to Sense: Welfare State Expectations, Privatisation and Private Law* (2001) 51.

[11] U Neergaard (2008), n 7 above, 88; see ECJ, Case C–350/07 *Kattner v Maschinenbau und Metall-Berufsgenossenschaft* [2009] ECR I–1513.

privatize former national state monopolies or statutory activities. However, behind the question of how far EU competences reach[12] lies the much more difficult issue of how to define the *conceptual* differences between public services, services of general interest, services of economic and non-economic interest, as well as universal services. It is this perspective that forms the focus of this chapter.

A. National Public Services and European SGEIs

Primary EU law does not know the category of 'public services'. This would appear to be very much a French category,[13] in contrast with German law that speaks of *Daseinsvorsorge*. Almost all Member States, at least the old ones, are familiar with particular types of services provided by the state or by state-owned companies, whatever the concrete legal category might be. In the former Communist countries, competences of the municipalities were often curbed and large public companies operating on a nation-wide scale were established.[14] These services are deeply rooted in national legal cultures and traditions.[15] Whenever the ECJ intervenes, whenever the European Commission takes action, it must be clear from the outset that privatization of former state-owned monopolies, or even less ambitious political projects like the restricting or reshaping of national public services, involves more than just changing the legal structure from public to private. Privatization bears a strong societal dimension. National state monopolies were often involved in sponsoring activities at the local community level. They were socially perceived not only as the provider of basic services but as donors financing all sorts of societal tasks, such as refurbishing schools and universities, and constructing sports arenas and public swimming pools. National statutory monopolies, particularly in countries like France, Germany, and Italy, functioned like a state within the state; they were—and to some extent still are—interwoven into the local community at the social and political level. Due to their very particular character, 'public services' cannot be totally disconnected from the public domain, despite all the privatization rhetoric.[16]

[12] Which is linked to definitions, see now U Neergaard, 'Services of General Economic Interest: The Nature of the Beast', Krajewski, Neergaard, and van de Gronden (eds), n 8 above, 17.

[13] See for details H Schweitzer, ch 2 in this volume; H Schweitzer, *Daseinsvorsorge, 'service public', Universaldienst Art 86 Abs 2 EG-Vertrag und die Liberalisierung in den Sektoren Telekommunikation, Energie und Post* (2001/2002); EM Garcia, 'Public Service, Public Services, Public Functions, and Guarantees of the Rights of Citizens: Unchanging Needs in a Changed Context' in M Freedland and S Sciarra (eds), *Public Services and Citizenship in European Law, Public and Labour Law Perspectives* (1998) 57, for a comparative analysis of the French, German and Spanish approach, also G Amato, 'Citizenship and Public Services—Some General Reflections' in M Freedland and S Sciarra (eds), *Public Services and Citizenship in European Law, Public and Labour Law Perspectives* (1998) 57, 145 for the different origins of public services in the common law and the continental law, also U Neergaard, n 7 above, 69 with further references from the literature.

[14] See for an insightful analysis of the situation in Poland before, during, and after communist times E Gromnicka, n 8 above, 17.

[15] U Neergaard, n 7 above, 71 with references.

[16] This is the major finding of our analysis of the implementation and enforcement of the EC Directives on electricity, gas, telecommunication and rail transport in a selected number of Member States: J Keßler/H-W Micklitz, *Kundenschutz auf den liberalisierten Märkten für Telekommunikation,*

The Treaty of Rome already contained the concept of '*services of general economic interest*' in Article 106(2) TFEU, empowering the Commission to exercise control over state monopolies under the competition rules. This article remained dormant until after the Single European Act. The European Commission then started to attack national statutory monopolies directly via the competition rules, and indirectly via the state aid rules, receiving strong support from the ECJ, at least in the beginning.[17] The European Commission and the ECJ thereby gave shape to what might be understood by 'services of general economic interest'. Both institutions were driven by the idea that statutory activities should be put in the hands of private competitors as they were thought to be better equipped than the state to offer high-quality services at competitive prices. The ideological ground for the privatization of public services was well prepared. The United States and the United Kingdom had demonstrated in the 1980s that transforming public services into competitive markets could produce better results for the market and for the citizen, ie consumers. In continental Europe there was increasing pressure on Member State governments to follow the US and UK example in due course.[18] The legal argument with which the ECJ managed to open up Pandora's box was the distinction between the economic nature of the statutory activity and the underlying public interests.[19] The ECJ used a similar legal construction in the field of intellectual property rights to overcome the boundaries of Article 345 TFEU.[20] Thus, the legitimacy of national public services remained unaffected, but the activities undertaken by the public services could be submitted to control under the Treaty provided they were 'economic'. The ECJ transferred the economic/non-economic divide developed in the field of market freedoms into competition and state aid law.[21] Two consequences of this approach were relatively easy to foresee: the ECJ and the European Commission would run into problems in defining where the line between economic and non-economic lies and, more profoundly, the economic/non-economic divide does not take the triangular relation into account.[22] The more deeply the European Commission and the ECJ became involved in the 'grey areas' of health care, education, and social security, the more acute these issues became. The introduction of Article 16 by the Treaty of

Energie und Verkehr—Vergleich der Konzepte, Maßnahmen und Wirkungen in Europa, VIEW Schriftenreihe, Band 23, 24, 25 (2008).

[17] See in particular the contribution of H Schweitzer and T Hervey in this volume, Chapters 2 and 7.

[18] In Germany, the Max-Planck-Institut in Hamburg and its former Director E-J Mestmäcker certainly played a key role; see E-J Mestmäcker, *Wirtschaft und Verfassung in der Europäischen Union* (2006).

[19] See W Sauter, 'Services of General Economic Interests and Universal Service in EU Law' (2008) European Law Review 167, 181. C Harlow, 'Public Services, Market Ideology and Citizenship' in M Freedland and S Sciarra (eds), n 13 above, 50, referring to the functional approach of treating public services as an activity in contrast to the institutional approach.

[20] S van Erp, *European and National Property Law: Osmosis or Growing Antagonism* (2006).

[21] Which does not mean that the notion of economic activities in both areas, market freedoms and competition, is the same, eg H Schweitzer, 'Competition Law and Public Policy: Reconsidering an Uneasy Relationship. The Example of Art 81', EUI Working Papers, 2007/3.

[22] See for the difficulties of were to define the demarcation line W Sauter, n 19 above; U Neergaard, n 7 above and for the triangular relationship see Part III.1 below.

Amsterdam (now Article 14 TFEU) was clearly meant to strengthen the role of the Member States in order to be able to properly perform and execute services of general interest in a spirit of social and territorial cohesion. The role and function of Article 14 (TFEU) are the subject of a heated academic debate. In the ECJ case law, Article 14 (TFEU) does not (yet) play a directly visible role, although Article 16 might have indirectly influenced the position of the European Commission and the ECJ regarding further privatization of national public services.

Two types of conflict need to be distinguished: first, how far would the ECJ go in paving the way for further privatization, even in sensitive areas like health care, education, research, and broadcasting, under reference to Article 106(2), and, second, whether and to what extent the ECJ and the European Commission would apply the EC rules on state subsidies to services which used to be public services and are now privatized but need financial support to execute a public service dimension.

The first type of conflict covers those situations where private competitors in a follow-on action refer to the new legal space that the European Commission has opened up by way of an infringement procedure against national state monopolies to challenge the privileged position of public-service providers or the cartel-like functioning of public and semi-public associations. In the late 1980s and the early 1990s, the ECJ did not take a consistent position and actually fed the hopes of private parties that EC competition law might become a tool to break up statutory monopolies even in the so-called grey areas. However, the ECJ gradually defined a more sophisticated approach. In a series of judgments from the 1990s the ECJ underlined that genuine state activity may be organized in public law form and that Article 106(2) does not allow for cherry picking of a profitable service by a private provider.[23] The overall lesson to be learnt from nearly 20 years of litigation around Article 106(2) might be that it would be difficult, if not impossible, for the ECJ to define via case law a genuine concept of 'services of general economic interest'. By and large the ECJ shied away from the most sensitive issues of health care and social security.[24] It is left for the EU legislator—if not the Treaty—to deregulate and privatize former national state monopolies, to define the categories of economic services which are of general interest, and to decide to what extent the most sensitive grey areas of public services may be submitted to EU law.

The second variant deals with conflicts between former public incumbents and the new competitor or between the respective Member States and private parties on which particular burdens are imposed to guarantee the supply of public services. Largely in compliance with the case law on Article 106(2), the ECJ took a hard line against all types of state subsidies which prevented private parties from gaining access to a market where public competitors, usually the former incumbents, held

[23] For a summary of the ECJ case law see N Reich, *Understanding EU Law* (2005) 160 et seq, more recently Case C–350/07 *Kattner v Maschinenbau und Metall-Berufsgenossenschaft* [2009] ECR I–1513 84 and 90; E Szyszczak, 'Public Service Provision in Competitive Markets' (2001) 20 *Yearbook of European Law* 35, 71 'cream skimming'.

[24] The solution to the question is the concept of undertaking, which excludes 'pure' social services: Case C–264/01 et al, *AOK Bundesverband* [2004] ECR I–2493; ECJ, Case C–350/07 *Kattner v Maschinenbau und Metall Berufsgenossenschaft* [2009] ECR I–1513.

a strong market position. *Ferring*,[25] decided in 2001, is regarded as the turning point. The ECJ followed AG Tizzano,[26] who strongly emphasized that neither Article 106(2) TFEU (then Article 90(2) EC) nor Article 107 TFEU (then Article 92 EC) had to be applied in cases in which the benefit given to those undertakings 'does not exceed what is strictly necessary to compensate the additional net costs which they incur in performing the public service obligations imposed on them'. In *Altmark*,[27] which concerned the admissibility of state aids for a private company for the execution of public service obligations, the ECJ confirmed its approach. It held that public subsidies intended to enable the operation of urban, suburban, or regional scheduled transport services do not fall within Article 107 TFEU if subsidies can be regarded as compensation for the services provided by the recipient undertakings in order to discharge public service obligations. Four criteria must be met:[28] (1) the recipient undertaking is actually required by law to discharge public service obligations and those obligations must have been clearly defined; (2) the parameters on the basis of which compensation is calculated must have been established beforehand in an objective and transparent manner; (3) the compensation must not exceed what is necessary to cover all or part of the costs incurred in discharging the public service obligations, taking into account the relevant receipts and a reasonable profit for discharging those obligations; (4) where the undertaking which is to discharge public service obligations is not chosen in a public procurement procedure, the level of compensation must have been determined on the basis of an analysis of the costs which a typical undertaking, well run and adequately provided with means of transport so as to be able to meet the necessary public service requirements, would have incurred in discharging those obligations, taking into account the relevant receipts and a reasonable profit for discharging the obligations.

There is a link between Article 16 EC introduced in 1999 (now Article 14 TFEU) and the ECJ's turning point in *Ferring* and *Altmark* in 2001 and 2003. The ECJ considerably increased the leeway of Member States to use state subsidies to guarantee public services, even if provided by private companies. Such an understanding has become even clearer through the new wording of Article 14 of the Lisbon Treaty. Here the words 'particularly economic and financial conditions' have been integrated.[29] Read together with the ECJ case law on Article 106(2) TFEU, the situation today seems to be that Member States have had to accept that the EC competition rules apply in the core area of services of general economic interest but they benefit from significant leeway in subsidizing either suppliers or consumers—provided they respect the four *Altmark* criteria. The interplay between

[25] Case C–53/00 *Ferring v Agence Centrale des organismes de sécurité sociale* (ACOSS) [2001] ECR I–9067 32.

[26] At 63.

[27] Case C–280/00 *Altmark Trans v Nahverkehrsgesellschaft* [2003] ECR I–7747.

[28] Mostly clearly in the tenor of the judgment.

[29] See Damjanovic and de Witte, n 6 above, 86 with reference to Winterstein, 'The Internal Market and Services of General Interests' in G Amato, H Bribosia, and B de Witte (eds), *Genesis and Destiny of the European Constitution* (2007) 645, 658.

the two sets of rules demonstrates the hybrid nature of public services, whereby neither the economic/non-economic nor the public/private law divide fully covers the complexity of the relationship.

There are two major concepts that need to be fine-tuned against each other—the *national concept of public services*, which is not coherent in its scope and density as it depends on the national cultural background and national traditions, and the *European concept of services of general economic interest*. The former is larger as it covers economic and non-economic services of general interest. However, beyond these rather banal findings there is ample room for all sorts of policy options, two of which deserve further investigation: (1) a sharpening of the demarcation line between economic and non-economic, and (2) the more ambitious project of developing a genuine European concept of public services, reframed in the terminology of universal services. The reform debate that preceded the adoption of the Treaty of Lisbon provides evidence in both directions.

B. The Distinction between Economic/Non-economic Services of General Interest

In the political debate on the revision of the Treaty, the Member States strengthened their efforts to build an ever thicker wall between their competences and those of the European Community. The Protocol to the Lisbon Treaty mentions for the first time 'non economic services of general interest' and confirms the Member States' competence. It reads as follows:

Article 2

The provisions of the Treaties do not affect in any way the competence of Member States to provide, commission and organise non economic services of general interest.

One might argue that such a rule should be integrated into a Treaty and not just relegated to a Protocol. However, even if the Member States had been prepared to take that path such a new treaty provision would not really have helped to clarify where the borderline should be situated. It remains for the ECJ to contrast the economic services of general interest laid down in Article 106(2) and reflected in Article 107 with the new rule in the Protocol that Member States retain competence for non-economic services of general interest. Thus, the added value of such a new rule might be rather limited. There is even a risk inherent in the Protocol that it could overrule the ECJ case law on equal access of non-national EU citizens to public employment and on the mobility rights of EU students.[30] One might wonder whether this really was the intention of the drafters.

The last 10 years have been marked by an increasing political influence of Member States on where to draw the line between EU and national competences, which is largely reflected in EU law. However, none of the Treaty amendments or

[30] Damjanovic and de Witte, n 6 above, 88; see for a full account of the development in a historical perspective MJ Elsmore and P Starup, 'Union Citizenship—Background, Jurisprudence, and Perspective: The Past, Present, and Future of Law and Policy' (2007) *Yearbook of European Law* 57.

the Protocols clarified what might be understood by public services, or services of economic—or non-economic—general interest.

The European Commission too stayed away from giving a clear-cut shape to these different concepts. Since 2003 the European Commission has published a number of communications, none of which is really helpful in clarifying conceptual issues nor in defining the current state of development under existing EC law. Largely in line with the common understanding of academia,[31] *Sauter*[32] listed the following services, whilst stressing that they should not be regarded as economic services of general interest in all Member States:

> River port operations, establishing and operating a public telecommunication network, water distribution, recruitment, basic postal services, maintaining postal service networks in rural areas, regional policy, port services, waste management, ambulance services, and basic health insurance.

From a constitutional point of view it would make sense simply to list the areas in which the Community and/or the Member States have competence. The Member States are not prepared to take that route and the European Commission intends to avoid setting the areas of competences in stone. Paradigmatic for the European Commission is the statement in the 2003 Green Paper on Services of General Interest, where it seeks a solution for conflicting concepts in the dynamics of the market and technology:[33]

> The range of services that can be provided on a given market is subject to technological, economic and societal change and has evolved over time . . . Given that the distinction is not static in time . . . it would neither be feasible nor desirable to provide a definite a priori list of all services of general interest that are to be considered non-economic.

The undertone of this statement is telling. The European Commission sets its hopes in that order: first on technological, second on economic, and third on societal change. Technological change in the telecommunication sector might, for instance, do away with the need to guarantee accessibility to public telephones. But what is the alternative? Technological change might overcome the need for physical accessibility to public phones through mobile phones, but technological change cannot resolve the second element inherent in accessibility, that citizen-consumers need to have the economic resources to buy a mobile phone and pay the tariffs.[34] Economic change has ties to both technological and societal change. Replacing public telephones with mobile phones implies a change in the market structure. Linking economic and societal change refers to an understanding of the kind of market we want to live in. Should the market alone guarantee access to these services or are there additional rules that need to be set down by the state? Does societal change imply that social exclusion becomes acceptable? This is certainly not

[31] See U Neergaard, n 7 above.
[32] Sauter, 'Services of General Economic Interests and Universal Service in EU Law' (2008) ELR 167, in particular fn 22.
[33] COM (2003) 270 final 14.
[34] For a clarification what is meant by citizen-consumer see Part III below.

in line with the long-term EU policy as set out in the Lisbon Council 2000.[35] Competition and social exclusion are strongly interrelated.

C. The Universality of the Concept of Universal Services

The European Commission obviously intends to avoid the slippery constitutional, ie competence, ground of distinguishing economic from non-economic services of general interest and from differentiating between (non) economic services of general interest and universal services.[36] For a fully fledged federal United States of Europe there would be an urgent need for such a clarification. For a European Union which stands on unstable constitutional—if any—ground, it seems indeed more realistic, and from an integrationist perspective more promising, to seek a bottom-up solution in the typical incremental approach[37] developed by the European Commission in bringing together the rules of the Treaty, the case law of the ECJ and secondary Community law where it has not only gained competence but has laid down elements of a new legal concept that can be generalized far beyond its relatively narrow concrete context.

The key to understanding the approach of the European Commission can be found in its 2003 Green Paper on Services of General Interest, which contains a whole chapter on 'universal service'. Again it is telling to examine the context in which the analysis is framed. The title of the chapter is 'Towards a Community Concept of Services of General Interest?', not economic services but all sorts of services. The first sub-chapter then deals with 'universal service' and provides the following account:[38]

> It is probably neither desirable nor possible to develop a single comprehensive European definition of the content of services of general interest. However, existing Community legislation on services of general economic interest contains a number of common elements that can be drawn on to define a useful Community concept of services of general economic interest. These elements include in particular: universal service, continuity, quality of service, affordability, as well as user and consumer protection. These common elements identify Community values and goals. They have been transposed into obligations in the respective legislations and aim to ensure objectives such as economic efficiency, social or territorial cohesion and safety and security for all citizens. They can also be complemented by more specific obligations depending on the characteristics of the sector concerned. Developed in particular for certain network industries they could also be relevant for social services.

The European Commission seems to contradict itself. On the one hand, universal services are said to constitute a mere element of SGEIs. This is true in so far as the different categories mentioned, 'continuity, quality affordability, consumer

[35] OJ [2002] C 137/2, see now COM (2010) 2020 3.3.2010, 'Europe 2020, A New Strategy for Smart, Sustainable and Inclusive Growth'.

[36] Critical on the lack of clarity and legal certainty, U Neergaard, 'Services of General Economic Interest: The Nature of the Beast' in M Krajewski, U Neergaard, and J van de Gronden (eds), n 8 above, 17, 49.

[37] JHH Weiler, 'The Transformation of Europe' (1991) 100 Yale Law Journal 2403; JHH Weiler, *The Constitution of Europe* (1999).

[38] COM (2003) 270 final, No 49 at 15.

protection'(!) have been developed in secondary Community law dealing with network industries.[39] This, however, is only half the truth. The key message is found in the title of the chapter and the last sentence of this quotation. Both suggest that these common elements are of importance far beyond the distinction between economic and non-economic services of general interest. The European Commission is developing a new concept in an area where it has gained competences. It then generalizes on the common elements, thereby intruding into areas where it lacks competence or where the competence of the EU is at the very least doubtful. The message is clearly spelt out, though it might remain unnoticed: 'they could also be relevant for social services'. The European Commission turns universal services into a general concept which might be extended to non-economic services of general interest.

What were politics in 2003 became law soon afterwards. The European Commission gained support for the adoption of the diverse Telecommunication Directives in 2002/2009[40] and the Energy Directives in 2003/2009.[41] Contrary to the 2003 Green Paper, the European Commission was able to base its 2007 Green Paper[42] on a relatively solid legal ground. The concept of universal services appears in the respective Directives and Regulations dealing with network industries. Whilst the language is far from clear, secondary EC law tends to use 'public services' and 'services of general interest' interchangeably, thereby confusing general European interests and national public interests.[43] The concept of universal services or more generally speaking the idea that the privatization of network industries must go hand in hand with obligations imposed on Member States to guarantee the availability of these former public services to each and every citizen has since then become relatively well established. The purpose of the 2007 Green Paper is therefore different. In light of the failure to integrate health care services in particular into Directive 2006/123/EC[44] on Services, the European Commission uses the Protocol of the Lisbon Treaty[45] and the concept of universal services to pave the way for further action in the social services field.[46] The language is rather tight and firm:[47]

> The capacity to combine the provision of services of general interest with the development of a European single market is particularly well illustrated by the series of sector-specific policies developed since the early 1990s for network industries such as telecommunications, energy, transport and postal services, which today represent more than 7% of the GDP and

[39] Directive 2002/22 on telecommunications, OJ [2002] L 108/51, Directive 2003/54 on electricity, OJ [2003] L 176/37; Directive 2003/55 on gas, OJ [2003] L 176/57; Directive 2008/6 on Postal Services OJ [2008] L 52/3.

[40] Directive 2002/22 on telecommunications, OJ [2002] L 108/51 (the Universal Services Directive), as amended by Directive 2009/136 OJ [2009] L 332/11.

[41] The second package: Directive 2003/54 on electricity, OJ [2003] L 176/37; Directive 2003/55 on gas, OJ [2003] L 176/57, the third package: Directive 2009/72 on electricity OJ [2009] L 211/55 and Directive 2009/72 on gas OJ [2009] L 211/94.

[42] COM (2007) 725 final.

[43] U Neergaard, n 7 above, 73.

[44] OJ [2006] L 376/36.

[45] See in more detail under IV.3.

[46] See the headlines of the Communication (2007) 725 final.

[47] COM (2007) 725 final, 6 (emphasis added).

5% of total employment in the EU. The gradual opening up of these sectors to competition went hand in hand with the definition of a number of *public service obligations for each sector, covering aspects such as universal service, consumer and user rights and health and safety concerns.*

More particularly on the role of universal services:[48]

Ensuring equal treatment and promoting universal access: Access to services of general economic interest is recognised as a right in the EU Charter on Fundamental Rights. This includes ensuring equal treatment between women and men and combating all forms of discrimination in accessing services of general economic interest. *Where an EU sector-specific rule is based on the concept of universal service, it should establish the right of everyone to access certain services considered as essential and impose obligations on service providers to offer defined services according to specified conditions, including complete territorial coverage and at an affordable price.* Universal service provides for a minimum set of rights and obligations, which as a general rule can be further developed at national level. *It is a dynamic concept, which needs to be updated regularly sector by sector.* Promoting access throughout the territory of the Union is essential for the promotion of territorial cohesion in the EU, as mentioned above in the case of social services. Territories with a geographical or natural handicap such as outermost regions, islands, mountains, sparsely populated areas and external borders, often face challenges in terms of access to services of general interest, due to the remoteness from major markets or the increased cost for connection. These specific needs must be taken into account.

The European Commission accepts that the concept of universal service rules are so tied to each relevant sector that they must be studied individually. This seems to be in line with the ECJ, which does not start from a universal concept of public services.[49] On the other hand, universal service rules are so variable that they present general ideas even beyond the relevant sectors. They could become constitutive for all efforts to liberalize economic and perhaps even non-economic services of general interest. They could develop into a new concept with far-reaching implications for private law.

In light of such a long-term perspective, the revised Article 14 TFEU gains importance. On the surface, Article 14 para (2) TFEU will introduce a new competence concurrent to Article 106(3) TFEU. The article, one might argue, would only codify what has become practice already. Since the European Commission is already today very reluctant in making use of its power under Article 106(3) TFEU and, if it does so, it integrates the European Parliament into the law-making process at an informal basis, the new competence basis in Article 14(2) TFEU does not seem to bring about major changes. However, Article 14(2) TFEU might legitimate the early attempt of the European Parliament to push the European Commission to propose a framework Directive on economic services of general interests.[50] Such a

[48] COM (2007) 725 final, 10 (emphasis added).

[49] See Case C–320/91 *Corbeau*, [1993] ECR I–2563 versus Case C–393/92 *Commune d'Almelo* Case [1994] ECR I–1508 and E Szyszczak, n 23 above, at 74; M Ross, 'A Healthy Approach to Services of General Economic Interest? The BUPA-Judgment of the Court of First Instance' 2009 (34) ELR 127, 133.

[50] See for a short re-construction of the initiative which goes back to 1998, U Neergaard, n 7 above, 112 et seq; now St Rodrigues, 'Towards a General EC Framework Instrument Related to SGEI? Political Considerations and Legal Constraints' in Krajewski, Neergaard, and van de Gronden (eds),

framework Directive would provide the opportunity to more deeply discuss the contract law parameters of universal services. However, the European Commission has suspended any further initiative for the time being.

3. The Hybridization of the Public/Private Law Divide in the Public Services Sector

In the high days of the welfare state, there was a clear distinction: the public sector = politics and the private sector = economics.[51] A reconstruction of the move from national public services to European-made universal services demonstrates that the distinction in EU law between economic and non-economic does not fully grasp the issues underlying that distinction. In the sectors at stake, trying to distinguish between non-economic and economic is simply a dead-end street, notwithstanding the legal means chosen, be they EU constitutional law or merely policy-making tools. What is really needed is to openly address the hybrid character of the public/private law divide in order to be able to determine the particularities of the sector that shape and influence the relationship between all parties concerned.[52] Only in this way is it possible to understand the constitutive elements of this new area of law in order to determine whether the concept of universal services contains elements that can be generalized beyond the field of network industries: what the European Commission would like to do, or what the relationships are between the 'new' law on universal services and the 'old' consumer law. Hybridization of the public service sector yields the concept of the *citizen-consumer*, who, due to the extension of entrepreneurial statutory activities, is no longer merely a citizen but likewise is not really a consumer because the state remains involved in the regulation of the public sector even after privatization.[53] The privatization of the welfare state changes the attitudes of citizens.[54] Thus, from now on I will refer to the consumer as the *citizen-consumer*, which demonstrates his or her hybrid status. The term 'customer' on the

n 8 above, 255; E Szyszczak, 'Legal Tools in the Liberalisation of Welfare Markets' in Neergaard, Nielsen, and Roseberry (eds), n 6 above, 279, 299.

[51] See for a deeper analysis of the impact of the expanding entrepreneurial state activities on the relationship between the state and the society E Picard, 'Citizenship, Fundamental Rights, and Public Services' in Freedland and Sciarra (eds), n 13 above, 83.

[52] C Scott, 'Services of General Interest in EC Law: Matching Values to Regulatory Technique in the Public and Private Sectors' (2000) ELJ 310 develops a regulatory model which takes the conflicting values into consideration.

[53] See in particular J Davies, *The European Consumer Citizen: A coherent, tangible and relevant notion of citizenship?*, PhD, Leicester, 2010; J Davies, 'Consumer Protection in a Normative Context: The Building Blocks of a Consumer Citizenship Practice' to be published in M Kenney and J Devenney (eds), *European Consumer Protection: Theory and Practice* (2010 forthcoming); M Everson and C Joerges, 'Consumer Citizenship in Post-national Constellations' in K Soper and F Trentmann, *Citizenship and Consumption* (2008), 154; Picard, n 52 above, 94; Amato, n 13 above, 153.

[54] E Szyszczak, 'Legal Tools in the Liberalisation of Welfare Markets', in Neergaard, Nielsen, and Roseberry (eds), n 6 above, 279, 285.

contrary refers to an intermediary status going back to the now-vanishing particular relationship between the entrepreneurial state and its citizens.

A. From a Bilateral to a Triangular Relationship

Traditional private law relationships are bilateral. Ideally, the parties negotiate the content of their contract as they so wish, within the boundaries set against the misuse of private autonomy in common law and civil law countries. Traditional bilateral private law making is anchored in economics. Consumer law led to the introduction of ever-increasing mandatory standards which limit the parties' freedom to contract.[55] Structurally speaking, the state, ie the European Union, intervened into private law relationships in order to correct market failures. Private law as consumer law enters politics via economics. The regulatory state, be it the nation state and/or the European Union, does not systematically monitor compliance with mandatory standards. This was and is left in principle to the private parties involved. There is, however, a growing tendency, and not only in the control of unfair contract terms,[56] to involve statutory agencies in enforcement.[57]

Universal service relations are not bilateral, a consequence which remains somewhat neglected in the case law of the ECJ.[58] Privatization suggests that this field of activity, formerly belonging to politics, has shifted to economics. Thus, ideally privatization would have to turn the former bilateral customer–state monopoly public law relationship into a bilateral citizen-consumer–supplier private law relationship. However, universal services lie in between economics and politics, in between the private/public law divide. The EC-privatized public services combine economics and politics. Teubner calls it a triangular relationship.[59] For our purposes, it is important to look at the new actors entering the scene in universal services. Before privatization the customer was provided with public services via the state directly or via statutory entities supervised and controlled by the state. After privatization the customer is faced with a completely new regulatory environment.

The universal service provider might still be the well-established incumbent, but the former incumbent has become at the same time a competitor in the market. The state and/or the government stay outside the market, deliberately distanced from the former customer. In the event of dissatisfaction, the potential addressees for the customer of universal services are the national regulatory agencies. The bilateral relationship has turned into a triangular relationship. The tensions between economics and politics, which seemed to be resolved when these services

[55] See for a rather traditional view J Basedow, 'Freedom of Contract in the European Union' (2008) European Private Law Review 901.

[56] See H Collins (ed), *Standard Contract Terms in Europe, A Basis for and a Challenge to European Contract Law* (2008).

[57] F Cafaggi and H-W Micklitz, 'Collective Enforcement of Consumer Law: A Framework for Comparative Assessment' (2008) European Review of Private Law 391.

[58] E Spaventa, 'Public Services and European Law: Looking for Boundaries' (2004) 5 *Cambridge Yearbook of European Legal Studies* 271.

[59] Teubner, n 10 above, 59.

were placed in the hands of the state (politics) a century ago, are reimported via privatization (economics) into the field of universal services. The simple fact that the privatization of public services produces universal services suffices to illustrate that the state cannot be rid of the problems inherent to public services by outsourcing them to private entities.[60] All sorts of new and old mismatches occur.

Seen from a private law perspective, the relationship between the customer and the state monopoly fell into the category of public law. There was no contractual freedom. The incumbent had to conclude the contract with each and every customer. Contractual relations were submitted to public law rules. Prices were guaranteed. Often, they were political prices, highly subsidized via taxes. In turn, the statutory monopoly benefited from privileges via tight restrictions on liability for injuries and damages.[61] Privatization may lead to a competitive market, but in this market not all competitors and customers are treated alike. The selected universal service provider is legally obliged to conclude a contract if a citizen-consumer so requests, provided that the citizen-consumer meets the necessary legal requirements to which the mandatory provision of the service is bound.[62]

The law on universal services is status-related at both ends, on the supplier and the customer sides. After privatization two levels of contractual relations could in theory co-exist in the former public sector: the citizen-consumer–supplier relation on the competitive market of former public services, where as a result of privatization the existing body of mandatory consumer law now fully applies,[63] and the citizen-consumer–universal service supplier relation, which is bound to even stricter requirements in relation to the freedom to contract and the freedom to shape contractual relations (*Abschlußfreiheit und Gestaltungsfreiheit*). The level of protection in universal services is higher than in citizen-consumer–supplier relations on the competitive market as it reaches beyond the limits set to the freedom of contract via standard terms legislation. Let us recall the clear-cut statement of the European Commission:

> Where an EU sector-specific rule is based on the concept of universal service, it should establish the right of everyone to access certain services considered as essential and impose obligations on service providers to offer defined services according to specified conditions, including complete territorial coverage and at an affordable price.[64]

[60] Garcia, n 13 above, 61: 'all the elements of the debate are still present in the current context'.

[61] See P Rott and B Butters, 'Öffentliche Dienstleistungen und Vertragsgerechtigkeit im Lichte des Gemeinschaftsrechts' (1999) VuR 75 (Teil 1) and 107 (Teil 2), B Butters, *Vertragsgerechtigkeit in der öffentlichen Versorgungswirtschaft* (2003); U Magnus and H-W Micklitz, *Liability for the Safety of Services* (2006).

[62] See for an attempt to overcome the dichotomy between public services and private services by way of developing new forms of public private partnership, A Rinken, *Alternativen zur Privatisierung, Das selbständige Kommunalunternehmen als Organisationsform der kommunalen Daseinsvorsorge am Beispiel der kommunalen Krankenhäuser* (2008).

[63] See the references to Directive 93/13 on unfair terms in Directives 2009/72 on electricity and 2009/73 on gas Annex A and Directive 2009/136 on telecommunications.

[64] COM (2007) 725 final, 10.

Obviously the addressees of the two sets of rules differ: on the one hand, there is the 'normal' citizen-consumer who chooses the most appropriate and mainly the cheapest provider in the now-privatized service sector. At the other end there are the addressees of the universal services, which may strictly speaking be broken down into two different categories: those who are uncoupled from territorial coverage but have the necessary resources, and those who are not able to pay the market price for the requested services independent of their domicile. Theoretically, both sets of legal relations could be kept separate from each other. However, new mismatches arise whatever the regulatory approach might be—a split concept differentiating between the two types of consumers or a unified concept, a one-size-fits-all approach, which treats all addressees alike. In line with EC terminology I will call the solvent consumer the circumspect consumer,[65] and the consumer who is in danger of social exclusion the vulnerable consumer.[66]

The circumspect consumer will claim to be treated as the vulnerable consumer. He or she may favour a maximization strategy, under which new and old consumer expectations generated in the field of public services are aggregated. Under the former state monopolies expectations were of low service and bad complaint management but high standards of equality, accessibility, continuity; after privatization new expectations associate better service and better quality at lower prices in addition to the level already achieved under the previous regime.[67] *Wilhelmsson*[68] raised the question whether these maximized expectations are legitimate[69] in the sense that they need to be respected in deciding whether the legal standards of universal services can be generalized even beyond their proper scope of application within the regulated market. However, if the standards generated with regard to universal services become the rule independent of the potential addressee, the circumspect and/or the vulnerable consumer, tensions arise with regard to the degree to which the invisible hand of the market shall decide on the price and the quality of the former public services. In the field of universal services they are subject to statutory regulation as a visible expression of the statutory responsibility to avoid social exclusion. Exactly this type of intervention constituted the primary target of privatization, at least with regard to those areas where the market forces are

[65] See with regard to its origins Weatherill, n 2 above, 430.

[66] See with regard to this concept Directive 2005/29 on unfair commercial practices, OJ [2005] L 149/22; T Wilhelmsson in G Howells, H-W Micklitz, and T Wilhelmsson, *European Fair Trading Law, The Unfair Commercial Practices Directive* (2006), ch 4, 111.

[67] See F Peraldi-Leneuf, 'Le Consommateur-Citoyen et la Mutation des Obligations de Service Public' in R Kovar and D Simon (eds), *Service Public et communauté européenne entre l'intérêt général et le marché*, Tome II: Approche transversal et conclusions, Actes du colloque de Strasbourg 17–19 October 1996. La documentation française (1998), Travaux de la CEDECE, who underlines that the notion of 'consommateur' bears an element of collectivity (l'intérêt collectif des consommateurs) different from the notion of client.

[68] See Wilhelmsson, n 8 above, and in Part 5, where I will study the question in more detail.

[69] See on the concept of legitimate expectations H-W Micklitz, 'Legitime Erwartungen als Gerechtigkeitsprinzip des europäischen Privatrechts' in L Krämer, H-W Micklitz, and K Tonner (eds), *Law and diffuse Interests in the European Legal Order, Liber amicorum Norbert Reich*, VIEW Schriftenreihe, Band 3 (1997), 245–78, H-W Micklitz, 'Social Justice in European Private Law' (1999/2000) *Yearbook of European Law* 167–204.

said to be the appropriate, if not the better, means of guaranteeing better services at lower prices. These mismatches are inherent to the privatization process. They demonstrate the hybrid character of privatized public services. It does not suffice to examine the bilateral relationship between the citizen-consumer and the now-privatized supplier, it is necessary to look more closely at the triangular relationship. Otherwise it is not possible to design a new law on universal services.

B. Interactions between the Citizen-Consumer, Universal Service Provider and State Relationship

The shift from a bilateral citizen-state monopoly to a triangular relation between the citizen-consumer, the universal service provider, and the regulatory agency transforms the social and economic environment between the citizen-consumer, the supplier, and the regulatory agency concerned. *Freedland* discusses the marketization of public services and distinguishes between *consumerization*, *marginalization*, and *economization*,[70] distinctions which do not yet cover the relationship between the citizen-consumer and the regulatory agencies that control and monitor the markets. Thus, a fourth category is needed, which I term *substitutionalization*.

Consumerization of the citizen-consumer/universal service provider relationship leads to an individualization of former collective relationships between state-owned public service providers and citizens. This is the consequence of the 'degeneration of collectivism into centralised corporatism' which legitimated the privatization of public services.[71] *Szyszczak*[72] has demonstrated that the privatization of public services affects the social behaviour of citizen-consumers and uncouples them from their local community. Citizen-consumers may no longer look to and feel bound to the local supplier whom they know and who might be involved in a number of local sponsoring activities, they may instead look for the cheapest supplier wherever it is located in their home country or, from an EC perspective, even from another Member State. *Consumerization* is taken to the extreme in the recent proposal for a Directive on Consumer Rights,[73] but elements of the shopper-consumer can also be found in every piece of regulatory EC law where the consumer is instrumentalized for the realization of the internal market or more particularly for the establishment of sectoral markets. Citizen-consumers are compensated for the loss of collective relationships in their community by being granted subjective rights.[74] This is the general response of EC law to the decoupling of the 'subject (the natural and the legal person)' from its own legal and social environment. However, the former collective relationship was a forced one, resulting from a lack of choice.

[70] M Freedland, 'The Marketisation of Public Services' in C Crouch, K Eder, and D Tambini (eds), *Citizenship, Markets and the State* (2001) 90.

[71] Harlow, n 19 above, 55.

[72] n 23 above, 47, and E Szyszczak, *The Regulation of the State in Competitive Markets in the EU* (2007).

[73] COM (2008) 614 final, 8.10.2008, see Micklitz and Reich, n 4 above, and Howells and Schulze (eds), n 5 above.

[74] See N Reich, *Bürgerrechte* (1999).

Privatization does not stop citizen-consumers from getting together and organizing themselves. Self-organization is now left to the civil society. This opens up new perspectives for organic solidarity in the sense of Durkheim.[75] What is really needed is an understanding of contract law as a means of shaping social relations that includes the trilateral dimension.[76] The question, however, remains as to what extent incentives, both of a legal and an economic nature, are needed to initiate self-organization in and for representing citizen-consumer interests.

Marginalization of the citizen-consumer/state relationship is a direct result of privatization. The baseline is the citizen-consumer/SGEI relationship, constructed as a market relationship. The changing relationship is reflected in the new language, where EC and national ministerial documents no longer refer to the government/citizen but to the government/consumer relationship.[77] The outsourcing of public services to the private arena, ie the delegation of statutory tasks to private actors, cannot, however, be fully achieved due to the Member States' obligation or right, depending on the regulated market at stake,[78] to establish a universal service provider. Through the selection and approval procedure, which might even end up granting exclusive rights, the universal service provider is much more closely connected to the state. From the citizen-consumer perspective, it is hard to overlook the distinction between normal competitors and the universal service provider which might at the same time be a competitor. The marginalization process is further enhanced by the Europeanization process. The nation state is no longer the true actor in regulated markets. Since the late 1980s, with the adoption of the White Paper on the Completion of the Internal Market,[79] law making and frame setting with regard to network industries lie in the hands of the European Community. Member States become mere implementers and enforcers of EU law and stay away from the role of political actors shaping policy in the respective sectoral market.[80] This does not mean that there is no leeway left to them. Secondary EC law sets only rather vague minimum standards.[81] Despite the strong European legal background citizen-consumers may nevertheless tend to hold

[75] R Münch, *Die Konstruktion der Europäischen Gesellschaft—Zur Dialektik transnationaler Integration und nationaler Desintegration* (2008); A somewhat shortened version will appear under R Münch, *European Governmentability. The Liberal Drift of Multilevel Governance* (2010).

[76] See for such an understanding of contract law H Collins, 'The Sanctimony of Contract' in R Rawlings (ed), *Law, Society and Economy, Centenary Essays for the London School of Economics and Political Science 1895–1995* (1997) 63, 75 et seq.

[77] See Teubner, n 10 above, 63; E Szyszczak, n 23 above, 65.

[78] Member States are obliged in the telecommunication sector, Art 3(1) Directive 2002/22 (remained unchanged in Directive 2009/136), in the postal sector, Art 3(1) Directive 2008/6, and the electricity sector, Art 3(3) Directive 2009/72; they may do so in the gas sector, Art 3(2) Directive 2009/72.

[79] COM (1985) 310 final.

[80] D Patterson and A Afilalo, *The New Global Trading Order—The Evolving State and the Future of Trade* (2008) are deliberately speaking of the national states as market states.

[81] See recital 46/50 Directive 2009/72 on electricity and recitals 44/47 of Directive 2009/72 on gas, Art 1(2) of Directive 2002/22 and Directive 2009/136 on telecommunications as well as recitals 16/19/34/47 Directive 2009/136; Art 3(1) and 3(6) of Directive 2008/6 on postal services; for a deeper analysis on this issue see Rott, n 8 above, 2005, 329 and 2009; Szyszczak, n 23 above, 58 and n 6 above, 289.

the state responsible and politically accountable, even for those actions where the state has given competence to the EU. The role of the nation state is more clearly visible where it decides to equip citizen-consumers with the necessary resources to pay for services they otherwise could not afford.

Substitutionalization refers to the independent regulatory agencies which serve as an intermediary between the citizen-consumer and the state. These regulatory agencies are a by-product of the EU-initiated privatization process. Before privatization the state did not only hold a monopoly, it also controlled the activities of its own monopoly mostly via the competent ministries. After privatization, when the state withdrew from the market, supervision and monitoring had to be reorganized. Over time EC law has put more and more pressure on Member States to establish independent agencies, which are in no way connected and bound to the competent ministries or the government.[82] The EC reacted thereby to the reluctance of Member States to give up political control over former incumbents. EC law, however, leaves it to the Member States to decide whether the monitoring and supervision should be entrusted to the competition authorities or to newly established independent regulatory agencies.[83] The majority of the Member States voted in favour of an independent separate regulatory agency, mainly due to the different tasks involved. Regulatory agencies had to establish a market for electricity or for telecommunications, competition authorities have to fight down distortions of competition in a workable market. In theory citizen-consumers could develop close and direct ties to 'their' competent national agency. Consumer-agency relations would then substitute citizen-government relations. This would presuppose that the regulatory agency establishes firm participation structures in decision making,[84] and accepts responsibility for the individual rights of citizen-consumers and not only for the workability of the respective sectoral market.[85] Even if these ties were established and even if societal relations could be established, the problem remains that the national regulatory agencies are integrated into the European regulatory networks. The 'formal' decisions are still taken at the Member State level, in that the regulatory agency accepts or refuses to deal with individual consumer complaints or more generally with individual consumer protection issues (the rights dimension of marginalization), but 'the material' basis of these decisions quite often results from a complicated coordination process of conflicting interests.[86]

[82] See Thatcher and Coen, 'Reshaping European Regulatory Space: An Evolutionary Analysis' (2008) Western European Politics 31.

[83] D Cameron, *Legal Aspects of EU Energy Regulation, Implementing the New Directives on Electricity and Gas Across Europe* (2007) and Kessler and Micklitz, n 16 above.

[84] See Harlow, n 19 above, 55.

[85] See Kessler and Micklitz, n 16 above; with regard to financial services J Kessler, H-W Micklitz, and N Reich (eds), *Institutionelle Finanzmarktaufsicht und Verbraucherschutz* (2010).

[86] See Lavrijssen and Hancher, 'Networks on Track: From European Regulatory Networks to European Regulatory "Network Agencies"' (2009) Legal Issues of Economic Integration 23; see also Thatcher and Coen, n 82 above; D Coen and M Thatcher, 'Network Governance and Multi-level Delegation: European Networks and Regulatory Agencies' (2008) Journal of International Public Policy 49; HCH Hoffmann and A Türk, 'The Development of Integrated Administration in the EU and its Consequences' (2007) ELJ 253.

Economization means the relationship between the universal service provider and the state. After privatization, service providers are subjected to financial accountability. As Teubner demonstrated, this is the field where economic rationality should dominate. However, due to the universal service dimension, the market mechanisms are partly suspended. If the EC imposes an obligation on service providers, via the Member States, to contract with disadvantaged citizen-consumers, a mechanism is needed under which these providers are compensated for the economic loss resulting from the fact that these citizen-consumers might not be able to pay the market price. Before and even during privatization national state monopolies used cross-subsidization[87] to balance out the gap between economically viable and non-viable economic services. As the competitive market structure becomes established, cross-subsidization vanishes, but the underlying problem remains. EC secondary Community law gives the Member States a large set of options for overcoming the discrepancies between economic and social rationality. The more general choice for the Member States to make is whether to subsidize the service providers or the citizen-consumer. If the Member States choose the first variant they must observe EC rules on state aids, with an abundant case law that sets boundaries for what Member States are allowed to do.[88] The second variant is exempted from EC state aids.[89] Much of the competence struggle at the EC level goes back to the Member States' intention to be freed from overly narrow legal constraints on using socially motivated state aids as a policy instrument in the field of public services.[90] Economists vote in favour of subsidizing citizen-consumers as a less intrusive intervention into the market.[91] If Member States are not willing or not able to subsidize either the service provider or the citizen-consumer, they may still impose obligations on the respective business sector to provide funds from which the service provider that accepts universal service obligations is compensated. This can be done via levies imposed on these companies,[92] although this form of taxation might have to face constitutional constraints as the principle of equal treatment is affected.[93] Such a mechanism might be regarded as a substitute for former cross-subsidization through the incumbent.[94] If the Member States impose universal services obligations on private companies without providing for statutory compensation, the circumspect citizen-consumers would have to pay for the vulnerable citizen-consumers. Whatever tool is chosen, the universal service

87 Case C–320/91 *Corbeau* [1993] ECR I–2563.

88 T Von Danwitz, 'State Aid Control over Public Services of General Interest' in Krajewski, Neergaard, and van de Gronden (eds), n 8 above, 81, and ch 4 in this volume.

89 See Art 107(2)(a) TFEU.

90 Damjanovic and de Witte, n 6 above, 86 with reference to Winterstein (2007) 658.

91 See A Petretto, 'The Liberalization and Privatization of Public Utilities and the Protection of User's Rights: The Perspective of Economic Theory' in Freedland and Sciarra (eds), n 13 above, 99; also Szyszczak, n 23 above, 59.

92 See in this regard *Ferring* Case C–53/00 [2001] ECR I–9067.

93 German Constitutional Court, 19 March 2003, 2 BvL 9/98 and 3 February 2009, 2 BvL 54/06 (CMA).

94 On the difficulties of identifying and controlling cross-subsidization via Art 102 TFEU see M Fehling, 'Problems of Cross-Subsidisation' in Krajewski, Neergaard, and van de Gronden (eds), n 8 above, 129.

obligation triggers redistributional effects either within the Member States or even across the borders.[95]

There is not much information available on how Member States are financing the universal services obligation. The Member States have to report to the European Commission on their progress in privatization, but with regard to financing the European Commission remains conspicuously reluctant.[96] The choice heavily affects the role and function of the citizen-consumer. If the latter is directly subsidized, the citizen dimension dominates; if the companies operating in the market have to finance the disadvantaged citizen-consumer via a compensation fund (*Ausgleichsfonds*) the consumer dimension prevails. Similar effects could be achieved via state aids granted to companies. If the 'richer' consumers have to finance the 'poorer' ones, the societal dimension dominates as economic solidarity is requested.

C. Implications for a Concept of Universal Services

Hybridization taken seriously implies that a legal concept of universal services would have to include the four dimensions of marketization: consumerization, marginalization, substitutionalization, and economization. Only such an all-embracing perspective allows a complete understanding of the implications that the concept of universal services has for private law matters.

Consumerization is perhaps the field in which the development of law and policy is most advanced, with regard to the addressee of the subjective rights and the prospective content of the contractual relationship. The Protocol to Article 14 TFEU addresses for the first time the needs and preferences of *users* and promotes *user rights*. It thereby goes beyond Chapter 3 of the 2003 Green Paper on universal services. The Commission obviously intends to combine horizontal consumer protection rules and particular sectoral rules.[97]

> In services of general interest, horizontal consumer protection rules apply as they do in other sectors of the economy. In addition, because of the particular economic and social importance of these services, specific measures have been adopted in sectoral Community legislation to address the specific concerns and needs of consumers and businesses, including their right to have access to high-quality international services. Consumer and user rights are set out in sector-specific legislation on electronic communications, postal services, energy (electricity, gas), transport, and broadcasting. The Commission's consumer policy strategy 2002–2006[98] has identified services of general interest as one of the policy areas where action is needed to ensure a high common level of consumer protection.

In the 2007 White Paper different notions of citizens, consumers, users, and customers stand side by side. It seems that the Commission starts from the premise that there are differences, but it makes no effort to define these differences nor to

[95] See in more detail Part 3C below.
[96] See for an analysis of the practice of the Member States, Kessler and Micklitz, n 16 above.
[97] COM(2003) 270 final, 18 (footnotes removed).
[98] A similar statement can be found in the consumer strategy 2007–2012; COM (2007) 99 final, 13.3.2007, 8, 11, and 12.

explain how they came about.[99] It says: '*Upholding user rights*: Citizens, consumer and user rights should be specified, promoted and upheld.' This reads as if user rights cover citizen and consumer rights. In a sense, such an interpretation is correct, as user rights might also be granted to non-citizens. But what is missing is the particular citizen dimension which results from the hybrid character of the former public services. The former citizen–state relation becomes clear in the obligation imposed via EC law on Member States to take appropriate measures to guarantee universal services and the bewildering mixture of citizen, consumer, and user in the EC policy documents and sectoral Directives. The European Commission does not discuss substitutes for the abolition of the communitarian element which was enshrined in the former citizen/local or regional public service provider relationship, perhaps with the exception of the electricity market. Here customers might get together in a buying group to negotiate a better price with the supplier.[100] This does not mean that there is no collective element at all in the EC consumer policy. However, it is shifted from *ex ante* influence to *ex post* monitoring and surveillance. The European Commission proposes collective actions for compensation of damages. However, this development is still at an early stage and does not particularly refer to the consequences of privatization in the public sector.[101]

Marginalization and *substitutionalization* should be read together. The state/citizen-consumer relationship might only matter in the event that the respective Member State decides to subsidize individual citizen-consumers so as to be able to pay the market price they could otherwise not afford. The relationship gains an EU law dimension if the state is not willing to treat its citizens and EU or even non-EU citizens equally. The ECJ has gone quite far in obliging Member States to subsidize EU citizens out of its budget.[102] Although to my knowledge no case law exists on this issue, the ECJ would probably challenge the compliance of national social aid rules meant to finance universal services which discriminate against EU nationals.[103] Much more important are the changes brought about by the establishment of regulatory agencies as intermediaries between citizen-consumers and their state. In its 2007 White Paper the European Commission indicates the set of issues to be given shape:[104]

> The capacity of consumers and users, including vulnerable or disabled persons, to take up their rights, especially their right of access, often requires the existence of independent regulators with appropriate staff and clearly defined powers and duties. These include powers of sanction, in particular the ability to monitor the transposition and enforcement of universal service provisions. These also require provisions for the representation and

[99] COM (2007) 725 final, 10.

[100] Art 3(3) of Directive 2009/72 on electricity.

[101] See COM (2008) 794 final, 27.11.2008.

[102] See in particular on the case law on transborder health care as well as on education Spaventa, n 58 above; M Dougan, 'Fees, Grants, Loans and Dole Cheques: Who covers the Costs of Migrant Education within the EU?' (2005) 42 CML Rev 943. However, this is not the place to discuss in depth the possible impact of the emerging case law in the educational sector on universal services. In Case C–158/07 *Förster* [2008] ECR I–8507, the ECJ underlined the limits of such transfer payments.

[103] In this context Case C–22/08 *Vatsouras* ECR [2009] I–nyr.

[104] COM (2007) 725 final, 10.

active participation of consumers and users in the definition and evaluation of services, the availability of appropriate redress and compensation mechanisms, and the existence of a review clause allowing requirements to be adapted over time to reflect new social, technological and economic developments. Regulators should also monitor market developments and provide data for evaluation purposes.

One might read into this statement that the European Commission would like to see the regulatory agencies established via secondary Community law in the field of network services not only as market supervision authorities but also as 'representatives' of the citizen-consumer interest, in that they look after individual citizen-consumers, and their rights, they adopt rules, either mandatory or non-mandatory,[105] and they monitor possibilities for enforcing their rights. However, secondary Community law, to the extent that it deals with regulatory agencies, does not, or does not yet, clearly impose on national regulatory agencies a legal obligation to look after the individual rights of citizen-consumers.[106] There is a gradual movement of EC secondary law in that direction, which might in the long run resolve the still existing discrepancies in the role and function of regulatory agencies in the Member States.[107] These can be divided largely into two groups: those where regulatory agencies are bound to supervise the market and reject any commitment towards individuals[108] and those where regulatory agencies are equally concerned with the workability of the market and the rights of individuals.[109]

The 2007 White Paper uses strong language on the need to include citizen-consumers in the decision-making process of the national regulatory agencies. This policy is in no way reflected in the secondary legislation dealing with privatization of the public sector. Therefore the degree to which citizen-consumers are represented by the regulatory agencies is entirely left up to the Member States. Again, there are large differences among the Member States. Those national agencies that look after the individual rights of citizen-consumers are generally speaking more inclined to grant citizen-consumers a right to participation and a stable forum in which they can raise their voices and defend their interests.[110] What is entirely missing in all EU documents is the European level which lies behind the national

[105] See with regard to national agencies as regulatory agencies in matters of private law, Kessler and Micklitz, n 16 above. They investigate the implementation of the respective EU Directives on energy, telecommunication and railway transport in France, Germany, Hungary, Italy, Sweden, Spain, and the United Kingdom under a common scheme. The books provide for a fuller account of the role of national agencies with regard to regulating directly or indirectly private law relations.

[106] See with regard to getting public authorities involved in collective complaints management C Hodges, *The Reform of Class and Representative Actions in European Legal Systems, A New Framework for Collective Redress in Europe* (2008), in particular ch 9.

[107] Of particular importance is the so-called third package on electricity, gas, and telecommunications.

[108] In particular Germany and France, see Kessler and Micklitz, n 16 above. There is a strong coincidence between the relationship of citizens towards the executive and the self-understanding of the executive; see with regard to the ways and means of citizens to get access to information and the way in which their national administrations are holding back H-W Micklitz (ed), *Informationszugang für Verbraucher in Europa und den USA, Recht und Praxis* (2009).

[109] In particular, the UK and the Nordic countries, see Kessler and Micklitz, n 16 above, and Micklitz (ed), n 108 above.

[110] See Kessler and Micklitz, n 16 above.

regulatory bodies. Citizen-consumers have no right to participate in the 'decision-making process' of the European regulatory network. By and large they may be heard at the discretion of the respective committee established under the comitology procedure.[111] However, the participation of citizen-consumers is in no way institutionalized and legally ensured. The recent initiative of the European Commission to set up European regulatory agencies in the field of energy and telecommunications would have been an occasion to take the 2007 policy statement seriously. However, whilst the respective agencies will now be established, they will not strengthen the rights of citizen-consumers at all.[112]

The weakest and by far the least developed of the four parameters of privatization is the *economization* process in the service provider state/agency relationship. The above-mentioned statement in the 2007 White Paper refers to the need for appropriate resources and staff to be able to monitor the transposition and enforcement of universal service provisions. However, the European Commission has not yet made any effort to develop a particular policy on the options of Member States on how to finance universal service obligations. Budget constraints might explain why European policy and European law are restricted to rather broad statements of what might and should be achieved by way of universal services. However, there is a clear tendency in the reform of the energy and telecommunication sectors by way of the third package to give the national regulatory agencies more specific duties to report to the Commission on the way in which the universal service is organized and applied in the Member States. *Neergard*[113] has rightly proposed the use of the open method of coordination as a regulatory device to examine more closely the various ways and means Member States have developed to finance universal services.

4. Constitutionalization of Universal Services

Universal services are integral to the constitutionalization process of private law relations.[114] Constitutionalization means that the contractual relations between the

[111] See Directive 99/468/EC, OJ [1999] L 184/23; H-W Micklitz, Regulatory Strategies on Services Contracts in EC Law in F Cafaggi and H Muir Watt (eds), *Regulatory Function of European Private Law* (2009) 16. However, Arts 290 and 291 TFEU have changed the regulatory framework of the comitology entirely.

[112] See the third package, telecommunication, COM (2007) 697 and 698 final, 13.11.2007; electricity COM (2007) 528 final, 19.9.2007—here a Common Position had been reached on 13.1.2009 nyr—and gas COM (2007) 529 final, 19.9.2007 and the Reg 2009/713 Agency on the Co-operation between Energy Regulators OJ [2009] L 211/1 and Reg 2009/1211 Body of European Regulators for Electronic Communications (BEREC) OJ [2009] L 337/1.

[113] n 7 above.

[114] See AC Ciachhi, G Brüggemeier, and G Commandé (eds), *Fundamental Rights and Private Law in the European Union, Volume II, Comparative Analysis of Selected Case Patterns* (2010 forthcoming, Cambridge University Press); O Cherednychenko, *Fundamental Rights, Contract Law and the Protection of the Weaker Party, A Comparative Analysis of the Constitutionalisation of the Contract Law with Emphasis on Risky Financial Transactions* (2008); C Mak, *Fundamental Rights in European Contract Law, A Comparison of the Impact of Fundamental Rights on Contractual Relationships in Germany, the Netherlands, Italy and England* (2008).

supplier and the citizen-consumer are ever more strongly subject to constitutional law. Here the rights rhetoric clearly dominates. The triangular relationship must therefore be reconstructed within the category of 'rights'. Whether these rights are individually enforceable or whether they must be regarded much more as 'principles' to be taken into account when interpreting the Treaty remains to be seen.[115] For the constitutionalization process both models are equally important.

It is clear that basic rights/human rights rhetoric and thinking affect the shaping of the contractual relationship. Most of the current debate focuses on the constitutionalization of private law within the Member States.[116] There is much less analysis available on the effects of the Treaty being understood as a constitution on private law relations.[117] In the EU, constitutionalization of universal services comes from two sides, from the impact of economic rights, ie from the market freedoms, from competition law and state aids on universal services on the one hand, and from social rights, from basic or human rights as enshrined in the Treaty or from the Fundamental Charter on the other. Both forces seem to work in different directions: economic rights in the direction of private autonomy; social rights, the basic and human rights in the direction of restricting private autonomy, thereby laying down standards of protection for the citizen-consumer.

However, such a dichotomy does not really fit into the hybrid character of universal services. The four market freedoms are still of limited importance in the area of universal services.[118] So far only the freedom to provide health care services across the border has gained importance. In a series of judgments the ECJ has taken a clear stand against restrictions which oblige the citizen-consumer to use the national health care system for ambulatory treatment.[119] The European Commission is currently trying to transform the case law of the ECJ into a binding instrument of law.[120] The freedom to provide service works to the benefit of the patient; usually it is the other way round. Service providers invoke the market freedoms to their benefit. More important in our context are Treaty provisions on competition and state aids. These two sets of rules do not work in one simple direction. The way in which they are construed requires a balancing of the rights of the new competitor, the old incumbent, and the state, which acts as a representative of citizen rights. In the third package on electricity, the European Commission formulated its credo in the following words:[121]

[115] With regard to the transformation of principles into rights see Picard, n 51 above, 90.

[116] See Cherednychenko, n 114 above; Mak, n 114 above, Ciachhi, n 114 above.

[117] See E Steindorff, *Gemeinschaftsrecht und Privatrecht* (1996); S Grundmann (ed), *Constitutional Values and Contract Law* (2008).

[118] For a more general understanding see N Reich, 'Horizontal Liability in EC law: Hybridization of Remedies for the Compensation in Case of Breaches of EC rights' (2007) 44 CML Rev 705.

[119] See for a recent account of the case law from the patient's perspective J Benedict, 'Die Liberalisierung der Gesundheitsversorgung in Europa. Die höchstrichterliche Entwicklung europäischer Patientenrechte aus dem Geist der Dienstleistungsfreiheit—oder zur Entdeckung des Binnenmarktes als Motor für die Entwicklung der mitgliedstaatlichen Sozialsysteme' (2008) Verbraucher und Recht 441; Spaventa, n 58 above; Hervey, ch 6, this volume.

[120] COM (2008) 414 final, 2.7.2008, also J Benedict and A Reich, 'Zum Vorschlag für eine Richtlinie über die Ausübung der Patientenrechte in der grenzüberschreitenden Gesundheitsversorgung' (2008) Verbraucher und Recht 448.

[121] See COM (2007) 386 final, 3(b).

Public service obligations are a necessary supplement to competition. If market forces alone do not meet society's general economic interest, governments have the right—and sometimes an obligation—to intervene.

Hybridization at the Treaty level means that the respective articles support the development of a legal concept of universal services which benefits from constitutional standing. A similar mixture of intertwined objectives might be found in the still rather weak set of human rights and fundamental rights impacting universal services.

A. The Triangular Relationship in a Constitutional Perspective

If we look at the triangular relationship from a citizen-consumer rights perspective, we may distinguish three different areas and three different sets of questions where the constitutionalization process matters to a highly different degree, even if we understand citizen-consumer rights to include individually enforceable rights as well as policy objectives.

The *consumerization* of the citizen-consumer/universal service provider relationship is clearly the area where the constitutionalization process is most visible. Via economic and via basic/human rights primary community law is giving shape to the constitutive elements of universal services. Two different sets of questions have to be distinguished: the rights versus principles and the vertical versus horizontal dimensions. Subjective enforceable rights can be much more easily derived from the economic freedoms. These rights may encompass a basic/human rights dimension. Whilst the ECJ has used the freedom of services as the trigger to grant citizen-consumer rights in transborder healthcare, it establishes indirectly a fundamental right to health care in that the services must be provided in a 'timely' manner and 'effectively'.[122] The addressees of such rights are predominantly states or statutory bodies. The transformation of public services into services of general economic interest and universal services enhances the importance of the horizontal dimension of economic and basic/human rights.[123] Gradually but steadily the effects of the constitutionalization process take shape.

Marginalization and *substitutionalization* instead have, at least in theory, a much stronger and more easily implemented subjective rights bias. The addressee of this process is the national regulatory agencies, which would be regarded under EC law as a state entity notwithstanding its independent regulatory status. Two different sets of rights might be discussed in this context: the right of citizen-consumers or consumer organizations to participate in administrative actions and the right of citizen-consumers to claim damages in the event that the competent regulatory agency has not taken or has taken insufficient action which harmed the citizen-consumer. Whilst the right to participate plays a prominent role in national and EC consumer policy programmes, this right has never reached the EU constitutional level. Article 169 TFEU (ex Article 153 EC) ensures the right of consumers to get together and to establish an association

122 Spaventa, n 58 above, 289.

123 See on this issue N Reich, 'Rights without Duties' *Yearbook of European Law* (2010, forthcoming).

which represents their interests.[124] But Article 169 is of little support when it comes to considering the existence of a general right to participate in administrative matters. Therefore, the position of the citizen-consumer largely depends on whether secondary Community law is formulated in such a way as to make sure that the regulatory agency in charge of the universal service is obliged under EC law to look after the interests of the individual citizen-consumers. *Peter Paul*[125] has set high standards for citizen-consumers to overcome that threshold. The existing secondary law points in that direction. The now adopted third package in energy and telecommunications[126] allows for arguing in favour of an individually enforceable right of citizen-consumers against the failing regulatory agency.[127]

Economization concerns citizen-consumers in so far as the question arises whether they have a right under EU law to claim financial support from their nation state if they cannot afford to pay the market price of the universal services. There is definitely a constitutional dimension here. Under EC law such a right could only be vested in an individual in his or her capacity as a citizen-consumer. The complicated question is whether EU law can establish a right to financial support for citizen-consumers who reside in a different Member State. This might only be possible to date within the boundaries of Article 18 TFEU (ex Article 12 EC). The Treaty, the Protocol to the Lisbon Treaty and the EU secondary Community law, particularly on network industries, is of little help here. These provisions cannot be read so as to grant a subjective right to citizen-consumers.[128]

Thus the constitutional dimension of universal services, reconstructed in a rights rhetoric, shows a rather poor record so far. It seems much more promising to examine the competition law and state aid rules on the one hand and on the other the social rights dimension as enshrined in the Protocol to the Lisbon Treaty and Article 36 of the Fundamental Charter to distil from primary community law in combination with secondary Community law a set of constitutive elements governing the law on universal services, in particular with regard to the citizen-consumer/service provider dimension. The triangular approach will not get lost, however, as the particular character of universal services still dominates private law relations even if it is not possible to constitutionalize the three sides of the triangle to a similar degree.

B. Constitutive Elements in Competition and State Aids Law

In *BUPA*[129] the CFI made a major effort to clarify, with reference to Article 106(2) and state aids, the criteria constitutive for the existence of universal services within SGEIs. *BUPA* still needs to be confirmed by the ECJ. So in a way the judgment

124 H-W Micklitz, P Rott, and N Reich, *Understanding EU Law* (2009) 26.
125 Case C–222/02 *Paul and others* [2004] ECR I–9425.
126 Directives 2009/72 on electricity, 2009/73 on gas and 2009/136 on telecommunications.
127 See with regard to financial services Kessler, Micklitz, and Reich (eds), n 85 above.
128 See on this question Rott, n 8 above (2005), 342.
129 Case T–289/03 *BUPA v European Commission*, [2008] ECR II–81 para 165, also Ross, n 50 above, and W Sauter, annotation (2009) 46 CMLR 269.

stands alone, but this attempt by the CFI deserves close attention as the judgment has no counterpart to date in the case law of the European courts.

BUPA deals with the question whether and to what extent private health insurers, which are the major competitors to the public health care regime, may be required to contribute to the national risk compensation fund. Their obligation depends largely on the question whether the services offered by private insurers may be regarded as universal services or not. The private law dimension underlying the case is that the CFI is considerably widening the meaning of universal services, taking it far beyond the boundaries of its agreed core which is the area of SGEIs. *BUPA* might gain, if it is confirmed, overwhelming importance for the scope and content of universal services obligations. Nowhere else have European courts so clearly underlined the Member States' leeway in defining public services, whilst at the same time insisting that public services which come under the scope of the Treaty respect certain *minimum* standards of protection to the benefit of the citizen-consumer.[130]

(1) The CFI uses the first *Altmark* criterion—that *the recipient undertaking is actually required to discharge public service obligations and those obligations have been clearly defined*—to draw a distinction between (i) universal services *in the strict sense*, ie services which respond to a need on the part of the whole population or which are to be supplied throughout the territory (universal coverage) and (ii) universal services *in the large sense*, where the service provider retains its autonomy to shape the substance and the price of the contract on the condition that it is obliged to offer certain services to all citizens who request them (no universal coverage).[131]

With this distinction the CFI considerably enlarges the meaning of universal services. The already adopted Directives on network industries do not fit into this categorization. So far secondary Community law seems to be united in the idea that universal services are devoted to full geographical coverage; this is true with regard to electricity and the use of public phones. Enlarging the definition bears risks and provides opportunities. The widening of scope allows all sorts of services to be brought under the category of universal services, thereby paving the way for a generalization of constitutive standards. The risk is that material standards of protection might be watered down.

(2) The *mandatory* character, ie the obligation to conclude a contract on request, is said to be constitutive for the existence of an SGEI independently of whether it is 'strict' or 'wide'. In contractual terms, universal services limit the freedom of the service provider to conclude a contract.[132] This in itself is not really new, but what matters is that the CFI undermines the overwhelming importance of that rule for the existence of universal services.

(186)... the concept of universal service, within the meaning of Community law, does not mean that the service in question must respond to a need common to the whole population or be supplied throughout a territory (see, in that regard, *Ahmed Saeed Flugreisen*, paragraph 181

[130] In the same vain Ross (2009), n 50 above, 134; Sauter, n 129 above, 281.
[131] See Ross, n 50 above, 136.
[132] Case C–64/06 *Cesky Telcom* [2007] ECR I–4887.

above, paragraph 55; *Corsica Ferries France*, paragraph 97 above, paragraph 45; and *Olsen v Commission*, paragraph 166 above, paragraph 186 et seq).... although those characteristics correspond to the classical type of SGEI, and the one most widely encountered in Member States, that does not preclude the existence of other, equally lawful, types of SGEIs which the Member States may validly choose to create in the exercise of their discretion.

(187) Accordingly, the fact that the SGEI obligations in question have only a limited territorial or material application or that the services concerned are enjoyed by only a relatively limited group of users does not necessarily call in question the universal nature of an SGEI mission within the meaning of Community law....

(3) The CFI draws a distinction between exclusive rights and the obligation to provide the service without taking costs into consideration and situations not providing for such a privileged status. Here it might suffice that the provider is mandated to offer certain services[133] which the citizen may but may not necessarily request. This seems to reflect the different Member State traditions as to whether public services are provided by monopolies or whether they are provided by private companies under statutory surveillance.[134] There is no mutual obligation on behalf of the citizen and the service provider. Compulsory membership is not required. The CFI opens the door for the crucial question of what type of services may come under the definition of situations in which an obligation to provide services suffices to regard them as universal.

(188) From the point of view of the operator entrusted with an SGEI mission, that compulsory nature—which in itself is *contrary to business freedom and the principle of free competition*—may consist, inter alia, particularly in the case of the grant of an *exclusive or special right*, in an obligation to exercise a certain commercial activity independently of the costs associated with that activity... In such a case, that obligation constitutes the counterpart of the protection of the SGEI mission and of the associated market position by the act which entrusted the mission. *In the absence of an exclusive or special right*, the compulsory nature of an SGEI mission may lie in the *obligation borne by the operator* in question, and provided for by an act of a public authority, *to offer certain services* to every citizen requesting them (emphasis added).

(195)... In effect, the universal and compulsory nature of the SGEI is not dependent on a reciprocal obligation to contract, that is to say, in this case, by compulsory... membership.... the *Albany* judgment, paragraph 101 above (paragraph 98 et seq) permits of no other interpretation...

(4) The services offered must not be determined in advance by the public authorities. The service provider may benefit from a certain leeway regarding the content and cost of the service. Therefore mandatory universal service obligations may be limited to the definition of *minimum quality standards*. Universal services and competition are not mutually exclusive. There shall be competition beyond a certain platform. This goes hand in hand with secondary Community law on network industries. The deeper question is to what extent the minimum character of universal services bears a discriminatory element or, to put it in different terms, whether the recipient of universal services must be satisfied with the minimum standards. The

[133] In the German version 'bestimmte Dienstleistungen', 189.
[134] Garcia, n 13 above, 61, 66, 71 and Amato, n 13 above, 147 and 150.

more procedural aspect is whether the standards should be determined in advance. It is not entirely clear from the judgment whether this should be the case in order to meet the transparency requirements set out in the *Altmark* judgment.[135]

(189) . . . the compulsory nature of the SGEI mission does not preclude a certain latitude being left to the operator on the market, including in relation to the content and pricing of the services which it proposes to provide. In those circumstances, a minimum of freedom of action on the part of operators and, accordingly, of competition on the quality and content of the services in question is ensured, which is apt to limit, in the community interest, the scope of the restriction of competition which generally results from the attribution of an SGEI mission, without any effect on the objectives of that mission.

(5) It is common ground that universal services do not require regulated prices.[136] All that the Member States have to guarantee under the respective Directives and regulations in line with the policy statements of the European Commission is that vulnerable consumers can afford universal services. The CFI goes rather far in granting precedence of competition over regulated prices without really discussing the affordability issue. This again is of utmost relevance for possible generalizations of the concept of universal services.[137] The key point is the question of universal character, not so much the calculation of price. All citizen-consumers might be able to cover the costs of a bank account, but they might not have access to it.[138] The judgment should not be overestimated. It might be that in the particular market segment which gave rise to the litigation 'unaffordable prices' did not really matter. But such a statement should not be generalized.

(202) . . . the fact that the prices of [the] services are neither regulated nor subject to a ceiling does not affect their universal nature either. . . . Owing to that uniformity of rates [prices] and to competition on rates [prices] between the different . . . insurers subject to . . . obligations, to the advantage of all insured persons, the risk of an excessive rate, which would be *economically unaffordable* for certain groups of persons, . . . seems to be very limited in practice. On the contrary, . . . community rating permits a *cross-subsidy of premiums* to the advantage of the most vulnerable insured persons, in particular the elderly and the sick, and ensures that they have easier access to . . . services, whereas such access would potentially be impeded, or indeed excluded, in a market in which rates were risk-based (emphasis added).

(6) There is a link between the affordability and the anti-discrimination issue. Both form an integral part of the EC policy and the secondary law on network industries. The key question is whether citizen-consumers suffer from discrimination if they cannot afford to pay for the service. The point then is whether and to what extent economic discrimination within universal services is permitted or not. The issue is well known and has so far largely been debated in the field of financial

[135] Case C–280/00, *Altmark Trans v Nahverkehrsgesellschaft* [2003] ECR I–7747.

[136] Note, however, the ECJ has considerably enlarged the leeway of Member States to regulate prices even in b2b relations: Case C–265/08 *Federutility* [2010] ECR I–nyr.

[137] See Part 8.

[138] H-W Micklitz, 'The Paradox of Access of Financial Services' (2010) European Journal of Consumer Law 7.

services.[139] The Directives and Regulations on secondary Community law do not provide much guidance on this issue.[140] The CFI analyses affordability and non-discrimination as two separate issues. With regard to non-discrimination it takes a very formal stand. Anti-discrimination means that the same service is offered at uniform and non-discriminatory rates. Such a reading of the anti-discrimination principle rejects any efforts to link it to the affordability dimension.[141] However, it is to be recalled that the ECJ took a similar perspective in labour law relations.[142]

(203) . . . The fact that certain potential users do not have the necessary financial resources to take advantage of all the [services] available on the market, in particular 'luxury' cover, does not undermine its universal nature provided that the service in question is offered at uniform and non-discriminatory rates and on similar quality conditions for all customers (see, to that effect, *Corbeau*, paragraph 131 above, paragraph 15; *Almelo*, paragraph 97 above, paragraph 48; and Case C–475/99 *Ambulanz Glöckner* [2001] ECR I–8089, paragraph 55).

(7) *BUPA* may be read as an attempt by the CFI to develop certain constitutive elements within the boundaries of SGEIs. This is particularly true with regard to *universal services in a wide sense.*[143] The demarcation line between universal services relations and 'normal' contractual relations is the legal obligation of the service provider to conclude a contract. The mandatory character of the service is crucial, in so far as the private autonomy, the autonomy to decide with whom to conclude a contract, is limited. Even such a restriction, however, must not necessarily be imposed on each and every service provider. The respective Member States may select one from among the different providers that shall be obliged to provide *certain services*—on request. The CFI confirms that universal service obligations are status-related. The legislation and contractual obligations affect only those companies or the single company in charge of providing certain services. This broad understanding leaves a lot of room for possible generalizations beyond the field of network industries. It might indeed become the basic unit for a new social European private law.

The criteria that the CFI is developing beyond and outside the obligation to conclude a contract are more problematic. The CFI seems to have in mind a model of contractual relations where mandatory minimum quality standards limit the freedom to shape a contract. The minimum character leaves room for market forces and competition beyond that minimum level—with regard to the quality of the service. The CFI, however, is very generous with regard to the question whether and to what extent the price of services is subject to control beyond the market

[139] In particular with regard to the question of whether there is a category such as social force majeure which the consumer may raise in order to fight down his or her insolvency, see T Wilhelmsson, 'Welfare State Expectations, Privatisation and Private Law' in Wilhelmsson and Hurri (eds), n 10 above, 3.

[140] In fact the so called network Directives do not touch the issue at all.

[141] See Sauter, n 130 above, 277.

[142] At least in so far as the ECJ rejected efforts to raise the level of the standards of protection, see H-W Micklitz, *The Politics of Judicial Co-operation* (2005) 247 with reference to *Smith v Advel* Case C–408/2 [1994] ECR I–4435, 4443.

[143] *BUPA*, n 129 above, 186.

forces. It neither explores the meaning of affordability nor anti-discrimination. Both belong to the core of universal services regulation, in policy and in secondary Community law. One way to look at the judgment is to stress its context. The broad reading of universal services allowed the CFI to admit that Ireland may impose an obligation on private insurers to contribute to the compensation funds, which serves to balance out the bad and the good risks. To this extent the CFI is in line with the ECJ, which does not allow cherry picking where only those services that are economically viable are privatized whereas non-economically viable services are left with the remaining public institutions.[144]

The regulatory technique of minimum standards is still the prevailing one in consumer contract law Directives. It is interesting to see that the European Commission intends to eliminate minimum standards in the revision of the consumer acquis,[145] thereby arguing that only a fully harmonized set of rules raises consumer confidence, whereas the European courts, in particular in non-harmonized markets, defend a totally different concept, one where regulation is restricted to minimum standards to leave room for competition. Universal services follow a different regulatory approach. So far the rights and duties of the parties within universal service contracts are very much determined by broader principles that deserve further concretization.[146] It is hard to imagine that the European Commission would propose a maximum approach to universal services relations. Even if the broad principles such as affordability, continuity, access and quality were turned into maximum standards, they would still need to be broken down into more concrete requirements. However, such a policy would already enhance possible mismatches between a status-bound law on universal services and those areas where fully harmonized consumer law applies, for instance in the energy and telecommunications markets.

C. Constitutive Elements in Fundamental and Human Rights

The EU legal order does not provide much input on fundamental and human rights which have an obvious and direct impact on universal services. I will limit my analysis to those rules which are of direct relevance in our context, the Protocol to Article 14 TFEU and Article 36 of the Charter on Fundamental Rights. The Protocol can only be used as a means to interpret the law. The situation is slightly more promising with regard to the Charter, independently from the classification of Article 36 as a subjective enforceable right or a defining principle. In *Promusica* the ECJ was prepared to take the Charter into consideration, although it did not yet form part of the European legal order.[147] With the entering into force of the Lisbon Treaty, Article 6 TFEU applies. In *Kücükdevici*[148] the ECJ held 'that Article 6(1)

[144] See N Reich, n 23 above, 160.
[145] See COM (2007) 614 final.
[146] See the references in fn 9.
[147] Case C–275/06 *Promusica* [2008] ECR I–271 61; see V Kosta, 'Internal Market Legislation and the Private Law of the Member States—The Impact of Fundamental Rights', EUI Working Paper 2009/22, *The Impact of the Internal Market on the Private Law of the Member States*, 25.
[148] Case C–555/07 [2010] ECR I–nyr para 22.

TEU provides that the Charter of Fundamental Rights of the European Union is to have the same legal value as the Treaties'. The key question would then be whether and to what extent secondary Community law refers to fundamental rights. The more recent Directives generally contain such a reference,[149] which suggests that the European Commission, the Parliament and the Council have checked the respective piece of law as to whether it is in compliance with the Charter on Fundamental Rights; quite to the contrary of the third package on telecommunications, electricity, gas as well as the EU Charter on the Rights of Energy Consumers.[150]

(1) The Protocol to Article 14 TFEU, which was adopted in June 2007 and added to the Treaty, contains a telling message that condenses the major findings of secondary EU law on network industries. Constitutionalization passes through different steps, from policy making to transformation into secondary Community law, and from there into a Protocol and perhaps sometimes even upgraded into the European Treaty. This is the European variant of 'constitutional law passes by, administrative law remains'.[151] The Protocol reflects to a large extent what has become existing secondary Community law in the last couple of years. In this way, it is not surprising that one might read *BUPA* as anticipating the Protocol without mentioning it.[152]

Article 1

The shared values of the Union in respect of services of general economic interest within the meaning of Article 16 EC Treaty include in particular:

- the essential role and the wide discretion of national, regional and local authorities in providing, commissioning and organising services of general economic interest as closely as possible to the *needs* of the users,
- the diversity between the various services of general economic interest and the differences in the needs and preferences of users that may result from different *geographical, social or cultural situations*,
- a *high level of quality, safety and affordability, equal treatment and the promotion of universal access and of user rights*. (Emphasis added.)

The introductory sentence contains a far-reaching message as it underlines that the Protocol expresses shared values of the Union. SGEIs are upgraded from a mere defence in Article 106(2) to a value which is shared by the Union as a whole, by the Member States and the EU. As such, the Protocol may one day be understood as a key element of an emerging European social model.[153] Does this entail direct effect of Article 106(2) TFEU?

[149] See, eg, the proposal of the Commission on a Directive on Consumer Rights, COM (2008) 614 final, 19, recital 66: 'This Directive respects the fundamental rights and observes the principles recognised, in particular by the Charter of Fundamental Rights of the European Union.'

[150] See COM (2007) 386 final, Damjanovic and de Witte, n 6 above, 84.

[151] Otto Mayer, *Deutsches Verwaltungsrecht*, Bd 1 (1924) Vorwort; see for an analysis of the development of a right to consumer safety H-W Micklitz, 'Consumer Rights' in A Cassese, A Clapham, and JHH Weiler (eds), *European Union—the Human Rights Challenge, Human Rights and the European Community: The Substantive Law, European University Institute* (1991) 53–110.

[152] Ross, n 50 above, 135.

[153] See Damjanovic and de Witte, n 6 above, 88.

The Protocol explicitly recognizes the prevailing diversity in the Member States. It inserts a new spirit into the relationship between Member States and the European Commission. So far the relationship is very much stamped by a clear definition of particular roles attributed to both sides. The European Commission is said to attack Member States' sovereignty in trying to cut back national public services, and the Member States have fought back for more than 10 years to defend national public services perhaps outside the established field of SGEIs. The European Commission appears to be the aggressor, and the Member States the defender. Indeed, the role of the Member States is often ambivalent as they instrumentalize the European Commission to initiate national privatization via the European level. Shared values and recognition of diversity unite the different positions within a new perspective.

The scope of the addressed services oscillates between SGEIs and universal services. The introductory sentence as well as the first two bullet points refer to SGEIs, the third explicitly mentions universal services. The two concepts are neither explained nor is any help provided in drawing a line between the two. In light of existing experience, the SGEIs may be broader but also narrower than the concept of universal services.[154] All three references are to some extent enshrined in the *Altmark* criteria. However, quite differently from *Altmark*, the Protocol lays down values which are shared by the Union as a whole. *Altmark* must be read much more as an attempt by the ECJ to strengthen the position of the Member States against an intruding EU law. The Protocol bears a different tone, a joint spirit.

(2) The *first* bullet point refers to the '*needs of the consumers*'. Private law theory was heavily debated in the 1980s and 1990s considering whether and to what extent private law should be shaped so as to meet the needs of citizens in market transactions, in particular in transactions between business and consumers.[155] One of the cornerstones of the debate was the issue of consumer overindebtedness and possible remedies for bringing the overindebted consumer back to business and back to social life.[156]

The *second* bullet point embeds SGEIs in the debate of whether and to what extent geographical, social, and cultural diversity matters. The Protocol confirms the case law of the ECJ at least with regard to cultural and social requirements[157] and pays tribute to the growing resistance against a unified European legal order that leaves no room for Member States' *geographical, social and cultural particularities*.[158] *Geographical* particularities refer to the differences between rural areas and dense populations in big city agglomerates, but also differences between flat lands near to the sea and mountains. Geographical particularities are related to the accessibility of services. *Social* particularities might allude to the different concepts

[154] See above, Part 2C.

[155] See T Wilhelmsson, *Critical Studies in Private Law* (1992).

[156] See, eg, U Reifner, 'Renting a Slave—European Contract Law in the Credit Society' in T Wilhelmsson et al (eds), *Private Law and the Cultures of Europe* (2007), 325.

[157] Case C–220/98 *Lifting* [2000] ECR I–117, 29: 'social, cultural or linguistic factors'.

[158] Wilhelmsson (ed), n 156 above.

of social welfare states in Europe[159] and the consequences which result from the leeway granted to Member States to define what SGEIs are and how to shape universal services in line with *Altmark* and maybe even *BUPA*. The Protocol recognizes the existence of multi-level welfare states.[160] The question remains as to what extent '*culture*' affects the concept of SGEIs and universal services. But what does this really mean? It is certainly not meant to become a gateway for all sorts of Member State measures to slow down privatization under the disguised need to protect cultural differences.

The *third* bullet point goes even further in that it refers to 'principles' that govern universal services in EU politics and in secondary Community law on network industries. These 'principles' are well known from secondary Community law. The Protocol gives them a quasi-constitutional outlook. There is a link between the needs of citizen-consumers and the principles set out in the third bullet point. Citizen-consumers *need* services at *affordable* prices. Needs cannot be separated from economic resources. Read this way, the interpretation given to affordability in the *BUPA* judgment is hardly in compliance with the Protocol.[161] Taking citizen-consumer needs into consideration sheds light on a new understanding of the principle of equal treatment. Affordability and equal treatment combined allow economic resources to become a criterion for interpreting existing EC law.

(3) The concept of SGEI found its way into Article 36 of the Charter of Fundamental Rights (proclaimed in December 2000) under the heading of solidarity, as follows:

> The Union recognises and respects *access to services* of general economic interest as provided for in national laws and practices, in accordance with the Treaty establishing the European Community, in order to promote the *social and territorial cohesion* of the Union. (Emphasis added.)

Article 36 of the Charter remains less specific than the Protocol. The article is certainly not meant to grant individual rights, at least not according to the majoritarian academic opinion.[162] On the other hand it does add further elements to the constitutional dimension of services of general economic interest: *access* as well as *social and territorial cohesion*. Article 36 even goes beyond the Protocol in that it more clearly stresses solidarity[163] in SGEIs. Social and territorial cohesion

159 See T Wilhelmsson, 'Varieties of Welfarism in European Contract Law' (2004) 10 ELJ 712.

160 See Neergaard, n 7 above, 103 and the various contributions in Sozialer Fortschritt, Unabhängige Zeitschrift für Sozialpolitik, Heft 1/2 Januar/Februar 1997; E Rieger and S Leibfried, *Limits to Globalization. Welfare States and the World Economy* (2003); H Obinger, S Leibfried, C Bogedan, P Starke, E Gindulis, and J Moser, *Welfare State Transformation. Small Countries—Big Lessons?* (forthcoming).

161 n 129 above, 202; Ross, n 50 above, 135.

162 Regarding the interpretation of this provision and its doctrinal qualification, J Baquero Cruz, 'Services of General Interest and EC Law' in G de Burca (ed), *EU Law and the Welfare State* (2005), 169, 178.

163 See M Ross, 'The Value of Solidarity in European Public Services Law' in Krajewski, Neergaard, and Van der Gronden (eds), n 8 above, 81; A Wunder, *The Usage of Solidarity in the Jurisdiction of the ECJ: Symbolism or a European Legal Concept?* LLM Thesis, EUI Florence, 2008.

is linked to the social and cultural particularities of EU Member States. The EU and the Member States—the shared values doctrine—will have to decide how much weight they will grant to social and territorial cohesion and how much to competition and utilitarian thinking. Neither the Protocol nor Article 36, and not even in combination with secondary EU law, presently allow shape to be given to the concept of social cohesion and solidarity. Solidarity is more than just symbolic; solidarity in the Treaty now bears a normative connotation. It might be used as a tool in interpreting the law and might serve as an adjudicatory benchmark.[164]

The more concrete limb of Article 36 is certainly 'access'. Access contains a threefold dimension: a technical, an economic and a social dimension. The technical side is enshrined in the geographical dimension. Access remains an empty tool if those who should have access are barred from requesting the respective universal services due to lack of resources. As such, access is linked to affordability and affordability is linked to continuity. A concrete understanding does not prohibit, but considerably reduces, the possibility of simply disconnecting vulnerable citizen-consumers from the net if they have not paid the bill.[165] The social element refers to those citizen-consumers who suffer from social exclusion. These are mainly vulnerable citizen-consumers. Contrary to the rules in the Protocol on social and territorial cohesion, access under Article 36, read together with the respective rules in secondary Community law, constitute subjective enforceable rights. In *Sabatauskas*[166] the ECJ did not decide on the right of access to consumers.[167] Although the ECJ leaves it up to the Member States to decide whether the supplier has a right to access under Article 20 of the electricity supply Directive, the Advocate General and the ECJ seemed inclined to go further if the right of the citizen-consumer was at stake. Such a reading could be backed by reference to the Anti-Discrimination Directives 2000/43, 2003/109, and 2004/113, which 'require access to and supply of goods and services available to the public'. Universal services come under the scope of those goods in respect of which these Directives intend to eliminate discrimination. As is well known, not all forms of discrimination are covered. One might wonder, however, to what extent it is possible to develop a 'general principle' out of the Directives in combination with Article 36 of the Charter, one which guarantees access, technically, economically and socially.[168]

[164] This is what Ross in Krajewski et al, n 163 above, 98 seems to have in mind.

[165] See on the overarching importance of access, affordability, and continuity in the new Member States M Bartl, 'The Affordability of Energy Supply' JCP (2010, forthcoming).

[166] See on the right to access under Art 20 of Directive 2003/54 in particular with regard to the right of access to universal services Case C–239/07 *Julius Sabatauskas* [2008] ECR I–7523, 47, AG Kokott at 35, 38; see case note by Pirstner-Ebner, 2009 EuZW, 15, 16 under 4.

[167] See Rott, n 8 above (2005), 342.

[168] S Weatherill, 'The "Principles of Civil Law" as a Basis for Interpreting the Legislative Acquis' (2010) ERCL 74.

5. Generalizations

The emerging law on universal services displays elements that differ considerably from the existing body of consumer law. The key difference is, indeed, as the CFI in *BUPA* clearly stated, that the respective universal services supplier is obliged to conclude a contract with vulnerable citizen-consumers. However, not only is the freedom to contract limited, but so too is the freedom to shape the rights and duties in the contract. The key difference between mandatory consumer law on the one side and the law on universal services seems to be an avoidance of economic discrimination. This concept becomes clear in the notion of access, affordability, and anti-discrimination. Economic discrimination is status-related; it is limited to the vulnerable consumer and it ties only the universal services provider.

Questions of generalizations emerge in different directions: with regard to the possible extension of universal services into the grey area of SGEIs; with regard to the extension beyond the grey area into the field of services traditionally seen as market-governed, but where the vulnerable consumer is equally dependent on access to services; and last but not least, with regard to the interaction between the law on universal services and traditional consumer law. Most articles to date discuss the question of whether consumer law might penetrate into the law on universal services. However, it might well be the other way around.

A. Beyond the Core of SGEIs—Universal Services in Health Care, Education, Social Security

It might be recalled that the Member States' position on the privatization of grey areas—to use *Neergaard's* terminology—is ambiguous. Whilst they are united in their rejection of EU intrusion into public services, they are divided with regard to the extent to which they introduce competitive elements into health care, education, research, and even social security. Some Member States, like Germany and the UK, have gone relatively far, particularly with regard to the health care system. The established regulatory mechanisms show a clear resemblance to the universal services approach. Service providers are obliged to conclude contracts. This is the dividing line between the free and universal services. Once the way is paved, the three parameters of marketization, in the words of Freedland, come to bear. *Consumerization* may be found in the national privatization laws which introduce binding minimum standards for certain services, on top of which competition might work, in terms of quality and price.[169] They all encourage citizen-consumers' choices and they are united in the *leitbild* of the circumspect citizen-consumer who has to set incentives by using new opportunities offered by the emerging markets.

[169] See with regard to health care in Germany H-W Micklitz, mit Anmerkungen von T Becker, A Oehler, M-B Pirokowsky, and L Reisch, *Stellung des Verbrauchers/Patienten im liberalisierten Gesundheitsmarkt*, Stellungnahme des Wissenschaftlichen Beirates Verbraucher und Ernährungspolitik beim BMELV, Mai 2008.

Marginalization is about to take place. Clear tendencies can be observed in the health care sector, in education, and research. What is missing so far is *substitutionalization*. Member States have not yet, or are not yet, discussing the establishment of new regulatory agencies in these emerging 'markets'. *Economization* is the necessary consequence of consumerization. Its effects are already becoming clear to varying degrees in the grey zone, in particular in the privatization of education.

The more the Member States move in the direction of marketization the shakier their resistance against EU intervention in the grey area becomes. Marketization will enhance transborder services. It is here that the EU might first intervene, as the recent draft on patient rights in transborder services shows. This Directive may become a blueprint for transborder education or transborder research as well. Seen from such a perspective, the European Commission seems indeed well advised not to set this development in stone and to rely on the further drift towards marketization.

B. Beyond the Core and the Grey Zone—Universal Services in Established Markets

The widening of universal services, even intruding into the grey areas, is still governed by the privatization ideology. Former state monopolies, former state services are gradually transformed into market services where competition rules apply, but where the market forces have to be tamed and counterbalanced via the introduction of universal services. Stretching the law on universal services beyond these boundaries and applying the constitutive rules in established markets would open up the possibility (for good or ill, depending on whether it is felt to be needed) of a new system of social private law outside the core areas of universal services on the one hand and traditional consumer law on the other.

A prime candidate, or perhaps even a test candidate, is the field of financial services, more particularly the question of whether the private banking sector is or shall be legally obliged to grant all citizens access to a private bank account.[170] This issue has been and is still widely debated in the Member States, and has now reached the EU level. The European Commission has launched an initiative to develop rules to help overcome resistance in the private sector in order to ensure that all citizen-consumers have access to a bank account.[171] The reason why the financial services sector is to come into the limelight of the universal service doctrine may be found in its history. Public and private banks stood and continue to stand side by side. The effects of an ever stronger marketization, as promoted by the European Commission, are most visible. It is here that consumerization is most developed, where substitutionalization is effectively operating, but where economization produces social exclusion. The key question is whether financial services are or can be legally obliged—under EC law—to conclude contracts with

[170] Scott, n 52 above, 313.

[171] <http://europa.eu/rapid/pressReleasesAction.do?reference=IP/09/224&format=HTML&aged=0&language=DE&guiLanguage=en> and Micklitz, n 138 above.

vulnerable consumers. It has been argued extensively that citizen-consumers need a bank account to be able to participate in the market and in society. Access then gains a constitutional dimension. Article 36 of the Charter is of little help as it mentions SGEIs only. The next candidate in that line of argument are the providers of the new information technologies. Access to the internet is becoming increasingly important. If citizen-consumers are barred from access, they are socially excluded.[172]

C. The New Law on Universal Services and the Old Consumer Law

Will the new law on universal services, a law which might intervene into the grey areas and might even intrude into services in established markets, become a safety net for vulnerable consumers who are no longer the addressees of the modernized EU consumer law that relies entirely on the consumer shopper to set incentives for further integration of the Internal Market? Or will the new law on universal services affect the old consumer law, thereby introducing into the existing body of consumer law a more 'social' element?

The cornerstone in the ongoing debate on the future of the consumer *acquis* will be whether the new sets of fully harmonized consumer law Directives will provide for particular rules on the protection of vulnerable consumers. So far such a double-headed approach has only been realized in the Directive on Unfair Commercial Practices. But none of the Directives which have been revised during the last couple of years in clear-cut areas of contract law and which strive for full harmonization—namely, Directive 2002/65 on distance selling, Directive 2008/48 on consumer credit, Directive 2008/122 on time sharing, nor the Proposal on Consumer Rights—target the vulnerable consumer. Seen this way, it seems indeed that consumer law is dying, at least the consumer law of the 1970s which was meant to protect the weaker party. The law on universal services could theoretically fill that gap.

A word of caution, however, is needed. Consumer law in the EU played a role as long as it was needed to open up and complete the Internal Market. The instrumental device became abundantly clear in *COS.MET*,[173] where market freedoms prevailed over consumer safety. A similar scenario is imaginable in the law on universal services which could be regarded as a by-product or alibi for the economization of statutory entrepreneurial activities. The universal service doctrine ends in a deadlock if it only serves to 'neutralize' public services[174] and turn citizens into consumers. The law on universal services—this is the lesson to be learnt from consumer law—can only become an integral part of a genuine European Social

[172] In that direction Szyszczak, n 23 above, 63 (public banks) and 71 (internet); Wilhelmsson, n 8 above, 154, and H-W Micklitz and A Oehler, *Consumer Policy in the Digital World* (2007), Scientific Advisory Board for Consumer, Food, and Nutrition Policies to the Federal Ministry of Consumer Protection, Food, and Agriculture, Germany, Berlin.

[173] Case C–470/03 *A.G.M. COS.MET* [2007] ECR I–2749 with note by N Reich, 'A.G.M. COS. MET or: Who is protected by EC safety regulation?' (2008) EL Rev 85.

[174] Sauter, n 130 above.

Model if it can be somewhat dissociated from the privatization logic and if the European Commission and the Member States recognize their joint responsibility for the vulnerable citizen-consumer. This implies that the European Social Model, of which universal services form an integral part, is limited to providing a regulatory framework, leaving room for shared values commonly implemented and for solidarity between national and EU citizens.

4

The Concept of State Aid in Liberalized Sectors

Thomas von Danwitz[*]

1. Introduction

The following reflections on the concept of state aid in liberalized sectors have, of course, been inspired by the particular intellectual appeal of this subject resulting from the indistinguishable combination of legal and economic elements which, like all crossbreeds, led to particularly original features and the need for a high degree of commitment to fully understand the nature of those developments. Less of intellectual but more of practical concern are the far-reaching economic, financial, and even political consequences with which we are faced when dealing with the subject of state aid in liberalized sectors. Already a first glance at the relevant jurisprudence tells us that it might not be easy to establish a clear-cut concept, since the Union Courts have only delivered a rather limited number of judgments in recent times of state aid features in liberalized sectors.

Beyond this interest in our subject lies a second dimension, which is of no lesser importance. After long years of discussion over the role of public services within the creation of the single market, the framework for public services has become more and more precisely defined after the elaboration of Article 16 in the Treaty of Amsterdam and particularly after its amendment by the Treaty of Lisbon. The new paragraph added to Article 16, now re-numbered as Article 14, empowers the Union legislator to establish principles and conditions in order to enable the Member States and the Union to provide, commission, and fund such services. This specific rule-making provision on the functioning of public services inserted in the Treaty, to which a specific protocol on services of general interest[1] has been added and which is accompanied by a Communication of the Commission,[2] constitutes a major change in the existing legal framework and, so far, the point

* Prof Dr Dr h c Thomas von Danwitz, DIAP (ENA, Paris), Judge of the Court of Justice of the European Union, Luxembourg/Cologne.

[1] See Treaty of Lisbon, Protocol No 26.

[2] Commission Communication 'Services of general interest, including social services of general interest: a new European commitment', COM (2007) 725 final.

of culmination in the fight for a specific legal status of public services. It goes without saying that this rule-making provision is designed to bear legislation specifically designed to meet the particular mission of public services and thereby, at least to a certain extent, replacing the predominant focus of the existing legal framework on competition rules and their implementation. Such an evolution could, of course, lead to a significant change to the existing framework, going far beyond the well-balanced solution adopted in the Constitutional Treaty.[3] But it will hopefully not limit the completion of the internal market in this field.

It is self-evident that these changes in the legal framework will become the predominant source of inspiration for legal scholars and will, once secondary legislation has been enacted, become more and more relevant for the status of public services and the legal appreciation of the conditions under which they operate. Given this perspective, it remains to be seen to what extent the relevant jurisprudence of the Court, in particular in *PreussenElektra*,[4] *Stardust Marine*,[5] *Chronopost*,[6] and *Altmark Trans*,[7] will continue to play a crucial role in this field. As you are certainly expecting a view from the Court on these matters and given the wide range of legal aspects having an impact on the mission and the functioning of public services, I will focus on the role of state aid control and its major challenges in this field. On the basis of some general remarks on the specific nature and difficulties of state aid control over public services, the major part of my presentation will be dedicated to the main elements of the established jurisprudence in respect to the problems arising from partially liberalized markets and in particular to the crucial question of cross-subsidization.

2. The Role of State Aid Control in the Process of Liberalization and Privatization

Undoubtedly, the purpose of privatization is to deprive state aid control of its principal object, a public undertaking. But, in order to achieve this goal, privatization has to be accomplished under conditions ensuring the competitive neutrality of the conducted privatization procedure. Typically, state aid control in the field of privatization gives rise to three different issues, all closely linked to the famous private investor test:

- first, the well-known phenomenon of 'dressing the bride' in order to make an undertaking more attractive to private investors;
- secondly, the famous dilemma of stranded costs: contributions or preferential treatments in order to compensate for investments or other engagements of

[3] See T von Danwitz, 'Die Rolle der Unternehmen der Daseinsvorsorge im Verfassungsentwurf' in J Schwarze (ed), *Der Verfassungsentwurf des Europäischen Konvents*, (2004) 251 et seq.
[4] Case C–379/98 *PreussenElektra* [2001] ECR I–2099.
[5] Case C–482/99 *France v Commission—Stardust Marine* [2002] ECR I–4397.
[6] Joined Cases C–83/01 P, C–93/01 P and C–94/01 *P Chronopost* [2003] ECR I–6993.
[7] Case C–280/00 *Altmark Trans* [2003] ECR I–7747.

formerly public undertakings which have become void under liberalized market conditions;
- thirdly, the old problem of how to assess whether the sale of a public undertaking is at market value or entails state aid.

Each of these problems would undoubtedly justify me concentrating my remarks on them individually. Instead, let me confine my remarks to the general statement that the settled case law on contributions aimed at making an undertaking more attractive to private investors[8] gives full guidance for the application of the private investor test in that respect. Nevertheless, the central question of whether a comparable private investor pursuing a structural policy which is guided by prospects of long-term viability leaves considerable scope for the assessment of each particular case. In contrast to that, there is only rather limited jurisprudence on the problem of stranded costs[9] and on the question of whether the sale of a public undertaking entails state aid.[10]

Finally, it should be noted that the general experience of state aid law to witness an incredible inventiveness of Member States, when it comes to original funding schemes and methods, is quite impressively confirmed in the field of privatization and liberalization. In the *AEM* case[11] the Court has already been asked to judge whether an increased charge for access to the national transmission grid only levied on certain undertakings in order to offset a particular advantage, which they presumably might have gained from liberalization constitutes state aid. Unfortunately, the preliminary reference did not contain sufficient factual information to conclude that the existence of state aid was established. I am convinced that Member States will also ensure in the future that the task of the Court will not end up in routine, but will continue to be faced with innovative systems of preferential treatment, which have to be monitored strictly under state aid rules.

3. The Competitive Environment

Despite the focus of my following remarks on state aid law, let me bring to your attention that state aid is not by a long way the only tool for Member States to favour a particular undertaking or a certain type of public services. In the preliminary ruling C–357/07 *TNT Post UK*,[12] the Court was faced with the question of VAT exoneration in favour of services carried out by public postal

[8] Eg Case T–157/01 *Dansk Busvognamænd* [2004] ECR II–917; Joined Cases T–129/95, T–2/96, and T–97/96 *Maxhütte* [1999] ECR II–17; Joined Cases C–278/92, C–279/92, and C–280/92 *Spain v Commission—Hytasa* [1994] ECR I–4103.

[9] Joined Cases C–128/03 and C–129/03 *AEM* [2005] ECR I–2861; C–206/06 *Essent Netwerk Noord* [2008] ECR I –5497.

[10] Case C–334/99 *Germany v Commission—Gröditzer Stahlwerke* [2003] ECR I–1139; C–280/92 *Spain v Commission—Hytasa* [1994] ECR I–4103.

[11] Joined Cases C–128/03 and C–129/03 *AEM* [2005] ECR I–2861.

[12] Case C–357/07 *TNT Post UK* [2009] ECR I–3025.

service operators under the circumstances of liberalization. The notion figuring in Article 13(A)(1)(a) of the Sixth VAT Directive received a self-evident interpretation in the good old days of the delivery monopoly for state-owned postal undertakings. Accordingly, the Court has held in 1985[13] under those circumstances that the public service operator was exempted from VAT including all offered services. Based on the assumption that the existence of a reserved market would constitute a prerequisite for such a VAT exemption, Advocate General Geelhoed proposed in 2003 under conditions of a partially liberalized market that the VAT exemption should only cover reserved market shares and not go beyond. Unfortunately, a withdrawal of the preliminary request made it impossible for the Court to render its judgment.

Under conditions of entirely liberalized markets the question today is asked from a different angle. On the one hand, it is quite evident that public postal services do merit a VAT exemption, even if those services are accomplished in a market environment by one or more operators. On the other hand, it is equally evident that such a VAT exemption of relevant services is of sufficient importance for the evolution of a competitive environment in postal markets to possibly produce distortions of competition. Therefore, the decision of the Court will, in any event, have to take the importance of public postal services and the maintenance of a high level of universal services into consideration as possible justification. Given these diverging goals, it will be revealing to see how the Court might strike the balance.

4. State Aid Control in Partially Liberalized Markets and Cross-Subsidization

Once a sector has been liberalized, it seems to be, at first glance at least, rather peculiar to look for a major role of state aid control under circumstances of liberalization. But in fact, state aid control is faced with quite a significant set of questions which go far beyond the traditional patterns of regional and sectorial state aid schemes or infrastructural support measures.[14] Particularly in sectors which have traditionally been shaped by public service obligations, it is not uncommon to see a Member State devoting continuous efforts to the development of this market according to priorities inspired by the general interest. The process of liberalization which we have experienced in the European Union in sectors such as telecommunications, postal services, energy supply, and public transportation since the 1990s has shown quite strikingly that Member States are in general not willing to pursue a strict 'hands-off' policy once public undertakings have been privatized and market

[13] See Case 107/84 *Commission v Germany* [1985] ECR 2655 para. 11.

[14] For the latter see C Koenig and S Kiefer, 'Public Funding of Infrastructure Projects under EC–State Aid Law' (2005) 3 EStAL 415 et seq.

conditions in these sectors have been liberalized.[15] The basic reason is simply to be found in the mere fact that those sectors continue to be perceived under a different angle than most other industrial or commercial markets, both by consumers and by public authorities. Those sectors are and will remain, for the foreseeable future, to be marked by the particular interest of consumers in services of general economic interest in terms of continuity, periodicity, and affordability.[16]

In consequence, public authorities continue to seek ways and means of ensuring that those consumer needs are met and, depending on traditional policy orientations, consider state subsidies and the maintenance of exclusive rights quite a legitimate way of ensuring that public policy priorities in delivering services of general economic interest are achieved. In that respect, it seems that Member States have not yet fully embraced the deeper logic of the concept of universal services which is designed to combine the continuous pursuit of public policy objectives with the conditions of a fully competitive market environment. This might explain why the liberalization process has in general been enacted on a step-by-step basis with a persistent tendency of maintaining certain exclusive rights of limited scope in postal services,[17] energy supply,[18] and public transport.[19] Beyond direct state subsidies designed to fulfil public service objectives, in particular the phenomenon of partially liberalized markets, be it a constant or a transitional one, most naturally gives rise to possible distortions of competition through cross-subsidization. The different manifestations in which cross-subsidization might occur are as numerous and possibly as diverse as the granting of state aid itself. The Court's practice already shows a quite significant range of different schemes, be it direct payments to compensate for public service obligations[20] or the levy of increased charges to finance public service missions,[21] logistical, and commercial, support to a subsidiary operating in a competitive market,[22] and the calculation of charges for the access and use of a transmission or a transport system[23] to a subsidiary.

A. The Role of State Aid Control in Partially Liberalized Markets

The undoubtedly highly technical nature of these examples, in particular when it comes to the allocation of costs, should not lead to the false conclusion that this

[15] See T von Danwitz, 'Der europäische Elektrizitätsbinnenmarkt zwischen Wettbewerbsorientierung und Wettbewerbsbeschränkung' in Jörg Ennuschat, Jörg Geerlings, Thomas Mann, and Johann Christian Pielow (eds), *Recht und Ordnung der Wirtschaft, Festsschrift für Peter J Tettinger* (2007) 703 et seq.

[16] Services of General Economic Interest—Opinion Prepared by the State Aid Group of EAGCP, 29 June 2006.

[17] Art 7(1) of Directive 97/67/EC as amended by Directive 2002/39/EC, OJ [2002] L 176/21.

[18] Art 3(8) of Directive 2003/54/EC OJ [1998] L 15/14.

[19] Art 10 of Directive 91/440/EEC OJ [1991] L 237/25.

[20] Case C–280/00 *Altmark Trans* [2003] ECR I–7747.

[21] Case C–340/90 *TNT Traco* [2001] ECR I–4109; Case C–526/04 *Laboratoires Boiron* [2006] ECR I–7529.

[22] Joined Cases C–83/01 P, C–93/01 P and C–94/01 P *Chronopost* [2003] ECR I–6993; Case T–613/97 *UFEX* [2006] ECR II–1531.

[23] Joined Cases C–128/03 and C–129/03 *AEM* [2005] ECR I–2861; Case T–266/02 *Deutsche Post v Commission* [2006] ECR II–1233.

subject-matter is too detailed to be deserving of particular attention. A closer look into the relevant jurisprudence and the academic research quite strikingly shows the considerable importance of these questions and the far-reaching consequences in economic and even in political terms.[24] The principal challenge facing Union Courts in the environment of liberalized and partially liberalized markets is to ask whether there is a specific role for state aid control, to define the scope of the powers of the European Commission in the assessment of state aid measures and to determine the nature and the extent of judicial review in this field. Fundamental questions altogether.

1. A 'Specific' Role for State Aid Control in Liberalized Sectors?

The starting-point of our reflections on the scope of state aid control in liberalized sectors is the basic question of whether state aid control has a specific role to play in liberalized areas. To put it in quite simple terms: my suggestion is that state aid control has no different role to play in liberalized sectors than in any other field. State aid control has to effectively ensure that Member States cannot create distortions of competition by aids which, first, are granted directly or indirectly through state resources and, secondly, are imputable to the state.[25] In view of the wide spectrum of ways in which aid can be granted, state aid control has to cover the entire range of possible configurations. In that respect, let me recall the settled case law according to which Union law cannot permit the rules on state aid to be circumvented by the creation of autonomous institutions or procedures charged with allocating state aid.[26]

But the purpose of state aid control of avoiding distortions of competition is not a self-sufficient objective which is on its own capable of justifying any given measure designed to improve conditions of competition in general. In that respect, it has to be stressed that a clear distinction must be drawn between the specific mandate of state aid control of avoiding selective distortions of competition by specific state intervention in granting state resources and a general, far-reaching regulatory mandate to maintain a level playing field for all undertakings active on the Internal Market. In particular, the improvement of competitive conditions as such between former public undertakings with enduring strong market positions in their home market and new competitors, be it new private undertakings or former public undertakings from other Member States, lies, as urgent as it might be for the realization of the Internal Market, beyond the Commission's mandate in matters of state aid control.[27] Cross-subsidization in general is subject to Article 102 TFEU

[24] The ongoing discussion on Community and national level instigated by the Court's decisions in cases like *Stardust Marine* and *Altmark Trans* and the resulting legislative initiatives may serve as examples.

[25] Case C–482/99 *France v Commission—Stardust Marine* [2002] ECR I–4397 para 24.

[26] See Case C–482/99 *France v Commission—Stardust Marine* [2002] ECR I–4397 para 23.

[27] B Vesterdorf, 'A Further Comment on the New State Aid Concept as this Concept Continues to be Reshaped' (2005) EstAQ 393, 398.

(ex Article 82 EC)[28] and specific regulatory rules for each sector come within the ambit of state aid rules only if state resources have been granted in a way which is imputable to the state.

Although the distinction between the general regulatory need for the realization of a level playing field in liberalized markets and the rather 'limited' function of state aid control is certainly less evident in practice, an important conclusion should be drawn from this differentiation. The regulatory standards contained in Regulations and Directives on the liberalization of a particular sector can go well beyond or stay behind the requirements of state aid control. Therefore, those standards as such cannot, it seems to me, be taken as valid criteria for decisions in state aid law without particular justification, which might of course be possible under given circumstances. This is why the Commission has rightly elaborated specific compensation standards in Article 5(2) of the decision taken on the application of Article 106(2) TFEU (ex Article 86(2) EC)[29] concerning the compensation granted to undertakings entrusted with the operation of services of general economic interest.

2. *Use and Abuse of State Resources—In Search of Imputability*

State aid control in liberalized sectors requires the granting of state resources in a manner which is imputable to the state. Quite evidently, both conditions must be met. All advantages financed by state resources constitute aid, irrespective of whether they are granted directly by the state or indirectly by a public or private body designated or established by the state.[30] By contrast, a selective measure that does not involve any direct or indirect transfer of state resources to undertakings may not be qualified an aid, even if it confers an undeniable advantage on certain undertakings.[31]

In quite a number of cases, the use of state resources has not been in question,[32] but the focus was rather on the question of whether the decision to grant those state resources can be attributed to the state and the measure therefore constitutes state aid. The conditions for such an imputability have been developed in the *Stardust Marine* judgment[33] on the basis of a realistic assumption. The Court states clearly that relations between the state and public undertakings are in general close and that it will therefore be very difficult for a third party to demonstrate in a particular case that aid measures taken by such an undertaking were in fact adopted on

[28] See T von Danwitz, 'Europarechtliche Grundlagen' in *Beck'scher PostG-Kommentar* (2002) 2nd edn, para 113 et seq.

[29] Decision 2005/842/EC on the application of Article 86(2) of the EC Treaty to State aid in the form of public service compensation granted to certain undertakings entrusted with the operation of services of general economic interest, OJ [2005] L 312/67.

[30] Case C–379/98 *PreussenElektra* [2001] ECR I–2099 para 58 with reference to the settled case law of the Court.

[31] Case C–379/98 *PreussenElektra* [2001] ECR I–2099 para 61.

[32] Case C–39/94 *SFEI* [1996] ECR I–3549 para 56; Case C–482/99 *France v Commission—Stardust Marine* [2002] ECR I–4397 para 32.

[33] Case C–482/99 *France v Commission—Stardust Marine* [2002] ECR I–4397 para 52.

instructions of public authorities.[34] The reference made in *Stardust Marine* to the circumstances of the case, and the context in which the measure was taken, has been criticized for being a rather vague notion.[35] But in fact, it seems hard to imagine how one could set up criteria once and for all relevant cases that could be significantly more precise.

In that respect, it seems to be more important to note that the Court has deployed great efforts on identifying indicators which might be relevant to establish that an aid measure adopted by a public undertaking is imputable to the state. Seen from this angle, it does not seem unreasonable to conclude that a merely formalistic approach fixing on the fact that an undertaking is legally placed under public control, would not be sufficient for drawing conclusions as regards the imputability of its decisions to the state. In making reference to the intensity of the supervision exercised by public authorities[36] and to the real possibilities of exercising a dominant influence,[37] *Stardust Marine* aims to achieve a realistic assessment of the particular legal and factual situation *in concreto* in which a public undertaking adopts a certain aid measure.[38] In the end, it is for the Commission and the Member States to demonstrate to the Court for what legal and factual reasons an aid measure should be considered imputable to the state or not. The jurisprudence will evolve in the light of this experience.

B. Cost Allocation—In Search of the 'Right' Standard

Ever since the ground-breaking study of *Faulhaber* on the phenomenon of cross-subsidization in public enterprises,[39] the pricing behaviour of public undertakings and their internal allocation of costs have become central features in proceedings on the abuse of a dominant market position. It should, however, be noted that *Faulhaber's* studies concerned wholly regulated industries.[40] Therefore, it might be worthwhile to do some research on the question to what extent his approach is transposable to state aid control over undertakings offering services both on reserved and on competitive markets.

In the early *Corbeau* judgment the Court concluded that cross-subsidization can be considered a generally justified behaviour in accordance with Article 106(2) TFEU (ex Article 86(2) EC), but added quite strongly that the exclusion of competition is not justified as regards specific services which are dissociable from

[34] Ibid, para 53 et seq—*Stardust Marine*.

[35] See Gahlleithner, 'Die Zurechenbarkeit von Handlungen öffentlicher Unternehmen an den Staat' (2002) European Law Reporter 271, 276; T Lübbig and T von Merveldt, 'Stardust Marine: Introducing Imputability into State Aid Rules—Plain Sailing into Calm Seas or Rowing Back into Shallow Waters?' (2003) ECLR 629, 632.

[36] Case C–482/99 *France v Commission—Stardust Marine* [2002] ECR I–4397 para 56.

[37] Ibid, para 57.

[38] See the reasoning of the CFI, Case T–613/97 *UFEX* [2006] ECR II–1531 para 166.

[39] GR Faulhaber, 'Cross-Subsidization: Pricing in Public Enterprises' (1975) American Economy Review 966; GR Faulhaber, 'Cross-Subsidization: Analysis with more than two Services' (2005) Journal of Competition Law and Economics, 441–448.

[40] GR Faulhaber, n 38 (1975), American Economy Review 966, 967.

services of general interest and meet special needs of economic operators for which the traditional postal services make no adequate offer.[41] The perception of cross-subsidization as subject to state aid rules is a more recent evolution, rather closely linked to the process of step-by-step liberalization giving rise to partially liberalized markets in which the cross-subsidization of liberalized market segments by using state resources originally designed to compensate for public service obligations has become a real danger for the creation of a competitive environment.[42]

1. Scope and Intensity of Judicial Review

Ever since the fundamental judgment in *Corbeau*, the Court has had quite a number of opportunities for developing its jurisprudence with regard to Article 106(2) TFEU (ex Article 86(2) EC). The general message of the judgments in *TNT Traco,*[43] *Chronopost,*[44] and *Ambulanz Glöckner*[45] seems to be quite clear. In particular, the Court pointed out clearly in *Chronopost* that the public network made available to Chronopost was clearly not a market network and would never have been created by a private undertaking. Accordingly, cost calculation and allocation in search of possible cross-subsidization have to be based on objective and verifiable elements[46] on the factual basis of the existing network.[47] The factual and legal difficulties for the Commission of meeting this standard may not be neglected, as the follow-on *UFEX* judgment of the CFI shows, in which the Tribunal annulled the contested decision of the Commission for defective reasoning. For the future, the rather detailed accounting standards of the Transparency Directive 2006/111/EC[48] and the cost calculation standards of the Commission decision on the application of Article 106 TFEU (ex Article 86(2) EC) to state aid in the form of public service compensation[49] should improve the factual conditions quite considerably to identify objective and verifiable elements for the required assessments relating to cross-subsidization.

In the *UFEX* judgment, the Tribunal addressed a rather fundamental question in stating that the Commission's calculation of the cost incurred in providing logistical and commercial assistance to a subsidiary involves, in the absence of analytical accounts, a complex economic appraisal for which the Commission enjoys a wide

[41] Case C–320/91 *Corbeau* [1993] ECR I–2533 paras 16–19.

[42] See L Hancher and J-L Buendia Sierra, 'Cross-Subsidization and EC Law' (1998) CML Rev 35, 901 et seq; D Triantafyllou, 'L'encadrement communautaire du service public' (1999) RTD Eur 21.

[43] Case C–340/90 *TNT Traco* [2001] ECR I–4109.

[44] Joined Cases C–83/01 P, C–93/01 P, 94/01 P *Chronopost* [2003] ECR I–6993.

[45] Case C–475/99 *Ambulanz Glöckner* [2001] ECR I–8089.

[46] Joined Cases C–83/01 P, C–93/01 P, 94/01 P *Chronopost* [2003] ECR I–6993 para 38.

[47] See Case T–613/97 *UFEX* [2006] ECR II–1531 para 131 and with respect to Art 82 EC see Case 27/76 *United Brands* [1978] ECR 207 para 248/257; Case C–323/93 *Centre d'insémination de la Crespelle* [1994] I–507 para 26 et seq.

[48] Commission Directive 2006/111/EC of 16 November 2006 on the transparency of financial relations between Member States and public undertakings as well as on financial transparency within certain undertakings, OJ [2006] L 318/17.

[49] Commission Decision of 28 November 2005 on the application of Article 86(2) of the EC Treaty to State aid in the form of public service compensation granted to certain undertakings entrusted with the operation of services of general economic interest, OJ [2005] L 312/67.

discretion. In consequence, the judicial review of that measure, even though comprehensive in principle as the CFI adds, is limited to manifest errors of assessment as well as the respect of procedural rules and the statement of reasons.[50] In the light of the complexities of cost calculation, this reasoning is fully understandable from any lawyer's and not only from a judge's point of view. In addition to that, we all know since the Court's reasoning in *TU München*[51] that a rather strict monitoring of the obligation to state reasons may in practice lead to a judicial review which is as strict as a comprehensive review in substantive terms.

But still, the question remains whether it would be compatible with Article 107 (1) TFEU (ex Article 87(1) EC) to assume that the Commission could lawfully, by a certainly non-arbitrary and most likely reasonable choice between different methods of calculation, come in one particular case to opposite conclusions as regards the existence of state aid. One could, of course, consider in line with the *UFEX* judgment that this would constitute a manifest error of assessment,[52] if that could be demonstrated to the Court. But again, would the same logic apply if not the existence of an aid, but only the amount were to differ considerably according to the choice of the calculation method? Where could one draw the line? In any event, we will follow with particular interest how the Commission will eventually justify for what reasons a particular cost-allocation standard has been chosen in one case while using a different cost-allocation standard in another case.

2. *The Cost Standard for Cross-subsidization*

When it comes to the central question of the 'right' cost standard for monitoring and detecting cross-subsidization, the interrelation of cost-accounting rules and the legal requirements of Union law deserve our full attention. Even if it might be in practice quite a self-evident starting point, it appears important to note that the allocation of costs has to be made on the basis of generally accepted cost accounting principles, as the Commission decision of 28 November 2005[53] states in Article 5 (2). This ensures that state aid control of cross-subsidization relies in the very first place on a 'best practice' approach, which is in particular completed by the requirements of the Transparency Directive.

On that basis, the opposing aims of the prohibition of any state aid in Article 107 (1) TFEU (ex Article 87(1) EC) and the necessity of ensuring workable conditions for public services according to Article 106(2) (ex Article 86(2)) and Article 14 TFEU (ex Article 16 EC) have to guide our reflections. The basic idea is to keep the prohibition of state aid effective, even if aid is granted by way of cross-subsidization. This purpose may, of course, not endanger the good functioning of public service operations, which enjoy a particular recognition in Union law. To me it seems

50 See Case T–613/97 *UFEX* [2006] ECR II–1531 para 128.

51 Case C–269/90 *Technische Universität München* [1991] ECR I–5469 para 26.

52 See Case T–613/97 *UFEX* [2006] ECR II–1531 para 138.

53 Commission decision of 28 November 2005 on the application of Article 86(2) of the EC Treaty to State aid in the form of public service compensation granted to certain undertakings entrusted with the operation of services of general economic interest, OJ [2005] L 312/67, fn 45.

quite inappropriate to strive for a hierarchical understanding of both values in terms of Union law. The challenge is rather to achieve practical solutions designed for an equivalent realization of both objectives. To my mind, the rationale of the jurisprudence in *Chronopost* seems to be rightly based on this balancing approach.

The formula for cost allocation used in *Chronopost* reflects quite clearly the commitment to a strict application of state aid rules without interfering with the conditions necessary for the operation of services of general economic interest, although this standard might indeed not have been written with the precision of a text book in business administration. Nonetheless, it becomes quite clear that the focus of the judgment is on the additional cost concept. Therefore, as the judgment states, prices charged to a subsidiary need to cover all the additional variable costs incurred in providing the assistance for a service in liberalized markets, an appropriate contribution to the fixed costs arising from the use of the existing postal network and an adequate return on capital investment used for competitive activities.[54] In my understanding, only those fixed costs can be taken into account which result from the actual use of the postal network for a particular competitive activity. Otherwise, this competitive activity would have to bear costs of services of general economic interest.

Admittedly, the Commission's decision on compensation of public services is not crystal clear in that crucial respect, when it states in Article 5(2)(c) that costs allocated to a service of general economic interest may cover the variable costs and 'a proportionate contribution to fixed costs common to both services of general economic interest and other activities'. But quite evidently, this provision can and has to be read in conformity with the requirements established in *Chronopost*, since they constitute an interpretation of primary law in Article 107(1) TFEU (ex Article 87(1) EC).

3. *Remaining Uncertainties*

Nevertheless, it is quite evident that the problem of cost allocation between services of general economic interest and competitive services has not fully been resolved by the existing jurisprudence. Details of considerable economic importance have so far not been brought to the attention of the Court and, therefore, have remained undecided yet. Questions relating to an eventual difference in calculating additional costs or incremental costs, to the degree of admissible standardization, to the time frame for calculation which is important for shifting the demarcation line between variable and fixed costs and, finally, to the consequences of a top-down as opposed to a bottom-up approach do not find an answer in the rules on state aid law. Consequently, they have not been reflected in the jurisprudence of the Court. It should, however, be noted that the Commission has made an effort to cope with these problems in a discussion paper on Article 102 TFEU (ex Article 82 EC).[55] Here again, it remains to be seen whether those standards are fully transposable to state aid law.

54 Joined Cases C–83/01 P, C–93/01 P, and C– 94/01 P *Chronopost* [2003] ECR I–6993 para 40.

55 DG Competition discussion paper on the application of Article 82 of the Treaty to exclusionary abuses, Brussels (December 2005), para 64 et seq, available at <http://ec.europa.eu/competition/antitrust/art82/discpaper2005.pdf>.

When it comes to the mission of Union Courts in that respect, it seems to be quite clear that enacting cost-allocation standards cannot be considered a genuine task of the judiciary and, beyond that, defining common rules for cost accounting and cost allocation in essence does not require a specifically legal reasoning. This only comes into play when the suitability and proportionality of such standards or the requirements of a homogeneous application respecting an equal treatment of all undertakings concerned give rise to legal doubts. But, in my perception, the elaboration of such standards in itself ought to be regarded as a non-judicial question which should be answered in accordance with generally recognized cost-accounting and cost-allocation standards. In that perspective, preference should be given to a best practice approach.

C. Procedural Consequences

What remains is the question of procedural consequences and in particular, how a party can eventually prove features of overcompensation. Since Member States enjoy, in general, procedural autonomy, the requirements of Union law are limited to the principles of equivalence and effectiveness. On this basis, in *Laboratoires Boiron* the Court has dealt with the delicate question of the burden of proof.[56] According to the findings of the Court, in a situation in which it is likely to be impossible or excessively difficult for the required evidence to be produced by a party, a national Court is required to use all procedures available under national law for this purpose, including the production of a particular document.[57] By this finding, the Court evidently responds to the need arising from a particular situation to make sure that a national court can verify a potential overcompensation.

There is indeed an undeniable need for such a procedural possibility in order to assess whether an alleged overcompensation in fact took place. But still, this judgment should not be taken as a general rule without limitations giving rise to all sorts of investigatory actions. It should rather be noted that the Court refers to the factual and legal circumstances in this specific case, where a national court had the power to order a party to produce a certain document. In particular, this judgment has not dealt with the protection of business secrets and the possibility of rejecting claims for the production of documents on such grounds.[58]

5. Conclusion

This overview over the jurisprudence of Union Courts on the concept of aid in liberalized sectors has been an occasion to identify the main challenges for state aid control in this field and to reflect the state of Union law jurisprudence. In essence, it

[56] Case C–526/04 *Laboratoires Boiron* [2006] ECR I–7529 para 51 et seq.
[57] Ibid, para 55.
[58] See *BVerfGE* 115, 205; T von Danwitz, 'Der Schutz von Geschäfts- und Betriebsgeheimnissen im Recht der Regulierungsverwaltung' (2005) DVBl 597.

seems to me that the jurisprudence is well established on a balanced approach which takes the necessities of a stringent state aid control seriously without neglecting the importance of maintaining the good functioning of services of general economic interest. In particular, let me draw three conclusions from the foregoing.

First, we have to acknowledge that state aid control is not a generally usable, unconditioned instrument of regulatory policy for realizing a level playing field in liberalized markets. State aid control is rather focused on the use and abuse of state resources in a competitive environment. In that respect, the role of state aid control in liberalized markets does not differ from the traditional mandate to render the prohibition of state aid in Article 107(1) TFEU (ex Article 87(1) EC) effective.

Secondly, the discussion of the issue of imputability has shown that Union Courts will have to live up to the basic standards established in *PreussenElektra* and in *Stardust Marine*. Quite evidently, these judgments have not provided us with a standard of review which is so easy to handle that most proceedings before the Commission and the Union Courts have or will become superfluous. But, as you well know, these judgments were not adopted to fulfil such unrealistic expectations and no future judgment will do so. The standards of review in state aid control need to be designed in a way which takes two aspects into account. A certain degree of flexibility is necessary to ensure a reasonable application in the Commission's practice and in particular in order to cover future evolutions. But a solid concept with a visible profile is indispensable to give Member States and public undertakings the orientation which they clearly need.

Thirdly, the jurisprudence of the Court has developed a realistic approach to cross-subsidization, which might still need some refinement and future evolution. In particular, judicial review will have to ensure a homogenous application of the criteria for cost allocation as they have been established in *Chronopost*. On that basis, procedural consequences, as they have been discussed in *Laboratoires Boiron* for the very first time, will certainly require more attention in the future.

5

The *Rüffert* Case and Public Procurement

*Christopher McCrudden**

1. Introduction

The 'posted-workers' cases of *Viking*,[1] *Laval*,[2] *Rüffert*,[3] and *Luxembourg*[4] have occasioned a considerable amount of commentary and assessment,[5] particularly surrounding the implications of these decisions for the future interpretation of the Posted Workers Directive[6] and Article 49 EC. The controversial nature of at least the first two decisions was widely predicted before the Court decided the cases.[7] In each of these cases, the European Court of Justice (ECJ) was called upon to strike a balance between the freedom to provide services and the protection of workers. Within that broad area, each of these cases has its own particular importance, and complexities, depending on the individual facts and context in which the case arose. *Rüffert* poses particular difficulties of interpretation because of the procurement context in which the case arose, an issue that has been relatively absent from much of the published commentary on the case so far.[8]

* I am grateful to Catherine Barnard, Nicholas Hatzis, Martin Trybus, Sacha Prechal, Paul Davies, Anne Davies, and Marise Cremona for reading and commenting on an earlier draft of this chapter.

[1] Case C–438/05 *International Transport Workers' Federation v Viking Line ABP* [2007] ECR I–10779.

[2] Case C–341/05 *Laval un Partneri Ltd v Svenska Byggnadsarbetareförbundet* [2007] ECR I–11767.

[3] Case C–346/06 *Rüffert v Land Niedersachsen* [2008] IRLR 467 (ECJ).

[4] Case C–319/06 *Commission v Luxembourg* [2008] IRLR 388 (ECJ).

[5] ACL Davies, 'One Step Forward, Two Steps Back? The *Viking* and *Laval* Cases in the ECJ' (2008) 37 Industrial Law Journal 125; Simon Deakin, 'Regulatory Competition in Europe after *Laval*' (2008) ESRC Centre for Business Research, Working Paper 364; S Prechal and S de Vries, 'Seamless web of judicial protection in the internal market?' (2009) 34(1) ELR 5; KD Ewing and John Hendy QC, *The New Spectre Haunting Europe—The ECJ, Trade Union Rights, and the British Government* (2009); Catherine Barnard, 'The UK and Posted Workers: the effect of *Commission v Luxembourg* on the territorial application of British labour law', (2009) 38 ILJ 122. For a more complete list of academic commentary, see <http://www.etui-rehs.org/en/Headline-issues/Viking-Laval-Rueffert-Luxembourg/2-Articles-in-academic-literature-on-the-judgements>.

[6] Directive 96/71/EC of the European Parliament and of the Council of 16 December 1996 concerning the posting of workers in the framework of the provision of services, OJ [1997] L 18/1.

[7] B Bercusson, 'The Trade Union Movement and the European Union: Judgment Day' (2007) 13 (3) ELJ 279.

[8] P Davies, 'Case C–346/06, *Rüffert v Land Niedersachsen* [2008] IRLR 467 (ECJ)' (2008) 37 ILJ 37; Richard Arthur, 'Third Case Unlucky: Ramifications of *Ruffert*', (2008) 8 (1) Federation News 12–14. But see the following which do consider aspects of the procurement issues involved: O Otting,

2. The Facts in *Rüffert*

The facts of *Rüffert* are somewhat complicated. A Lower Saxony law (the *Landesvergabegesetz*)[9] provided that public building contracts over a threshold amount of €10,000 would only be awarded by Lower Saxony public authorities to contractors who agreed to abide by a contract condition applicable to the main contractor, and all subcontractors.[10] This contract condition required that those employed on the contract would be paid at least at the level of the rates of pay applying to the place where the contract was performed, set out in the relevant collective bargaining agreement that was applicable.[11] The purpose of the law was to prevent undercutting of wages.[12] Sanctions for breach of the contract condition were set out in the legislation, consisting of financial penalties and possible termination of the contract.[13]

'Case Comment: Compulsory social standards for public contracts as a restriction on the freedom to provide services: *Dirk Rüffert v Land Niedersachsen* (Case–346/06)' (2008) Public Procurement Law Review 193; S Arrowsmith and P Kunzlik, 'Introduction—a note on *Rüffert v Land Niedersachsen*', in S Arrowsmith and P Kunzlik (eds), *Social and Environmental Policies in EC Procurement Law: New Directives and New Directions* (2009); Richard Arthur, '*Rüffert* and *Luxembourg*: The Posted Workers' Directive and ILO Convention 94' in Ewing and Hendy, n 5 above, 36–48.

[9] The Law of Land Niedersachsen on the award of public contracts (Landesvergabegesetz Nds., 'the Landesvergabegesetz'). The translations of the provisions in the following footnotes are taken from the ECJ's judgment.

[10] Paragraph 4(1) of the Law provides:

> The contractor may assign to subcontractors services for which his establishment is set up only where the contracting authority has given written consent in a given case. The tenderers are required at the stage they lodge their tenders to state which services are to be devolved to subcontractors. In so far as services are assigned to subcontractors, the contractor must also undertake to impose on the subcontractors the obligations laid down in Paragraphs 3, 4 and 7(2) applicable to contractors and to monitor compliance with these obligations by the subcontractors.

[11] Under Paragraph 3(1) of the Law:

> Contracts for building services shall be awarded only to undertakings which, when lodging a tender, undertake in writing to pay their employees, when performing those services, at least the remuneration prescribed by the collective agreement at the place where those services are performed and at the time prescribed by the collective agreement. For the purposes of the first sentence, the term 'services' means services provided by the principal contractor and by subcontractors. The first sentence shall also apply to the award of transport services in local public transport.

[12] The preamble to the Law states:

> The Law counteracts distortions of competition which arise in the field of construction and local public transport services resulting from the use of cheap labour and alleviates burdens on social security schemes. It provides, to that end, that public contracting authorities may award contracts for building works and local public transport services only to undertakings which pay the wage laid down in the collective agreements at the place where the service is provided.

[13] Paragraph 8 of the Law provides:

> (1) In order to ensure compliance with the obligations under Paragraphs 3, 4 and 7(2), public contracting authorities shall agree with the contractor for each case of culpable non-fulfilment a contractual penalty of 1%, and in the case of several cases of non-fulfilment a

In 2003, a contract for the building of a prison was awarded to Objekt und Bauregie GmbH & Co KG (hereafter OB), a German company, at the cost of about €8.5 million. The relevant collective agreement was the Building and Public Works Collective Agreement. OB subsequently subcontracted to PKZ Pracownie Konserwacji Zabytków sp. zoo (hereafter PKZ), which was a Polish undertaking with a branch in Germany. PKZ brought in Polish workers hired in Poland to work on the site. There was an alleged substantial breach by PKZ of the contract condition regarding minimum rates of pay, established by the collective agreement. The firm was accused of paying the 53 employees only 46.57 per cent of the minimum wage that was applicable. The contract was subsequently terminated by both Lower Saxony and OB.

Litigation was initiated by both Lower Saxony and OB against each other. Lower Saxony issued a penalty notice against OB. Lower Saxony's argument was that OB was in breach of its undertaking regarding the rates of pay to be paid at the site, and should therefore pay the relevant penalty. OB's claim was for payment of the proportion of the contract price that reflected the work undertaken until the termination of the contract. In effect, the first instance state court (the *Landgericht Hannover*) decided that both parties were correct, to some extent, and awarded a sum of money to OB in compensation for work completed to date, but then deducted the same amount from the award of compensation as an offset in payment of the penalty for OB's failure to comply with the contract condition regarding pay rates. OB subsequently went into liquidation but the litigation continued in the name of Rüffert, who was OB's liquidator.

The primary issue when the litigation went on appeal to the state higher (appeal) court (the *Oberlandesgericht Celle*) was whether a deduction from OB's claim based on the penalty was impermissible. OB argued in the domestic court that the deduction was impermissible because the Lower Saxony law was contrary to European Community (EC) law, viz Article 49 EC. This provides: 'Within the framework of the provisions set out below, restrictions on freedom to provide services within the Community shall be prohibited in respect of nationals of Member States who are established in a State of the Community other than that of the person for whom the services are intended.' The effect of the contract requirements, it was alleged, was to make it more difficult for a Polish contractor

contractual penalty of up to 10%, of the contract value. The contractor shall be obliged to pay a contractual penalty under the first sentence also in the event that there is non-fulfilment on the part of a subcontractor used by it or a subcontractor used by that subcontractor, unless the contractor was not aware or could not have been aware of the non-fulfilment. Where the contractual penalty imposed is disproportionately high, the contracting authority may reduce it to the appropriate amount at the request of the contractor. (2) The public contracting authorities shall agree with the contractor that failure to satisfy the requirements referred to in Paragraph 3 by the contractor or his subcontractors and any non-fulfilment stemming from gross negligence or repeated non-fulfilment of the obligations laid down in Paragraphs 4 and 7(2) will entitle the contracting authority to terminate the contract without notice. (3) Where an undertaking is proved to have failed to fulfil its obligations under this Law as a result, at least, of gross negligence or on a repeated basis, the public contracting authorities may exclude it from the award of public contracts within their field of competence for a period of up to one year.

to be able to compete with German contractors. The state higher court referred the issue to the ECJ. The question referred to the ECJ was as follows:

Does it amount to an unjustified restriction on the freedom to provide services under the EC Treaty if a public contracting authority is required by statute to award contracts for building services only to undertakings which, when lodging a tender, undertake in writing to pay their employees, when performing those services, at least the remuneration prescribed by the collective agreement in force at the place where those services are performed?

3. German Procurement Context

Before turning to consider the decision of the ECJ, it is important to appreciate some particular aspects of the German political and legal context of the *Rüffert* case. The *Rüffert* case arises from the law of one of the German states (or *Länder*). Procurement law in Germany is governed by federal, state, and municipal legal provisions. At the federal level, Part IV of the *Gesetz gegen Wettbewerbsbeschränkungen* (GWB), the (Federal) Act against Restraints on Competition, contains the basic principles of public procurement.[14] The use of public procurement to advance social and political agendas is controversial in many countries but perhaps nowhere to such a degree as in Germany. Trybus has described the issue as 'subject to a fierce political debate' in Germany.[15] The two main political groupings in Germany have tended to align themselves on different sides of the divide. The centre-right group of Christian Democrats (CDU/CSU) and Liberals (FDP) was mostly against the inclusion of social criteria, whereas the centre-left camp consisting of the Social Democrats (SPD) and Greens was more favourable. The post-communist Left Party was also more favourable. As Trybus observes: '[t]his debate has not been decided yet.'

This debate is reflected in the new federal legislation, which was passed in 1998 to reform the whole procurement process and to bring German law into compliance with EC law, the Act coming into force on 1 January 1999. The Act was a compromise between the *Bundestag* (the 'main' chamber of Parliament, at the time dominated by the CDU/FDP, favouring the draft prepared by the Government) and the *Bundesrat* (the generally weaker, but for this kind of legislation almost equally powerful chamber of Parliament, representing the 16 *Länder*, at this time mainly dominated by the SPD). This 1998 Act transferred the legal regulation of public procurement from the States Budgetary Law Act, where it was fragmentarily laid down before, to the GWB.[16] The inclusion of the procurement reform in this Act was seen as indicating 'a remarkable shift of perspective', since previously public

[14] M Trybus, 'Study on Social Considerations in Public Procurement', Country Report for the Federal Republic of Germany, 11 June 2008, 1 (available at: <http://ec.europa.eu/social/main.jsp?catId=331&langId=en&newsId=417&furtherNews=yes>).

[15] Ibid.

[16] GWB, §§ 97 to 129.

procurement requirements 'were intended only to safeguard correct and economic administration of public money, not to protect competitors or competition'.[17]

The Act laid down several principles for awarding public sector contracts, which until then were only either included in administrative rules (*VOL* and *VOB*),[18] or deemed to be valid but unwritten. One set of rules, which was upgraded from the level of *VOL* and *VOB* to the level of formal legislation, concerned the substantive criteria according to which the public administration had to award its contracts.[19] These provided that the public body primarily procured goods, buildings, and services according to rules by way of competition and in a transparent procurement procedure. The participants in the procurement process were to be treated equally, unless a prejudicial treatment is explicitly required or allowed by virtue of this statute. The interests of the *Mittelstand* (the class of small and medium-sized businesses, in contrast to large-scale industry) were to be regarded appropriately, primarily by dividing the contract into smaller parts. Paragraph 7 provided that tenderers are entitled to claim conformity by the public body with the procurement rules. Paragraph 7 has been seen as the crucial part of the reform over all, because this provision and the additional system of judicial remedies for the protection of this claim made this whole field of law justiciable, whereas before it was in the unsupervised discretion of the administration.[20]

For the purposes of this chapter, however, it is paragraph 4 that is most important. Paragraph 4 provided that contracts are awarded to professional, competent, and reliable companies (other or further requirements are only allowed, if they are provided for by federal or *Länder* legislation). The lowest bid is to be accepted. This provision was one of those that were the result of a compromise between the *Bundesrat* and the *Bundestag*.[21] The original draft prepared by the federal government was stimulated by the controversy about social aims in procurement procedures. The federal government's draft contained an authorization to implement secondary aims only on the basis of federal statutes, not *Länder* statutes. The federal government may have been afraid that the *Länder* would be less willing to comply with EC standards, and that EC law compliance would be easier to ensure if only one jurisdiction (the federal one) were competent. The *Länder* argued, through their representative at the federal level, the *Bundesrat*, that social aims should be allowed to be determined and implemented by *Länder* statutes as well. And the *Bundesrat* succeeded, as can be seen in § 97 (4) GWB. The *Bundesrat* managed to achieve another goal. The original federal Government draft of § 97 (4), the second part of the sentence, read: '*Further* requirements are only allowed, if

[17] B Spiesshofer and M Lang, 'The New German Public Procurement Law: Commentary and English Translation of the Text' (1999) 8 Public Procurement Law Review 103.

[18] *Die Verdingungsordnung für Leistungen (VOL)* (Regulations on Tender Procedures for Supplies and Services), and *Die Vergabe- und Vertragsordnung für Bauleistungen (VOB)* (Regulations on Tender Procedures for Public Works) provided detailed *administrative* rules for tender procedures in the absence of legislative provisions.

[19] It is located in the first paragraph of the part of the GWB regarding public procurement, § 97.

[20] Ibid, at CS104.

[21] The history of the legislation of this provision is described by C Benedict, *Sekundärzwecke im Vergabeverfahren* (2000), 4, 107 et seq.

they are provided for by federal statute.' Now it reads: '*Other or* further requirements . . . ' By this wording, the Act allowed the general replacement, not only the supplementation of the requirements and criteria mentioned in § 97 (4), GWB, first part of the sentence.

However, the purpose of § 97 (4) GWB, second part of the sentence, is, in general, a restrictive one. In contrast to the former legal situation, promoting procurement linkages by public procurement requires a formal Act of Parliament (either at the federal or *Länder* level), and cannot be done, as was so often in the past, by internal Circular, ordinance, oral order or plain custom. In order to protect public administration and its practice from too speedy an alteration of the legal situation, the *Bundesrat* did, however, manage to install a transitional provision for § 97 (4) GWB, last part of the sentence. Until June 2000 the promotion of secondary aims in public procurement was allowed even without statutory provisions. After June 2000, these measures could not be undertaken on administrative authorization alone, but had to be based on a (state or federal) Act of Parliament.[22]

4. German Controversies concerning the *Tariftreuegesetz*

One of the main areas of discussion about the incorporation of social aims into public procurement was whether public sector contracts should be given only to companies that declared that they paid wages according to the collectively agreed wages (*tarif*) in the area in which the contract was carried out. Several public authorities wanted to be able to award contracts only to those tenderers who would agree to be bound by the collectively agreed rate for the area. The purpose of the loyalty declaration was to ensure that only those bidders were allowed to take part in the procurement procedure who, no matter where they were from, declared that all the employees involved in the performance of the contract, and all employees of possible subcontractors, were paid and treated in accordance with the local wage system.

In July 2002, the federal government proposed a law that obliged companies seeking to obtain public contracts to pay their employees the collectively agreed rate, but this was rejected by the *Bundesrat*.[23] However, several *Länder* upgraded their previously administratively provided requirement to the level of (state) Act of Parliament. The legal situation has become complex, as rules relating to the award of public contracts have been inserted into various state statutes dealing primarily with other issues.

According to the 2007 BMWI Study in 2002, at page 13,[24] eight states of Germany introduced a Compliance with Collective Bargaining Agreements Act (German: Tariftreu-

[22] See in general M King, *Die Zulässigkeit vergabefremder Regelungen* (2000); C Benedict, *Sekundärzwecke im Vergabeverfahren* (2000).

[23] European Industrial Relations Observatory online, available at: <http://www.eiro.eurofound.ie/2000/08/inbrief/DE0208201N.html>.

[24] Gutachten Nr. 2/07 Öffentliches Beschaffungswesen, Wissenschaftlicher Beirat beim Bundesministerium für Wirtschaft und Technologie, Berlin, December 2007, available at: <http://www.wissenschaftlicher-beirat.de>.

gesetze) after the Federal Parliament (Bundestag) had rejected such a law on the federal level. In the states of Schleswig-Holstein and Hamburg these laws had only a limited application period. In the State of North Rhine-Westphalia the respective act was abolished in 2006 after a Study of the Sozialforschungsstelle Dortmund (Social Research Unit Dortmund) had evaluated the law for the period of 2004 to 2005. This Study found that that 70 per cent of the districts (German: Kreise) and 96 per cent of the municipalities did not review compliance with the law. Moreover, 80 per cent of contracting authorities found it very difficult to differentiate between different types of collective bargaining agreements and 70 per cent informed that it was difficult to review any calculations and to correctly implement the law. 70 per cent of the construction companies complained about the task of reviewing compliance with the law actually being transferred to the general contractor. Also on the basis of these findings the 2007 BMWI Study argued strongly against the *Tariftreuegesetze*. As the Federal Parliament rejected a *Tariftreuegesetz*, at least the State of North Rhine-Westphalia has abolished its law, the law in other states has an 'expiry date' and will not be renewed, and as anyway only half of the German states ever had such a law it can be assumed that this kind of law will soon be very rare in Germany.[25]

5. *Tariftreuegesetz* in the German Constitutional Court

Despite the apparent authorization in the GWB for requirements linking procurement with social issues, these requirements in the *Länder* encountered considerable legal difficulty. Prior to the federal reform legislation, equivalent requirements were held unlawful by the Federal Procurement Supervisory Committee and the Federal Cartel Office.[26] In July 1999 Berlin was the first *Land* to pass an Act of Parliament on public procurement after the reform legislation. The law concerning collective agreements, contained in the Berlin Contract Award Act, included a requirement that tenderers had to agree to pay the collectively agreed rate, if they were awarded the contract. The newly installed judicial review provided a basis for challenging this and in January 2000 the Federal Supreme Court (*Bundesgerichtshof* (BGH)) decided a case concerning this requirement in the Berlin procurement legislation.[27] The BGH was of the opinion that the crucial issue was whether or not the requirement in the Berlin Procurement Act was valid. It was invalid if it violated the Basic Law or other federal law. In its decision, the BGH held the requirement in the Berlin Procurement Act to be invalid, on the grounds that it violated § 97 (4) GWB, and that the *Land* had no jurisdiction over collective bargaining issues. Only the German Constitutional Court (*Bundesfervassungsgericht*, or BVerfG) was allowed to decide the constitutionality of the legislation, however, and for that reason the BGH submitted the case to the BVerfG. By the time the issue went to the BVerfG, several state procurement laws required tenderers to show that their

[25] M Trybus, 'Study on Social Considerations in Public Procurement', Country Report for the Federal Republic of Germany, 11 June 2008, 1.

[26] H-J Priess and C Pitschas, 'Recent German Public Procurement Case Law: Bodies Governed by Public Law and Social Criteria Unrelated to Public Procurement Rules' (1999) 8 Public Procurement Law Review 120, 121.

[27] The decision is published in Der Betrieb 2000, 465 et seq.

employees were paid wages that were not below those set forth in the applicable local collective labour agreements.[28]

In July 2006, between the time that the reference was made to the ECJ and the decision by the ECJ in the case, the BVerfG held this stipulation constitutional under German law.[29] The law concerning collective agreements was compatible with the Basic Law and with other federal law. Berlin had the authority to issue the provision; the statute violated neither fundamental rights nor other federal law.

The regulation on respect for collective agreements did not encroach on the area protected by the right to form associations in Article 9(3) of the Basic Law. The obligation to respect collective agreements did not restrict the right of the enterprises involved in the procurement proceedings to remain out of the association concluding the collective agreement. The statute also did not exert any coercion or significant pressure to join. It was unlikely that an entrepreneur, not bound by the collective agreement, would feel forced to join the association concluding the collective agreement in order to be able to influence the conclusion of future collective agreements by which the entrepreneur would subsequently be bound. The fundamental right not to form associations did not protect against the legislature taking the results of agreements concluded by associations as the starting point of statutory provisions. Furthermore, the obligation to respect collective agreements did not lead to state legislative activity taking place in an area in which the agreements reached autonomously between the social partners via collective bargaining took priority. The local collective remuneration agreements did not become part of the employment contracts of the workers deployed in carrying out the public contract by virtue of the state ordering their validity, but subsequent to implementation by the employers of the obligation to respect collective agreements in individual employment contracts.

The regulation on respect for collective agreements contained in the Berlin Contract Award Act also did not violate the fundamental right to occupational freedom in Article 12(1) of the Basic Law. The protection afforded by the right to occupational freedom was affected since the regulation on respect for collective agreements concerned contractual freedom in the field of business guaranteed by Article 12(1). The legislative provision also encroached on the fundamental right to occupational freedom. But, this encroachment on the right to occupational freedom was constitutionally justified. The Berlin legislature had pursued constitutionally legitimate goals by enacting the regulation on respect for collective agreements. The obligation incumbent on tenderers for a public contract to respect collective agreements was a suitable means to achieve the goals pursued by the Act, and the statutory regulation on respect for collective agreements was necessary to achieve the goal. Finally, impairing the right to occupational freedom by means of the obligation to respect collective agreements was also suitable.

[28] Eg § 3 Hamburg Award Law of 18 February 2004, GVBl. 2004 No 12, p 97; § 1 (1) Berlin Award Law of 9 July 1999, GVBl. No 28, p 369; § 3 Bavarian Public Works Award Law of 28 June 2000, as amended, GVBl. 2000 No 15, p 364.

[29] Judgment of 11 July 2006—1 BvL 4/00. Translation taken from Venice Commission translation of case, available at: <http://codices.coe.int/NXT/gateway.dll?f=templates&fn=default.htm>.

The obligation to respect collective agreements imposed on construction companies concerned a major guarantee of the right of occupational freedom protected by Article 12(1) of the Basic Law. The freedom to freely negotiate the remuneration agreements with workers and sub-contractors was a major element of exercising an occupation. These contractual conditions determined the economic success of the enterprises, and were therefore characteristic of the activity serving to create and maintain livelihoods protected by Article 12(1).

The weight of the encroachment was, however, reduced by the fact that the obligation to pay the collectively agreed wages did not follow directly from a statutory order, but from an individual decision to submit a declaration of loyalty to collective agreements in order to obtain a public contract. The impact of the obligation to respect collective agreements was also restricted to the individual public contract. Only the content of the employment contracts of the workers deployed in implementing the respective public contract was prescribed, and then only for those working hours during which they were actively implementing the public contract.

By contrast, the justifying reasons, which caused the legislature to enact the provision submitted for review, had considerable weight. The fight against unemployment in conjunction with guaranteeing the financial stability of the system of social security was a particularly important goal, and the legislature must be afforded relatively broad latitude for its realization, particularly in difficult labour market conditions. This public interest, which the regulation on respect for collective agreements tried to accommodate, took on overriding significance. The weighing in favour of the public interests carried out by the legislature was unobjectionable. The limit of acceptability for tenderers for a public contract, which were only to undertake to apply remuneration rates in accordance with collective agreements in parts of their entrepreneurial activity, was not exceeded in the light of the greater insight of the important goals of the regulation on respect for collective agreements.

Nor did the unequal treatment agreements of those tenderers who did not submit a declaration of respect for collective agreements, and hence did not receive public contracts, in comparison with those tenderers who met the condition contained in the provision submitted for review, did not violate the principle of equality set out in Article 3(1) of the Basic Law. It was justified by the particularly important public interest described, which inspired the *Land* legislature to enact the statutory provision. The regulation on respect for collective agreements was also compatible with other federal laws.

6. The ECJ's Judgment in *Rüffert*

The German Constitutional Court explicitly left to one side the EC dimensions of the *Tariftreuegesetz*. Nor did the Berlin law involve the application of the *Tariftreuegesetz* in a situation of posted workers. So the issue presented to the ECJ in *Rüffert* was significantly different in some ways from the German Constitutional

Court's decision, and in many ways it was a difficult one for the ECJ. How should the balance be struck between national labour standards and allowing effective cross-border competition in service provision in contexts where the foreign service provider wanted to take advantage of its lower wage rates and bring its own workers onto the contract?

The approach that the Member States took to the issue had earlier been addressed in the Posted Workers Directive. The Court, at the urging of the European Commission, and several Member States that submitted observations, agreed to take the Posted Workers Directive into account, and not confine its decision to Article 49 EC. There is some ambiguity, however, in the exact role of the Posted Workers Directive in the *Rüffert* case. In the *Laval* case, it appears clear that the approach that the Court took was to view the Posted Workers Directive as providing a test as to whether a law that was contested as contrary to Article 49 EC might be regarded as justified. On one reading, the Court in *Rüffert* appears to have taken this approach also, starting from the position that the Lower Saxony law constituted a prima facie breach of Article 49 EC and then examining whether the Posted Workers Directive provided a safe haven for the contested law. There is an alternative reading of the Court's approach in *Rüffert*, however, which is that the Court regarded the Posted Workers Directive as providing a test as to whether there was a breach of Article 49 EC itself.

In any event, whichever reading is adopted, the Court makes clear that it will regard the Posted Workers Directive as a key to determining the acceptability of the contested law under the Treaty. This is a sensible, and understandable, move on the part of the Court. It is clear that, whilst not bound by the compromise reached, it was important that the Court at least consider the political compromise that the Posted Workers Directive represents when it is interpreting the Treaty in a context in which posted workers are involved. To do otherwise would be to undermine the legislative role of the Council and Parliament. The Court, therefore, spends a considerable part of the judgment exploring the implications of the Directive.

The Posted Workers Directive applies (Article 1) 'to undertakings established in a Member State which, in the framework of the transnational provision of services, post workers . . . to the territory of a Member State.' 'Posting' arises when, according to Article 1(3)(a), undertakings engaged in the transnational provision of services, 'post workers to the territory of a Member State on their account and under their direction, under a contract concluded between the undertaking making the posting and the party for whom the services are intended, operating in that Member State, provided there is an employment relationship between the undertaking making the posting and the worker during the period of posting.' These conditions were assumed to have been met in this case, and neither the Advocate General nor the Court discussed the matter further.

In these situations, under Article 3(1), Member States 'shall ensure that, whatever the law applicable to the employment relationship, the undertakings . . . guarantee workers posted to their territory the terms and conditions of employment' covering a set of matters provided for in the Directive:

(a) maximum work periods and minimum rest periods; (b) minimum paid annual holidays; (c) the minimum rates of pay, including overtime rates; this point does not apply to supplementary occupational retirement pension schemes; (d) the conditions of hiring-out of workers, in particular the supply of workers by temporary employment undertakings; (e) health, safety and hygiene at work; (f) protective measures with regard to the terms and conditions of employment of pregnant women or women who have recently given birth, of children and of young people; (g) equality of treatment between men and women and other provisions on non-discrimination.

The Directive provides that the minimum rates of pay referred to in paragraph 1(c) are 'defined by the national law and/or practice of the Member State to whose territory the worker is posted'. In the *Rüffert* case, the relevant provision is (c) concerning 'minimum rates of pay'. This has been seen as among the most controversial standards to be included in the Directive.[30]

There are four ways in which Member States can satisfy the requirement ('shall ensure') that workers are to be guaranteed protection of these labour standards:

(1) The labour standards are provided for in laws, regulations and/or administrative provisions. These standards must be applied by the host state to posted workers.

There was considerable debate over how far beyond this the Directive should go, involving, in particular, the issue of whether 'labour standards derived from collective agreements should be included and, if so, standards derived from which sorts of collective agreements'.[31] The result of this debate was that collective agreements were specifically included as a source of legal obligation, but only in the context of the building industry, which was the case in *Rüffert*. In this context, there are three somewhat different sorts of collective agreements that are listed:

(2) The labour standards are included in a collective agreement or arbitration award relating to the building industry that has been 'declared universally applicable'. A collective agreement or arbitration award which has been 'declared universally applicable' means a collective agreement or arbitration award which must be observed by all undertakings in the geographical area and in the profession or industry concerned. These standards must be applied by the host state to posted workers.
(3) Where there is no system of declaring collective agreements universally applicable, the labour standards are included in a collective agreement relating to the building industry that has been concluded by the most representative union and employer organizations at the national level and has been applied throughout the national territory, subject to the proviso that other national undertakings in (otherwise) similar positions are treated equally.
(4) Where there is no system of declaring collective agreements universally applicable, the labour standards are included in a collective agreement relating to the building industry that is generally applicable to all similar undertakings in the

[30] P Davies, 'Posted Workers: Single Market or Protection of National Labour Law Systems?' (1997) 34 Common Market Law Rev 571, 579–80.
[31] Ibid, 580.

geographical area and in the industry concerned, subject to the proviso that other national undertakings in (otherwise) similar positions are treated equally.

The ECJ held that:

(1) did not apply in the context of the *Rüffert* case, because the Lower Saxony law did not itself set out the wages rates but merely referred to the collective agreement;

(2) did not apply because the collective agreement in issue was not declared universally applicable under the available German law for declaring collective agreements to be universally applicable,[32] and anyway the agreement could not be so treated since there was no evidence that the collective agreement must be observed by all undertakings in the geographical area and in the profession or industry concerned;

(3) and (4) did not apply since there was a system in place in Germany for declaring collective agreements universally applicable, and it was not used in this case, and in any event they would not apply since the agreement was not generally applicable to similar undertakings since only a parts of the construction sector falling within the geographical area was covered, ie those parts of the construction industry covered by public sector construction contracts.

The ECJ appears to conclude, therefore, that the provisions of the Directive would not protect the contested Lower Saxony law unless some further provision of the Directive did so. The most obvious candidate was Article 3(7), which provides that the provisions we have been examining 'shall not prevent application of terms and conditions of employment which are more favourable to workers'.[33] This was interpreted by Germany in its legal submissions in *Rüffert*, and by Advocate General Bot in his Opinion in *Rüffert*,[34] to mean that the host state could provide posted workers with terms and conditions of employment that were more favourable to workers than the ones examined so far. The ECJ, however, disagreed. This provision did not apply in this case, because the provision applied only where the *home country*'s laws or collective agreements provided that workers recruited on their territory and posted to another Member State should have better terms and conditions of employment than other workers were accorded in the sending country, or where the company recruiting the posted workers applied better

[32] The federal German law had a system of declaring collective agreements universally applicable and had in fact declared a minimum wage agreement for the construction industry to be universally applicable (*TV Mindeslohn*), but the collective agreement at issue in *Rüffert* was another collective agreement that had not been declared universally applicable, and provided for a higher minimum wage than that in the (federally recognized) collective agreement.

[33] Art 3(10) did not apply because (a) the Lower Saxony legislation did not concern 'terms and conditions of employment on matters other than those' provided for explicitly in the Posted Workers Directive since it involved wages, and (b) did not concern 'terms and conditions of employment laid down in the collective agreements or arbitration awards . . . concerning activities other than' building work, since it concerned a construction contract.

[34] AG Opinion, para 83.

terms and conditions of employment. Neither Poland nor PKZ had done so in this case, and so Article 3(7) did not apply.

7. Justifying Prima Facie Breaches of Article 49 EC

Even though the Posted Workers Directive did not 'save' the Lower Saxony law, was that law nevertheless able to be justified under Article 49 EC directly? The Court in previous cases adopted a three-part test that it applied to the question of justification:

(1) Is there a *legitimate aim* recognized by Community law?
(2) Is the measure *suitable* for achieving that legitimate aim?
(3) Is the measure *necessary* for achieving that legitimate aim?

Taken together, these form one variety of the ever-present 'proportionality' test. Of this three-part test, only the first two are really in issue in *Rüffert*.[35]

First, are the reasons advanced by the Member State capable of constituting 'overriding requirements relating to the public interest',[36] or 'imperative requirements in the general interest'?[37] In *Rüffert*, Lower Saxony advanced three principal justifications as legitimate aims:

(a) that the state measure was justified by the objective of protecting workers;
(b) that the measure was justified by the objective of supporting union autonomy through support for collective bargaining;
(c) that the measure was justified by the objective of ensuring the financial balance of the social security system, which would be damaged if reduced contributions were to be paid into the system because of reduced wages being paid to workers contributing to that system.

Of these, the Court clearly regarded the first as the principal justification. In *Guiot*,[38] the Court held that 'the public interest relating to the social protection of workers in the construction industry may . . . because of the conditions specific to that sector, constitute an overriding requirement justifying such a restriction on the freedom to provide services'.[39]

The second issue in the justification process involves asking whether there is a nexus between the objective of the measure adopted and the actual achievement of

[35] The third issue in justification is whether the objective sought could be accomplished by less restrictive means, 'they must not go beyond what is necessary in order to attain it'. *Gebhard*, para 37. See also Case C–19/92 *Kraus v Land Baden-Wuerttemberg* [1993] ECR I–1663, para 32. The Court in *Rüffert* does not really consider this issue.

[36] Joined Cases C–369/96 and C–376/96 *Arblade* et al [1999] ECR I–8453, paras 33 and 34.

[37] Case C–55/94 *Reinhard Gebhard v Consiglio dell'Ordine degli Avvocati e Procuratori di Milano* [1995] ECR I–4165.

[38] Case C–272/94 *Michel Guiot and Climatic SA* [1996] ECR I–1905.

[39] Ibid para 16; in Case C–222/95 *Société Civile Immobilière Parodi v Banque H Albert de Bary et Cie* [1997] ECR I–3899, para 32, the Court held that consumer protection could constitute a public interest ground for this purpose.

the objective in practice; 'they must be suitable for securing the attainment of the objective which they pursue'.[40] The main question the Court was confronted with in *Rüffert* was whether the provisions in issue in fact protected the interests of the posted workers. The test set out in *Finalarte*[41] was whether, 'viewed objectively, the rules in question in the main proceedings promote the protection of posted workers'.[42] To do this:

> it is necessary to check whether those rules confer a genuine benefit on the workers concerned, which significantly adds to their social protection. In this context, the stated intention of the legislature may lead to a more careful assessment of the alleged benefits conferred on workers by the measures it has adopted.[43]

Do the legal requirements 'in fact pursue the public interest objective of protecting workers employed by providers of services established outside Germany'?[44]

The suitability of the contested measure for ensuring the objective of protecting workers was not convincing, held the ECJ, applying very similar criteria to those it had already applied in the context of considering the Posted Workers Directive. The contested measure applied to only part of the construction sector falling within the geographical area, since the legislation applied solely to government contracts in that sector, and the collective agreement was not declared universally applicable. The Member State had not shown why this limitation to government contracts was 'necessary'.[45]

In any event, the rate of pay guaranteed was greater even than that provided for in the *national* legislation transposing the Posted Workers Directive. For the same reasons, the Court was unwilling to accept that the measure was justified by the objective of supporting union autonomy. And no convincing evidence was presented on the financial issues involved to support the social security argument.

8. Reactions to *Rüffert*

The reaction to *Rüffert* was immediate and, in particular from trade union sources such as the ETUC,[46] hostile, since they saw the case as part of the *Viking* and *Laval* set of cases, which they had earlier condemned. These criticisms sometimes focused on the implications for the use of procurement, pointing to the possibly deleterious

[40] *Gebhard*, n 37 above, para 37. See also Case C–19/92 *Kraus v Land Baden-Wuerttemberg* [1993] ECR I–1663, para 32.

[41] Joined Cases C–49/98, C–50/98 to C–54/98, and C–68/98 to C–71/98 *Finalarte Sociedade de Construção Civil Ld* [2001] ECR I–7831.

[42] Para 41.

[43] Para 42.

[44] Para 49.

[45] Nicholas Hatzis has suggested (personal communication) that the ECJ appears to have adopted an 'under-inclusiveness' analysis, meaning that a law may be unacceptable under the 'suitability' element of the proportionality test if it leaves outside its scope conduct that should have been included, given the legitimate aim sought to be advanced.

[46] ETUC, '*Rüffert* case: ETUC warns that ECJ's judgement is destructive and damaging', 3 April 2008.

effects on specific projects, such as the Greater London Authority's London Living Wage, and the similar programmes established by the Olympic Delivery Authority. Trade union influence led, in turn, to further developments. *Rüffert* appears to have been used by the successful 'no' campaigners in Ireland's June 2008 referendum campaign on the ratification of the Lisbon Treaty to support an argument that the EU was undermining social protections.[47] Think-tanks involved with European policy organized day-long discussions of the *Viking-Laval-Rüffert* set of cases.[48] The European Parliament took up the issues posed by *Viking*, *Laval*, and *Rüffert* as a package, pressing the European Commission and Council of Ministers for answers to questions about the implications of the cases,[49] publishing an own-initiative report by the Employment Committee on the issues involved,[50] and adopting a Resolution that was critical of the judgments.[51] The European Commission first sought to deal with the controversy by focusing on the narrower issues involved in implementation of the Posted Workers Directive,[52] but then subsequently organized a Stakeholders' Meeting in Brussels to debate the wider issues involved.[53]

For someone dissatisfied with the result in *Rüffert*, there were, essentially, two possible routes for dealing with the deleterious consequences of the case. The first was political: to proceed on the basis that the Community should adopt legislative changes to deal with the case. This approach garnered significant support among trade unions and others on the left of the political spectrum on the basis that the issues in *Rüffert* were essentially political issues that should be taken back either from an aggressively liberal (economically) ECJ,[54] or from a Court that had understandably filled a vacuum left open by the previous failure of political will.[55] This political approach involved two possible sets of legislative changes.[56] One approach was to amend the Posted Workers Directive itself, for example by

[47] 'Employers back "yes" vote but unions divided on Lisbon Treaty', EIROnline, 2008/07; EU court judgments affecting Irish treaty campaign, *Euobserver.com*, 6 May 2008.

[48] See, eg, the debate organized by Notre Europe and the European Trade Union Institute, 'Viking-Laval-Rüffert: Economic freedoms versus fundamental social rights—where does the balance lie?', July 2008, available at: <http://www.notre-europe.eu/en/viking-laval-rueffert>.

[49] European Parliament, Written question P–2404/08; Written question E–4129/08; Written question E–29963/08.

[50] Report on Challenges to collective agreements in the EU, Committee on Employment and Social Affairs (Rapporteur: Jan Andersson), 30 September 2008 (A6–0370/2008).

[51] European Parliament resolution of 22 October 2008 on challenges to collective agreements in the EU (2008/2085 (INI)).

[52] Commission Recommendation of 3 April 2008 on enhanced administrative cooperation in the context of the posting of workers in the framework of the provision of services, OJ [2008] C 85.

[53] See 'EU states eye political response to *Laval* court ruling', EurActiv, 10 October 2008, available at: <http://www.euractiv.com/en/socialeurope/eu-states-eye-political-response-laval-court-ruling/article-176245>.

[54] See, eg, J Kvist, 'Rocking the boat—again', in Notre Europe/ETUI debate, n 48 above, 3: 'Politics must be taken away from the Court and given back to elected politicians.' See also M Höpner, 'Political answers to judicial problems? Europe after *Viking*, *Laval* and *Rüffert*', ibid.

[55] R Dehousse, 'Laval & Co: law and politics in EU social policy' in Notre Europe/ETUI debate, n 48 above, 4, concluding: 'Short of an agreement on a legislative solution, it is the ECJ line of reasoning that will prevail.'

[56] See, eg, the campaign by the British trade union, Amicus, available at: <http://www.amicustheunion.org/lavalvikingruffert/default.aspx>.

reverting to the approach proposed by the Commission when the Directive was first drafted, of setting an initial period when none of the host state mandatory provisions would apply and thereafter to apply all the host state mandatory rules.[57] The problem with this option was that the existing Directive is a compromise between alternative rationales for the adoption of the Directive in the first place.[58] At that moment, the compromise meant that various different interests could support it for different reasons. Seeking greater clarity was likely to involve upsetting the carefully calibrated political fudge that the Directive represents.

The second ('legislative') option, of amending the Treaty, had two different facets. One was to rely on ratification of the Lisbon Treaty to accomplish the needed reform, by way of reinforcing the importance of social policy, including the importance of collective bargaining, through the incorporation of the EU Charter of Fundamental Rights in the Lisbon Treaty. The difficulty with this option was that it relied heavily on a necessarily untested provision of great breadth but possibly insubstantial depth. The alternative Treaty amendment option involved the incorporation of an entirely new provision in the Lisbon Treaty, such as the 'social protocol' requested by the ETUC,[59] with all the uncertainties that that would involve. Each of these legislative options was fraught with difficulty and these difficulties resulted in considerable scepticism concerning their viability being expressed by government ministers from several Member States at the European Commission's October 2008 Forum.[60]

Assuming, therefore, that no legislative changes are likely to be implemented, at least in the short to medium term, what can be done? Again, there are different ways of addressing the issues involved in *Rüffert*, but all involve a significant attempt at persuading the ECJ to revisit the main issue addressed in *Rüffert*: the scope for Member State action using public procurement where posted workers are engaged. In this context, there are several sub-issues that might be addressed in subsequent interpretation. What, exactly, is the basis for the prima facie breach of Article 49 EC?[61] In *Rüffert*, the prima facie breach of Article 49 EC was largely assumed by all the parties, and there was little, if any, empirical evidence substantiating the allegedly deleterious effect of the law on out-of-state (particularly Polish) contractors. The almost complete lack of attention paid to this issue in *Rüffert*, however, does not give great grounds for optimism that this approach would result in a significantly different conclusion, particularly if an interpretation of *Rüffert* is adopted in which the Court is seen as holding that breach of the Posted Workers Directive is sufficient to find a breach of Article 49 EC. Given that, future litigation would need to explore how far it will be possible to argue that the protection of the Posted Workers Directive applies because the circumstances in the new case differ

[57] See, eg, Harlem Désir (PSE), European Parliament Debates, 2 September 2008.

[58] See P Davies, n 30 above.

[59] ETUC Proposal for a 'Social Progress' Protocol, available at: <http://www.etuc.org/IMG/pdf_social_progress_protocolEN.pdf>. Free Movement of Labour: Forum Addresses Controversies Regarding Posting of Workers, European Social Policy, 12 November 2008.

[60] See, eg, speeches by Sven-Otto Littorin, Minister for Employment, Sweden, and by François Biltgen, Minister of Labour and Social Affairs, Luxembourg.

[61] See S Deakin, n 5 above, 6.

from those in *Rüffert*, for example because the collective agreement relied on has been applied by administrative provisions. Even if this is found to be possible, however, it is still the case that Article 49 EC applies.

We cannot escape, it seems, from the central aspect of the approach adopted by the ECJ in *Rüffert* that raises such significant problems in the future: the approach taken to issues of justification under Article 49 EC. There are at least two different ways in which this issue may be approached. One approach is to seek to persuade the Court to attach more weight to the employment protection issues involved, for example by arguing that the matters of employment protection listed in the Posted Workers Directive are matters of human rights, rather than 'merely' workers' interests. We have seen in other cases in the past that when the Court identifies one of the interests involved in the balancing process involved in assessing justification as involving questions of 'human dignity', the Court is willing to consider them weightier.[62] The other approach, and the one on which I shall concentrate in the remainder of this chapter, is to persuade the Court that it underestimated the procurement aspects of the case. Those considering the *Rüffert* case tend to see the case through the lens of the Posted Workers Directive rather than as one concerned with public procurement, and that is too blinkered an approach, in my view.

9. *Rüffert* as a Procurement Case

Central to the problems that *Rüffert* causes for the use of procurement to ensure minimum wages in the context of posted workers is the scepticism of the Court of Justice about the use of the procurement mechanism itself. If the Court is to be persuaded to adopt a more progressive stance in future *Rüffert*-type cases, it will only be if the Court can be persuaded that the use of procurement is justified as a delivery mechanism even where the coverage of the employment condition in issue is thereby limited to only a part of the sector in which the contract operates. We have seen in the discussion of the ECJ's judgment that a recurring theme was incredulity that Lower Saxony should choose the procurement tool to advance wages that were above the minimum in Germany, rather than another mechanism which would cover all workers in the construction industry in the area involved.

Meeting this point head on will also be important if another possible implication of the *Rüffert* case materializes in practice. It is possible to argue that *Rüffert* raises the more general issue of the application of Article 49 EC to the inclusion of social (and, indeed, environmental) linkages in procurement beyond the context of posted workers. It is arguable that if the test applicable to procurement linkages in general is the same as that applied in *Rüffert*, ie whether such measures impose 'an additional economic burden that may prohibit, impede or render less attractive

[62] Case C–36/02 *Omega Spielhallen- und Automatenaufstellungs-GmbH v Oberbürgermeisterin der Bundesstadt Bonn* [2004] ECR I–9609. I do not attempt to explore this issue here. For an analysis of dignity-based arguments and their roots (*inter alia*) in the movement for workers' rights, see C McCrudden, 'Human Dignity and Judicial Interpretation of Human Rights' (2008) 19 (4) EJIL 655–724.

the provision of their services in the host Member State',[63] such linkages would constitute a restriction within the meaning of Article 49 EC.[64] The Member State would then need to argue that it was nevertheless justified, according to the three-part test described earlier. If the ECJ subsequently held that the interpretation of Article 49 EC in *Rüffert* should be seen as independent of the Posted Workers Directive, then the Court's scepticism in *Rüffert* of using public procurement as a mechanism for the delivery of the social policy would apply generally, thus calling into question all those social linkages that were not also obligatory beyond the procurement contractor.[65] Not only does the *Rüffert* case thus pose a problem for the use of procurement linkages in the posted workers context, but (possibly) more generally.

10. The Missing Side of the Triangle: The EC Procurement Directives

It is clear that the tension between social and economic interests, and between domestic and transborder interests, is not only played out in the case law of the ECJ in its interpretation of the four freedoms, and in the provisions of the Posted Workers Directive. In a series of Procurement Directives too, the Community has had to face up to how to resolve, or at least manage, the tension between the social and the economic functions of public procurement, and between domestic policy making and transnational freedom of action. Surprisingly, there is no reference by the ECJ to any part of the large corpus of legislation and case law that constitutes EU procurement law in *Rüffert.*

I argued in *Buying Social Justice*[66] that, although the legal resolution of tensions between the economic and the social usages of public procurement was still work in progress, with many uncertainties remaining, a continuous adaptation of procurement regulation in the EU had progressively given greater domestic regulatory space to procurement linkages as a method of enforcement of Community social policy. I argued, in particular, that this emerging *modus vivendi* was effectively constructed by the Court of Justice, usually in the teeth of opposition from the European Commission. Legal interpretation, particularly by the Court of Justice, played a major role in mediating the tensions between the more extreme proponents of procurement liberalization and the desire to continue to utilize procurement for social uses. In cases from *Beentjes*[67] to *Nord-Pas-de-Calais*,[68] the Court of

[63] Para 37 of the ECJ judgment.

[64] Arrowsmith and Kunzlik, n 8 above, 1, argue that the appropriate test is not this, but what they consider to be the narrower test of whether the measure is directly or indirectly discriminatory. In practice, it may not matter much which test is applied, given the potential breadth of the concept of indirect discrimination used by the ECJ, and given the sketchiness of the analysis undertaken in determining whether a prima facie case has been determined (under either test).

[65] Arrowsmith and Kunzlik consider that the *Rüffert* judgment is confined to the posted workers context, n 8 above, 6.

[66] C McCrudden, *Buying Social Justice: Equality, Government Procurement, and Legal Change* (2007).

[67] Case C–31/87 *Beentjes v The Netherlands* [1988] ECR 4635.

[68] Case C–225/98 *Commission v France* [2000] ECR I–7745 (*Nord-Pas-de-Calais*).

Justice had tended to view the issue of procurement not in isolation from, but as part of the larger economic and social role that the Community had adopted. Effectively what the Court did was to stop the onward march of a purely commercial approach to government procurement, and allow a space for politics in which other interests could compete. Although at first extremely resistant to the Court's approach, by the end of the 1990s the Commission substantially bought into the Court's approach, and in an important Communication[69] set out its approach to the existing Directives in some detail, which (after some modification) was incorporated into legislation in new Directives.

The Procurement Directives have somewhat the same function as the Posted Workers Directive: they provide a politically acceptable set of rules by which the principles set out in general terms in the Treaty can be operated. In both cases, the Treaty remains in play and is by no means replaced. The Court is willing to view the provisions of the Posted Workers Directive as clear indicators of how the political interests in the Community consider that the balancing of the various interests involved should be resolved, and to read the Treaty and the Directive harmoniously. Indeed, the Court in *Rüffert* says that its view that the Posted Workers Directive effectively sets the parameters of what the Treaty permits, 'is confirmed by reading it in light of Article 49 EC, since that Directive seeks in particular to bring about the freedom to provide services, which is one of the fundamental freedoms guaranteed by the Treaty'.[70] Directive 2004/18/EC of the European Parliament and of the Council of 31 March 2004 on the coordination of procedures for the award of public works contracts, public supply contracts and public service contracts ('the Public Sector Directive') is as clearly based on the four (economic) freedoms as the Posted Workers Directive. Indeed, the legal base for the Posted Workers Directive and the Public Sector Directive was the same: Article 47(2) and Article 55.[71] Just as it was clear that the Court should attempt to ensure a harmonious reading of the Posted Workers Directive and the Treaty in this context, so too the Court should have had regard to the Procurement Directives in much the same way. The more obvious it is that the Posted Workers Directive was relevant, the more puzzling is the sidestepping of the Procurement Directives. It is even more peculiar that the Procurement Directives do not feature in *Rüffert* when we realize that the Procurement Directives themselves directly address the posted workers' issue, thus establishing a triangle of relevant EU legal provisions in a *Rüffert*-type case.[72]

[69] Commission, 'Community Law Applicable to Public Procurement and the Possibilities for Integrating Social Considerations into Public Procurement' OJ [2001] C–333/27.

[70] Para 35.

[71] Preamble 1: 'Having regard to the Treaty establishing the European Community, and in particular Article 47(2) and Article 55 and Article 95 thereof'.

[72] The Directives permit the incorporation of certain exclusions into the qualifications expected of tenderers before they are allowed to proceed to make a qualifying bid at all. These are referred to in the Directives as 'criteria for qualitative selection'. Both Directives specify that '[a]ny economic operator may be excluded from participation in a contract where that economic operator' falls into one or more categories that are regarded as unacceptable for a potential contractor with government. The two most relevant for our purposes relate to 'professional misconduct'. Economic operators may be excluded if

Unlike the Court, the Advocate General did mention the Procurement Directives. In his Opinion, he identified the relevant EC procurement provision in force at the time of the events that gave rise to the dispute as Council Directive 93/37/EEC of 14 June 1993 concerning the coordination of procedures for the award of public works contracts.[73] The value of the contract in issue was above the threshold for the application of the 1993 Directive, and the Directive therefore applied. By the time of the Advocate General's Opinion, this Directive had been replaced by the Public Sector Directive of 2004,[74] for which the implementation period expired on 31 January 2006.[75] He referred to both Directives as relevant to the interpretation of Community law on the disputed issues, and in the remainder of the article I follow his lead in this respect. In particular, he specifically rejected the view (adopted by the ECJ) that the Lower Saxony measures could not be justified because they applied only to workers on some public contracts: 'while it is true that the aim of public procurement is above all to meet an identified administrative need for works, services or supplies, the award of public contracts also authorizes the attainment of other public interest requirements, such as environmental policy, or, as in the present case, social objectives.'[76]

11. Compliance with Collective Agreements Establishing Employment Conditions

The Advocate General rightly pointed out that that Directive 93/37/EEC 'does not regulate the performance of public contracts', by which he means that the Directive only regulates the stage up to the award of the contract, and not the 'execution of the contract'.[77] The requirements that Lower Saxony imposed on OB were in the form of a 'contract performance condition' which came into effect after the award of the contract. That said, the Advocate General quoted Article 23 of the Directive

the operator 'has been convicted by a judgment which has the force of res judicata in accordance with the legal provisions of the country of any offence concerning his professional conduct', Art 45(2)(b), Public Sector Directive, or 'has been guilty of grave professional misconduct proven by any means which the contracting authorities can demonstrate', Art 45(2)(c), Public Sector Directive. Non-compliance with national law obligations implementing the Posted Workers Directive 'may be considered to be grave misconduct or an offence concerning the professional conduct of the economic operator concerned, liable to lead to the exclusion of that economic operator from the procedure for the award of a public contract', Recital 34, Public Sector Directive. These provisions demonstrate clearly that the posted workers issue was clearly in the minds of the legislators at the time of the adoption of the new Directives. It was also clear to academic commentators at the time the Public Sector Directive was passed that there was a close relationship between public procurement and the Posted Workers Directive more broadly; see P Davies, n 30 above.

[73] OJ [1993] L 199/54.

[74] OJ [2004] L 134/114.

[75] Germany had not implemented Directive 2004/18/EC by the deadline, see M Trybus, 'The morning after the deadline: the state of implementation of the new EC Public Procurement Directives in the Member States on February 1, 2006' (2006) 15 Public Procurement Law Review 82–90.

[76] Para 132.

[77] Para 17.

relating to the information on working conditions to be respected during the performance of a public contract (which we shall return to consider below). The Advocate General 'note[d]' that Article 23 'is not without interest in the present case because it expresses the notion that the performance of the work following the award of a public contract must comply with the employment protection provisions and the working conditions in force in the place where the work is to be carried out'.[78] Having said that, however, the Advocate General continued:

> I shall not, however, go further in interpreting Directive 93/37, because that directive is of no assistance with regard to the central issue raised by the question from the court of reference, namely determination of the employment conditions which may, in compliance with Community law, be imposed for the performance of a public contract in a situation where workers are posted in the framework of the provision of services.

This underestimates the importance of these provisions, in my view.

Equivalent provisions were included in the Procurement Directives currently in force. Although somewhat badly drafted, the Recitals to both the Public Sector Directive and Directive 2004/17/EC of the European Parliament and of the Council of 31 March 2004 coordinating the procurement procedures of entities operating in the water, energy, transport and postal services sectors (the 'Utilities Directive') make clear that, provided that they themselves comply with EU law, and are applied in a way which complies with EU law, Member States may, by general legislation for example, require that those carrying out a public procurement contract should comply with 'laws, regulations and collective agreements' that are in force and deal with 'employment conditions' during the performance of the contract.[79] This simply reflects numerous ECJ decisions both prior to and subsequent to the enactment of the Directives.

These provisions in Directive 93/37 and the 2004 Directives followed closely the equivalent provisions in the Procurement Directives introduced during the previous period of sustained procurement reform during the 1980s and early 1990s. These provisions were proposed by the Commission in order to meet recommendations of the European Parliament, but the debate over their content and their effect was influenced by the *Rush Portuguesa* case. This was one of the earliest 'posted workers' cases considered under the Treaty prior to the introduction of the Posted Workers Directive, and was decided in March 1990.[80] In *Rush Portuguesa*, the Court adopted a broad statement of compatibility between Community law and the application of host state labour law to home state contractors:

> Community law does not preclude Member States from extending their legislation, or collective labour agreements entered into by both sides of industry, to any person who is employed, even temporarily, within their territory, no matter in which country the

[78] Para 59.

[79] Recital 34, Public Sector Directive; Recital 45, Utilities Directive.

[80] Case C–113/89 *Rush Portuguesa Ld v Office national d'immigration* [1990] ECR I–1417. See, in general, McCrudden, n 66 above, 327–30.

employer is established; nor does Community law prohibit Member States from enforcing those rules by appropriate means.[81]

The Commission, which was considering reform of an earlier Utilities Directive, appears to have specifically considered the working conditions article in light of the judgment, and declared it consistent with the ECJ's decision.[82]

It was therefore well known at the time of the passage of the 1993 Works and the 2004 Directives that one of the most controversial questions was how far it was consistent with EU law for Member States to require compliance with such rules where the contractor brought workers from another EU state to carry out the contract. The controversy was whether the application of such national rules meant that the effect would be to discourage 'posting of workers' from states that had a lower legal standard of employment conditions and safety at work conditions, and would thus discriminate in effect against out-of-state contractors: precisely the issue in *Rüffert*. Most importantly, the political actors regarded the working conditions article in the Procurement Directives as one of the set of provisions of Community law that indicated how Member States should deal with the posted workers issue. The provision was intended to take advantage of the *Rush Portuguesa* judgment's broad support for the application of domestic labour law. In addition, it indicated the legislators' view that public procurement was one of the 'appropriate means' of enforcing domestic labour law in the context of posted workers. In this respect, the Advocate General in *Rüffert* failed to stress the close connections between the Treaty, the Posted Workers Directive, and the Procurement Directives.

Having shown the relevance of the 2004 procurement directives, we can now turn to consider their content in somewhat greater detail. A contracting authority:

> may state in the contract documents, or be obliged by a Member State so to state, the body or bodies from which a candidate or tenderer may obtain the appropriate information on the obligations relating to . . . the employment protection provisions and to the working conditions which are in force in the Member State, region or locality in which the works are to be carried out or services are to be provided and which shall be applicable to the works carried out on site or to the services provided during the performance of the contract.[83]

Contractors might be expected to know relevant legislation and employment rules in the country where they intended to operate, but in the interests of transparency it is clearly better if contracting authorities help contractors by informing them where the appropriate information may be obtained.

The Directives also provide that a contracting authority that supplies this information

> shall request the tenderers or candidates in the contract award procedure to indicate that they have taken account, when drawing up their tender, of the obligations relating to

81 Point 18.
82 COM (90) 301 of 12 July 1990, para 11(f).
83 Art 27(1), Public Sector Directive; Art 39(1), Utilities Directive.

employment protection provisions and the working conditions which are in force in the place where the works are to be carried out or the service is to be provided.

The purpose of this is linked to the fear that contractors may seek to reduce their levels of employment protection in order to be able to submit a lower bid. This provision requires contracting authorities at least to require tenderers to indicate that they have taken the legal requirements 'into account' when drawing up the tender. It is clearly considerably less stringent than a requirement that tenderers must cost full compliance with the legislation when drawing up the tender, or requiring contracting authorities not to award contracts to those bidders that do not comply with employment legislation. We shall see, however, that although this more stringent approach is not included, contracting authorities do have some further discretion to attempt to ensure that tenderers intend to comply with employment legislation. These are equivalent to the provisions that the Advocate General 'noted', and interpreted but did not apply because they did not address the issue of *what* employment conditions were acceptable under the Treaty.

12. Abnormally Low Tenders

The Advocate General failed to consider adequately several other provisions of the Directive that may have been of assistance when taken together with these 'notice' requirements. The provisions regarding abnormally low tenders are also highly relevant. The first observation to make about these provisions is that they assume that contracting authorities may reject a tender as 'abnormally low'. This means that a tender is considered to be in some way aberrant if it does not reflect the full cost that the tender should include. An example would be where the tenderer was being subsidized by another Member State to such an extent that it was able to reduce the cost of its tender significantly enough to be more attractive in comparison with those firms not so subsidized.

Although based on the presumption that abnormally low tenders may be rejected, the Directives provide only for procedures that the contracting authority must adopt before the tender is actually rejected on the ground that it is abnormally low, hence the rather strange phrasing of the provisions in question.[84] They provide: 'If, for a given contract, tenders appear to be abnormally low in relation to the goods, works or services, the contracting authority shall, before it may reject those tenders, request in writing details of the constituent elements of the tender which it considers relevant.' The details may relate 'in particular' to 'compliance with the provisions relating to employment protection and working conditions *in force at the place where the work, service or supply is to be performed*' (emphasis added), among other factors. Each case should be treated on its merits; there should be no automatic exclusion; and tenderers should have the opportunity to rebut the case against them.[85]

[84] Art 55, Public Sector Directive; Art 57, Utilities Directive.
[85] Case C–103/88 *Costanzo* [1989] ECR1839.

The provisions of the Directives indicate, somewhat obliquely, that the tenderer's compliance with the 'provisions relating to employment protection and working conditions in force at the place where the work, service or supply is to be performed' may be one such factor.[86] This is important as it indicates that the Directive adopts the idea that some methods of competition, including ignoring provisions relating to employment protection that are legally required, may be unfair competition. We saw in the previous paragraphs that there was a concern that contractors should not engage in cost cutting to the extent of undermining employment legislation requirements. May contracting authorities go further than simply applying the 'notice and request' provisions regarding compliance with domestic employment law, discussed above? A key indication that they may is provided in Article 27 itself, which explicitly provides that the provisions regarding the giving of notice 'shall be without prejudice to the application of the provisions . . . concerning the examination of abnormally low tenders'.[87] Had the Advocate General and the Court taken a more systematic approach to the interpretation of the Procurement Directives, a picture would have emerged that was much more sympathetic to the goals ostensibly pursued by Lower Saxony.

13. Use of Contract Conditions

Later in his Opinion, the Advocate General returned to consider another provision of the Procurement Directives. He did so in the context of his consideration of the argument advanced by the Commission that 'if the objective of [Lower Saxony] is truly to protect workers, it should extend this type of measure to all workers in the industry'.[88] One of the reasons that the Advocate General resisted this line of argument was based on the procurement dimensions of the case. As he pointed out,[89] Article 26 of the Public Sector Directive (and, with minor differences, Article 38 of the Utilities Directive) provides for the inclusion of additional contract conditions:

> Contracting authorities may lay down special conditions relating to the performance of a contract, provided that these are compatible with Community law and are indicated in the contract notice or in the specifications. The conditions governing the performance of a contract may, in particular, concern social and environmental considerations.

This provision incorporates into the Directive the previous case law of the Court that extends back as far as 1988, in the *Beentjes* case.[90] On the basis of these provisions, the Advocate General adopted the view that 'the award of public contracts . . . authorises the attainment of other public interest requirements, such as environmental policy or, as in the present case, social objectives'.[91] According to the Advocate General, the major limits imposed on the use of such social

[86] Art 55(1)(d), Public Sector Directive; Art 57(1)(d), Utilities Directive.
[87] Art 39, Utilities Directive is in similar terms. [88] Para 127. [89] Para 133.
[90] Case 31/87 *Beentjes* [1988] ECR 4635. [91] Para 132.

conditions were that they should not be discriminatory, and that they should be transparent, quoting one of the recitals to the Directive which states that: '[c]ontract performance conditions are compatible with this Directive provided that they are not directly or indirectly discriminatory and are indicated in the contract notice or in the contract documents.'[92] The Advocate General went on to hold that 'the contract performance condition [laid down in the Lower Saxony law] ... complies with the principle of non-discrimination on the basis of nationality, and ... complies with the principle of transparency' and is therefore consistent with Community law.[93]

There is evidence that some members of the Court may have misunderstood this provision of EU procurement law quite profoundly and, as a result, may not have taken the procurement context of the case seriously enough. Although he was not sitting as a judge in the Second Chamber at the time of the *Rüffert* decision, Judge Thomas von Danwitz of the European Court of Justice gave a press interview in September 2008 in which he was asked why the Court in *Rüffert* had not referred to the Procurement Directives, given their inclusion of references to the protection of social and environmental policies. His response was interesting and important. He considered the reference to social and ecological aspects in the Procurement Directives to be in the nature of an 'exception', which should be narrowly construed, like all exceptions. He was not persuaded that this exception should be used to circumvent the Posted Workers Directive and to place the market access for the new European Union countries in jeopardy.[94]

On the face of it, this is a reference to Article 26 of the Public Sector Directive (and, with minor differences, Article 38 of the Utilities Directive), the provision to which the Advocate General referred. Judge von Danwitz's characterization of this provision as an exception, which must be narrowly construed, is peculiar. The use of contract conditions focuses attention on the stage after the contract has been awarded. It does not attempt to exclude potential contractors on the basis of their previous activities. Instead, it requires that whoever is awarded the contract must comply with certain conditions in carrying out the contract once it is awarded. This model presents all contractors with the same requirement that the contractor must sign up to. The Advocate General and the Court both consider that in the contested law Lower Saxony made use of just such a contract condition. If the approach adopted by Judge von Danwitz was also shared by other members of the Court who did participate in the *Rüffert* case, then viewing the references to the ability to include social and environmental considerations as 'exceptions' risks radically undermining the consensus on which the Procurement Directives was based.

[92] Fn 43, quoting Recital 33 to the preamble of the Public Sector Directive.

[93] Para 134.

[94] 'Die Hinweis auf soziale und ökologische Aspekte bei der öffentlichen Auftragsvergabe ist eine Ausnahmeklausel, die wie alle Ausnahmeklauseln eng auszulegen ist. Ich fände es nicht überzeugend, mit ihr die Systematik der Entsenderichtlinie auszuhebeln und den Marktzugang für die neuen EU-Länder infrage zu stellen.' 'Kritik ist nicht berechtigt', *Taz.de*, 12 September 2008, available at: <http://www.taz.de>.

More specifically, it underestimates another feature of these provisions in the new Directives. We have seen that a major thrust of the Court's concerns was based on a scepticism that procurement clauses could justifiably require contractors to protect workers beyond what the ordinary law of the land required. Yet the Procurement Directives make clear that this use of procurement was precisely what the legislators of the Procurement Directives expected. A close reading of the recitals demonstrates that the use of contract conditions to require contractors to abide by obligations that would not apply to them in any event, because they are not in generally applicable legislation, was expected. Recital 33 of the Public Sector Directive (again with minor differences in the Utilities Directive)[95] sets out some further indications of what is envisaged as included in the concept of a 'social consideration'.

> They may, in particular, be intended to favour on-site vocational training, the employment of people experiencing particular difficulty in achieving integration, the fight against unemployment... For instance, mention may be made, amongst other things, of the requirements... to recruit long-term job-seekers or to implement training measures for the unemployed or young persons, *to comply in substance with the provisions of the basic International Labour Organisation (ILO) Conventions, assuming that such provisions have not been implemented in national law, and to recruit more handicapped persons than are required under national legislation*'(emphasis added).

The recitals thus specifically cite as examples two contract conditions that had not been made obligatory under domestic law.

14. Relevance of ILO Conventions

The reference to the ILO Conventions should also have alerted the Court to the potential significance of ILO Convention 98. It is clear from the text of the Procurement Directives that the drafters of the Directives engaged with several Member States' ILO obligations and sought to create a degree of synchronization. Unfortunately, neither the Advocate General nor the Court recognized this.

Since the 1930s the ILO has been concerned with the issue of labour standards in public works. In 1936, the Conference adopted the Reduction of Hours of Work (Public Works) Convention. This applied to 'persons directly employed on building or civil engineering works financed or subsidized by central Governments'. It provided for a normal working week of 40 hours, overtime work up to a limit of 100 hours in any year and overtime wage rates of not less than 25 per cent in excess of normal rates. This Convention was more concerned with the ILO's perception that a reduction in the hours of work should help to reduce unemployment than with any general concern with labour conditions on government contracts as such. Public contracts were a focus of attention because, in the case of public contracts, the 'decision is a matter for administrative action, and there is no occasion for

[95] Recital 33, Public Sector Directive; Recital 44, Utilities Directive.

legislation or protracted negotiations with employers' and workers' organizations or any other procedure such as might delay the establishment of a shorter working week in an employment not directly under the control of the Government'.[96] In 1937, the Conference adopted the Public Works (National Planning) Recommendation, which included provisions regarding the rates of wages of workers on public works. Rates of pay 'should be not less favourable that those commonly recognised by workers' organizations and employers for work of the same character in the district where the work is carried out'.

After the Second World War, the ILO focused on ensuring that government contractors would not undermine collectively agreed pay rates adopted by other employers not engaged in government contracting. By then, the ILO had identified a 'tendency towards the internationalization of the fair wages clause'.[97] For example, during the War, the United States had inserted labour and social clauses in contracts for the procurement of strategic material from other countries.[98] The British Colonial Development and Welfare Act 1940 made approval of certain grants conditional on the maintenance of certain labour standards.[99]

After the usual procedure of reports and comments, the International Labour Conference adopted the Labour Clauses (Public Contracts) Convention, 1949 (Convention No 94) in 1949.[100] This provided that workers employed under contracts for certain construction works, the manufacture of goods, the shipment of supplies or equipment, and the supply of services awarded by a central public authority were to be protected. States which were parties to the Convention were required to include clauses in these public contracts ensuring these workers wages (including allowances), hours of work, and other conditions of labour which were not less favourable than those established by collective agreement, arbitration award or national laws for work of the same character in the trade or industry concerned in the district where the work was performed.[101] The Convention also required the establishment and maintenance of an adequate system of inspection and the imposition of remedies and sanctions in case of non-compliance with the terms of the labour clauses. This, in turn, contributed to several states adopting such provisions in their domestic legislation.

Coincidentally, in 2008 the ILO's Committee of Experts produced the first comprehensive General Survey on the application of Convention 94, concluding

[96] International Labour Conference, 19th session, Report VI (vol 1): Reduction of Hours of Work (ILO, Geneva, 1935), 20.

[97] International Labour Conference, 31st session, Report VI(b)(1): Wages: (b) Fair Wages Clauses in Public Contracts (ILO, Geneva, 1947), 5.

[98] See further for discussions leading to the adoption of this Convention: International Labour Conference, 1948.

[99] International Labour Conference, 31st session, Report VI(b)(1): Wages: (b) Fair Wages Clauses in Public Contracts (ILO, Geneva, 1947), 5.

[100] See further for discussions leading to the adoption of this Convention: International Labour Conference, 31st Session, 1948, Wages: (b) Fair Wages Clauses in Public Contracts, Reports: VI(b)(1) and (2) and Supplement (ILO, Geneva, 1947 and 1948).

[101] Art 2(1) and (2). See H K Nielsen, 'Public Procurement and International Labour Standards' (1995) 4 Public Procurement Law Review 94.

that it still had important current relevance.[102] Unfortunately, however, the report was published before the ECJ had delivered its judgment in *Rüffert* and the authors of the report relied on the Advocate General's Opinion to argue that there was no conflict between the Convention and EU law.[103] The ECJ's judgment was announced just before the Annual Conference of the ILO at which the Report was to be debated. Unsurprisingly, when the Annual Conference considered the General Survey, the ECJ's decision was assessed, with employers and unions taking radically different positions both on the acceptability of the result in *Rüffert*, and also on what, if anything, should be done about it.[104]

Although Germany never ratified this Convention, the Lower Saxony Law is a classic example of the type of domestic legislation that was enacted in compliance with the Convention. A significant number of EU Member States have ratified the Convention: Austria, Belgium, Bulgaria, Cyprus, Denmark, Finland, France, Italy, Netherlands, Spain, and (until 1992, when it denounced its ratification) the United Kingdom. In addition, Norway, a member of the European Economic Area, has ratified the Convention. Eleven states, therefore, are affected by a decision that has the potential to undermine a piece of domestic social protection, without the Convention even being mentioned in the Opinion of the Advocate General, or in the judgment of the ECJ.

15. Equal Treatment

More detailed consideration of *Rüffert* from a procurement point of view would have highlighted another aspect of the case and provided a way of addressing it. It is a noteworthy feature of the case that there are several different sets of inequalities that are in play.

There is, first, the inequality that the Commission emphasized before the Court: that between *workers* in the construction industry who are employed on private sector construction projects, who do not have the advantage of the higher wage levels of those working on public sector construction projects, due to the Lower Saxony contract conditions. This is also the inequality that the Court consistently emphasizes in its judgment.[105] There is another inequality in play, however, not involving inequality between the workers, but inequality between (actual and potential) *contractors*. Prior to *Rüffert*, inequality between German firms and Polish firms resulted (allegedly) from the inability of the Polish firms to be able to compete

[102] ILO, Labour Clauses in Public Contracts: Integrating the social dimension into procurement policies and practices (ILO, Geneva, 2008).

[103] Ibid, 96.

[104] International Labour Conference, Provisional Record, 97th Session, Geneva, 2008, Third item on the agenda: Information and reports on the application of Conventions and Recommendations, Report of the Committee on the Application of Standards, C. Reports requested under Art 19 of the Constitution, Labour Clauses (Public Contracts) Convention (No 94) and Recommendation (No 84), 1949, especially paras 116–21.

[105] Para 40.

with German firms if they are disabled from taking advantage of their comparative advantage based on the lower wage costs payable to Polish workers compared with German workers. A primary concern of the Court is also with this inequality.[106]

It is not surprising that the ECJ appears to have been primarily concerned with the effects of the contested measure on the Polish workers, and the Polish contractors. After all, the anticipated effect of the measure was that it would keep the Poles out of the German market, and it has been a central element of EU law that the purpose of the four freedoms is to ensure that open markets prevail in which economic operators are able to use whatever competitive advantages they have in order to engage in transnational economic competition. And, as part of the Single Market programme, the 2004 Public Procurement Directives are also clearly in that frame of reference: competition is at the heart of Community procurement rules, just as it is at the heart of the four freedoms generally. This approach concentrates on equality being primarily equal treatment as between different EU nationals, and attempts to protect the foreign national attempting to enter a foreign market.

The effect of the *Rüffert* judgment was, however, to create another set of inequalities: as between *workers*, there is inequality between Polish workers who are working on public sector contracts who (after *Rüffert*) do *not* receive the higher wage, and German workers working alongside the Polish workers on the same contract, who *do* receive the higher wage. This is the inequality that the Advocate General emphasized in his Opinion.[107] In addition, as between *contractors*, the Court's decision also creates another inequality. Following the decision, German firms that have to pay a higher wage cost than Polish firms are at a comparative disadvantage to the Polish firms in being able to bid successfully for a contract that includes price as one of the areas of competition between tenderers. Home firms will thus be treated 'worse' (by not being able to avoid the effect of 'home' labour conditions in the procurement context), whereas 'non-home' firms are able to avoid (some) of these labour costs.

If the only focus of attention under the Procurement Directives were the prohibition of discrimination against EU nationals, then the answer would be (relatively) simple: the ECJ should focus on the first set of inequalities. However, the equality principle is not so constrained in the Procurement Directives. For the Court, equal treatment precludes comparable situations from being treated differently, and different situations from being treated in the same way,[108] unless the treatment is objectively justified.[109] This is a general principle, not limited simply to securing non-discrimination on grounds of nationality. The case in which the ECJ first articulated the idea that the principle of equal treatment 'lies at the very

[106] Para 37.
[107] Para 131.
[108] Case 106/83 *Sermide SpA v Cassa Conguaglio Zucchero* [1984] ECR 4209, para 28. See also Opinion of AG Van Gerven delivered on 15 September 1993, Case C–146/91 *Koinopraxia Enoseon Georgikon Synetairismon Diacheir iseos Enchorion Proionton Syn. PE (KYDEP) v Commission* [1994] ECR I–4199.
[109] See, eg, Case C–189/01 *Jippes v Minister van Landbouw, Natuurbeheer en Visserij* [2001] ECR I–5689, para 129 and Case C–149/96 *Portugal v Council* [1999] ECR I–8395, para 91.

heart of the [procurement] directive'[110] illustrates the point. In the *Storebaelt* case,[111] the Court held that 'observance of the principle of equal treatment of tenderers requires that all the tenders comply with the tender conditions so as to ensure an objective comparison of the tenders submitted by the various tenderers'.[112] It therefore considered that the principle of equal treatment precluded *Storebaelt* from taking into consideration a tender where the tender did not comply with the fundamental conditions stipulated by the authority in the tender documents.[113] This aspect of the case had nothing to do with non-discrimination on the basis of nationality.

An interpretation of equal treatment that regards it as simply another way of expressing a prohibition of discrimination on grounds of nationality therefore misunderstands the complexity of the concept, as used by the Court in the procurement context. The question that the Court requires to be addressed is the broader one that concentrates on preventing comparable situations from being treated differently, and different situations from being treated in the same way. The issue then becomes one of determining when the situations are 'comparable'. In the *Storebaelt* case, the Court emphasized the importance of 'the development of effective competition in the field of public contracts'[114] and this has led Sue Arrowsmith to suggest that tenderers are 'comparable' when the entities are in a 'comparable competitive position'.[115]

The Recitals to the Procurement Directives are relevant to the issue.[116] Recital 2 of the Public Sector Directive and Recital 9 to the Utilities Directive both state that the Directives are 'based on' several principles that 'derive' from the four freedoms set out in the Treaty, including 'the principle of equal treatment [and] the principle of non-discrimination'. Four points are immediately apparent: first, non-discrimination appears to be a concept that is separable from equal treatment, with the latter being a broader concept (a point made clear in Recital 9 of the Utilities Directive, which states that 'the principle of non-discrimination is no more than a *specific expression*' of the principle of equal treatment). Second, there is no apparent limit to the scope of the principle of equal treatment as applying only to equal treatment on the basis of nationality. When the Directives wish to make clear that only non-discrimination on the basis of nationality is to be included, then they say so explicitly.[117] Third, the Procurement Directives are not a complete instantiation of the appropriate relationship between the 'equal treatment' principle and public procurement; they do not incorporate the whole of the equal treatment principle; the equal treatment principle more broadly should be integrated into their interpretation. Fourth, there is nothing in the Procurement Directives that should lead to a conclusion that equal treatment only in its first dimension is appropriate to be taken into account. As Recital 2 of the Public Sector Directive explicitly states:

[110] Para 39, *Storebaelt*.
[111] Case C–242/89 *Commission v Denmark* ('*Storebaelt*') [1993] ECR I–3353.
[112] Para 37. [113] Para 43. [114] Para 33.
[115] Arrowsmith, n 3 above, para 7.7. [116] Ibid, para 12.43.
[117] Eg Art 3, Public Sector Directive.

the provisions of the Directive 'should therefore be interpreted in accordance with both the aforementioned rules and principles and other rules of the Treaty'. Both Article 2 of the Public Sector Directive and Article 10 of the Utilities Directive state clearly and simply: 'Contracting authorities shall treat economic operators equally and non-discriminatorily and shall act in a transparent way.' After *Rüffert*, it is not at all clear that all economic operators (German and Polish) are being treated equally and non-discriminatorily, given the clear disadvantage to the German firms of being required under domestic law to pay higher wages than their (foreign) competitors. Yet again, looking more closely at the procurement context should have given the Court a somewhat different perspective.

16. What Difference Would It Have Made?

Concentrating on the differing perspectives that would have been brought into clearer focus if the Procurement Directives had been properly taken into account assumes that this would have affected the approach the Court should have taken. But it is arguable that, even if the Court had been fully briefed on the procurement dimensions of the case, it would have made little difference because in any event the Court's Article 49 analysis would have trumped the Procurement Directives and the Court would therefore have determined the issue in the same way.

Given that it didn't happen, it is impossible to know what the Court would have made of the *lex specialis* argument, and it is mere speculation whether the Court would have altered its approach or its conclusion, but in my view it is at least arguable that the Court could well have viewed its Article 49 analysis somewhat differently. At this point, we need to return to the earlier analysis and remind ourselves that the key issue on which the Court found the challenged law not to be justified was because it was not 'suitable' to achieve the legitimate aim pursued by the law in question. It was not suitable because it sought to target only part of the group of workers in question: those employed in firms that would be covered by public procurement contracts. Taking a 'procurement perspective', as it might be called, the under-inclusiveness looks rather different than it does in the absence of such a perspective. The Recitals (indeed, the history of EU public procurement) have been largely based on a recognition that public procurement can be used to impose on contractors obligations that are not generally applicable to others that are not contractors, because of the additional functions that public procurement is considered to have, such as reflecting important public values.

Given that perspective, what otherwise appears to be mere arbitrariness in targeting only those firms with a procurement contract now becomes a much more understandable, targeted use of a special regulatory tool, which is surely enough to pass not only the 'suitability' test, but also the 'necessity' test. Public procurement is an area in which Member States must be given some discretion to decide how social policies, which are accepted to be legitimate social policies, and indeed further policies that several Member States have committed themselves to in international agreements, may best be implemented. At this point in the analysis, the ECJ's earlier procurement case law becomes highly relevant, given the high degree of tolerance the Court accorded to these uses of procurement. In addition, as we have seen, this use of public procurement in Germany has gone through scrutiny in a variety of democratic processes, as well as by the German courts.

17. Conclusion

There is a major problem with the approach that the ECJ took to the resolution of the *Rüffert* case. The Court essentially ignored the procurement dimensions and context of the case, and thereby missed an important aspect of the set of relevant legal materials that it should have addressed. There is a useful concept that is used in the legal systems of some countries which goes by the name of '*per incuriam*', literally translated as 'through lack of care', which means that a court has arrived at its decision in ignorance of some relevant legal provision or jurisprudence that should have been taken into account.[118] The decision of the ECJ in the *Rüffert* case is *per incuriam* in this sense. In its apparent rush for consistency with the recent decisions in *Laval* and *Viking*, ignoring anything that stood in its way, even its own previous judgments, it has risked undermining the coherence of the corpus of EC law relating to procurement linkages, a corpus of law that the Court itself partly constructed, and of which it should have been justly proud. Ralph Waldo Emerson wrote: 'A foolish consistency is the hobgoblin of little minds, adored by little statesmen and philosophers and divines.' We must now, unfortunately, add 'and (at least some) judges of the European Court of Justice' to the list.

In this chapter, I have examined the procurement context of the *Rüffert* case that the Court ignored, and considered the implications of the case for the future use of procurement to advance social policies. In particular, I aimed to re-examine whether a central argument I advanced in *Buying Social Justice*, that the EU was in the process of creating a *modus vivendi* between the economic and social dimensions of public procurement, needs to be reconsidered. On first reading, the ECJ's decision in *Rüffert* tends to indicate that my argument was over-optimistic, and that the ECJ has considerably rolled back on its previous efforts at helping to construct a workable compromise. The fact that it has done so, however, without once mentioning the corpus of pre-existing law on procurement means that we are confronted with two potentially conflicting strands of ECJ judgments on procurement linkages: the older judgments of the Court stretching from *Beentjes* through to *Nord-Pas-de-Calais*, a strand adopted in the interpretation of the Directives and the Treaty in the procurement context, versus a newer strand represented in *Rüffert*. Undoubtedly, the Court will be called on to choose between these two strands on a future occasion. It should not be too proud to accept that *Rüffert* was *per incuriam* and that it should restore its earlier strand of decisions.

[118] Eg in *R v Northumberland Compensation Appeal Tribunal, ex parte Shaw* [1951] 1 All ER 268, a divisional court of the King's Bench Division declined to follow a Court of Appeal decision on the ground that the decision had been reached *per incuriam*.

6

Public Service Media and Market Integration: A Differential Application of Free Movement and State Aid Rules?

Roberto Mastroianni

Introduction

It is well established, both in the case law of the European Courts and in academic literature, that the regulation of the EU internal market is nothing short of an unremitting balancing exercise between conflicting interests. On the one hand lies the principle of free movement, ie the cornerstone of the entire internal market construct, whereby service providers lawfully operating in one Member State must enjoy unrestricted access to the markets of all the other Member States; on the other hand, there are certain aims in the general interest that simply cannot be overlooked, as they often embody politically sensitive issues of particular concern for national authorities and their constituencies.

The regulation of audiovisual media services, and in particular of public service media, is no exception. Whilst market integration is, save for some relevant exceptions and limitations, the foremost concern in the framework of the Union rules applying to audiovisual media services in general, public interest considerations seem to take precedence in respect of public service media. The main focus of this work is *how* this prevalence is enshrined in legislation and is affirmed in the case law of the European Courts. Public service media, being a subset of the broader sector of the 'services in the general interest', embodies a specificity that calls for the application of a special set of rules, different from the ones governing audiovisual media services provided on a commercial basis. Unlike other public utilities, however, it will be shown that, in respect of public service media, its specificity results not so much in the provision of *different rules*, but rather in a *differential application and interpretation* of the common rules on free movement and, in particular, on state aids.

To this end, the first part of the present work will briefly examine the legal framework applying to audiovisual media services and in particular to public service media. It is, instead, on the latter that the second part of this contribution will focus, with a view to emphasizing the specificities in the application of the rules of state aids in the field of public service media.

1. Internal Market Rules, Television Broadcasting and the Special Framework for Public Service Broadcasting

A. Treaty Provisions on Free Movement, Namely of Services (Articles 56–57 TFEU (Ex Articles 49–50 EC)

The Treaty provisions on free movement are possibly the most straightforward market integration device devised by the drafters, even though they tend to concern audiovisual media services in general, rather than public service media in particular.

As early as 1974 the Court of Justice delivered a key ruling as to the classification of audiovisual media services within the framework of the four freedoms: in *Sacchi* it stated that the transmission of television signals, including those in the nature of advertisements, fell within the scope of the Treaty provisions on services.[1] Whilst this characterization might appear rather self-evident nowadays, it was a relevant finding at the time as it clarified that Article 56(1) TFEU (ex Article 49(1) EC) covers not only situations in which the provider of the service temporarily crosses a border in order to provide a service (the so-called active provision of services),[2] but also cases where it is the service itself that crosses the border, whilst both provider and recipient remain in their respective Member States (the so-called correspondence services).

Moreover, it was in the context of a television broadcasting case that the ECJ clarified that the notion of remuneration set out in Article 57 TFEU (ex Article 50 EC) does not require the service to be paid for by those for whom it is performed: in *Bond van Adverteerders* the ECJ took the view that the activity engaged in by cable network operators, consisting in relaying to network subscribers the television programmes sent to them by the broadcasters established in other Member States, did constitute a service, even though its costs were borne by network subscribers in the form of subscription fees rather than by the said broadcasters.[3] Again, this finding was somewhat unexpected, as in its earlier rulings, notably *Humbel*, the ECJ had insisted on the presence of a 'direct economic link'[4] between the provider and the recipient of the service.[5]

[1] Case 155/73 *Giuseppe Sacchi* [1974] ECR 409, para 6.

[2] K Böttcher and O Castendyk, 'Comment on Art 49 EC', in O Castendyk, E Dommering, and A Scheuer (eds), *European Media Law* (2008) 92.

[3] Case 352/85 *Bond van Adverteerders and others v The Netherlands State* [1988] ECR 2085, para 17. See the case notes by M De Blois (1990) CML Rev 371; G Friden, 'The *Bond van Adverteerders* Case and Recent Legal Developments in EEC "Television Law"' (1990) 3 Leiden Journal of International Law 231.

[4] C Barnard, *The Substantive Law of the EU* (2005) 335.

[5] Case 263/86 *Belgian State v René Humbel and Marie-Thérèse Edel* [1988] ECR 5365. It is worth noting, however, that in Case C–159/90 *SPUC v Grogan* [1991] ECR I–4685 the Court apparently

Articles 34–36 TFEU (ex Articles 28–30 EC) also come into play, since, as the Court noted in *Sacchi*, the 'trade in material, sound recordings, films, apparatus and other products used for the diffusion of television signals are subject to the rules relating to freedom of movement for goods'.[6] However, national rules governing television advertising have often been regarded as falling outside the scope of the Treaty provisions on goods insofar as they can be characterized as 'certain selling arrangements' within the meaning of paragraph 16 of the *Keck* judgment, viz 'so long as those provisions apply to all relevant traders operating within the national territory and so long as they affect in the same manner, in law and in fact, the marketing of domestic products and of those from other Member States'.[7] Accordingly, in a number of cases the ECJ subjected national rules governing advertising to undergo a dual scrutiny, both under Article 34 TFEU (ex Article 28 EC) and under Articles 56–57 TFEU (ex Articles 49–50 EC), as it can be seen in *Leclerc-Siplec*[8] and in *De Agostini.*[9]

What is worth emphasizing at this juncture is that the Treaty provisions on the free movement of services and, where applicable, those on goods embody a significant momentum towards market integration, as their application results in a model of quasi-absolute home state control. Not only do they contain a proscription on both discriminatory and merely restrictive national measures (ie those 'liable to hinder or make less attractive the exercise of fundamental freedoms', according to the wording used in *Gebhard*)[10] but, as Kaldellis put it, they place a significant burden of proof on Member States also at the level of justification: whilst in the case of establishment national measures are permissible unless it is shown that one of the four *Gebhard* conditions is not met, in service cases it is for Member States to prove that any and all those requirements are satisfied.[11]

B. The Initial Agnosticism: Constraints on Market Integration, Restrictive Measures and Overriding Reasons in the General Interest

In spite of the momentous market integration potential embodied by the Treaty provisions on services and goods, it is fair to say that, for a period of about 25 years

disregarded its earlier *dictum* in *Bond van Adverteerders* by engaging in a close scrutiny of the presence of an economic link.

[6] Case 155/73 *Sacchi*, n 1 above, para 7.

[7] Joined Cases C–267/91 and C–268/91 *Criminal proceedings against Bernard Keck and Daniel Mithouard* [1993] I–6097.

[8] Case C–412/93 *Société d'Importation Edouard Leclerc-Siplec v TF1 Publicité SA and M6 Publicité SA* [1995] I–00179.

[9] Joined Cases C–34/95, C–35/95, and C–36/95 *Konsumentombudsmannen (KO) v De Agostini (Svenska) Förlag AB (C–34/95) and TV-Shop i Sverige AB (C–35/95 and C–36/95)* [1997] ECR I–03843.

[10] Case C–55/94 *Reinhard Gebhard v Consiglio dell'Ordine degli Avvocati e Procuratori di Milano* [1995] I–04165, para 37. To that effect, see also Case C–442/02 *CaixaBank France* [2004] ECR I–8961, para 11; and Case C–298/05 *Columbus Container* Services [2007] ECR I–10451, para 34.

[11] E Kaldellis, 'Freedom of Establishment v Freedom to Provide Services: An Evaluation of Case-law Developments in the Area of Indistinctly Applicable Rules' (2001) 28 (1) Legal Issues of Economic Integration 23.

from the signature of the Treaty of Rome, those provisions remained dormant. The opening up of national broadcasting markets was fiercely opposed by Member States. Indeed, television broadcasting activities, and mass-communication in general, have always been considered a politically sensitive sector, where strong interests are at stake: the safeguard of pluralism (*TV 10*),[12] the protection of consumers against abuses of advertising or the maintenance of a certain level of programme quality (*ARD*),[13] the application of copyright legislation (*Coditel*),[14] the protection of culture (*Bond van Adverteerders*),[15] to mention but a few.

The paramount importance of those public interest reasons called for, at least until the 1980s, far-reaching safeguard measures at the national level, ranging from rules on the contents of television broadcasts to outright bans on television advertising and even to legal monopolies over television broadcasting. Restricting measures of such a magnitude clashed with the very essence of the European internal market construct and were soon brought to the attention of the Court of Justice, which, at least in its early rulings, espoused a rather agnostic approach vis-à-vis national regulation.

As to the issue of monopolies, it must be recalled that they fall within the notion of 'special or exclusive rights' within the meaning of Article 106 TFEU (ex Article 86(1) EC) and, for the purposes of competition law, they may constitute a dominant position. It is well established in the case law of the European Courts that the mere granting of a legal monopoly is not a *per se* violation of Article 106 TFEU (ex Article 86(1) EC) *juncto* Article 102 TFEU (ex Article 82 EC) provided that the enterprise which has been granted special or exclusive rights is not *led to abuse* its dominant position.[16] It is thus little wonder that when the Italian statutory broadcasting monopoly was brought before the Court in *Sacchi*, the latter took the view that nothing in the Treaty prevented Member States, for considerations of public interest, of a non-economic nature, from removing radio and television transmissions, including cable transmissions, from the field of competition by

[12] Case C–23/93 *TV10 SA v Commissariaat voor de Media* [1994] ECR I–4795.

[13] Case C–6/98 *Arbeitsgemeinschaft Deutscher Rundfunkanstalten (ARD) v PRO Sieben Media AG, supported by SAT 1 Satellitenfernsehen GmbH, Kabel 1, K 1 Fernsehen GmbH* [1999] ECR I–07599.

[14] Case 262/81 *Coditel SA, Compagnie générale pour la diffusion de la télévision and others v Ciné-Vog Films SA and others* [1982] ECR 3381.

[15] Case 352/85 *Bond van Adverteerders*, n 3 above.

[16] See, to that effect, Case C–41/90 *Klaus Höfner and Fritz Elser v Macrotron GmbH* [1991] ECR I–1979 para 34, where the ECJ held that a Member State which has conferred an exclusive right to carry on that activity upon the public employment agency is in breach of Art 106(1) TFEU (ex Art 86 (1) EC) where it creates a situation in which that agency cannot avoid infringing Art 102 TFEU (ex Art 82 EC). See also Case C–163/96 *Criminal proceedings against Silvano Raso and Others* [1998] ECR I–00533, para 27 and Case C–475/99 *Firma Ambulanz Glöckner v Landkreis Südwestpfalz* [2001] ECR I–8089, para 39 where the Court employed a slightly different language focusing on the issue whether the undertaking in question by exercising the exclusive rights granted to it is 'led to abuse its dominant position' or when such rights 'are liable to create a situation in which that undertaking is led to commit such abuses'. Similarly, in Case C–179/90 *Merci convenzionali porto di Genova SpA v Siderurgica Gabrielli SpA* [1991] ECR I–5889, para 17 the Court held that a Member State is in breach of Art 106 (1) TFEU (ex Art 86(1) EC) and Art 102 TFEU (ex Art 82 EC) when such rights 'are liable to create a situation in which that undertaking is induced to commit such abuses'.

conferring on one or more undertakings an exclusive right to carry out those activities.[17] The Court, however, did not fail to remind that in the performance of those activities, statutory monopolists remained subject to the prohibitions against discrimination and to Article 106 TFEU (ex Article 86(1) EC).[18]

The ruling in *ERT* provided further guidance as to the scope of statutory monopolies and the permissible restrictions associated with it.[19] In the first place, the Court took the view that the Treaty articles on *goods* are no bar to the granting of exclusive rights relating to television broadcasting and of exclusive authority to import, hire or distribute materials and products necessary for that broadcasting, provided that this does not result in discriminatory practices as between domestic products and imported products. Likewise, the ECJ ruled that the Treaty provisions on *services* preclude national rules which create a monopoly comprising exclusive rights to transmit the monopolists' broadcasts and to retransmit broadcasts from other Member States where such a monopoly gives rise to discriminatory effects to the detriment of broadcasts from other Member States, unless those rules are justified by reference to one of the express derogations laid down in the Treaty. Article 106 TFEU (ex Article 86(1) EC), in turn, prohibits the granting of an exclusive right to transmit and an exclusive right to retransmit television broadcasts to a single undertaking, where those rights are liable to create a situation in which that undertaking is led to infringe Article 102 TFEU (ex Article 82 EC) by virtue of a discriminatory broadcasting policy which favours its own programmes, unless the application of Article 106 TFEU (ex Article 86 EC) obstructs the performance of the particular tasks entrusted to it.

Finally, the Court added that where a Member State seeks to justify measures which are likely to obstruct the exercise of the freedom to provide services, such justification must be interpreted in the light of the general principles of law and in particular the freedom of expression, as embodied in Article 10 of the European Convention on Human Rights.[20] As noted by some commentators,[21] this may call into question the *per se* legality of broadcasting monopolies, since in *Lentia* the European Court of Human Rights found that public monopolies impose the greatest possible restriction on the freedom of expression and are thus normally disproportionate and can only be justified where they correspond to a pressing need.[22]

Turning to the issue of advertising rules, the order for reference in *Debauve* concerned the compatibility of a Belgian ban over television advertising with

[17] Case 155/73 *Sacchi*, n 1 above, para 14. Cf C Cicala, 'Esercizio del diritto ed abuso di posizione dominante', (1989) *La funzione amministrativa* 430; NMH: 'Cable Television in Italy', (1975) The Journal of Business Law 72.

[18] Case 155/73 *Sacchi*, n 1 above, para 14.

[19] Case C–260/89 *Elliniki Radiophonia Tiléorassi AE and Panellinia Omospondia Syllogon Prossopikou v Dimotiki Etairia Pliroforissis and Sotirios Kouvelas and Nicolaos Avdellas and others* [1991] ECR I–02925.

[20] Ibid, para 44.

[21] K Böttcher, O Castendyk, 'Comment on Art 49 EC', in O Castendyk, E Dommering, and A Scheuer (eds), n 2 above, at 91–92, footnote 16.

[22] ECtHR, 24 November 1993, *Lentia*, Application 13914/88, 15041/89, 15717/89.

Articles 56–57 TFEU (ex Articles 49–50 EC).[23] Not only did the Court answer in the affirmative, but it went so far as to state that, *in the absence of any harmonization* of the relevant national laws, each Member State retained the power 'to regulate, restrict or even totally prohibit television advertising' in its territory on grounds of general interest, even if that prohibition extends to such advertising originating in another Member State.[24] Arguably, this finding reversed the principle of Home-State control normally applicable to services in favour of a model of Host-State control, thus legitimizing the segmentation of the common market along national boundaries.

C. The Green Paper 'Television Without Frontiers': Laying the Foundations for a European Legal Order for Public Service Broadcasting

In the early 1980s market integration in the broadcasting sector appeared nothing short of a chimera. The 1984 Green Paper *Television Without Frontiers* revealed the existence of 10 different national broadcasting markets, dominated, albeit to different degrees, by public undertakings, often enjoying special or exclusive rights.[25] What is striking is that Union law, at the time, allowed for the perpetuation of that situation: under the *Sacchi* doctrine, public broadcasters could be legitimately sheltered from competition at the national level;[26] according to the *Debauve* ruling, the divergence of national legislations as to the protection levels of general interest aims afforded a reliable protection against foreign broadcasters allowing for far-reaching restrictive measures.

But the mood began to change, gradually at first, then with increasing tempo. Heads of State and Government at the Copenhagen European Council in 1982 stated that the completion of the internal market was a high priority, a pledge reaffirmed at the Fontainebleau (June 1984), Dublin (December 1984) and Brussels (March 1985) Councils which culminated in the publication of the celebrated White Paper *Completing the Internal Market* in June 1985.[27]

With specific reference to the broadcasting sector, appeals to put an end to the protectionist policy hitherto pursued by Member States came, at first, from the European Parliament, which both in the Hahn Report and in the van Minnen Opinion expressed concerns over the adverse effects of the national control over mass media on the freedom of information and, ultimately, on the development of a European identity.[28]

[23] Case 52/79 *Procureur du Roi v Marc JVC Debauve and others* [1980] ECR 833. See the case note by N March Hunnings, (1980) CML Rev 553, 564–569.

[24] Case 52/79 *Debauve*, n 23 above, para 15.

[25] Commission, '*Television without Frontiers*, Green paper on the establishment of the common market for broadcasting, especially by satellite and cable', COM (1984) 300 final, 63–105 (hereinafter: the TWF Green Paper).

[26] Cf A Ruffilli, 'Estensione del monopolio della RAI-TV alla TV via cavo e abuso di posizione dominante ex art. 86 CEE', (1976) II Rivista di diritto industriale 3–35.

[27] Commission, '*White Paper on completing the Internal Market*', COM (1985) 310 final.

[28] Both resolutions are cited in the TWF Green Paper, n 25 above, 2.

The TWF Green Paper is usually cited by scholarly authors as the document that paved the way for the much more popular, and to some extent controversial, Television Without Frontiers Directive. Whilst this role is indisputable, the Green Paper is of paramount importance for the purposes of this work insofar as it lays down some of the key principles governing the application of Union law to public service broadcasting. In particular, the said document clarified the Commission's interpretation of three Treaty provisions, ie Articles 54(2), 51(1), 106(2) TFEU (ex Articles 48(2), 45(1), and 86(2) EC), which could bring public service broadcasting outside the scope of Union law.

Article 54(2) TFEU (ex Article 48(2) EC) defines the notion of 'Companies or firms' for the purpose of the application of the Treaty provisions on establishment and services[29] as comprising 'companies or firms constituted under civil or commercial law, including cooperative societies, and other legal persons governed by public or private law, *save for those which are non-profit-making*' (emphasis added).

Since some of the undertakings entrusted with the operation of public service broadcasting at the time were run on a non-profit basis,[30] it could be argued that those undertakings fell outside the scope of the Treaty provision on establishment and services. The Commission thus deemed it appropriate to specify the wording 'non-profit-making' under Article 54(2) TFEU (ex Article 48(2) EC) should not be interpreted literally by reference to company law, but rather it was a Union law concept applying to the companies that take part in commercial life, namely that carried on 'an *economic activity*'. In so doing, the Commission clearly espoused a functionalist, effect-based approach: 'its objective', the Commission further noted, 'might have to do with information, culture, or sport [. . .] but once this is linked to a commercial or commercially relevant activity, the company is within the scope of the Treaty.'[31]

The Commission then persuasively linked the notion of 'profit-making' within the meaning of Article 54(2) TFEU (ex Article 48(2) EC) to that of 'remuneration' referred to in Article 57 TFEU (ex Article 50 EC) in the framework of the definition of the Union concept of service; likewise, it expressly stated that public service broadcasters were 'undertakings' for the purpose of Article 106 TFEU (ex Article 86 EC), as in *Sacchi* the Italian and the German Government had argued, albeit to no avail, that RAI's public service attributions precluded its classification as an undertaking and deprived its activity of its purported economic nature. With the benefit of hindsight, it can be observed that the notion of 'undertaking' within the meaning of Article 106 TFEU (ex Article 86 EC) (as well as of Articles 101 and 102 TFEU (ex Articles 81 and 82 EC)), that of 'profit-making' set out in Article 54(2) TFEU (ex Article 48(2) EC) and that of 'remuneration' found in Article 58 TFEU

[29] Art 54 TFEU (ex Art 48 EC) is part of Chapter 2 'Right of Establishment', but also applies to the subsequent chapter on service by virtue of the reference set out in Art 62 TFEU (ex Art 55 EC).

[30] According to the TWF Green Paper, n 25 above, 205, several broadcaster organizations operated without a view to making a profit for their owners at the time: *inter alia* in Italy the RAI, in Denmark DR, in Greece ERT 1, in Ireland RTE, in the United Kingdom the BBC and IBA.

[31] TWF Green Paper, n 2 above, 206.

(ex Article 50 EC) substantially overlap,[32] insofar as they all have been found to be connected with the notion of 'economic activity',[33] ie any activity consisting in offering goods and services on a given market.[34]

Article 51 TFEU (ex Article 45(1) EC) takes 'activities which in that State are connected, even occasionally, with the *exercise of official authority*' outside the scope of the Treaty provisions on establishment and, by virtue of the reference set out in Article 62 TFEU (ex Article 55 EC), on services. In the TWF Green Paper the Commission dealt at length with the issue whether public service broadcasters qualify for that exemption. In this connection, the Commission recalled AG Mayras' definition of 'official authority' as arising from the sovereignty and majesty of the state and implying, for those who exercise it, 'the power of enjoying the prerogatives outside the general law, privileges of official power and powers of coercion over citizens'.[35] Noting that national broadcasting organizations at the time were 'not placed over the people they deal with', but rather at the same level, that they did not issue binding legal acts and did not exercise compulsion,[36] the Commission concluded that the whole broadcasting sector was not connected with the exercise of official authority.[37]

The TWF Green Paper dealt at length with Article 106(2) TFEU (ex Article 86 (2) EC), addressing in detail the various elements of that provision. The first issue that arose is whether the broadcasting organizations operating in the Member States at the time could be regarded as 'undertakings' within the meaning of the said provision, a query that the Commission answered in the affirmative relying on the ECJ judgment in *Sacchi*.

The second requisite for the application of Article 106(2) TFEU (ex Article 86(2) EC) to broadcasting organizations is that those undertakings be 'entrusted'

[32] A Arena, 'Il servizio pubblico come eccezione nel contesto della liberalizzazione degli scambi commerciali: Unione Europea ed OMC a confronto' (PhD thesis, Università degli Studi di Napoli 'Federico II' 2008), 93.

[33] As to Arts 101, 102, and 106 TFEU (ex Arts 81, 82, and 86 EC), see the ECJ finding in Höfner, n 16 above, para 21: 'in the context of competition law, [...] the concept of an undertaking encompasses every entity engaged in an economic activity'. The parallel between the concept of 'profit-making' within the meaning of Art 54 TFEU (ex Art 48(2) EC) and that of 'economic activity' was drawn by the same Commission in the TWF Green Paper, as explained above. Finally, the concept of 'remuneration' under Art 57 TFEU (ex Art 50 EC) was put on a par with that of 'economic activity' by Art 4(1) of Directive 2006/123/EC of the European Parliament and of the Council of 12 December 2006 on services in the internal market, OJ [2006] L 376/36: '"service" means any self-employed *economic* activity, normally provided *for remuneration*, as referred to in Article 50 of the Treaty' (emphasis added); moreover, the Commission's *Handbook on implementation of the Services Directive*, 10, specifies that, in order to constitute a 'service', an 'activity' must normally be '*provided for remuneration; in other words, it must be of an economic nature*'.

[34] Joined Cases C–180/98 to C–184/98 *Pavel Pavlov and Others v Stichting Pensioenfonds Medische Specialisten* [2000] ECR I–06451, para 75. See also Case 118/85 *Commission v Italy* [1987] ECR 2599, para 7, and Case C–35/96 *Commission v Italy* [1998] ECR I–3851, para 36.

[35] Case 2/74 *Reyners v Belgium* [1974] ECR 664.

[36] It is worth mentioning, however, that both the three Belgian broadcasting bodies and RTE in Ireland had been granted the power to acquire land by compulsory purchase: even though that activity did constitute exercise of official authority, it did not change the nature of public service broadcasting, as those powers were 'severable' from the other activities carried out by broadcasting organizations.

[37] TWF Green Paper, n 2 above, 203.

with the operation of a service of general economic interest, an assignment that requires an 'act of sovereignty' or an 'act of the public authority' such as a statute, royal charter or decree conferring the public service and governing the broadcasters' activities and relations with the public authorities. Conversely, the mere granting of an authorization, concession or licence to organize broadcasting without the simultaneous conferment of public task does not constitute an act of sovereignty so as to trigger the application of Article 106(2) TFEU (ex Article 86(2) EC).

The Commission then turned to the notion of 'services of general economic interest' presenting a series of convoluted arguments pointing to one basic statement: a broadcaster may be considered to be entrusted with the operation of services of general economic interest only where the relevant national law governs the activities of the undertaking, 'ie *the particular tasks assigned to it*', in such a way that they are to be recognized under Union law as being in the general economic interest. Put differently, it all boils down to the broadcaster's remit, whose general interest connotation is not incompatible with the economic nature of the activity pursued by the broadcaster.

The Green Paper also dealt with the principles governing the application of Article 106(2) TFEU (ex Article 86(2) EC). On that occasion such a provision was referred to as a 'conditional exception', ie an exception dependent on a prior examination of the consequences of the application of the individual Treaty rules to the undertaking concerned. It is thus for the Commission, on a case-by-case basis, to determine whether the application of those rules would obstruct the performance of the general interest task assigned to that undertaking. Almost as an afterthought, the Commission seemed to establish a presumption that the application of the rules on free movement does not in principle obstruct the performance by public service broadcasters of their own task.

The priority on the Commission's agenda to ensure freedom of retransmission across the national borders is also apparent in the Commission's interpretation of the last sentence of Article 106(2) TFEU (ex Article 86(2) EC), whereby the development of trade must not be affected, as a consequence of the exemption set out in that provision, to such an extent as would be contrary to the interests of the Union. The Green Paper states quite clearly that, in the field of broadcasting, the interests of the Union consist in achieving the minimum of freedom of movement for broadcasts between the Member States and of interstate freedom of transmission and reception for citizens throughout the Union. The foundations for a far-reaching harmonization measure in the field of broadcasting had been thus laid.

D. The Television Without Frontiers Directive: Market Integration and the Impact on Public Service Broadcasting

The commitment made by the TWF Green Paper was honoured, only five years later, by the so-called Television Without Frontiers Directive (Directive 89/552/ EEC, hereafter: the TWF Directive), amended for a first time by Directive 97/36/

EC and, lately, by Directive 2007/65/EC, which also changed its name to 'Directive on Audiovisual Media Services'.[38] Perhaps the most significant novelty brought about by Directive 2007/65/EC concerns the scope of the harmonized provisions. Directive 89/552, both in its original and its 1997 version, only covered 'television broadcasting' (ie linear audiovisual media services) provided for simultaneous viewing on the basis of a programme schedule set by the broadcaster; whereas the new Directive also applies to on-demand (non-linear) audiovisual media services, which enable the viewing of programmes at the moment chosen by the user and at his or her individual request on the basis of a catalogue of programmes selected by the media service provider.

The TWF Directive first approximated the legislation of Member States in certain sensitive sectors of the broadcasting activity, namely the promotion of European works (Articles 16–18 of the AVMS Directive, Consolidated text), television advertising (Articles 19–26), the protection of minors (Article 27), the right of reply (Article 28). Moreover, Member States are allowed to take measures to ensure that broadcasters under its jurisdiction do not broadcast on an exclusive basis events which are regarded as being of major importance for society (Article 14) and are required to ensure that any broadcaster established in the Union has access to those events for the purpose of short news reports on a fair, reasonable and non-discriminatory basis (Article 15).

Having achieved the harmonization of national provisions, the Directive set up a system of Home-country control for the subject-matters falling within its scope: it is for the transmitting state to ensure that audiovisual media services providers under its jurisdiction comply with the rules applicable to audiovisual media services

[38] The text of the AVMS Directive was recently consolidated into Directive 2010/13/EU, OJ L 95/1. On the TWF Directive and its amendments see A Tizzano, 'La direttiva CEE sulla "televisione senza frontiere"' (1990) IV Foro It 92; R Mastroianni, 'Il diritto comunitario e le trasmissioni televisive', (1990) Dir. comun. scambi internaz. 170; V Salvatore, 'Quotas on TV Programmes and EEC Law' (1992) CML Rev 967; G Strozzi and R Mastroianni, '*La disciplina comunitaria delle trasmissioni televisive e la recente legislazione italiana*' (1993) IV Foro It 141; D Dörr and H Hümmerich, *Die Revision der EG-Fernsehrichtlinie* (1994); B de Witte, 'The European Content Requirement in the EC Television Directive—Five Years After' (1995) *The Yearbook of Media and Entertainment Law* 101; R Mastroianni, 'La revisione della direttiva "televisione senza frontiere"' (1999) DRT 185; G Votano, 'TV europea senza frontiere, atto secondo, in Dir. Informaz. Informat.' (1997) 985; P Keller, 'The New Television without Frontiers Directive' in E Barendt (ed), *Yearbook of Media and Entertainment Law 1997/8* (1998) 176; BJ Drijber, 'The Revised Television Without Frontiers Directive: Is It Fit for the Next Century' (1999) CML Rev 87; A Meyer-Heine, 'Les apports de la nouvelle directive 'Télévision sans frontières' du 30 juin 1997 entrée en vigeur le 31 décembre 1998' (1999) Rev. trim. dr. eur. 95; A Jones, 'Television Without Frontiers' in *Yearbook of European Law* (2000) 299; R Mastroianni, 'Convergenza e disciplina dei contenuti: verso la seconda revisione della direttiva "televisione senza frontiere"' in G Morbidelli and F Donati (eds), *Comunicazioni: verso il diritto della convergenza?* (2003) 51; 'Die Zukunft der Fernsehrichtlinie / The Future of the "Television without Frontiers" Directive', *Proceedings of the conference organised by the Institute of European Media Law (EMR) in cooperation with the European Academy of Law Trier* (ERA), Schriftenreihe des Instituts für Europäisches Medienrecht (EMR), Band 29, (2005); J Harrison, L Woods, *European Broadcasting Law and Policy* (2007); J W van den Bos, 'No Frontiers: The New EU Proposal on Audiovisual Media Services' (2006) Ent Law Rev 109; O Castendyk and K Böttcher, *The Commission Proposal for a New Directive on Audiovisual Content: A Feasible Solution?*, [2006] Ent L Rev 174; O Castendyk, E Dommering, and A Scheuer (eds), *European Media Law* (2008); I Katsirea, Public Broadcasting and European Law (2008); R Mastroianni, *La direttiva sui servizi di media audiovisivi* (2009).

intended for the public in that Member State (Article 2(1)), as well as with harmonized rules set out in the Directive. The requirement that the originating Member State should verify that broadcasts comply with national law as coordinated by the Directive is sufficient to ensure free movement of broadcasts without secondary control on the same grounds in the receiving Member States (Recital No 36). Those states, indeed, must ensure freedom of reception and cannot restrict retransmissions on their territory of audiovisual media services from other Member States for reasons which fall within the fields covered by the Directive (Article 3(1)).

Member States can derogate from the obligation not to restrict retransmission only in two cases: in respect of television broadcasting, if a broadcast coming from another Member State 'manifestly, seriously and gravely' infringes the Directive provisions on the protection of minors or the ban on incitements to hatred, subject to the requirements set out in Article 3(2); in respect of on-demand audiovisual media services, for a number of public interest reasons set out in Article 3(4).

The transmitting state might deem that the harmonized provisions provide an insufficient protection. For this reason the Directive allows Member States to require media service providers under their jurisdiction to comply with more detailed or stricter rules in the fields coordinated by the AVMS Directive (Article 4(1)).

In sum, the TWF Directive and its successor, the AVMS Directive, are chiefly market integration instruments.[39] However, the overriding requirements Member States once successfully invoked before the ECJ, as shown in *Debauve*, are not entirely neglected in the name of the internal market imperatives; rather, a balance between those conflicting instances is struck by the Union legislature. This is the case, for instance, with the freedom to provide advertising services, which is counterpointed by the overriding requirement of protecting viewers from excessive advertising:[40] what the TWF and the AVMS Directives do is to achieve a regulatory bargain by establishing minimum advertising limits (Article 23). Thus, whilst the TWF and AVMS Directives are undoubtedly internal market measures, as reflected in the choice of their legal basis (ie then Article 47(2) EC (now, after amendment, Article 53(2) TFEU), which applies to services by virtue of the reference set out in Article 62 TFEU (ex Article 55 EC)), they simultaneously pursue the so-called flanking policies.[41] This is the case of culture, as demonstrated by the provisions concerning the promotion of the European audiovisual production contained in the TWF and AVMS Directives.[42]

[39] This is expressly stated in the preamble: 'whereas disparities in national legislations may impede the free movement of broadcasts within the Community and may distort competition within the common market [...] Whereas all such restrictions on freedom to provide broadcasting services within the Community must be abolished under the Treaty'.

[40] Case 6/98 *ARD v Pro Sieben* ECR I–7599.

[41] See, notably, B de Witte, 'Non-market values in internal market legislation' in NN Shuibhne (ed), *Regulating the internal market* (2006) 68.

[42] The promotion of culture as a flanking policy reflects the wording of the Treaty: Art 167(4) TFEU (ex Art 151(4) EC) requires the Union to 'take cultural aspects into account in its action under other provisions of this Treaty', yet to this end it empowers the Council only to adopt 'incentive measures, excluding any harmonisation of the laws and regulations of the Member States'.

Turning to the impact of the TWF Directive on public service broadcasting, it must be noted, in the first place, that such a Directive did not go unnoticed by Member States' public broadcasters: the Home-State control principle set out therein opened up to foreign competition formerly secluded national broadcasting markets, thus threatening to undermine the financial position of the incumbent broadcasting organizations.[43] Secondly, it is noteworthy that the TWF Directive, in line with the arguments of the TWF Green Paper, provided no exemption for public broadcasters, which thus fell within the scope both of the Treaty rules on free movement and of the secondary legislation aimed at facilitating the application thereof by way of approximation of national legislations.[44] In the third place, the horizontal approach adopted by the TWF Directive resulted in the imposition even on commercial broadcasters of requirements pursuing general interest aims. If thus public broadcasters were subject to the same rules as commercial ones, the question arose as to the legitimacy of the privileges they enjoyed in terms of preferential access to broadcasting frequencies, financial assistance by way of subventions or licence fees revenues etc. This in turn prompted the development of a Union notion of public service broadcasting.

E. Crisis and Reconstruction of the Legal Notion of Public Services: The Case of Broadcasting

The fortunes of the Union notion and regulation of public service broadcasting can be better understood in the broader framework of the Union approach to public utilities. Public services have long had a marginal role in the Union agenda and, in fact, they have been, for at least a quarter of a century, mostly ignored for the purposes from free movement provisions and competition law.[45]

The picture starts to change from the beginning of the 1980s: the attainment of the internal market gained new momentum thanks to the Commission's White Paper *Completing the Internal Market*[46] which, complemented by the introduction of majority voting in several key areas by the Single European Act (1986), constituted the basis for several significant liberalization initiatives in the late 1980s and early 1990s. At the same time, the Commission and the Court started applying competition law and state aids provisions to public utilities with an increasing frequency. The general feeling at the time was that Union action was aimed mainly at opening up the markets for public utilities, leaving little room for

[43] R Craufurd Smith, 'Getting the Measure of Public Services: Community Competition Rules and Public Service Broadcasting' (1997) *Yearbook of Media and Entertainment Law* 147–175.

[44] It is worth noting, though, that in practice the right recognized by Art 4 of the Directive with regard to broadcasters which fall into their jurisdiction is often exercised by Member States to impose additional and specific obligations to public broadcasters.

[45] G Napolitano, 'Towards a European Legal Order for Services of General Economic Interest' (2005) 11 (4) EPL 566.

[46] White Paper from the Commission to the European Council COM (85) 310 final 'Completing the Internal Market' [1985] dated 12 June 1985.

broader social and political considerations, thus threatening to bring to a close the *service public* tradition.[47]

Partly reconsidering its approach, the Commission in 1996 issued its first Communication on Services of General Interest[48] emphasizing the necessity to strike a balance between liberalization and the general interest objectives entrusted to services of general economic interest, thus establishing the tenets for the EU legal order for public utilities.[49] Indeed, following this new approach, several Directives have been approved in various sectors; the significance of services of general (economic) interest as shared values of the Union, already highlighted in the ECJ case law,[50] has been acknowledged in Article 14 TFEU (ex Article 16 EC) introduced by the Treaty of Amsterdam,[51] and their basic principles have been further clarified in a series of Commission soft-law documents.[52]

The Union approach to public service broadcasting followed a similar path. As mentioned above, the liberalization process brought about by the adoption of the TWF Directive in 1989 called for the definition of the differential element that could justify the privileges Member States bestowed upon public service broadcasters, thus placing commercial ones at a competitive disadvantage. This caused the attention to shift, both at the national and at the Union level, on the 'specific tasks' entrusted to public service broadcasters, ie their 'remit', and their 'specific role' in the attainment of the democratic, social, and cultural needs of each society and to the need to preserve media pluralism.

There was no lack of acknowledgment for the specificity of public service broadcasting both by Member States and by EU institutions. By far the most important, because of its binding nature and its rank in the hierarchy of legal sources, is the Protocol on the system of public broadcasting in the Member States attached to the Treaty of Amsterdam (1997), which contains a number of 'interpretative provisions', whose meaning will be analysed in further detail in the next section, clarifying the way in which Treaty provisions were to be applied in this particular sector.[53] In this connection it is also worth mentioning the Report from the high-level

[47] G Napolitano, n 44 above.

[48] Commission Communication COM (96) 443 'Services of General Interest in Europe' OJ [1996] C 281/3, 4.

[49] M Ross, 'Article 16 EC and Services of General Interest: from Derogation to Obligation?' (2000) 25 (1) ELR.

[50] Judgment of the Court of 27 April 1994, *Municipality of Almelo and others v NV Energiebedrijf Ijsselmij*, Case C–393/92, [1994] ECR I–01477; Judgment of the Court of 5 October 1994, *Société Civile Agricole du Centre d'Insémination de la Crespelle v Coopérative d'Elevage et d'Insémination Artificielle du Département de la Mayenne*, Case C–323/93 [1994] ECR I–05077.

[51] See also Art 36 of the Charter of Fundamental Rights, Art III–122 of the Treaty Establishing a Constitution for Europe, and Art 14 TFEU.

[52] Commission Communication COM (2000) 580 'Services of General Interest in Europe' OJ [2000] C 17/4; Report to the Laeken European Council COM (2001) 598 final 'Services of General Interest' [2001] presented by the Commission on 17.10.2001; Green Paper; Commission Communication to the European Parliament, the Council, the European Economic and Social Committee and the Committee of the Regions COM (2004) 374 final 'White Paper on services of general interest' [2004] Bull. 5, point 1.3.25.

[53] See R Mastroianni, 'Il Protocollo sul sistema di radiodiffusione pubblica' (1998) 2–3 Il Diritto dell'Unione Europea, 533–539.

group on audiovisual policy chaired by Commissioner Oreja (1998), which emphasized the important role played by public service broadcasting 'in promoting cultural diversity in each country, in providing educational programming, in objectively informing public opinion, in guaranteeing pluralism and in supplying, democratically and free-of-charge, quality entertainment'. The importance of public service broadcasting for social, democratic, and cultural life in the Union was also reaffirmed in the Resolution of the Council and of the Representatives of the Governments of the Member States, Meeting within the Council of 25 January 1999 concerning public service broadcasting. Finally, the European Commission in 2001 issued a Communication on the application of State aid rules to public service broadcasting, which was replaced by an updated version in July 2009.[54]

2. The Specificity of Public Service Broadcasting in the Application of the Rules on State Aids

A. State Aid Rules and the Functioning of the Internal Market in the Field of Broadcasting

The application of the Treaty rules on state aids to public service broadcasting provides some invaluable insights as to how their specificity, acknowledged on several occasions, affected in fact the application of substantive provisions of Union law.[55]

By and large, Member States finance public service broadcasting according to two broad categories of funding schemes: 'single-funding' and 'dual-funding'. The former relates to those systems in which the transfer of state resources, in whatever form, constitutes the sole source of the broadcasting organization entrusted with public service obligations.[56] As far as 'Dual-funding' systems are concerned, conversely, public financing is coupled by, to different extents, revenues from commercial activities, typically the sale of advertising space or the provision of premium contents to the viewers.

[54] Commission communication on the application of state aid rules to public service broadcasting, OJ [2001] C 320/5 (hereafter: 'The 2001 Broadcasting Communication'); Commission communication on the application of state aid rules to public service broadcasting, OJ [2009] C 257/1 (hereafter: 'The 2009 Broadcasting Communication').

[55] Cf *ex multis* A Antoniadis, 'The Financing of Public Service Broadcasting' in M Sanchez Rydelski (ed), *The EC State Aid Regime: Distortive Effects of State Aid on Competition and Trade* (2006), ch 23; A Bartosch, 'Annotation on Case C–156/98, *Federal Republic of Germany v Commission*', (2001) 38 CML Rev 1285; AF Bavasso, 'Public Service Broadcasting and State Aid Rules: Between a Rock and a Hard Place', (2002) 27 ELR; S Coppieters, 'The Financing of Public Service Broadcasting' in A Biondi/P Eeckhout/J Flynn (eds), *The Law of State Aid in the European Union* (2004); R Craufurd Smith, 'State Support For Public Service Broadcasting: The Position under European Community Law', (2001) Legal Issues of Economic Integration 3; D Tambini and J Cowling (eds), *From Public Service Broadcasting to Public Service Communications* (2004); I Katsirea, *Public Broadcasting and European Law* (2008) 321.

[56] See the 2001 Broadcasting Communication, n 53 above, para 45.

It is almost self-evident that the two categories of commercial revenues are, by the same token, the element that makes the provision of non-public service broadcasting commercially viable. Public service broadcasters are thus at a competitive advantage over their commercial counterparts, whose legitimate concern would be that the incumbent public broadcasters might have an incentive in engaging in exclusionary practices, such as undercutting the price of advertising space or of the access to audiovisual contents.[57] This, in turn, would not only entail distortions of competition, but might also jeopardize the attainment of the European internal market, insofar as incumbent public broadcasting organizations usually enjoy dominant positions the abuse whereof might effectively prevent competitors established in other Member States from entering 'their own' national markets, thus restoring a pre-TWF Directive scenario.[58]

The establishment of a clear legal framework governing the provision of public funding to public service broadcasters is thus no less essential for the functioning of the internal market than the elimination of restrictions to the free movement of services achieved through the approximation of national legislations and the application of the Treaty rules of free movement. The flipside of the commonality of aims existing between state aid and free movement rules is the necessity, in both cases, to strike a balance between the imperatives of the internal market and some general interest aims, strongly felt at the national level, namely the need to address the democratic, social, and cultural needs of each society and to the need to preserve media pluralism.

It is well-established in economic literature that the provision of programmes aimed at addressing those needs is likely to result in a market failure:[59] broadcasts aimed at linguistic minorities, concerning niche sports or allowing the equal representation of political forces are, almost by definition, unlikely to attract large audiences. This results in advertising revenues often insufficient to compensate the costs incurred for their provision or, alternatively, in minor demand if those broadcasts were supplied on a premium basis. Those programmes, however, are usually regarded as 'merit goods' having positive externalities, let alone their sensitive nature in the governments' political agenda.[60] Since the market does not provide for sufficient incentives for their provision, public intervention is in order: this calls for their characterization as 'public services', their exemption from the ordinary legal framework, and possibly their funding through state resources.

[57] See 'Getting the Measure of Public Services: Community Competition Rules and Public Service Broadcasting' (1997) *Yearbook of Media and Entertainment Law*, 148–149.

[58] This scenario has been thoroughly examined by the Commission in the TWF Green Paper.

[59] See, eg, PO Steiner, 'Program Patterns and Preferences, and the Workability of Competition in Radio Broadcasting', (1952) The Quarterly Journal of Economics, vol 66(2), 194–223; M Spence and B Owen, 'Television Programming, Monopolistic Competition, and Welfare' (1977) The Quarterly Journal of Economics, vol 91(1), 103–126; ST Berry and J Waldfogel, 'Free Entry and Social Inefficiency in Radio Broadcasting' (1999) RAND Journal of Economics, vol 30(3), 397–420.

[60] On the notion of merit goods, see RA Musgrave, 'A Multiple Theory of Budget Determination' (1957) FinanzArchiv, New Series 25(1), 33–43; AK Sen, 'Rational Fools: A Critique of the Behavioral Foundations of Economic Theory' [1977] Choice, Welfare and Measurement, 84–106.

B. The Framework Governing the Financing of Public Service Broadcasting: Article 107(3)(d) TFEU (ex Article 87(3)(d) EC)

The Union rules on state aids reflect the considerations above under a number of aspects. First and foremost, the concerns about competition being distorted and the functioning of the internal market being jeopardized by public funding are addressed by Article 107(1) TFEU (ex Article 87(1) EC), which indeed declares incompatible with the common market aids granted by Member States that 'distort competition by favouring certain undertakings', in so far as they 'affect trade between Member States'. General interest aims and the ensuing need to allow for the financing of public services designed to pursue those goals are, instead, addressed by three distinct groups of rules: (i) the *Altmark* rule of reason in Article 107 (1) TFEU (ex Article 87(1) EC); (ii) the express derogations under Article 107(2) and (3) TFEU (ex Article 87(2) and (3) EC); and (iii) the conditional exemption set forth in Article 106(2) TFEU (ex Article 86(2) EC).

The order of the items in the list above reflects the one followed by the Commission and the EU Courts in the assessment of the legality of public service broadcasting state aid schemes.[61] Nonetheless, it is worth dealing with paras 2 and 3 of Article 107 TFEU (ex Article 87 EC) in the first place, as they only have a very limited impact on the issue of the financing of public service broadcasting. Those provisions, indeed, enumerate certain categories of state aids, which are, or may be considered to be, compatible with the internal market. For the purpose of this work, however, regard must be had exclusively to Article 107(3)(d) TFEU (ex Article 87(3)(d) EC), whereby aids designed to promote 'culture and heritage conservation', which do not affect trading conditions and competition in the EU to an extent that is contrary to the common interest, may be regarded as compatible with the common market. That provision is to be read in conjunction with Article 167 TFEU (ex Article 151 EC): paragraph 1 thereof requires the Union to contribute to the flowering of the cultures of the Member States, while respecting their national and regional diversity and at the same time bringing the common cultural heritage to the fore; Article 167(4) TFEU (ex Article 151(4) EC), moreover, provides that the Union shall take cultural aspects into account in its action under other provisions of this Treaty, in particular in order to respect and to promote the diversity of its cultures.

The said provisions, taken together, seem to imply a duty on the part of the Commission to accord sympathetic consideration to the culture-related measures adopted by Member States when assessing their compatibility with the common market within the framework of the rules on state aids.[62] On the contrary, the European Commission took the view that the derogation contained in Article 107

[61] Cf the 2001 and 2009 Broadcasting Communications, n 53 above.

[62] See to that effect Jens-Daniel Braun, 'Article 87 EC' in O Castendyk, E Dommering, and A Scheuer (eds), European Media Law (2008) 220.

(3)(d) TFEU (ex Article 87(3)(d) EC) be construed narrowly[63] and insisted, especially it its earlier decisions, that state measures have a cultural rather than an economic focus as an eligibility requirement for exemption under Article 107(3)(d) TFEU (ex Article 87(3)(d) EC).[64] Even though, in subsequent decisions, the Commission conceded that culture-related measures might have also economic aspects and that the presence of the latter did not rule out *per se* the applicability of the said derogation,[65] it was uncompromising in requiring that the cultural interests pursued overweigh the distortions of competition brought about by the measure concerned.[66]

Furthermore, the Commission has consistently held that the educational and democratic needs of a Member State have to be regarded as distinct from the promotion of culture, thus refusing to apply the derogation under Article 107(3)(d) (ex Article 87(3)(d) EC) in cases where Member States failed to provide for a separate definition and funding of state aid designed to promote culture. As a result of the following, it is thus unsurprising that in some proceedings the Commission discarded the application of the derogation at issue impliedly.[67]

C. 'Favouring' Certain Undertakings: The Four Conditions in *Altmark* and Their (Limited) Relevance in the Broadcasting Sector

The public service characterization of the remit entrusted to a specific broadcaster may also have an impact on the classification of the transfer of state resources as a state aid within the meaning of Article 107(1) TFEU (ex Article 87(1) EC). According to the wording of such provision, to qualify as state aid it is necessary that the measure favours the recipient, in the sense that the latter receives an advantage of any valuable kind; conversely, if the measure merely constitutes compensation for the services provided in order to discharge public service obligations, it cannot be regarded as a state aid. As AG Jacobs pointed out in *GEMO*,[68] this 'compensation approach' is contrasted by another possible reading of the provision in question, the so-called 'state aid approach', whereby funding granted to an undertaking for the performance of general interest obligations is always a state aid within the meaning of Article 107(1) TFEU (ex Article 87(1) EC), but it

[63] See the 2001 Broadcasting Communication, para 29; the 2009 Broadcasting Communication, para 37; see also State Aid N 548/2001, 13 February 2002, 6; Decision 2006/513/EC, DVB-T, OJ [2006] L 200/14, para 122.

[64] See, eg, Commission Decision 1999/133/EC, CELF, OJ [1999] L 44/37 (52).

[65] See Commission, Staatliche Beihilfe Nr. N 3/98, Decision of 14 June 1999, Filmförderung, 6; Commission, Ayuda de Estado N 458/04, 14 December 2004, Espacio Editorial Andaluza Holding, para 15.

[66] C Koenig and J Kühling, 'Mitgliedstaatliche Kulturförderung und gemeinschaftliche Beihilfenkontrolle durch die EG-Kommission', (2002) EuZW 197, 202.

[67] See F Mortensen, 'Altmark, Article 86(2) and Public Service Broadcasting' (2008) 2 European State Aid Law Quarterly 240.

[68] Opinion of Advocate General Jacobs delivered on 30 April 2002, Case C–126/01 *Ministère de l'Économie, des Finances et de l'Industrie v GEMO SA* [2003] ECR I–13769 paras 93–106.

may be justified under Article 106 TFEU (ex Article 86(2)) EC insofar as it is necessary and proportionate to discharge those obligations.

The early case law of the European Courts provided little guidance as to the correct approach,[69] due to its relevant inconsistencies: the ruling in *ADBHU*[70] followed the compensation approach; *Banco Exterior de España*,[71] *FFSA*,[72] and *SIC*[73] instead were based on the state aid approach; in *Ferring* the Court went back to the compensation thesis.[74] As far as public service broadcasting is concerned, it is noteworthy that the Commission in its first Communication on the application of state aid rules to public service broadcasting (2001) expressly espoused the state aid approach.[75]

The landmark *Altmark* ruling brought the debate to a close in favour of the compensation approach, yet dampened it by the provision of four such stringent cumulative requirements. First, the recipient undertaking must actually have public service obligations to discharge, and the obligations must be clearly defined. Second, the parameters on the basis of which the compensation is calculated must be established in advance in an objective and transparent manner. Third, the compensation cannot exceed what is necessary to cover all or part of the costs incurred in the discharge of the public service obligations, taking into account the relevant receipts and a reasonable profit. Fourth, where the undertaking which is to discharge public service obligations, in a specific case, is not chosen pursuant to a public procurement procedure which would allow for the selection of the bidder capable of providing those services at the least cost to the community, the level of compensation must be determined on the basis of an analysis of the costs which a typical undertaking, well run and adequately equipped so as to be able to meet the necessary public service requirements, would have incurred in discharging those obligations.

Some commentators wondered whether those onerous conditions left any room for Article 106(2) TFEU (ex Article 86(2) EC) in cases involving the financing of services of general economic interest.[76] In the field of public service broadcasting the answer is arguably in the affirmative: the Commission's decisions in state aid cases in that sector actually reveal that, even post *Altmark*, the real focus of the legal analysis has been Article 106(2) TFEU (ex Article 86(2) EC) rather than the notion of 'favouring' within the meaning of Article 107(1) TFEU (ex Article 87(1) EC).

[69] See C Rizza, 'The Financial Assistance Granted by Member States to Undertakings Entrusted with the Operation of a Service of General Economic Interest' in A Biondi, P Eeckhout, and J Flynn (eds), *The Law of State Aid in the European Union* (2004) 67 et seq; A Sinnaeve, 'State Financing of Public Services: The Court's Dilemma in the *Altmark* Case', (2003) EStAL 351, 352 et seq.

[70] Case 240/83 [1985] ECR 531, para 16–21 of the judgment.

[71] Case C–387/92 [1994] ECR I–877, para 21 of the judgment.

[72] Case T–106/95 *FFSA and Others v Commission* [1997] ECR II–229.

[73] Case T–46/97 [2000] ECR II–2125. It is worth noticing that prior to the judgment in *SIC*, the EFTA Court had already applied the state aid approach in Case E–4/97 *Norwegian Bankers' Association v EFTA Surveillance Authority*, judgment of 3 March 1999.

[74] Case C–53/00, judgment of 22 November 2001.

[75] Para 19.

[76] See Mortensen, '*Altmark*, Article 86(2) and Public Service Broadcasting', n 66 above, 242.

In particular, it appears that the second and the fourth *Altmark* conditions have proved difficult to meet in cases concerning the financing of public service broadcasters.[77] With specific regard to the fourth condition, this is little wonder, as it requires that the undertaking entrusted with the general interest mission be selected through a public procurement procedure or, alternatively, that the level of compensation be determined on the basis of an analysis of the costs in which a well-run and adequately equipped typical undertaking would have incurred.

As to the 'typical undertaking' test, several Member States have argued that the application thereof is impossible in the field of broadcasting, as there are no comparable undertakings that can be employed as a benchmark to the actual public service broadcasters. Indeed, not only are those obligations usually not carried out by private companies, but their very content varies considerably among the various Member States.[78] Equally utopian is the public procurement requirement: the existing public service broadcasters have all, with the exception of TV 2 in Denmark, been established prior to the EU accession of their respective Member State, thus it would be simply unrealistic to require the Member State to revoke their entrustment of the public service broadcasting remit and to call for new tenders.[79]

D. Should Public Service Broadcasting Be Entrusted on the Basis of Competitive Tendering? Some Considerations on the Recent CFI Ruling in SIC

The public procurement requirement laid down in the fourth *Altmark* condition was recently referred to by the Court of First Instance in *SIC*,[80] where the applicant had argued that the failure to award the public television service to the Portuguese broadcaster RTP on the basis of competitive tendering should have prevented the Commission from finding that the funding granted to RTP could benefit from the exemption under Article 106(2) TFEU (ex Article 86(2) EC). To this end, the applicant relied on the Commission's communication on concessions under Community law,[81] the Commission's interpretation of the *Telaustria*[82] judgment contained in its *XXXIst Report on Competition Policy—2001*,[83] the ECJ ruling in *Teckal*[84] and the fourth *Altmark* condition.

[77] Ibid. In 2008 the author pointed out that since the *Altmark* judgment was delivered, in none of the 17 decisions of the Commission had the four criteria been met. If regard is had to the latest decisions, such as State Aid C13/2008 United Kingdom, Decision of 11.02.2009 *Aid to Channel 4 linked to digital switchover* or State Aid N287/2008 Denmark Decision of 04.08.2008 *Rescue Aid to TV2/Danmark A/S*, apparently his findings still hold true today. See also Case T–354/05 *TFI v Commission of the European Communities* [2009] ECR II-471, para 124–147 of the judgment.

[78] Ibid, 244.

[79] Ibid.

[80] Case T–442/03 *SIC—Sociedade Independente de Comunicação, SA v Commission of the European Communities* [2008] ECR II–01161.

[81] Commission interpretative communication on concessions under Community law, OJ [2000] C 121/2, 2–3.

[82] Case C–324/98 *Telaustria and Telefonadress* [2000] ECR I–10745.

[83] (SEC (2002) 462 final).

[84] Case C–107/98 *Teckal* [1999] ECR I–8121.

The judgment by the CFI is, admittedly, of limited importance as to the interpretation of the fourth *Altmark* requirement, as that plea was declared inadmissible on procedural grounds. Conversely, in its lengthy ruling, the CFI developed some lines of argument providing valuable insights as to the 'specificity' of public service broadcasting.

In the first place, the CFI, recalling its earlier ruling in *Olsen*,[85] held that it is not apparent either from the wording of Article 106(2) TFEU (ex Article 86(2) EC) or from the case law on that provision that a service of general economic interest may be entrusted to an operator only as a result of a tendering procedure. Thus, the absence of competitive tendering cannot have the result that state funding of the undertaking entrusted with the operation of the service of general interest must be regarded as incompatible with the common market, but would, at most, have justified the Commission in bringing an action under Article 258 TFEU (ex Article 226 EC).

It is plain to see how this finding alone would have sufficed to reject the applicant's plea. The CFI, however, did not content itself with that, but, in order to clear up any potential misunderstandings, went on to demonstrate why the Portuguese Republic was 'in no way' required to organize a competitive tendering prior to the award of the public broadcasting service to RTP.

First, the CFI observed that the public service contracts concluded between the Portuguese Republic and RTP could not be regarded as 'concessions' within the meaning of the communication referred to by the applicant. Secondly, it held that even though RTP was a concession holder, the communication stated expressly that, 'in the audiovisual sector, account should be taken of the [Amsterdam Protocol]',[86] thus acknowledging 'the specific nature of broadcasting' and 'exemp [ting] that sector from the general rule'.

The CFI then took a small detour mentioning a passage of the Communication according to which it did not concern 'acts concerning non-economic activities such as obligatory schooling or social security'.[87] But should public service broadcasting be regarded as a service of general *non-economic* interest? The CFI conceded that it was not the case, but somewhat cryptically added that 'it must none the less be pointed out that that classification as an SGEI is explained more by the de facto impact of public service broadcasting on the otherwise competitive and commercial broadcasting sector, than by an alleged commercial dimension to broadcasting'.

Going back to the main argument, the CFI recalled the Amsterdam Protocol and held that such 'specific status' for public service broadcasting is the basis for the freedom accorded to Member States in the award of broadcasting services of general economic interest, which explains and justifies the fact that a Member State cannot be required to have recourse to competitive tendering for the award of such service, 'at least where it decides to ensure that public service itself through a public

[85] Case T–17/02 *Olsen v Commission* [2005] ECR II–2031, para 239.
[86] Commission interpretative communication on concessions, n 81 above, footnote 29, eighth subpoint of point 2.4.
[87] Ibid, second indent of the fifth subpoint of point 2.4.

company', as in the case at issue. Finally, as to the ECJ judgments in *Telaustria* and *Teckal*, the CFI considered them irrelevant, again, due to 'the specific features of that sector and the particular objectives pursued by Member States when they define and organise broadcasting'.[88]

The ruling by the CFI in *SIC* is better understood in the broader context of the case law concerning the award of concessions of cross-border interests. In this connection, the Court was ready to disregard legal classifications in order to enable the services market to be opened up to competition and to achieve the broadest possible application of the rules instituting and guaranteeing the proper operation of the Single Market, namely the rules prohibiting any discrimination on grounds of nationality, the rules on the free movement of goods, freedom of establishment, freedom to provide services, as well as those governing the granting of special and exclusive rights. As a result, public authorities granting concessions of cross-border relevance are presently bound by a number of obligations—especially in terms of transparency, non-discrimination, mutual recognition and proportionality—that previously only applied to the award of public procurement contracts falling within the scope of the relevant EC Directives.

This framework provides a possible explanation for the CFI's otherwise almost unintelligible zeal in assessing the legality of the entrustment of the public broadcasting service in *SIC*: arguably, the CFI sought to take pre-emptive action to prevent the obligations imposed on the authorities awarding public procurement contracts, that had already spilled over into the field of concessions having a cross-border relevance, from creeping into the revered sector of public service broadcasting. To this end, the CFI, apart from its sibylline reference to the purported non-economic nature of that activity, relied on one main argument: the 'specificity' of public service broadcasting acknowledged by an instrument of primary EU law, viz the Amsterdam Protocol. As will be illustrated in greater detail in the following section, the relevance of the Protocol for public service broadcasting is twofold, as it provides the framework for the interpretation of Union law in cases involving that activity and, in some cases, exempts that sector 'from the general rule'.

E. Article 106(2) TFEU (Article 86(2) EC) and the Definition of the Public Service Broadcasting 'Remit': The Role of the Amsterdam Protocol

Article 106(2) TFEU (ex Article 86(2) EC) constitutes the backbone of the Union legal framework for public utilities. It exempts the undertakings entrusted with the operation of services of general economic interest from the Treaty rules, insofar as the application of such rules would obstruct the performance of the particular tasks assigned to them, provided that the development of trade is not affected to such an extent as would be contrary to the interests of the Union.

[88] Case T–442/03 *SIC*, n 79 above, para 155.

Article 106(2) TFEU (ex Article 86(2) EC) affords a horizontal conditional exemption: 'horizontal' insofar as it can exempt the provision of a given service of general economic interest from *any* Treaty rule, even though this section will focus on its application in conjunction with the ban on state aids set out in Article 107(1) TFEU (ex Article 87(1)); 'conditional' insofar as it does not bring a given sector outside the scope of the Treaty altogether, but only precludes the application of those rules to the extent necessary to guarantee the effective fulfilment of the general interest mission. Put differently, the application of Article 106(2) TFEU (ex Article 86(2) EC) is subject to a strict *proportionality assessment*, which in turn calls for a clear definition of the mission entrusted to the undertaking concerned.[89]

A key principle governing services of general economic interest is that of their *freedom of definition* entrusted to Member States. Put differently, it is neither for the Union legislature nor the case law of the European courts to determine which services should be regarded as services of general economic interest: that is a task for Member States, whose definitions can only be subject to control by the Commission in case of manifest error. However, in every case, for Article 106(2) TFEU (ex Article 86(2) EC) to apply, the public service mission needs to be *clearly defined*[90] and must be *explicitly entrusted* through an act of public authority (including contracts).[91] This is necessary not only to improve transparency and legal certainty, but chiefly to allow the Commission to carry out its proportionality assessment.[92]

That of services of general economic interest, therefore, may well be defined as 'a notion in search of a content', which is to be filled by Member States according to the principle of freedom of definition, but, at the same time, it must be regarded as a 'container', insofar as such freedom of definition is, at least to a degree, constrained by the Commission's control in case of manifest error.[93] The exercise of this power, in turn, calls for the establishment at the Union level at least of some basic requirements, of the core features of the notion of services of general economic interest. In this connection, some guidance is provided by the CFI ruling in *BUPA* and by two soft-law documents issued by the Commission.

As to the latter, regard must be had in the first place to the 2001 Communication *Services of General Interest in Europe*, whereby the Commission held that services of general economic interest 'are different from ordinary services in that public authorities consider that they need to be provided even where the market may not have sufficient incentives to do so'. Even more straightforward is the Opinion Prepared by the State Aid Group of EAGCP on Services of General Economic Interest (2006), where the latter are defined as 'economic activities that public

[89] Communication from the Commission, 'Services of general interest in Europe' (2001/C 17/04), para 23.

[90] See Commission Decision 2005/842/EC of 28 November 2005 on the application of Article 86 (2) of the EC Treaty to State aid in the form of public service compensation granted to certain undertakings entrusted with the operation of services of general economic interest (notified under document number C (2005) 2673) OJ [2005] L 312/67, Recital No 8.

[91] Case C–159/94 *EDF* [1997].

[92] Communication, 'Services of general interest in Europe', n 88 above, para 22.

[93] See A Arena, n 32 above, 93.

authorities identify as being of particular importance to citizens and that would not be supplied (or would be supplied under different conditions) if there were no public intervention'. The Opinion then expressly refers to the economic theory concept of 'market failures' and identifies their most common causes: externalities and public goods. Relying on the economic theory, the Opinion spells out three principles that should guide the EU policy in the field of state aids: (i) state aids are legitimate responses to market failures; (ii) state aids should not lead to undue market distortions, thus cost-effectiveness should not be overlooked; (iii) intervention is warranted only if its expected benefit, in terms of improving market outcomes, outweighs the expected cost of intervention, thus state aid should only be used as a remedy for market failures if it is the best feasible remedy. It is thus fair to contend that one of the basic requirements of the notion of service of general economic interest is that of market failure: if the market does have sufficient incentives to provide such service, then its characterization as a service of general economic interest would be vitiated by a manifest error.

In its recent judgment in *BUPA*[94] the CFI held that even though Member States have a wide discretion when determining what they regard as services of general economic interest, they are required to ensure that such general interest mission satisfies certain minimum criteria, such as the presence of an act of the public authority entrusting the operators in question with such a mission and the universal and compulsory nature of that mission. Furthermore, the Member State must indicate the reasons why it considers that the service in question, because of its specific nature, deserves to be characterized as a service of general economic interest and to be distinguished from other economic activities.

With reference to public service broadcasting, the basic document illustrating the Commission's view as to the application of Article 106(2) TFEU (ex Article 86 (2) EC) is undoubtedly the 2001 *Communication on the application of State aid rules to public service broadcasting*, which in this connection lays down three conditions that apparently substantially reflect those set out in the 2001 Communication *Services of general interest in Europe*: (i) the service in question must be a service of general economic interest and clearly defined as such by the Member State (*definition*); (ii) the undertaking in question must be explicitly entrusted by the Member State with the provision of that service (*entrustment*); (iii) the application of the ban on state aid must obstruct the performance of the particular tasks assigned to the undertaking and the exemption from such rules must not affect the development of trade to an extent that would be contrary to the interests of the Union (*proportionality test*). The Communication further requires, with reference to the first condition, that the definition of the public service mandate be 'as precise as possible' so as to allow the Commission to carry out its proportionality assessment under Article

[94] Judgment of the Court of First Instance (Third Chamber, extended composition) of 12 February 2008, *British United Provident Association Ltd (BUPA), BUPA Insurance Ltd and BUPA Ireland Ltd v Commission of the European Communities* Case T–289/03 [2008] ECR II–00081. For comments, see notably A Biondi, '*BUPA v Commission*' (2008) European State Aid LQ 401; W Sauter, (2009) CML Rev 269; M Ross, 'A healthy approach to services of general economic interest? The *BUPA* judgment of the Court of First Instance' (2009) ELR 127.

106(2) TFEU (ex Article 86(2) EC):[95] again this reiterates an obligation referred to in the Communication *Services of general interest in Europe* that had been affirmed 20 years earlier by ECJ in *Züchner*.[96] Paragraph 2 of the Broadcasting Communication, moreover, seems to impliedly refer to the market failure criterion in recalling that when the broadcasting markets were opened to competition, Member States considered that public service broadcasting should be maintained, 'as a way to ensure [. . .] the satisfaction of needs that private operators would not necessarily fulfil to the optimal extent'.

If regard be had exclusively to these passages of the said Communication, it would be fair to conclude that the Commission's approach to the application of Article 106(2) TFEU (ex Article 86(2) EC) in state aid cases involving public service broadcasting is fully in line with the broader framework applying to all other services of general economic interest. Conversely, with specific reference to the definition of the general interest mission (or 'remit', as it is usually referred to in the field of broadcasting), whilst the rules remain formally the same, their application and interpretation in the broadcasting sector differ significantly.

Paragraph 33 of the 2001 Broadcasting Communication, indeed, provides that Member States, in exercising their competence to define the public service mandate, 'generally speaking' should take account of the Union concept of services of general economic interest, but, due to the 'specific nature' of the broadcasting sector, 'a wide definition, entrusting a given broadcaster with the task of providing balanced and varied programming in accordance with the remit, while preserving a certain level of audience, may be considered, in view of the interpretative provisions of the Protocol, legitimate under Article 106(2) TFEU (ex Article 86(2) EC)'. Such a definition, according to the Broadcasting Communication, 'would be consistent with the objective of fulfilling the democratic, social and cultural needs of a particular society and guaranteeing pluralism, including cultural and linguistic diversity' as set out in the Amsterdam Protocol.

As one commentator aptly observed, in so doing the Commission espoused a *functional* understanding of the public service broadcasting remit, impliedly discarding the market failure criterion referred to in connection with other services of general economic interest: so long as a given service is 'directly related to the democratic, social and cultural needs of each society and to the need to preserve media pluralism' it can be regarded as part of the public service broadcaster's remit, even if the market does offer sufficient incentives for its provision on a commercial basis.[97]

The Commission applied this approach in a number of state aid decisions involving public service broadcasting. In *BBC News 24*, for instance, the Commission found that the provision of a 24-hour news service could be considered as 'addressing the democratic and social needs of society' because it provided a wider coverage of news topics and a greater degree of depth in the analysis of events

[95] For a recent application of Art 106(2) in the field of State aids to public broadcasters, see judgment of the General Court of 1 July 2010, Joined Cases T–568 and 573/08, *M6 and TF1 v European Commission*, nyr.

[96] Judgment in Case 172/80 *Züchner* [1981] ECR 2021.

[97] V Wiedemann, 'Public Service Broadcasting, State Aid, and the Internet: Emerging EU Law' (2004) 4 European State Aid LQ 596.

compared to the existing news programmes broadcast by the BBC.[98] In *BBC Licence Fee* (2003), moreover, the Commission cleared the financing of nine new BBC digital channels for radio and television as they were 'addressing the same democratic, social and cultural needs of the society'.[99]

In a controversial article published in 2004, two DG Comp civil servants expressed their concern that such a broad definition of the remit could entail the so-called 'mission-creep', ie the hypertrophic expansion of the activities of public service broadcasters to neighbouring markets, such as the Internet, where traditional justifications for public service broadcasting do not apply.[100] In the (linear) broadcasting sector, for instance, it is widely accepted that the remit can comprise both popular programmes, such as soccer matches, and cultural broadcasts on the assumption that the viewer will continue to watch the latter after the former. The inclusion of popular programmes in the public service broadcaster's remit, however, would no longer be justified if those broadcasts were offered in the framework of a special-interest channel, where no cultural programmes are scheduled.[101]

It was about at that time that the Commission apparently departed from its earlier broad definition of the broadcasting remit in cases involving online services to espouse a market-failure-based approach. The seminal case was *BBC Digital Curriculum*,[102] in which the BBC sought to rely on its licence fees to finance the provision of educational services over the Internet. Even though educational services had been part of the BBC's remit for decades, the Commission considered their online provision as a new service and thus regarded their financing through the licence fees as a new aid. What is striking, however, is that when the Commission assessed the compatibility of that aid with the internal market under Article 106(2) TFEU (ex Article 86(2) EC) it did not refer to the Amsterdam Protocol and even though, on the facts, it eventually considered the educational aim of the new service as a suitable justification, it stressed that it reached such a conclusion only because the remit had been so narrowly defined as to ensure no harm to competitors and as to distinguish the BBC's online services from the offers of commercial competitors. As held by one commentator, the subsequent Dutch and Danish decisions further elaborated those findings thus reversing the burden of proof, insofar as it was the Member State that was required to show that there was a need for these new services and that they were of a special character, viz that they were not also offered by commercial broadcasters.[103]

The recent CFI judgment in *TV2*,[104] however, arguably brought the debate over the market failure model to a close[105] by rejecting the argument put forward by two

[98] State aid NN 88/98 *BBC News 24*, OJ (2000) C 78 para 50.

[99] State aid N 631/2001 *BBC Licence Fee*, OJ (2003) C 23.

[100] S Depypere and N Tighcelaar, 'The Competition's state aid policy on activities of public service broadcasters in neighbouring markets' (2004) 2 Competition Policy Newsletter 19.

[101] Ibid, 22.

[102] State aid N 37/2003 *BBC digital curriculum*.

[103] V Wiedemann, 'Public Service Broadcasting, State Aid, and the Internet', n 95 above, 599.

[104] Judgment of the Court of First Instance (Fifth Chamber) of 22 October 2008, Joined Cases T–309/04, T–317/04, T–329/04, and T–336/04 *TV 2/Danmark A/S and Others v Commission of the European Communities*, nyr.

[105] This is the view of M Ridinger, 'The Public Service Remit and the New Media', (2009) 6 IRIS Plus 10.

Danish commercial broadcasters, SBS and Viasat, that, in the case of a public service broadcaster enjoying dual-funding, its remit can only cover non-profitable broadcasts, as otherwise it would be inevitably led to depress advertising prices in order to reduce the profits of the commercial operators. The CFI, in contrast, took the view that the public service broadcaster's ability to provide a wide range of programming and to seek to reach wide audiences descends directly from the Protocol and cannot be called into question by the fact that the public service broadcaster also collects advertising revenues.[106] Indeed, quoting the 2001 Broadcasting Communication, the CFI pointed out that one issue is the definition of the public service remit, quite another is the financing mechanism chosen to provide those services.[107] Then, so as to leave no uncertainties, the CFI expressly embraced a functional understanding of the remit by affirming that a service of general economic interest 'is defined, *ex hypothesi*, in relation to the general interest which it is designed to satisfy and not in relation to the means of ensuring its provision'.[108]

The ruling in *TV2*, moreover, arguably leaves no room for the 'distinctiveness' of the services provided by the public service broadcaster as a precondition for their inclusion in its remit. Viasat, indeed, sought to challenge the legality of the Commission's decision on the compatibility with the common market of the aids granted to TV2 on the assumption that the Commission failed to compare TV2's programme schedule with that of its commercial competitors. In the applicant's view, such a comparative assessment would have revealed that the public service broadcaster's programming was no different from that of Viasat or SBS. The CFI, in turn, harshly rebuked this line of reasoning which, in fact, would have made the definition of the remit dependent, through a comparative analysis of programming, on the range of programming offered by the commercial broadcasters. Conversely, the CFI took the view that Member States cannot be constrained by the activities of the commercial television channels when they define the remit of public service broadcasting.[109]

The *TV2* judgment, along with that in *SIC*[110] and the 2009 Broadcasting Communication,[111] provides persuasive authority for a 'qualitative definition' of the remit entrusting a given broadcaster with the obligation to provide a wide range of programming and a balanced and varied broadcasting offer. *S'il faut parler bien franc*, TV2's remit definition was, arguably, as vague as it could be: to provide as a public service 'through television, radio, Internet and the like, a wide range of programmes and services comprising news coverage, general information, education, art and entertainment'. Danish law also provided that '[TV2's broadcasting] range shall aim to provide quality, versatility and diversity'.

[106] Ibid, paras 106–107.
[107] Ibid, para 108.
[108] Ibid.
[109] Ibid, para 123.
[110] Judgment in Case T–442/03, *SIC v Commission*, n 79 above, para 201. See also para 211, where the CFI held that these qualitative criteria are 'the justification for the existence of broadcasting SGEIs in the national audiovisual sector' and that there was 'no reason for a widely defined broadcasting SGEI which sacrifices compliance with those qualitative requirements in order to adopt the conduct of a commercial operator'.
[111] Notably para 47 thereof.

The Commission, in its decision, had taken the view that '[a]lthough TV2's broadcasting obligation is of a qualitative nature and rather widely defined, . . . this wide definition of the operator's task [is] in line with the Broadcasting Communication'. The CFI, in turn, conceded that the definition chosen by the Danish authorities was 'broad since, being essentially qualitative, it le[ft] the broadcaster free to establish its own range of programmes', but determined, contrary to the applicant's contention, that it was 'perfectly clear and precise: to offer the entire Danish population varied television programming which aims to provide quality, versatility and diversity'.[112]

Whilst such a finding may prompt some to advocate the use, as it is common in WTO Appellate Body and Panel reports,[113] of dictionary definitions for such obscure terms as 'clear' and 'precise', others may rejoice upon learning that such a leeway in the definition of the remit reflects the editorial independence public service broadcasters enjoy from political authority in the choice of programmes, as per Article 11 of the EU Charter on Fundamental Rights and Article 10 ECHR.[114]

The 2009 Broadcasting Communication, apart from acknowledging the CFI rulings above, seems to introduce an additional requirement in affirming that a manifest error in the definition of the remit would occur 'where State aid is used to finance activities which do not bring *added value* in terms of serving the social, democratic and cultural needs of society'.[115] This condition is, albeit under a different guise, reiterated with reference to the use of state aids by public service broadcasters to provide premium audiovisual services over new distribution platforms. According to the Broadcasting Communication, the presence of a direct remuneration element does not *per se* take those services out of the public service remit, so long as they are addressing the democratic, social and cultural needs of the society and do not entail disproportionate effects on the market. The Commission, however, leaves this complex determination to Member States, which are called to carry out such an *ex ante* assessment as to whether significant new audiovisual services envisaged by public service broadcasters meet the requirements of the Amsterdam Protocol by way of an open public consultation.[116]

3. Conclusion

As acknowledged both in the 2001 and in the 2009 Broadcasting Communications, 'public service broadcasting, although having a clear economic relevance, is not comparable to a public service in any other economic sector'. Indeed, no other

[112] Ibid, para 117.

[113] See, eg, *Chile—Price Band System and Safeguard Measures Relating to Certain Agricultural Products* AB–2007–2 Report of the Appellate Body of 7 May 2007, para 29, footnote 49, where the Chilean Government relied on the definitions of 'liable' and 'contemplate' contained in WR Trumble and A Stevenson (eds), *Shorter Oxford English Dictionary*, Vol 1 (5th edn 2002), 499 and 1583.

[114] Ibid, para 118.

[115] 2009 Broadcasting Communication, para 49, emphasis added.

[116] Ibid, paras 84–85.

service 'has access to such a wide sector of the population, provides it with so much information and content, and by doing so conveys and influences both individual and public opinion'. In other words, public service broadcasting, whilst potentially falling in the scope of the Treaty provisions on free movement, competition, and state aids, is a public service like no other, is an exception to the exception.

This explains why the impact of Union law on public service broadcasting has chiefly been indirect. The AVMS Directive provides a clear example: it neither regulates nor mentions public service broadcasting, yet it had a significant impact on it by establishing a legal framework in which commercial broadcasters could thrive. That of the AVMS Directive and of the less-known TVWF Green Paper has been, on balance, the Commission's most courageous leap towards the liberalization of public service broadcasting, as it significantly contributed to the dusk of the age of broadcasting monopolies.

Ever since then, the EU legislature, and the Commission and the Courts alike, have shown a remarkable deference vis-à-vis those broadcasting organizations, most of which predate the accession to the EU of the Member State they are established in. Their joint bid for sporting events through the EBU Eurovision Scheme was exempted from competition law.[117] Likewise, their preferential or guaranteed access to broadcasting frequencies was never challenged.[118]

Where Union law is progressively gaining ground, public service broadcasting comes through unscathed. This is the case of broadcasting concessions: whilst the Commission and the European Courts are endeavouring to extend the application of the principles of transparency, non-discrimination, and mutual recognition beyond the scope of the Public Procurement Directives adopted by the European legislature, the CFI was ready to affirm that public service broadcasting must not be entrusted on the basis of competitive tendering.

The same holds true in the field of state aids, and more generally of services of general interest. Also in this case, the Commission and the European Courts are toiling to lay down the foundations of a Union legal order for public utilities which does not encroach on the prerogatives of Member States. Notions such as 'services of general interest', 'universal service', and 'public service obligations' are being outlined in the Commission's soft-law documents, underpinned by the economic concept of market failure and fleshed out by judgments such as *BUPA*. Yet, nothing of the foregoing applies to public service broadcasting, whose mission, in a functional perspective, can be broadly defined in qualitative terms and can even include clear-cut market activities (the premium on-demand contents), leaving it to 'open public consultations' at the national level to strike a balance between their 'added value' and their impact on the market.

[117] *Re the Application of the European Broadcasting Union* (93/403/EEC), 11 June 1993, [1995] 4 CMLR 56.

[118] See, however, the case law on 'must-carry' obligations imposed on private cable operators to the advantage of certain broadcasters, where the relevant legislation was found to be necessary and proportionate to pursue cultural objectives: Case C–250/06 *United Pan-Europe* [2007] ECR I–11135; Case C–336/07 *Kabel Deutschland Vertrieb und Service*, nyr.

From a legal perspective, all of this is made possible by recourse to an item of primary legislation, the Amsterdam Protocol, capable of exempting public service broadcasting from any rule of Union law as well as of aligning the interpretation and application thereof with the 'specificity' of the sector at issue. From a political perspective, it would be fair to say that, as far as broadcasting is concerned, Member States have played and will play a key role even to the detriment of full market integration—which is to be welcomed, so long as the Council of Europe's calls[119] for media pluralism and independence of public service broadcasters from political influence are taken seriously.

[119] See *inter alia* Parliamentary Assembly of the Council of Europe, Recommendation 1641 (2004) on Public service broadcasting.

7

If Only It Were So Simple: Public Health Services and EU Law

Tamara K Hervey[*]

1. Introduction

Public health services are both a potent symbol and an important test for the European Union and its legal order. Public health services symbolize—sometimes with almost 'iconic' status—historical European political settlements reflecting values of community, solidarity, substantive equality, and respect for human dignity; and a commitment to eradicate the worst effects of extreme poverty and to care collectively at state level for the weakest and most in need within a particular state. For at least as long as what is now the EU has been in existence, and in spite of apparently being in almost continual 'crisis', European public health services have, in essence, proved remarkably durable in supporting these values, and translating them into practical reality. However, across the EU, European models of public health service provision are now, to greater and lesser extents, in transition from their 1950s post-Fordist foundations, or from the legacies of communism. Public health service provision in Europe now needs to adapt itself meet the 21st-century challenges of economic downturn, public budgetary constraints, calls for greater efficiency and evidence-based healthcare. These changes need to be made within the constraints of the EU's legal order.

At the foundation of the EEC, public health services were conceived as totally distinct and separate from the areas of free trade and fair competition that the Treaty of Rome sought to establish. The creation of the internal market is a matter for EU decision making; social matters, such as public health services, were to be left within the scope of national sovereignty. In successive revisions of the Treaties, the governments of the Member States have restated this constitutional

* University of Sheffield, UK. I am grateful to Marise Cremona; my colleagues in Sheffield, especially Tawhida Ahmed; Annamaria La Chimia; the participants at the EUI summer school 2008, the conferences *Health Care and EU Law*, Nijmegen, October 2009 and *European Economic and Social Constitutionalism*, Leeds, September 2009; and my collaborators in E Mossialos, G Permanand, R Baeten, T Hervey (eds), *Health Systems Governance in Europe: the role of EU law and policy* (2010), especially Rita Baeten.

arrangement, with perhaps increasing shrillness.[1] The Court of Justice of the European Union (the Court) ostensibly confirms this legal position, stating frequently that 'the organisation and delivery of healthcare services is the responsibility of the Member States'.[2] Public health services, in the sense of the systemic structures for medical treatment and social care provided within national healthcare systems, are conceived as outside the scope of EU competence, and are therefore a matter for national law alone.[3]

Perhaps the separate spheres approach could be defended as legally accurate in the 1950s and 1960s, when EU internal market and competition law had yet to develop through the Court's jurisprudence,[4] and when there was very little EU-level legislation covering the products and services of healthcare.[5] But even then, and increasingly so now, as well as being important parts of national welfare systems, some healthcare goods (pharmaceuticals, medical devices) are traded and healthcare services (medical treatment, insurance) provided within markets, and using market models and structures (such as provision by a choice of competitors, payment according to what the market will bear) within and increasingly across the Member States of the EU. Admittedly, these markets are highly regulated.[6] But where goods and services are traded, there is scope for EU internal market and competition law to apply, at least in principle. The distinction between 'the economic' (constitutionally a matter for the EU) and 'the social' (constitutionally a matter for the Member States) has been shown to be increasingly untenable.[7]

It follows that the application of EU law to public health services is based on a more complex set of relationships than the Treaty on the Functioning of the European Union (TFEU) and Court suggest. Among the complexities, we might consider the following: first, increasingly, the health of a population has been recognized as an important economic indicator of human capacity.[8] If health is a

[1] Art 129 EC; Art 152(4) EC; Art 168(7) Treaty on the Functioning of the European Union (TFEU).

[2] See, eg, Case C–238/82 *Duphar* [1984] ECR 523, para 16; Cases 159 and 160/91 *Poucet and Pistre* [1993] ECR I–637, para 6; Case C–70/95 *Sodemare* [1997] ECR I–3395, para 27; Case C–120/95 *Decker* [1998] ECR I–1831, para 21; Case C–158/96 *Kohll* [1998] ECR I–1931, para 17; Case C–157/99 *Geraets-Smits and Peerbooms* [2001] ECR I–5473, para 44.

[3] Arts 4 and 5 TEU, Art 6 TFEU (ex Art 5 EC).

[4] Some of the significant decisions of the Court in the context of public health services include Case C–159/90 *Society for the Protection of Unborn Children Ireland v Grogan* [1991] ECR I–4685 confirming that health services fall within Art 49 EC; and the case law discussed in detail below, but of course the Court's general jurisprudence concerning the direct effect and supremacy of EU law is also crucial to this development; see, seminally, JHH Weiler, 'The Transformation of Europe' 100 Yale Law Journal (1991) 2403.

[5] Among the early legislation in this category is Directive 65/65/EEC on proprietary medicinal products OJ Sp Ed 1965–66 I, 24. See T Hervey and J McHale, *Health Law and the European Union* (2004), ch 8.

[6] See, eg, the regulation discussed in J McHale, M Fox, M Gunn, S Wilkinson, *Health Care Law* (2006); J Montgomery, *Health Care Law* (2002) (both UK); H Nys, *La Médicine et Le Droit* (1995) (Belgium); L Westerhäll, *Medical Law: An Introduction* (1994) (Sweden).

[7] B de Sousa Santos, *Toward a New Common Sense: Law, Science and Politics in the Paradigmatic Transition* (1995), 284.

[8] See, eg, David Byrne, Commissioner for Health and Consumer Protection, *Enabling Good Health for All: A reflection process for a new EU health strategy* (2004), 5, 7, 35. Economic growth relies upon

'factor of production' as well as a fundamental social right, how do public health services sit within the European constitutional settlement? Second, although, according to the Court, matters concerning the design of public healthcare systems are for the Member States, whereas the operation of public healthcare systems may be subject to internal market law,[9] of course, the distinction between design, organization, structure or essence, on the one hand, and everyday operation or exercise, on the other hand, is not a bright-line distinction. What is (and is not) permissible in terms of practical operation of a (healthcare) system has fundamental implications for the design or structure, or even the very essence, of that system. Third, the EU does have an explicit competence in the field of public health,[10] which is related to public healthcare services, not least in that preventative public health measures may reduce burdens on healthcare systems. Fourth, through its 'Open Method of Coordination' for social protection and social inclusion ('OMC social'),[11] the EU contributes to a 'steering' process, involving peer review of national policies against common objectives, some of which involve public

the good health of populations, as one of the factors of production (labour). At a micro level, the costs of an unhealthy labour force include the direct cost of sickness payments, but also the costs of replacement workers and lower productivity for the employer. At a macro level, a population can only increase its labour capacity if it is healthy enough to do so. The link between health and economic prosperity has been a theme underlying the World Health Organization's Annual Health Reports; see especially WHO, *Making A Difference* (1999), ch 1, which describes the consequences of improved human health for economic growth. See also DE Bloom and D Canning, 'Public Health: The Health and Wealth of Nations' (2000) 287 Science 1207:

> The positive correlation between health and income per capita is one of the best-known relations in international development. This correlation is commonly thought to reflect a causal link running from income to health... Recently however another intriguing possibility has emerged: that the health–income correlation is partly explained by a causal link running the other way—from health to income. Several mechanisms... could account for this relation. *Productivity.* Healthier populations have higher productivity.... *Education.* Healthier people who live longer have stronger incentives to invest in developing their skills.... *Investment in physical capital.* Improvements in longevity create a greater need for people to save for their retirement. Insofar as increased savings lead to increased investment, workers will have access to more capital and thus incomes will rise.... *'Demographic dividend'.* The transition from high to low rates of mortality and fertility has been dramatic and rapid in many developing countries in recent decades.... An initial surge in the numbers of young dependents gradually gives way to an increase in the proportion of the population that is of working age. As this happens, income per capita can rise dramatically....

[9] See V Hatzopoulos, 'Health Law and Policy: The Impact of the EU', in G de Búrca, *EU Law and the Welfare State* (2005) 112; V Hatzopoulous, '*Killing* National Health and Insurance Systems but *Healing* Patients? The European Market for Health Care Services after the Judgments of the ECJ in *Vanbraekel* and *Peerbooms*' (2002) 39 CML Rev 683. This echoes the Court's finding in Case C–438/05 *Viking* [2007] ECR I–779, para 40: 'in the areas which fall outside the scope of the Community's competence, the Member States are still free, in principle, to lay down the conditions governing the existence and exercise of the rights in question, the fact remains that, when exercising that competence, the Member States must nevertheless comply with Community law' (see, by analogy, in relation to social security, Case C–120/95 *Decker*, n 2 above, paras 22 and 23, and Case C–158/96 *Kohll*, n 2 above, paras 18 and 19; in relation to direct taxation, Case C–334/02 *Commission v France* [2004] ECR I–2229, para 21, and Case C–446/03 *Marks & Spencer* [2005] ECR I–10837, para 29).

[10] Art 168 TFEU (ex Art 152 EC).

[11] Commission Communication, 'A renewed commitment to social Europe: Reinforcing the Open Method of Coordination for Social Protection and Social Inclusion', COM (2008) 418 final.

healthcare service indicators.[12] All of these features of the EU's current legal order lead to the conclusion that the relationships between public health services and EU law are not simple.

This chapter explores those complex and unfolding relationships. It begins with a discussion of 'public health services' in the context of the EU's Member States in the 21st century. It then considers the current position of the relationships between EU law and public health services in two broad areas of EU law:[13] EU competition, state aids, and public procurement law; and EU law on free movement of the factors of production, focusing on the free movement of services.[14] For the purposes of this chapter, public procurement law is discussed alongside state aids law, rather than as part of free movement law, because of the close practical relationships between the application of the two regimes in this area. Throughout, the chapter seeks to illuminate how the structures of EU law affect its relationships with public health services. One important feature of these relationships is a move from the conceptualization of public health systems as holistic entities, towards the idea that states provide, or create the conditions for the provision of, a set of atomized public health services. Finally, the chapter brings together the strands, to illuminate the nature of those structures, and to discuss why they are problematic as a basis for the future development of both EU law and public health service provision within the EU and its Member States. I conclude by proposing some lines for a more promising development of EU law, to be explored in more detail in future research. To the extent that public health services are an example of welfare services more generally, my conclusions apply to the ongoing general debate about 'social Europe', and the relationship between internal market law and social welfare or solidarity.[15]

[12] See Commission Communication, 'Working together, working better: A new framework for the open coordination of social protection and inclusion policies in the European Union', COM (2005) 706 final; Social Protection Committee, 'Portfolio of Overarching Indicators and streamlined Social Inclusion, Pensions and Health Portfolios', Brussels 7 June 2006; Social Protection Committee, 'Portfolio of Overarching Indicators and streamlined Social Inclusion, Pensions and Health Portfolios', April 2008 update, Brussels, April 2008. See also Art 168(5) TFEU, which confirms that the EU has competence to carry out actions to coordinate health policies, and to adopt incentive measures designed to protect and improve human health.

[13] Vassilis Hatzopolous was one of the first scholars to recognize that an implication of the case law on free movement of patients is the application of EU competition, state aids, and public procurement law to public health services; see V Hatzopoulos, '*Killing* National Health and Insurance Systems but *Healing* Patients: The European Market for Health Care Services after the Judgments of the ECJ in *Vanbraekel* and *Peerbooms*' (2002) 39 CML Rev 683.

[14] Space precludes discussion of the developing body of EU public health law. For discussion of this see, eg, A Gilmore, T Hervey, and M McKee, 'Public Health Policies', in E Mossialos, G Permanand, R Baeten, and T Hervey (eds), *Health Systems Governance in Europe: the role of EU law and policy* (2010); T Hervey and J McHale, *Health Law and the European Union*, n 5 above, ch 9; E Randall, *The European Union and Health Policy* (2001).

[15] See, seminally, F Scharpf, 'The European Social Model: Coping with the Challenges of Diversity' (2002) 40 Journal of Common Market Studies 645; more recently F Scharpf, 'Legitimacy in the Multilevel European Polity' FPIfG Working Paper 09/1, available at: <http://www.mpifg.de/publications/workingpapers>; C Joerges, 'European Economic Law, the Nation-State and the Maastricht Treaty' in R Dehousse (ed), *Europe after Maastricht: An Ever Closer Union* (1994); more recently, C Joerges and Rödl, 'On the "Social Deficit" of the European Integration Project and its Perpetuation through the ECJ judgments in *Viking* and *Laval*' RECON Online Working Paper 2008/06, available at: <http://www.reconproject.eu/projectweb/portalproject/RECONWorkingPapers.html>; C Offe,

2. Public Health Services in the Member States of the EU

The phrase 'public health services' can be read in two ways. Public health services are services concerning the health of populations.[16] Public health[17] covers matters such as communicable diseases; managing risks to health in areas such as sanitation, air and water quality and food safety; preventative healthcare measures, such as vaccinations or screening; health education and the promotion of good health in areas such as diet and other lifestyle choices. All the Member States of the EU pursue public health policies, and have measures of public health law to support them.[18] In accordance with the Member States' obligations under the Treaty on European Union,[19] these laws and policies must comply with measures of EU law. The EU has an explicit competence in public health, and has adopted numerous measures of public health law.[20]

The focus of this chapter is the alternative reading of the phrase. Public health services means the health services and medical treatments that are offered to the public, made available through a systemic arrangement of various public and quasi-public relationships, rather than private contracts. Every Member State of the EU has a system that makes such provision for its citizens and indeed for others resident within its borders. At least arguably, each Member State of the EU is under an obligation in international law to provide such health services, in order to protect and secure the 'right to health' within its territory.[21]

Funding for public health services is usually thought of in terms of a binary model: either a 'social insurance' 'Bismarckian' model or a taxation-based 'Beveridgean' national health system. Although it is difficult to categorize precisely, just under one half of the current Member States of the EU fall into the latter type, and just over one half into the former.[22] On a social insurance model, healthcare is paid

'The European Model of "Social" Capitalism: Can it Survive European Integration?' (2003) 11 Journal of Political Philosophy, 437; L Moreno and B Palier, 'The Europeanisation of Welfare: Paradigm Shifts and Social Policy Reforms' in P Taylor-Gooby (ed), *Ideas and Welfare State Reform in Western Europe* (2005); G Davies, 'The process and side-effects of harmonisation of European welfare states', Jean Monnet Working Paper, No 02/06, 1–64, available at: <http://centers.law.nyu.edu/jeanmonnet/papers/06/060201.pdf>.

16 See LJ Donaldson and RJ Donaldson, *Essential Public Health* (2003).

17 In 1920, CEA Winslow, Yale's first Chairman of Public Health, defined public health as 'the science and art of preventing disease, prolonging life and promoting health through the organized efforts and informed choices of society, organizations, public and private, communities and individuals'. CEA Winslow, 'The untilled field of public health' (1920) 2 Modern Medicine 183.

18 For a discussion of the relevant UK law, see J Montgomery, *Health Care Law* (2003), ch 2.

19 Art 4(3) TEU (ex Art 10 EC).

20 Eg, measures on blood and human organ safety adopted under now Article 168 TFEU; many of the measures of the common agricultural policy concern phytosanitary and veterinary health; the body of EU food law concerns public health. For further discussion, see Hervey and McHale, n 5 above, ch 9.

21 This obligation arises from Council of Europe Treaties, in particular the European Social Charter and Revised European Social Charter, not from membership of the EU. For further discussion, B Toebes, *The Right to Health as a Human Right in International Law* (1999).

22 M Flear, *Does the Free Movement of Persons Cause Change in Healthcare Systems?* Unpublished PhD thesis, University of Nottingham, Nottingham, UK, 2006; V Hatzopoulos, in G de Búrca (ed)

for by compulsory insurance. In the first instance, people are insured by reference to their membership of a professional group or employment sector, industry, organization, or company. Sickness insurance funds (with manifestations in law as either public or private bodies) hold contributions from both the employer and the employee. Those who are not employed are covered by schemes that 'fill the gaps'. The sickness insurance funds contract with hospitals, clinics, and other healthcare providers, who again may be public or private bodies. The Beveridge model starts from citizenship, rather than economic activity. Everyone is covered, because of their citizenship (or presence in the national territory[23]). The system is financed by the state, through state taxes. Healthcare facilities such as hospitals and clinics are generally speaking public institutions.

Like all models, Bismarck and Beveridge form ideal types, not representations of reality. No individual national public healthcare system conforms directly to either of the ideal types. Moreover, the ideal types refer to the foundation of European social welfare systems,[24] rather than the way that European welfare settlements are currently developing. All the Member States currently face challenges to their healthcare systems. These include the health and long-term care needs of older populations, such as the recent prevalence of chronic disease over infectious disease; changing patient expectations, such as the demand for access to new health technologies; and a situation of 'permanent welfare austerity',[25] as employment patterns, and thus contributions to welfare institutions, are changing, and economic and monetary union requires budgetary constraints, while at the same time a healthy population is seen as a key component of a competitive economy.[26] In response to these challenges, all the EU Member States use different combinations of policy measures in their public healthcare systems, using features of the ideal types to different extents. In the case of several Member States, this policy mix includes experimenting with elements of market-based models for some public healthcare delivery. National public healthcare systems differ in terms of the funding mix,

(2005), n 9 above; W Palm, J Nickless, H Lewalle, and A Coheur, *Implications of Recent Jurisprudence on the Coordination of Health Care Protection Systems* (2000); J Marreé and PP Groenewegen, *Back to Bismarck: Eastern European Health Care Systems in Transition* (1997); Z Ferge, 'Welfare and 'Ill-fare' Systems in Central and Eastern Europe' in R Sykes, B Palier, and PM Prior (eds), *Globalization and European Welfare States: Challenges and Change* (2001), 127–52; WHO, EC (World Health Organization, European Commission), *Health Status Overview for Countries of Central and Eastern Europe that are Candidates for Accession to the European Union* (2002).

[23] As in the case of the National Health Service in the UK.

[24] P Baldwin, *The Politics of Social Solidarity: Class Bases of the European Welfare State 1875–1975* (1990).

[25] P Pierson, 'Coping with Permanent Austerity: Welfare State Restructuring in Affluent Democracies' in P Pierson (ed), *The New Politics of the Welfare State* (2001).

[26] M Rhodes and Y Mény, 'Europe's Social Contract Under Stress' in M Rhodes and Y Mény (eds), *The Future of European Welfare* (1998); R Freeman and M Moran, 'Reforming Health Care in Europe' (2000) 23(2) Western European Politics 35; M Kleinman, *A European Welfare State? EU Social Policy in Context* (2001); H Schwartz, 'Round up the Usual Suspects!: Globalization, Domestic Politics, and Welfare State Change' in P Pierson (ed), *The New Politics of the Welfare State* (2001); T Marmor, R Freeman, and K Okma, 'Comparative Perspectives and Policy Learning in the World of Health Care' (2005) 17 Journal of Comparative Policy Analysis 1, 2–3; P Pestieau, *The Welfare State in the European Union: Economic and Social Perspectives* (2006).

logistics of payment for healthcare and medical treatment, locus of administration, legal status of healthcare institutions and providers, organization of access to healthcare, and coverage of medical treatments.

Healthcare funding in the EU is mainly provided through progressive taxation or income-related social contributions or after-premium financial compensation, risk pooling and risk selection prohibition, and adequate risk adjustment across insurers and regions, or a combination of the two. Every national public healthcare system within the EU relies on taxation to some extent; equally all rely on insurance (including private insurance) to some extent. Private funding, including co-payments for some public healthcare services, also plays a role in all systems. Healthcare is paid for either under a refund/reimbursement system or under a benefits-in-kind system. Under a reimbursement system, patients choose their healthcare provider (sometimes from a closed list), and then the sickness fund repays the expense.[27] Under a benefits-in-kind system, healthcare and treatment are free for the patient at the point of receipt.[28]

Some Member States administer their public healthcare system at national or central level. Others organize the administration of public healthcare at sub-national levels.[29] Healthcare institutions, such as hospitals, clinics, and sickness funds, and healthcare providers, including medical professionals across a wide range of disciplines, have different relationships to the state, ranging from those governed by private law relationships to state ownership or employment by the state. Healthcare systems employ different gate-keeping mechanisms concerning access to secondary and especially tertiary healthcare.[30] Some use a system of referral by general practitioner at the primary level; other systems involve more choice for the patient or consumer. Significant differences between public healthcare systems of the Member States also include, for instance, what medical treatment and long-term social care patients are entitled to under what circumstances in each state, or region; where medical treatments are provided (hospital, clinic, or outpatient treatment); and who provides a particular medical treatment (specialist practitioner, general practitioner, nurse, health visitor).[31]

[27] Broadly speaking, this is the case, for instance, in France, Belgium, and Luxembourg.

[28] Broadly speaking, this is the case in Beveridgean systems, and in some sickness insurance systems, such as Austria and Germany.

[29] For instance, Ireland has a centralized national health service; Denmark, Sweden, Finland have more decentralized national health services.

[30] Traditionally, there are three levels of healthcare: primary, secondary and tertiary. Primary is at local level, administered through family doctors and general practitioners. Secondary is at municipal level (or area for rural coverage), provided by small hospitals, clinics, and specialized practitioners, such as health visitors and midwives. Tertiary is at regional or even national level (depending on the size of the state, and how centralized the system is). Healthcare is provided through large hospitals, specialized hospitals, and university clinics.

[31] Rich data on the Member States' public healthcare systems is available in the documentation for the healthcare OMC, launched in October 2004, and in the healthcare strands of the OMC on social protection and social inclusion, within which the healthcare OMC was included from 2006. The 2005 National Preliminary Reports of the Member States under OMC-health; the 2006–08 National Action Plans under OMC-health; and the 2008–2010 National Strategy Reports on Social Protection and Social Inclusion can all be found at <http://ec.europa.eu/employment_social/spsi/strategy_reports_en.htm> (accessed 2 March 2009). There is also rich data in the European Observatory on Health Care Systems, *Health Care Systems in Transition* studies (1999), available at:

Notwithstanding these significant differences, all the Member States of the EU converge on one ideational point. All the public healthcare systems of the Member States of the EU operate on the principle of universal access to necessary healthcare, irrespective of the ability of the patient to pay. In this respect, all Member States uphold the internationally recognized 'right to health'. As part of their national welfare systems,[32] all their public healthcare systems operate on the basis of solidarity.

Solidarity is a concept found within both social democratic and Christian democratic traditions of European politics, as well as in Roman Catholic social teaching and Protestant ethics, all of which underpin the development of the welfare state in European countries.[33] Stjernø has defined solidarity as 'the preparedness to share resources by personal contribution to those in struggle or in need and through taxation and redistribution organised by the state'.[34] All the public healthcare systems of the Member States of the EU, as part of their welfare systems, embody solidarity in the sense of being based on taxation and redistribution (through social insurance) organized by the state. In the context of healthcare systems,[35] solidarity implies universal coverage, in the sense that everyone is included in the system; mandatory affiliation in the sense that no one may opt out of the system; and mandatory acceptance, in the sense that sickness insurance funds or national health systems may not exclude some categories of persons. In terms of the funding of systems, solidarity implies income-related contributions, independent of the extent to which the contributing patient uses or will use the system. Solidarity consequently implies cross-subsidization between healthy and unhealthy, rich and poor, and also across different age groups.[36] Solidarity also implies that, as coverage is based on the medical needs of the patient, all patients are treated equally, regardless of their contributions to the system.

<http://www.euro.who.int/observatory/Hits/TopPage>. For further discussion of the differences between the public healthcare systems of the Member States of the EU, see, eg, M McKee, E Mossialos, and R Baeten, *The Impact of EU Law on Health Care Systems* (2002); E Mossialos and M McKee, *EU Law and the Social Character of Health Care* (2002); V Hatzopoulos in G de Búrca (ed) (2005), n 9 above; M Steffen (ed), *Health Governance in Europe: Issues, Challenges and Theories* (2005).

[32] On the relationships between welfare systems and social policy and healthcare, see V Hatzopoulos, in G de Búrca (ed), 2005, n 9 above.

[33] See S Stjernø, *Solidarity in Europe* (2005); G Esping-Andersen, *The Three Worlds of Welfare Capitalism* (1990); P Baldwin, *The Politics of Social Solidarity: Class Bases of the European Welfare State 1875–1975* (1990).

[34] Ibid, 2. On the roles of 'solidarity' in EU law see M Ross, 'The Value of Solidarity in European Public Services Law' in M Krajewski, U Neergaard, and J Van de Gronden (eds), *The Changing Legal Framework for Services of General Interest in Europe* (2009); M Ross, 'Promoting Solidarity: From Public Services to a European Model of Competition' (2007) 44 CML Rev 1057; N Boeger, 'Solidarity and EC competition law' (2007) 32 ELR 319.

[35] See W Palm, 'Voluntary Health Insurance and EU Insurance Directives: Between Solidarity and the Market' in M McKee et al (eds), *The Impact of EU Law on Health Care Systems* (2002), 196–7; V Hatzopoulos, in de Búrca (ed), n 9 above, 118.

[36] Given that both poverty and old age are significant indicating factors for ill health see, eg, N Daniels, *Just Health: Meeting Health Needs Fairly* (2008), especially ch 13; J Sachs, *The End of Poverty* (2005), especially chs 1, 12, 13.

These solidarity features of national healthcare systems and health insurance systems in the Member States underpin their public nature. They are not simply organized on the basis of private activity within (regulated) markets (although they include such activity);[37] they also involve public institutions—such as public hospitals—taxation, and mandatory social insurance. The solidarity features also underpin the national nature of national healthcare systems.[38] In the absence of EU-level redistributional competences, healthcare within Europe is systemically organized at national, regional, and local levels, with cross-subsidization and redistribution of resources based on national solidarity, focused on shared social responsibility for the well-being of one's co-citizens within each Member State. Within Europe, healthcare, in common with other welfare entitlements, is not based on pan-European solidarity. This is one of the reasons that application of EU law can be problematic for public health services. Free movement law presumes that openness of markets across the EU will bring benefits: European public health services assume systems that are closed to those outside that particular state.

But notwithstanding the universal access principle, and the underlying concept of solidarity, it is important to remain aware of the significant differences between the public healthcare systems of the Member States. The relationship between EU law and public healthcare systems differs, depending upon the specific details of the system at issue. This chapter provides an overview of the areas of EU law that have had or are likely to have an effect upon or apply to public healthcare systems. However, without a detailed knowledge of the specific elements of a specific healthcare system, it is not possible to predict in the abstract the effect of EU law on the ground in a particular Member State. Generalizations about such effect should be treated with caution. They are defensible only at the systemic level, which is the subject of this chapter. With that proviso in mind, the chapter now turns to consider the relationships between public health services and EU competition, state aids, and public procurement law.

3. Competition, State Aids, and Public Procurement Law

A. EU Competition Law

EU competition law applies to 'undertakings', and prohibits 'agreements, concerted practices' (essentially cartels) 'which have as their object or effect the prevention, restriction or distortion of competition within the common market'[39] and 'abuse of dominant position within the common market or in a substantial part of it'

[37] Indeed solidarity may be seen as rationale or justification for regulation; see T Prosser, 'Regulation and Social Solidarity' (2006) 33 Journal of Law and Society 364.

[38] See G Davies, 'The process and side-effects of harmonisation of European welfare states', Jean Monnet Working Paper, No 02/06, 11–12.

[39] Art 101(1) TFEU (ex Art 81(1) EC). An exemption is available under Art 101(3) TFEU (ex Art 81(3) EC).

(essentially monopolies).[40] A special exemption applies to 'public undertakings and undertakings to which Member States grant special or exclusive rights'.[41] If such undertakings are 'entrusted with the operation of services of general economic interest', they are only subject to the Treaty rules, including Articles 101 and 102 TFEU (ex Articles 81 and 82 EC), 'insofar as the application of such rules does not obstruct the performance, in law or in fact, of the particular tasks assigned to them'.[42] All these matters have been developed through a significant body of case law of the Court of Justice of the European Union, and also Commission Decisions and soft law guidance.[43] Since 2004, the system of enforcement of EU competition law has been decentralized, so that national competition authorities are now the primary means of enforcement.[44]

As noted above, public healthcare systems in the Member States of the EU have been developed on the basis of principles of solidarity. Solidarity implies a fundamentally different perspective to that of competition law. For instance, providing healthcare on a basis of equal access according to medical need may be achieved by restricting the power of individual consumers to buy healthcare services on a market in accordance with their ability to pay. A competitive market approach allocates goods and services in society in accordance with willingness to pay for those goods or services, to encourage efficient production of goods or provision of services at the lowest possible cost. It also encourages consumer choice, through ensuring open access to a market of competing suppliers. Nothing in EU law prevents Member States from organizing their public healthcare systems on the basis of solidarity. However, if a Member State chooses to bring 'market elements' into its healthcare system, then in principle EU competition law will apply.[45] In response to the various challenges noted above, several of the Member States have been experimenting with 'market models' within their public healthcare provision, to increase efficiency and to realign the balance between responsibility of the family, the state, and the market for healthcare.[46]

Whether EU competition law prohibits an element, practice or provision within a public healthcare system depends upon three stages of legal analysis. First, is the body responsible an 'undertaking'? EU competition law applies only to undertakings, so this first stage of analysis operates as a filter to remove many practices or provisions of public healthcare systems from the scope of EU competition law.

[40] Art 102 TFEU (ex Art 82 EC).

[41] Art 106 TFEU (ex Art 86 EC).

[42] Art 106(2) TFEU (ex Art 86(2) EC).

[43] See, for a detailed discussion, D Goyder, J Goyder, and A Albors-Llorens, *Goyder's EC Competition Law* (2009); R Whish, *Competition Law* (2008); A Jones and B Sufrin, *EC Competition Law* (2007); G Monti, *EC Competition Law* (2007).

[44] Council Regulation 1/2003/EC on the implementation of the rules on competition laid down in Arts 81 and 82 of the EC Treaty, OJ [2003] L 1/1.

[45] See T Prosser, 'EU Competition Law and Public Services' in E Mossialos et al (eds) (2010), n 14 above; T Prosser, *The limits of competition law: markets and public services* (2005).

[46] This is particularly the case for three 'front-runner' Member States: Germany, Netherlands, and the UK; also to some extent Hungary. See T Hervey, 'The European Union's Governance of Health Care and the Welfare Modernization Agenda' (2008) 2 Regulation and Governance 103.

Second, is a 'service of general economic interest' involved? If so, an exemption from the basic Treaty rules may be engaged. Third, is the restriction on competition proportionate? Even if the exemption from Treaty rules is *prima facie* engaged, there may be a legitimate reason to justify departure from those rules. This exemption, in common with many exceptions to basic EU law norms, is subject to a proportionality test. Part of the difficulty in determining how EU competition law could apply to bodies or practices within public healthcare systems is that the relevant principles of EU competition law have mainly been developed in the context of case law concerning other services of general economic interest,[47] and there are relatively few Court decisions concerning public healthcare systems. This is partly because it was assumed for a long time that EU law did not apply to public health systems, although, as we will see, this assumption is increasingly problematic.

1. Is the Relevant Body an 'Undertaking'?

Faced with the question as to whether a public healthcare provider, or a body which pays for public healthcare (for example, a sickness fund under a social insurance system) is an 'undertaking' in the sense of EU competition law, a court or national competition authority must consider the following. The legal test for an 'undertaking' is whether the body is engaged in an 'economic activity', regardless of the legal status of the body or the manner in which its activities are financed.[48] An 'economic activity' is the offering of goods and services in a market.[49] A body may be an undertaking for some activities but not for others, in particular not where the body exercises official authority.[50] The Commission takes the view that 'matters . . . such as compulsory basic social security schemes' are not carried out by undertakings.[51] Whether an activity is 'economic' for these purposes depends on whether it is organized on the basis of 'social solidarity'.[52] These rules have been

[47] Particularly the 'classic' services of general economic interest, such as transport and communications.

[48] Case C–41/90 *Höfner and Elser* [1991] ECR I–1979; Cases C–180/98-C–184/98 *Pavlov v Stichting Pensioenfonds Medische Specialisten* [2000] ECR I–6451, para 75.

[49] Case 118/85 *Commission v Italy* [1987] ECR 2599, para 7; Case C–35/96 *Commission v Italy* [1998] ECR I–3851, para 36; Cases C–180/98 to C–184/98 *Pavlov v Stichting Pensioenfonds Medische Specialisten* [2000] ECR I–6451, para 75; Case 475/99 *Ambulanz Glöckner v Landkreis Südwestpfalz* [2001] ECR I–8089, para 19. See O Odudu, *The Boundaries of EC Competition Law* (2006), 26–45.

[50] Case 118/85 *Commission v Italy* [1987] ECR 2599, para 7.

[51] *Green Paper on Services of General Interest* COM (2003) 270 final, para 45; Prosser, in Mossialos et al (eds) (2010), n 45 above. This view is underpinned by the Court's rulings in Case C–364/92 *Eurocontrol* [1994] ECR I–43 (air traffic regulation); Case C–343/95 *Calì* [1997] EC I–1588 (pollution surveillance).

[52] Cases C–159 and 160/91 *Poucet and Pistre* [1993] ECR I–637 (compulsory social security scheme not an 'undertaking'); Case C–218/00 *INAIL* [2002] ECR I–691 (compulsory worker compensation scheme not an 'undertaking'); Cases C–264/01, C–306/01, C–355/01 *AOK Bundesverband* [2004] ECR I–2493 (sickness insurance funds not 'undertakings'); contrast Case C–244/94 *FFSA*, [1995] ECR I–4019 (voluntary supplementary pension insurance scheme was an 'undertaking'); Case C–67/96 *Albany International* [1999] ECR I–5751, Case C–115/97 *Brentjens* [1999] ECR I–6025, Case C–219/97 *Bokken* [1999] ECR I–6121, Cases C–180/98 to C–184/98 *Pavlov* [2000]

applied in the public healthcare sector in two relatively recent cases: *BetterCare Ltd v Director of Fair Trading*[53] and *FENIN*,[54] which illustrate their operation.

In the *BetterCare* case, the UK Competition Appeal Tribunal was asked to decide whether the Director General of Fair Trading, who administers the Competition Act 1998, which implements EU competition law in the UK, had correctly decided that a local authority was not acting as an undertaking when it purchased care services. The local authority concerned, the North and West Belfast Health and Social Services Trust, had purchased nursing and social care services, in Better-Care's residential homes, under a standard contract. The local authority itself also provided such residential nursing and social care services, in the same market. In BetterCare's view, the contract for the care services offered unreasonably low prices and unfair contract terms. BetterCare therefore complained to the Director General of Fair Trading, on the grounds that the contract breached the UK Competition Act, in particular that part of the Act that implements Article 82 EC (now Article 102 TFEU),[55] concerning abuse of a dominant position. The Director General of Fair Trading found that the local authority was not acting as an 'undertaking', and therefore did not fall within the Act. BetterCare challenged that decision.

The Competition Appeal Tribunal found that the local authority *was* acting as an 'undertaking'. Approaching the case in the manner that, in their view, the Court of Justice of the European Union would approach it, and seeking a decision consistent with the Court's case law,[56] the Tribunal rejected the arguments of the Director General of Fair Trading. These were to the effect that the activity concerned was only the purchase of nursing and residential care for elderly people who lack the means of their own to pay. This was, in the Director General of Fair Trading's view, an 'exercise of official authority', the discharging of the local authority's statutory duty to provide social care, not an economic act. It was irrelevant that the local authority also provided nursing and residential care; in doing so it was also discharging its statutory duty and in no way competing with BetterCare in an economic market. The local authority would be an undertaking, according to the Director General of Fair Trading, when providing residential care services to residents who could fund the full cost of their care, but not when providing those services to residents who cannot afford them, which is an act of 'social solidarity'.

ECR I–6451 (pension fund with optional membership, capitalization, and benefits in proportion with contributions was an 'undertaking'); Case C–475/99 *Ambulanz Glöckner v Landkreis Südwestpfalz* [2001] ECR 8089 (medical aid organization providing ambulance services was an 'undertaking').

[53] [2002] CAT 7. For other examples of national competition authorities applying the Court's jurisprudence on this subject see, eg, JW Van de Gronden, 'Purchasing Care: Economic Activity or Service of General (Economic) Interest?' (2004) 25(2) ECLR, 87, in particular at 90 (Germany); Decision of the Spanish National Anti-Trust Tribunal, 29 January 1997, *Cruz Roja Española* (Expte R 179/96); *Kilpailuvirasto*, 17 March 2000, dnro 343/61/1997 (Finland); Decision No 358 of the competition authority of 12 October 1994 in *FDB v Southern Health Board* (Ireland); and the examples in J Lear, E Mossialos, and B Karl, 'EU Competition Law and Health Policy', in E Mossialos, G Permanand, R Baeten, and T Hervey (eds), n 14 above.

[54] Case C–205/03 P [2006] ECR I–6295.

[55] UK Competition Act 1998, s 18.

[56] [2002] CAT 7, paras 31–2.

The Tribunal agreed that some acts of the local authority, such as for instance refusing to register a home as licensed to contract with the authority to provide residential care, would be an exercise of official authority, not economic acts.[57] Distinguishing *Eurocontrol*[58] and *Cali*,[59] the Tribunal found that a public body (here a local authority) empowered to provide residential and nursing care engages in 'economic' activity when it contracts out the provision of such care to the private sector. The establishment of the North and West Belfast Health and Social Services Trust, like its counterparts, the NHS trusts in Great Britain, had the objective of facilitating efficient management and a more market-orientated approach within the public national healthcare system. The system of contracting out of residential care was supposed to produce a more competitive outcome with a wider choice for patients through competition between providers. Providers of residential care, be they private or voluntary homes, or the local authority itself, do so on the basis that they will recover their costs from the residents, or a proportion of the cost that the patient can afford, under the national statutory regime. When the local authority acquired places in BetterCare's residential care homes on this basis, it was entering into contracts for services in a market. The prohibition on 'abuse of a dominant position' applies to unfair purchase prices or unfair trading conditions imposed by a dominant buyer, just as it does to unfair purchase prices imposed by a dominant seller. Likewise, the potential abuse of applying dissimilar conditions to equivalent transactions with other trading parties, is not limited to sellers, but may equally apply to buyers. Moreover, the Tribunal found that the local authority was also active as a seller of services on the relevant market.[60] The transactions on this market were 'economic activities' carried out on a commercial basis: indeed the Tribunal found that 'the supply of residential care or nursing services by what appear to be some thousands of independent providers to NHS trusts and local authorities all over the United Kingdom is in a real sense 'big business'.[61] It was not relevant that the activities of providing residential care were (largely) funded by taxation. Merely being entrusted with a public interest task (such as providing residential care to the elderly) does not prevent a body from being an 'undertaking'. Nor does the mere fact of providing social care to the elderly, many of whom cannot afford to pay for the care themselves, make the activity one of 'social solidarity' in the sense of the case law of the Court. An 'economic' activity does not have to be a 'for-profit' activity, and the Court has been very clear about that principle in its case law.[62] The activities of the local authority had both a 'social

[57] [2002] CAT 7, paras 168–71.

[58] Case C–364/92 *SAT Fluggesellschaft v Eurocontrol* [1994] ECR I–43. In a later case involving Eurocontrol, Case T–155/04 [2006] ECR II–479, 7, the Court of First Instance took a different approach, but the European Court of Justice (Case C–113/07 P, [2009] ECR I–26 March 2009) has since ruled that the CFI erred in finding that Eurocontrol's activity was an 'economic' activity, see para 80.

[59] Case C–343/95, *Cali & Figli v Servizi Ecologici Porto di Genova* [1997] ECR I–1547.

[60] [2002] CAT 7, paras 200–1.

[61] [2002] CAT 7, para 199.

[62] [2002] CAT 7, para 249: 'it is clear from the judgments of the court and decisions of the European Commission that neither the aim of "making profits", nor the achievement of that aim, is an

dimension' and a 'business dimension'. 'Solidarity', in the sense of cases such as those involving compulsory social security schemes, was not present here. Rather the only 'solidarity' present here was in the very general sense that public funds are available to support elderly persons in need of care. This is not 'solidarity' between the local authority and its independent providers, such as BetterCare, and thus did not deprive the contractual relationships between those parties of their commercial nature.

In its reasoning, the UK Competition Appeal Tribunal interprets the Court's case law[63] as establishing that:

> there is a sharp distinction between activities which are to be classified as 'economic' in character, and those where the state 'acts in the exercise of official authority':... The latter activities are outside the scope of the competition rules.

Likewise acting within a competitive market and acting in the context of social solidarity are sharply distinguished in the structure of the Tribunal's reasoning, and indeed in the case law of the Court upon which it relies.

This sharp distinction is also found in *FENIN*,[64] concerning an association of undertakings (Federación Española de Empresas de Tecnología Sanitaria) which market the medical goods and equipment used in both public and private Spanish hospitals. FENIN complained to the Commission that the 26 bodies which run the Spanish national health service were abusing a dominant position in the sense of Article 82 EC (now Article 102 TFEU). The abuse included systematically taking an average of 300 days to pay debts to its members, even though they settled debts to other suppliers much more quickly—a discriminatory practice which was feasible because of their dominant position in the Spanish market for medical goods and equipment. The Commission rejected the complaint, on the basis that the bodies concerned were not acting as 'undertakings' when they ran the public healthcare service. This was because the purchasing activities of the Spanish national health service could not be separated from their activities in providing the public service of healthcare to the Spanish people. FENIN challenged this decision under Article 230 EC (now Article 263 TFEU).

The Court of First Instance[65] held that FENIN was not an 'undertaking'. Its reasoning was thus: it is the nature of the activity that matters, not the nature of the

essential ingredient to the concept of "an undertaking"': see, eg, Film Purchases by German television stations (OJ 1989 L 284/36); *FFSA*, n 52 above, para 21 of the judgment; and *Pavlov*, n 48 above, para 117 of the judgment. 'In addition, in *Höfner & Elser*, the Bundesanstalt, which was held to be an undertaking, did not make profits, and provided its services for free. In *Ambulanz Glöckner*, medical aid organizations, such as the German Red Cross, which ran the public ambulance service, were non-profit making, but were none the less held to be undertakings. In our view, the central point is again to be found at para 21 of the judgment in *FFSA*, n 52 above, namely that if the activities in question are capable of generating the effects which the competition rules are designed to prevent, the fact that the activities are not profit-making is neither here nor there.'

[63] In particular Case C–343/95 *Calì* [1997] ECR I–1547, para 16.

[64] [2006] ECR I–6295.

[65] Case T–319/99 *FENIN* [2003] ECR III–357. Now the 'General Court'.

body itself.[66] The activity consisting in offering goods and services on a given market is the characteristic feature of an 'economic activity', not the business of purchasing as such. The nature of the purchasing activity must be determined according to whether or not the subsequent use of the goods amounts to an 'economic activity'.[67] Here, the organization purchased goods not to offer them for sale as part of an economic activity, but for a different activity, providing healthcare within the Spanish national healthcare system—one of purely public service.

On appeal, the Court agreed:

> The Court of First Instance rightly deduced . . . that there is no need to dissociate the activity of purchasing goods from the subsequent use to which they are put in order to determine the nature of that purchasing activity, and that the nature of the purchasing activity must be determined according to whether or not the subsequent use of the purchased goods amounts to an economic activity.[68]

When the body concerned purchased medical goods and equipment from FENIN's members, this activity was not an 'economic activity' separate from the subsequent use to which those goods purchased were put, that is, the provision of services in the public healthcare system.[69]

BetterCare and *FENIN* can be distinguished on the basis that in *BetterCare* the local authority, as well as acting as a buyer of services, was also a supplier of services on the same market as BetterCare, whereas in *FENIN* the bodies running the Spanish national health service were only purchasing goods, not acting as suppliers of goods in the same market at the same time.[70] However, the reasoning of the UK Competition Appeal Tribunal in *BetterCare* does not rely on this distinction. Rather, the Tribunal found that the prohibition on 'abuse of a dominant position' applies not only to dominant sellers within a market, but also to dominant buyers. In this respect, therefore, the *BetterCare* case must be regarded as having been overruled by the later *FENIN* case.[71] The question of whether the provision of healthcare services by the Spanish national health service (the use to which the medical goods and equipment were put) could *itself* be an 'economic activity' was not put before the Court in *FENIN*. It was dealt with by the Advocate General,

[66] Para 35. [67] Para 36. [68] Para 26.

[69] Interestingly, Hatzopoulos, in Mossialos et al (eds) (2010), n 14 above, notes that there may be some inconsistencies in the application of this legal test by national competition authorities. The Polish Office for Competition and Consumer Protection, in a decision of March 2007, censured the National Health Fund, whose task is to ensure health services to insured persons (a traditional public authority task), for abusing its dominant position by fixing below-cost contracting prices for dentists.

[70] Relying on this distinction, the Office of Fair Trading closed cases alleging infringements of competition law concerning public bodies that were only engaged in purchasing in a particular market and not engaged in the direct provisions of goods and services in that market, Policy Note 1/2004, *The Competition Act 1998 and Public Bodies*. See T Prosser in Mossialos et al (eds) (2010), n 14 above.

[71] When the Office of Fair Trading retook the decision that had been overturned by the Competition Appeal Tribunal, it found that the local authority had not breached competition law, as it was not responsible for setting the prices paid to independent care homes. Rather, prices were set by the health board and Northern Ireland Government department. As they did not offer goods or services in a market when doing so, but instead allocated public funds in order to discharge social functions, they did not act as 'undertakings'. See T Prosser in Mossialos et al (eds) (2010), n 70 above, and N Boeger and T Prosser, 'The United Kingdom' in M Krajewski et al (eds), n 34 above, 367.

who reasoned, by reference to the case law on the free movement of services, that the act of providing free-at-the-point-of-receipt healthcare could be an 'economic' act in some circumstances, but that the Court had insufficient facts before it to make a determination on this point.[72] This particular point of law must therefore be regarded as open. While it may seen inconceivable from the point of view of public healthcare services traditions within the Member States of the EU that hospitals providing healthcare to patients, usually free at the point of receipt to those patients, within a public healthcare system, could be 'undertakings' in the sense of EU law, Hatzopoulos[73] warns that this legal conclusion is not certain. Both the European Commission[74] and the influential German national competition authority[75] have implied that public hospitals can be 'undertakings'.

However, even though the rulings can be distinguished on this point, they do adopt the same *overall* approach to the first stage in the question of the application of EU competition law to public healthcare provision: whether there is an 'undertaking'. The approach is to adopt a sharp distinction between the 'economic' and the 'social', between competition and solidarity, between acts taken by 'undertakings' and those that are an 'exercise of public authority'. As Advocate General Maduro explains in *FENIN*:

> In effect, the State assumes two distinct roles, depending on whether it is acting as an operator on a market or whether it is acting for political purposes, inspired by considerations of solidarity.[76]

Put this way, the approach seems appropriate. Where a Member State makes the choice to operate its public healthcare service on a 'social solidarity' footing, then public healthcare institutions will not be covered by EU competition law. If, however, as was the situation in the UK as seen in the *BetterCare* case, a Member State seeks to increase management efficiency in its healthcare system through introducing market models of choice and competition between providers, then competition law will apply, as the public healthcare institutions at issue (along with any private or voluntary institutions providing healthcare) will be acting as 'undertakings'. As Advocate General Maduro puts it in *FENIN*:

> the power of the State which is exercised in the political sphere is subject to democratic control. A different type of control is imposed on economic actors acting on a market: their

[72] See paras 39–57.
[73] In Mossialos et al (eds) (2010), n 14 above.
[74] In its '*Altmark* Decision', Commission Decision 2005/842/EC, on the application of Art 86(2) of the EC Treaty to State aid in the form of public service compensation granted to certain undertakings entrusted with the operation of services of general economic interest, OJ [2005] L 312/67, see discussion below, which states that monies given to all hospitals (publicly or privately owned) are (justified) state aids.
[75] In a decision of March 2005, Bundeskartellamt, 23 March 2005, Rhön-Klinikum AG, Landkreis Rhön-Grabfeld, Decision B10-123/04, reported and commented by H Bergmann and F Röhling in (2007) E-Competitions Law Bulletin, <http://www.concurrences.com/abstract_bulletin_web.php3?id_article=12733>, in which a merger between two public hospitals was blocked. By definition, therefore, the hospitals must have been classified as 'undertakings' subject to merger control law.
[76] Para 27.

conduct is governed by competition law. But there is no justification when the State is acting as an economic operator, for relieving its actions of all control.[77]

The problem with this approach, however, is that the roles and concepts are *not* as distinct as the structure of the jurisprudence implies. Both Prosser[78] and Sauter[79] have also identified this objection to the current law on 'undertakings', as applied in the context of public healthcare systems within the Member States. The distinction between 'markets' and 'solidarity' is not a dichotomous distinction: different types of market involve different levels of competition, and so a more subtly differentiated application of EU competition law would be more responsive to changing policy contexts within the Member States. Where Member States seek to experiment with market models—which they are being encouraged to do both by the various challenges necessitating change in provision of public healthcare services and by the processes of the OMC-social, which encourage 'efficiency' *inter alia* in public healthcare systems—they are unlikely to seek to move from a totally 'public', solidarity-based provision to one that is totally based on free competition within a market.[80] Rather, Member States are likely to seek to phase in competitive elements, perhaps only within one part of the system, in order to protect both the stability of the healthcare system as a whole, and to allow for a period of adjustment or transition. In other words, it is not an 'on-off' switch; it is a question of degree. As the Advocate General in *FENIN* and the UK Competition Appeal Tribunal both point out (although they are unable to rely on this observation, given the current structure of the law), a body, and a specific activity of a body, may play *both* market *and* non-market roles; the activities of the bodies concerned had *both* a 'social dimension' *and* a 'business dimension'.

2. *Is a 'Service of General Economic Interest' Involved?*

The fact that developing policies and practices within Member States involve public bodies which might arguably be appropriately controlled through EU competition law as applied by courts and tribunals, but equally might arguably be appropriately

[77] Para 26.

[78] Prosser in Mossialos et al, eds, n 45 above, 324:

> ...it is unclear just how much competition needs to be introduced into a national system to make activities subject to competition law. After all, there are markets and markets, some highly regulated and others operating more freely; for example, the United Kingdom health service internal market, introduced by the Conservative Government in the 1980s, looked very different from the textbook competitive market for consumer products.

[79] W Sauter, 'Services of general economic interest and universal service in EU law' (2008) 33 ELR 167, 168:

> ...the binary system...complicates efforts to introduce competition either gradually or partially. That is a problem because phasing in competition in hitherto sheltered markets is frequently not only a political necessity but also desirable from the perspective of system stability. In a liberalisation context it will often be preferable not to force a 'big bang' but to provide for an adjustment period or transition mechanism, or to experiment with greater or smaller degrees of market freedom in different market segments.

[80] Although this is precisely the kind of approach that has been adopted in various public sectors by many developing countries; see N Klein, *The Shock Doctrine* (2007).

controlled through democratic political processes, is reflected in Article 106(2) TFEU (ex Article 86(2) EC). This provides:

Undertakings entrusted with the operation of services of general economic interest . . . shall be subject to the rules contained in the Treaties, in particular to the rules on competition, in so far as the application of such rules does not obstruct the performance, in law or in fact, of the particular tasks assigned to them. . . .

The second stage of legal analysis, in determining the relationship between EU competition law and public healthcare, is therefore whether a 'public undertaking' or an 'undertaking to which Member States grant special or exclusive rights'[81] falls within Article 106(2) TFEU. This question itself involves considering whether a 'service of general economic interest' is engaged; whether there has been an act of entrustment of the operation of such a service; and whether the challenged practice—the particular tasks assigned to the body concerned—would be obstructed by the application of EU competition law.

An understanding of how Article 106(2) TFEU might be interpreted and applied to public health services within the Member States needs to take account of the ongoing, and highly contested, development of EU law and policy on 'services of general interest'.[82] In terms of hard law, Article 14 TFEU (ex Article 16 EC), which provides that both the EU and the Member States must 'take care' that 'services of general economic interest operate on the basis of principles and conditions . . . which enable them to fulfil their missions' was originally added to the EC Treaty by the Treaty of Amsterdam.[83] However, the legal status of Article 14 TFEU remains unclear,[84] and it is explicitly stated to be 'without prejudice to' Article 106 TFEU.[85] There is no case law or legislative definition of 'service of general economic interest'.[86] This is partly so that the question of what is such a

[81] Art 106(1) TFEU (ex Art 86(1) EC).

[82] H Schweitzer, 'Services of General Economic Interest: European Law's impact on the role of markets and of Member States', ch 2, this volume; M Krajewski et al (eds), n 34 above; M Krajewski, 'Providing Legal Clarity and Securing Policy Space for Public Services through a Legal Framework for Services of General Economic Interest: Squaring the Circle?' (2008) 14 European Public Law 377; L Hancher, 'Community, State and Market' in Craig and de Búrca (eds) *The Evolution of EU Law* (1999); M Ross, n 34 above; Prosser in Mossialos et al (eds), n 45 above; Lear and Mossialos in Mossialos et al (eds) (2010), n 14 above.

[83] See L Flynn, 'Competition Policy and Public Services in EU Law' in D O'Keeffe and P Twomey, *Legal Issues of the Amsterdam Treaty* (1999).

[84] See M Ross, 'Article 16 EC and Services of General Interest: From Derogation to Obligation' (2000) 25 ELR 22; Banquero Cruz, 'Beyond Competition: Services of General Interest and European Community Law' in G de Búrca (ed), n 9 above; M Ross, n 34 above, 1070.

[85] There is also a Protocol annexed to the Treaty, which provides that Art 16 'shall be implemented with full respect for the jurisprudence of the Court of Justice, inter alia as regards the principles of equality of treatment, quality and continuity of such [public] services'.

[86] There are a few Directives on specific sectors, such as natural gas, electricity, postal services and electronic communications, adopted under Art 86(3) EC. Sauter, n 79 above, 177–8, concludes that these demonstrate that the key feature is an obligation to provide a universal service, defined in terms of (enforceable) rights and deliverables and separated from the remaining part of the sector concerned (which is liberalized).

service is left to each Member State to determine, in its own circumstances, and partly because the concept changes over time.[87]

In contrast to the Court, the Commission has used what is now Article 14 TFEU as a springboard for significant policy activity. The Commission has sought to distinguish between 'services of general economic interest' and 'services of general interest',[88] a concept picked up in the Treaty of Lisbon[89] which appears to cover a wider category of public services than that covered by Article 106(2) TFEU. The non-economic aspects of services of general interest appear to fall outside the scope of the Treaty altogether.[90] In its Green Paper on Services of General Interest,[91] the Commission provides some definitional indicators for the broad category. Common elements are 'universal service, continuity, quality of service, affordability, user and consumer protection'.[92] Universal service means 'to guarantee access for everyone, whatever the economic, social or geographic situation, to a service of specified quality at an affordable price'.[93] Universal service 'establishes the rights of everyone to access certain services considered as essential and imposes obligations on service providers to offer defined services according to specified conditions including complete territorial coverage and at an affordable price.'[94] These criteria would apply to many, if not most, elements of national public healthcare systems in the Member States. However, they would not apply to all healthcare services: for instance, they would not apply to non-clinically indicated plastic surgery, nor perhaps to enjoying a single occupancy room in a hospital. Perhaps even more confusingly, the Commission has more recently focused on 'social services of general interest',[95] a different sub-category of 'services of general interest', which includes various social welfare services, including health services.[96] More recently, in its Communication on the proposed Protocol on Services of General Interest,[97] annexed to the Treaty of Lisbon, the Commission notes that social services of general interest, such as health services, may be classed as 'economic' or 'non economic'.[98] Health services are one of a number of specific sectors in which the Commission plans to bring forward future initiatives.[99]

[87] Sauter, n 79 above, 174–5.

[88] 'Commission Communication on Services of General Interest' OJ [1996] C 281/3; and OJ [2001] C 17/4; 'Commission Green Paper on Services of General Interest', COM (2003) 270 and Commission, 'White Paper on Services of General Interest', COM (2004) 374.

[89] Treaty of Lisbon, Protocol on Services of General Interest.

[90] See M Ross, n 34 above, 1058; Treaty of Lisbon, Protocol on Services of General Interest, Art 2: 'The provisions of the Treaties do not affect in any way the competence of Member States to provide, commission and organise non-economic services of general interest.'

[91] COM (2003) 270 final.

[92] COM (2003) 270 final, 15.

[93] COM (2003) 270 final, 4.

[94] European Commission, White Paper, 'Services of general interest', COM (2004) 374 final, 8.

[95] European Commission, 'Implementing the Community Lisbon Programme: Social Services of General Interest in the European Union', COM (2006) 177 final.

[96] Although these were shelved for separate, later discussion, see Ross, n 34 above, fn 7, 1058.

[97] European Commission, 'Services of general interest, including social services of general interest: a new European commitment', COM (2007) 725 final.

[98] COM (2007) 725 final, 5.

[99] The work of the Commission on cross-border healthcare services, which resulted in the proposal for a Directive on Patients' Rights in Crossborder Health Care, COM (2008) 414 final, arguably already contributes to this plan.

Although the Member States are free to determine what is a service of general economic interest, in order for Article 106(2) TFEU to apply, the Commission takes the view that the public service mission of the undertaking must be clearly defined, and 'explicitly entrusted through an act of public authority'.[100] Thus a body seeking to rely on the application of Article 106(2) TFEU must show that it has been entrusted with a legitimate public service task. Ideally, there must be a specific act of entrustment, defining the mission, scope, and conditions under which the service of general economic interest is to be provided.[101] However, it appears that the existence of a service of general economic interest may be derivable from the broader legal context.[102] The details of the legal test have been made clear in the context of state aids (to be discussed below). If the beneficiary of the money is not formally entrusted with a service of general economic interest, the money will be classified as a 'state aid' to an 'undertaking' under the EU state aids regime.[103] The choice by a Member State of the undertaking to which to entrust with an obligation to provide a service of general economic interest is subject to EU public procurement law.[104]

The question of whether the application of EU competition law would obstruct the performance of the tasks entrusted to the body concerned—in other words whether the restrictions imposed are consistent with the task of performing the legitimate public service task—has been considered by the Court in its case law. The case law turns to the third stage of legal analysis outlined above: whether the restriction on competition is proportionate.

3. Is the Restriction on Competition Proportionate?

Advocate General Jacobs has summarized the approaches of the Court in three different types of cases concerning whether the grant of an exclusive right to an undertaking entrusted with a service of general economic interest is a proportionate restriction on competition.[105] In the first type of case,[106] the state-created monopoly, *in conjunction with additional structural features*, created an inducement to abuse a dominant position, or made abuses very likely. In these cases, the exclusive right was not compatible with EU law. The Court adopts an 'absolute competition' approach:[107] a mere grant of a legal monopoly is a violation in and of itself of

[100] COM (2000) 580 final.

[101] Case T–289/03 *BUPA Ireland* [2008] ECR II–81, paras 181–2.

[102] Case C–157/94 *Commission v Netherlands (Dutch Electricity Monopoly)* [1997] ECR I–5699; the Commission has decided that health insurance companies in Ireland and the Netherlands were providing a service of general economic interest, even though there was no specific act of entrustment, in decisions involving risk equalization schemes of health insurance companies; see Sauter, n 79 above, 184–5.

[103] Sauter, n 79 above, 184. See Case C–280/00 *Altmark* [2003] ECR I–7747.

[104] See further below.

[105] In Case C–67/96 *Albany International* [1999] ECR I–5751, paras 395–420.

[106] Case C–260/89 *ERT* [1991] ECR I–2925; Case C–179/90 *Port of Genoa* and Case C–163/96 *Raso* [1998] ECR I–533.

[107] D Edward and M Hoskins, 'Article 90: Deregulation and EC Law. Reflections arising from the XVI FIDE Conference.' (1995) 32 CML Rev 157.

Article 106(1) TFEU, since the Member State necessarily places the undertaking in a dominant position, free of the normal market constraints, so that it is by definition able to pursue abusive practices. In a second, similar, type of case,[108] the state did no more than grant an exclusive right, but because of the specific economic context and the nature of the services involved, the monopolist could not avoid abusing its dominant position. The abuse took the form of *manifest* failure to meet demand. Again, in these (exceptional) cases, the exclusive rights were not compatible with EU law, and no exemption was granted. The Court adopts a 'limited sovereignty' approach:[109] Member States are free to grant legal monopolies, so long as the operation of the monopoly does not have the *necessary* consequence of contravening the competition law rules of the Treaty.

In principle, where an undertaking is concerned with public healthcare services, if the state grants monopoly rights, within a structural context to make abuse of that dominant position likely, or if a grant of a monopoly right makes abuse unavoidable, then those lines of case law will apply. However, most cases are likely to fall into the third category, where the Court undertakes a balancing process between the objective public interest justifying the monopoly or anti-competitive practice, and the restriction on competition.[110] In these cases, the Court adopts a 'limited competition' approach:[111] Member States may create undertakings that operate in ways that breach Articles 101 and 102 TFEU (ex Articles 81 or 82 EC) only where this is justified by a legitimate national objective, and where the consequent restriction of competition is limited to what is necessary to achieve this objective. In other words, Article 106(2) TFEU is subject to a proportionality test.

The application of this legal principle in the context of public healthcare systems is illustrated by *Ambulanz Glöckner.*[112] Ambulanz Glöckner is a private firm providing ambulance services, both for emergency and non-emergency patients. It applied to the public authorities of the German *Land* of Rheinland-Pfalz for an authorization to provide emergency ambulance services, and patient transport services, which are reimbursed by the relevant public health insurance funds. This authorization was refused, in part because the two medical aid organizations entrusted with the public ambulance service in the area (the German Red Cross and the Maltese Aid Service) showed that they were already operating at a loss, and so if another provider entered the market, then it was argued that the user charges would have to increase.

The question before the Court was whether the exclusive granting to those two medical aid organizations of the authorization to provide ambulance services was a

[108] Case C–41/90 *Höfner and Elser v Macrotron* [1991] ECR I–1979; Case C–55/96 *Job Centre* [1997] ECR I–7119.

[109] Edwards and Hoskins, n 107 above.

[110] Case 155/73 *Sacchi* [1974] ECR 409; Case C–320/91 *Corbeau* [1993] ECR I–2523; Case C–393/92 *Almelo* [1994] ECR I–1477; Case C–266/96 *Corsica Ferries France* [1998] ECR I–3949; Case C–340/99 *TNT Traco v Poste Italiane* [2001] ECR I–4109; Case C–67/96 *Albany International* [1999] ECR I–5751. See also Opinion of the AG in Joined Cases C–264/01, C–306/01, C–354/01, and C–355/01 *AOK* [2004] ECR I–2493.

[111] Edwards and Hoskins, n 107 above.

[112] Case C–475/99 [2001] ECR I–8089.

breach of EU competition law—in particular was it an abuse of a dominant position under what is now Article 102 TFEU? Or did what is now Article 106 (2) TFEU apply? Were the German Red Cross and the Maltese Aid Service 'undertakings entrusted with services of general economic interest' whose performance of their tasks would be obstructed if EU competition law were to apply?

The Court dealt first with the question of whether the provision of ambulance services was an economic activity—in other words, whether the German Red Cross and the Maltese Aid Service were 'undertakings'. The Court concluded that they were,[113] reasoning that because the activity of providing emergency transport services and patient transport services has not always been, and is not necessarily, carried on by public authorities, this was a service, for remuneration from users, on a market, and hence the activity was an economic activity, for the purposes of the test as to whether they were 'undertakings' under EU competition law.[114]

The Court then found that the relevant national law had conferred a special or exclusive right on the undertaking, because only a limited number of undertakings were authorized to provide the service, and this affected the ability of other undertakings to provide the service within the same geographical area.[115] Further, there was an abuse of a dominant position, as the application of the national law, which required consultation with the German Red Cross and the Maltese Aid Service before granting an authorization to an independent operator such as Ambulanz Glöckner, limited markets to the prejudice of consumers.[116] The question then was, was the grant of exclusive rights to the German Red Cross and the Maltese Aid Service proportionate under what is now Article 106(2) TFEU?

On the application of Article 106(2),[117] the issue was whether the exclusive rights were necessary to ensure that the German Red Cross and the Maltese Aid Service could perform the tasks entrusted to them.[118] If that could be shown to be the case, it would be permitted under Article 106(2) TFEU. The Court agreed with its Advocate General (Jacobs) that the revenue from non-emergency transport offset the costs of providing emergency transport, and that was what made the service economically viable. If private operators were to be allowed to enter the market, this would affect how much that cross-subsidization could continue, and ultimately jeopardize the quality and reliability of the public service.[119] This is similar to the 'no cream-skimming' argument found in several earlier cases on what is now Article 106(2) TFEU, to the effect that Article 106(2) TFEU protects the 'economic equilibrium' of public service provision, which would be upset if further private operators were permitted to enter the market and take the more profitable elements of it, undermining the solidarity-based cross-subsidization that the grant of special or exclusive rights permits.[120] The 'no cream-skimming' argument would not be available only if it could be shown that the undertakings entrusted with the operation of the public ambulance service were manifestly unable to satisfy

113 Para 22. 114 Para 20. 115 Paras 24 and 25. 116 Para 43.
117 Paras 51–65. 118 Para 56. 119 Para 61.
120 See, eg, Case C–320/91 *Corbeau* [1993] ECR I–2523.

demand.[121] This was factually contested, and the Court therefore left it for the national court to decide.

The Court's application of the proportionality test under Article 106(2) TFEU is obviously crucial in terms of the substantive outcome of specific cases of its potential application. As Sauter points out,[122] there are two versions of the proportionality test. In the milder version, a measure that is *prima facie* suitable to achieve the task in hand, and is not manifestly disproportionate, is permissible. In the strict version, only the least restrictive means of achieving an objective are permissible, and the relevant body must show that no other imaginable measure could achieve that objective with a lesser detrimental effect on competition. As Article 106(2) TFEU is an exception to a general rule, we might expect the strict version of the proportionality test to apply, that is, an exemption from the general principles of EU competition law is available only to the extent strictly necessary for performing the public service functions concerned. Actually, Sauter argues, unless the area is one where the Member States are pre-empted from action, because a norm of EU law occupies the field, the standard is whether the measure is manifestly inappropriate, having regard to the objective to be achieved (the milder version of the test). This argument relies on a case involving the common agricultural policy,[123] and on the 1997 *Electricity* cases,[124] in which the Court held that 'in the absence of a common policy in the area concerned', the milder version of the proportionality test should apply. However, it could be said either that there *is* a common policy in the area concerned, that is to say competition policy applies; or that there are now emerging norms of EU law occupying the field of healthcare policy. Whatever the merits of Sauter's argument,[125] the mild version of proportionality was applied in *Ambulanz Glöckner*. In other words, the Court did not ask whether there was no other way to achieve the public interest aim involved (provision of 24-hour emergency ambulance services, and non-emergency ambulance services) that was less restrictive of competition. Rather, it respected the national approach to the mix between public and private provision, within the specifics of the national health insurance system. It found that the approach of the law was not 'manifestly inappropriate', or at least would only be so if the demand for the service was not being satisfied by the undertakings with exclusive rights.[126]

As is the case with the question of whether a body operating within a public service sector, such as healthcare, is an undertaking, again the Court's jurisprudence is based upon a sharp distinction. The application of Article 106(2) TFEU is predicated on the prior question of whether there is a 'service of general economic

[121] Para 62.

[122] Sauter, n 79 above, 186.

[123] Case C–331/88 *R v Ministry of Agriculture, Fisheries and Food, ex parte FEDESA* [1990] ECR I–4023.

[124] Case C–157/94 *Commission v Netherlands (Dutch Electricity Monopoly)* [1997] ECR I–5699; Case C–158/94 *Commission v Italy (Italian Electricity Monopoly)* [1997] ECR I–5789; Case C–159/94 *Commission v France (French Electricity and Gas Monopoly)* [1997] ECR I–5815.

[125] And he notes that it needs further investigation; see p 188.

[126] The Court of First Instance has applied the 'manifestly appropriate' test to Art 86(2) EC more recently in Case T–289/03 *BUPA Ireland* [2008] ECR II–81.

interest'. Either there is, or there is not. Where services are provided, as in the case with healthcare services, within a context where some of the services, or some elements of a service, might properly be considered as 'public', representing 'services of general economic interest', whereas others might better be considered 'private', add-on services, purchased by the consumer, then again this binary legal structure does not capture the reality on the ground. However, given that it is Member States who have the power to define the contours of healthcare entitlements under their public healthcare systems, the approach of EU law that it is for Member States to say what constitute 'services of general economic interest' is appropriate. Likewise, we might say that the 'mild' version of the proportionality test constitutes the appropriate check on national policies or procedures that might be anti-competitive. This is not because of the lack of EU norms 'occupying the field', but because of the constitutional position of healthcare within the EU's multilevel legal order. The approach of the Court here, as we shall see later, is in stark contrast to the way the Court applies the proportionality test in the context of free movement of services.

B. EU State Aids and Public Procurement Law

Alongside the EU's anti-cartel and anti-monopoly abuse laws are the measures of EU competition law concerning state aids to undertakings, and a significant body of EU law on public procurement. If in some circumstances public healthcare services are services traded by undertakings on a market, there must be regulation of the way that public money reaches this market. This is the function of state aids and public procurement law, which, as Hatzopoulous notes, are two sides of the same coin.[127] While the rules of public procurement apply to public contracting entities, to prevent states *indirectly* favouring particular undertakings in an anti-competitive manner, state aid rules apply where state resources are transferred *directly* to undertakings in a way which disrupts fair competition. Therefore, logically, as both rules seek to achieve the same aim, the rules apply alternatively, and not simultaneously.[128] However, this logic applies only to the specific area of public procurement rules, and not to free movement rules in general.[129] Free movement rules, such as Article 34 TFEU (ex Article 28 EC), can apply to state aids.[130]

[127] Hatzopoulous in Mossialos et al (eds) (2010), n 14 above; see also C Bovis, 'Financing Services of General Interest in the EU: How do Public Procurement and State Aids Interact to Demarcate between Market Forces and Protection' (2005) 11 ELJ 79; A Bartosch, 'The Relationship between Public Procurement and State Aid Surveillance—the toughest standard applies' (2002) 39 CML Rev 551.

[128] See Hatzopoulous, ibid, citing Case C–280/00 *Altmark* [2003] ECR I–7747 as authority, in particular the fourth criterion for when a transfer of state resources is not a state aid—when it has been transferred following 'a public procurement procedure which would allow for the selection of a tenderer capable of providing those services at the least cost to the community'. Compliance with public procurement rules and procedures therefore precludes application of the state aids rules.

[129] The rules on public procurement are an application of free movement rules and must be interpreted in the light of the Treaty: see, eg, Case C–225/98 *Commission v France* [2000] ECR I–7445, Opinion of the Advocate General, para 76. The legal basis of the relevant secondary legislation also confirms its purpose as securing free movement within the internal market.

[130] Case C–21/88 *Du Pont de Nemours Italiana* [1990] ECR I–889.

Article 107 TFEU (ex Article 87 EC) prohibits aid granted by a Member State which distorts or threatens to distort competition, in so far as it affects trade between Member States, unless the Treaties provide otherwise.[131] There is an obligation on Member States to notify the Commission of state aids that might be unlawful in EU law.[132] Several kinds of state aids that are considered beneficial to the EU either are[133] or may be[134] permitted, following notification to the Commission and a procedure of authorization. Article 107 TFEU applies to aids 'granted by a Member State or through state resources'.[135] The nature of the body through which aid is provided is irrelevant, and Article 107 TFEU covers aid granted by regional authorities.[136] The aid must confer an economic advantage on an undertaking.[137] It must favour a certain undertaking or the producer of certain goods.[138] A general social welfare scheme or system does not constitute an 'aid'.[139] Finally, the aid must distort competition and affect trade between Member States. This is similar to the legal test for the application of Articles 101 and 102 TFEU. If aid strengthens the financial position of one undertaking compared to others within the EU, then trade between Member States is affected. A potential effect is sufficient. On the other hand, as long as the effects of a subsidy are confined to one Member State, the matter is for national law. The role of Article 107 TFEU is to protect against distortions of competition at EU level. The application of Article 107 TFEU to undertakings operating within national public healthcare systems thus depends on the existence of undertakings that either do, or could, operate across borders to provide such services. As the EU market in healthcare services opens up, for instance following litigation on freedom to provide services

[131] Joined Cases T–447/93 and T–448/93 *AITEC v Commission* [1995] ECR II–1971. For examples of state aids, see M Evans and Martin in 'Socially Acceptable Distortion of Competition: Community Policy on State Aid' (1991) 16 ELR 7; C Quigley, 'The Notion of a State Aid in the EEC' (1988) 13 ELR 242; J-D Braun and J Kuehling, 'Article 87 and the Community Courts: from revolution to evolution' (2008) 45 CML Rev 465.

[132] Art 108 TFEU (ex Art 88 EC), Council Regulation No 659/1999 of 22 March 1999 laying down detailed rules for the application of Art 93 of the EC Treaty, OJ [1999] L83/1, as amended.

[133] Art 107(2) TFEU (ex Art 87(2) EC).

[134] Art 107(3) TFEU (ex Art 87(3) EC).

[135] Cases C–72 and 73/91 *Sloman Neptun* [1993] ECR I–887; Case C–189/91 *Kirsammer-Hack* [1993] ECR I–6185; Cases C–52 to 54/97 *Viscido v Ente Poste Italiane* [1998] ECR I–2629. Where a Member State holds shares in a private company, this is an 'aid' if the undertaking could not have obtained the amounts in question on the ordinary capital market (the 'hypothetical private investor test'): Case 323/82 *Intermills SA v Commission* [1984] ECR 3809; Case C–142/87 *Belgium v Commission (Tubemeuse)* [1990] ECR I–959.

[136] Case 323/82 *Intermills SA v Commission* [1984] ECR 3809; Cases 67, 68, and 70/85 *Kwerkerij Gebroeders Van der Kooy v Commission* [1998] ECR 219.

[137] This is a wide test. It covers not only positive aid, but also measures which mitigate the charges on an undertaking. Advocate General Jacobs, in C–256/97 *DMT* [1999] ECR I–3913, explained that the crucial point is whether the undertaking obtains a benefit which it would not have received in the normal course of events on the private market.

[138] For discussion of the Court's approach to this point, see M Ross, 'State Aids: Maturing into a Constitutional Problem' (1995) 15 *Yearbook of European Law* 79.

[139] Case C–256/97 *Déménagements-Manutention Transport* [1999] ECR I–3913; Case C–75/97 *Commission v Belgium (Maribel)* [1999] ECR I–3671.

and freedom of establishment,[140] it becomes increasingly easy to show that this is the case.

Article 106(2) TFEU concerning services of general economic interest provides an important exemption from the rules and procedural requirements (obligation to notify) of Article 107 TFEU. Where there is a legitimate service of general economic interest, a payment made by the state to an undertaking as compensation for that service will arguably not constitute a state aid. If there is no state aid at all, there is (obviously) no need to notify the Commission, which is an important practical ramification. Until its *Altmark* Decision[141] in 2003, the Court applied two different approaches to its analysis in such cases (although the outcomes converged): the 'state aid approach'[142] (there is an aid, but it can be justified) and the 'compensation approach'[143] (there is no aid, as the undertaking does not receive an uncompetitive advantage, merely remuneration for a service rendered).[144] Now, as we will see, the Commission has provided what is effectively a 'block exemption' for compensation for the provision of certain categories of public service.

The EU legislation on public procurement[145] is found in a series of Directives,[146] which establish a system of technical rules about contracts for public goods, works or services, concerning matters such as advertising through standard form notices, negotiations with bidders, selection of tenderers, award procedures, and award criteria (lowest price, or most economically advantageous tender), where the value of the contract is above certain thresholds.[147] There are also 'compliance Directives', establishing a duty on Member States to provide effective remedies for breaches of the public procurement rules, in particular by entitling suppliers to damages, interim remedies, and set-aside of unlawful decisions.[148] Under Directive 2004/18/EC, contracts for health and social services are not subject to the full range

[140] See Hatzopoulous in Mossialos et al (eds), n 127 above, noting that *Kohll* and its progeny are 'the tip of the iceberg' in terms of the implications of EU law for public healthcare systems.

[141] Case C–280/00 [2003] ECR I–7747, see below.

[142] See, eg, Case T–106/95 *FFSA* [1997] ECR II–229.

[143] See, eg, Case C–53/00 *Ferring* [2001] ECR I–9067.

[144] See Opinion of the Advocate General, Case C–126/01 *GEMO* [2003] ECR I–13769.

[145] See S Arrowsmith, *The Law of Public and Utilities Procurement* (2005).

[146] EP and Council Directive 2004/17/EC coordinating the procurement procedures of entities operating in the water, energy, transport, and postal services sectors, OJ [2004] L 134/1; EP and Council Directive 2004/18/EC on the coordination of procedures for the award of public works contracts, public supply contracts and public service contracts, the 'General' Procurement Directive, OJ [2004] L 134/114. Directive 89/665/EEC of the Council of 21 December 1989 on the coordination of the laws, regulations and administrative provisions relating to the application of review procedures to the award of public supply and public works contracts, OJ [1989] L 395/33; and Directive 92/13/EEC of 25 February 1992 coordinating the laws, regulations and administrative provisions relating to the application of Community rules on the procurement procedures of entities operating in the water, energy, transport and telecommunications sectors, OJ [1992] 76/14. Both Directives have recently been amended by Directive 2007/66/EC of the EP and the Council of 11 December 2007, OJ [2007] L 335/31.

[147] See S Arrowsmith, 'The Community's Legal Framework on Public Procurement: The Way Forward at Last?' (1999) 36 CML Rev 13.

[148] See Directive 89/665/EEC OJ [1989] L 395/33 as amended by Directive 92/50/EEC and Directive 92/13/EEC OJ [1992] L 76/7.

of public procurement rules. They are only subject to the rules in Article 23 of the Directive on technical specifications to be used in tender documents and the rules in Article 35(4) on publication of notices.[149] There is therefore no obligation under the Directives for prior advertisement or to follow the detailed procedures for competitive tendering for health and social services contracts.

However, the specific and technical rules of the Directives are not the only source of EU public procurement law or internal market law that might apply to public health services. The Court has held that general principles of non-discrimination and equal treatment, transparency (which essentially means adequate publicity), proportionality, and mutual recognition[150] apply to public contracting authorities when public contracts are awarded to economic operators,[151] or wherever public money, or indeed non-financial limited public resources, such as a fixed number of licences,[152] are put onto the market. So although the EU legislature leaves public health sector organizations free to procure goods, works, and services by whatever procedure they deem appropriate, this is now constrained by the Court's jurisprudence, based on general principles of internal market law, which requires 'adequate publicity, extended mutual recognition and, most importantly, does not allow for clauses that would exclude, directly or indirectly, operators from other Member States'.[153] This is the case also for contracts for goods, works or services that fall below the thresholds set by the Directives.[154]

The public procurement rules cover central, regional, municipal, and local government departments, bodies covered by public law, and public undertakings.[155] A 'body governed by public law' in this context can take any legal

[149] Art 21. See Hatzopoulos in Mossialos et al (eds), n 127 above: mixed contracts (which involve the provision of both health and social care and other Annex IIA services) should be awarded on the basis of which element of the contract has the highest value, Directive 2004/18/EC, Art 22; see also the Court's judgment in Case C–475/99 *Glöckner* [2001] ECR I–8089.

[150] Case C–225/98 *Commission v France, Nord Pas de Calais* [2000] ECR I–7445; Case C–324/98 *Telaustria* [2000] ECR I–7287; Case C–458/03 *Parking Brixen* [2005] ECR I–8612; Case C–231/03 *Coname* [2005] ECR I–7287 Case C–234/03 *Contse* [2005] ECR I–9135. See also Commission Communication on the 'Community Law Applicable to Contract Awards Not or Not Fully Subject to the Provisions of the Public Procurement Directives' OJ [2006] C 179/2, which interprets this case law.

[151] An 'economic operator' is 'any natural or legal person or public entity or group of such persons and/or bodies which offers on the market, respectively, the execution of works and/or a work, products or services', Directive 2004/18/EC, Art 1(8). In-house relationships are excluded from the application of the procurement rules, see Case C–107/98 *Teckall* [1999] ECR I–8121.

[152] Joined Cases C–338/04, C–359/04, and C–360/04 *Placanica* [2007] ECR I–1891.

[153] See further Commission Communication on the 'Community Law Applicable to Contract Awards Not or Not Fully Subject to the Provisions of the Public Procurement Directives' OJ [2006] C 179/2. Hatzopoulos, n 149 above.

[154] See, eg, Case C–6/05 *Medipac* [2007] ECR I–4557, in which the Court applied internal market law to a contract with the general hospital of Heraklion, Greece, for surgical sutures with a value below the thresholds; contrast Case C–532/03 *Commission v Ireland (Ambulance Services)* [2007] ECR I–11353, in which the Court found that the Commission had not made out its case that internal market law should apply to a contract with the Irish Eastern Regional Health Authority for ambulance services.

[155] Directive 2004/18/EC, Art 1(9). Annex III includes a non-exhaustive list of entities deemed by the Member States to be 'contracting authorities'. Some Member States include very broad categories of healthcare bodies, eg *établissements publics hospitaliers* (public hospitals) (France); others include specific bodies, such as the various Belgian sickness insurance funds.

form,[156] for instance, it can be a public entity, or a private company in national law. The conditions are that the entity must have legal personality, be owned, controlled or financed for the most part by (an emanation of) the state, and be established to meet 'needs in the general interest, not having an industrial or commercial character'.[157] So if an entity meets those three conditions, where it contracts for goods, works or services, it is subject to public procurement law. If, on the other hand, a genuinely competitive regime (a matter of both law and fact) applies to a public undertaking, then it is excluded from the operation of the public procurement rules altogether.[158] The essential question is whether the body meets needs in the general interest (will be subject to public procurement law), or has a commercial character (will be subject to competition law, including state aids law). The Court in *Altmark*[159] seemed to have made explicit the relationship between state aids law and public procurement law. This was followed by the Commission in the '*Altmark* package'.[160] According to these provisions, a measure is not a state aid in the sense of Article 107 TFEU if four cumulative conditions are met:

1. there must be actual and clearly-defined public service obligations;
2. the monies/compensation must be calculated in advance on the basis of objective and transparent criteria;
3. the compensation must be strictly necessary, taking into account what the body will receive for the service and what is a reasonable profit;
4. where the undertaking is not chosen through a public procurement tendering process, the level of compensation must be calculated by reference to an efficient undertaking, what costs would it have incurred, to meet the public service requirements, taking into account a reasonable profit.[161]

However, the Court of First Instance, when applying the *Altmark* criteria in the 2008 *BUPA Ireland* case,[162] modified the third and fourth criteria. Rather than the need to show that the compensation was necessary to discharge a public service

[156] Case C–360/96 *BFI Holding* [1998] ECR I–6821.

[157] Directive 2004/18/EC, Art 1(9). For a discussion of the definition see C Bovis, 'Recent Case Law Relating to Public Procurement: A Beacon for the Integration of Public Markets' (2002) 39 CML Rev 1025, 1037–43.

[158] See Case C–392/93 *R v HM Treasury ex parte British Telecommunications plc* [1996] ECR I–1631; Case C–360/96 *BFI Holding* [1998] ECR I–6821; Cases C–223 and 260/99 *Agorà* [2001] ECR I–3605; Case C–44/96 *Mannesmann* [1998] ECR I–73.

[159] Case C–280/00 [2003] ECR I–7747.

[160] Directive 2005/81/EC OJ [2005] L 312/47, which requires 'any undertaking that enjoys a special or exclusive right granted by a Member State pursuant to Art 86(1) of the Treaty or is entrusted with the operation of a service of general economic interest pursuant to Art 86(2) of the Treaty, that receives public service compensation in any form whatsoever in relation to such service and that carries on other activities' to maintain separate accounts of activities for which it receives compensation from other activities. Commission Decision 2005/842/EC on the application of Art 86(2) of the EC Treaty to State aid in the form of public service compensation granted to certain undertakings entrusted with the operation of services of general economic interest OJ [2005] L 312/67 and Notice OJ [2005] C 297/04.

[161] Case C–280/00 *Altmark*, paras 89–93; Commission Decision 2005/842/EC, Recital 4.

[162] Case T–289/03 *BUPA v Commission* [2008] ECR II–81.

obligation, the Court simply found that the test was whether the compensation was calculated on the basis of elements which are 'specific, clearly identifiable and capable of being controlled'.[163] Rather than the procurement process or efficiency requirements, the Court found that it was enough to show that the compensation provided was neutral with regard to inefficiencies.[164]

The context in *BUPA Ireland* was a very different type of state aid to the reimbursement of a loss-making public transport route at issue in *Altmark*.[165] The case concerned a challenge brought by BUPA Ireland to a Commission Decision concerning the application of what is now Article 107 TFEU to the risk equalization scheme in the Irish health insurance market.[166] Ireland has a taxation-funded national healthcare system. As an alternative, the Voluntary Health Insurance Board provides a private health insurance scheme. Around 50 per cent of the Irish population have private health insurance. In 1997, following Irish legislation liberalizing the Irish private health insurance market, BUPA Ireland entered the Irish market for private health insurance, as a competitor to the Voluntary Health Insurance Board. BUPA Ireland had a market share of around 15 per cent, with the Voluntary Health Insurance Board having the other 85 per cent.

The relevant national law also made provision for a 'risk equalization scheme'. The scheme essentially provides that private health insurers who have lower risks than the average should pay into a central fund. Those insurers who have higher risks than average should receive monies from that central fund. Effectively, this meant transfer of funds from BUPA Ireland to the Voluntary Health Insurance Board. The question arose as to whether this was a state aid, contrary to Article 107 TFEU.

The Commission thought not. Either it was not a state aid at all, or it was compatible with the common market under what is now Article 106(2) TFEU. It was intended as compensation for the obligation to provide services in the general economic interest, imposed on all private health insurance providers in Ireland, so as to ensure that everyone in Ireland could receive private health insurance at an affordable price. In other words, it was organized on the basis of solidarity, in the context of a public service, rather than being an unwarranted interference in a market. In the alternative, the Commission found that even if it was a state aid, it was compatible with the common market under Article 106(2) TFEU.

BUPA Ireland challenged this Commission Decision before the Court of First Instance. The CFI applied the *Altmark* conditions, but in modified form ('*Altmark de luxe*'[167]). The CFI held first that it was up to Ireland to define what a 'public service'/'service of general economic interest' is. The CFI then found that 'an SGEI mission' would be present if the service provider is obliged to contract, without

[163] Para 237.
[164] Para 256.
[165] See para 237: 'the operation of the system is radically different from that of the compensation systems forming the subject matter of the judgments in *Ferring* and *Altmark*'.
[166] Commission Decision C (2003) 1322 final of 13 May 2003, State aid N 46/2003—Ireland—Risk equalization scheme in the Irish health insurance market.
[167] W Sauter, 'Annotation of Case T–289/03 *BUPA*' (2009) 46 CML Rev 269, 282.

being able to reject the other contracting party.[168] They found that this was the case for all private health insurance providers in Ireland, including the Voluntary Health Insurance Board. Insurers were obliged to: (i) offer a private medical insurance contract to everyone who requests it (the 'open enrolment obligation');[169] (ii) offer the private medical insurance services at a uniform rate, whatever the personal circumstances and medical history of the insured person (the 'community rating obligation');[170] (iii) renew contracts when the insured person sought to renew them (the 'lifetime cover obligation');[171] and (iv) reimburse for healthcare by reference to the national rules on minimum benefits (the 'minimum benefits obligation').[172] The first of the *Altmark* criteria was met. On the second *Altmark* criterion, the Court found that even though the economics of calculating the payments was complex, there were objective and transparent criteria for calculating the compensation.[173]

The implications of a literal application of the third *Altmark* criterion would have been that if BUPA could show that the compensation that the Voluntary Health Insurance Board was not 'strictly necessary', the measure concerned would have been a state aid. The CFI, however, rejected BUPA's argument that the compensation to the Voluntary Health Insurance Board under the risk equalization scheme was not necessary because the Voluntary Health Insurance Board could avoid burdens under the community rating obligation by partitioning the market in health insurance according to the risk insured, in accordance with a commercial strategy.[174] It also rejected the argument that, because there was no direct link between, on the one hand, the costs to the Voluntary Health Insurance Board of complying with the open enrolment, community rating, lifetime cover and minimum benefits obligations, and, on the other hand, the amount of compensation paid to the Voluntary Health Insurance Board under the risk equalization scheme, the scheme was not 'strictly necessary'.[175] The aim of the risk equalization scheme was not to compensate costs of specific services, but rather to equalize the additional burdens where one healthcare insurer has a negative risk profile, compared to the average market risk profile.[176] Thus the risk equalization scheme does not correspond to the situation envisaged by the third *Altmark* condition,[177] cannot fulfil that condition,[178] and so, according to the CFI, the Commission did not err in finding the risk equalization scheme necessary and proportionate.[179] This aspect of the CFI's ruling in *BUPA Ireland* shows sensitivity to the *systemic* structures of the Irish public healthcare system, rather than focusing upon a strict and literal application of EU state aids law rules.

Likewise, the CFI modified the fourth *Altmark* criterion. The risk equalization scheme does not intend to provide compensation for the cost of providing a specific healthcare insurance service. Because of this, the situation does not correspond to

[168] Para 190. [169] Irish Health Insurance Act, 1994, s 8.
[170] Irish Health Insurance Act, 1994, s 7. [171] Irish Health Insurance Act, 1994, s 9.
[172] Irish Health Insurance Act, 1994, s 10.
[173] Paras 215 and 217. [174] Paras 229–32. [175] Paras 233–36.
[176] Para 235. [177] Para 241. [178] Para 237. [179] Paras 242–3.

that envisaged by the requirement that, if there has been no tendering process, the level of compensation must be calculated by reference to an efficient undertaking, and what costs it would have incurred to meet the public service requirements, taking into account a reasonable profit. Rather, the CFI was satisfied that 'the compensation provided for by the risk equalization was neutral by reference to any costs associated with inefficiency incurred by certain private medical insurance insurers'.[180]

Cases such as *Altmark* and *BUPA Ireland* link with the case law on what is an 'undertaking' under what are now Articles 101 and 102 TFEU (the 'economic activity' being related to receiving compensation for profit, as against costs, in the third and fourth of the *Altmark* criteria) and in particular with the case law on the application of what is now Article 106(2) TFEU, on services of general economic interest, which logically must be a similar (if not identical) concept to 'public service' in the first of the *Altmark* criteria.[181] The Commission's 'Community framework for State aid in the form of public service compensation'[182] elaborates the four criteria, granting a 'block exemption' to state aid in several categories of services of general economic interest, including 'public service compensation granted to hospitals . . . carrying out activities qualified as services of general economic interest by the Member State concerned'.[183] The principal practical significance of a grant of state resources being exempt from the state aids provisions is that there is no obligation to notify that grant to the Commission.[184] In terms of its broader conceptual significance, the main contribution of the *BUPA Ireland* case is the CFI's wide view of what constitutes a service of general economic interest, at least in the healthcare context.[185]

C. What Is the Relationship between EU Competition Law and Public Health Services?

Because health services can be delivered on the basis of purely private relationships, healthcare *per se* is not a 'need in the general interest, not having an industrial or commercial character'. Private hospitals and clinics, and independent healthcare professionals will fall outside public procurement law, and be subject to competition law, including state aids law. Many healthcare sector cases involving competition law concern the supply of pharmaceuticals or medical devices.[186]

[180] Para 256. The relevant national law was subsequently struck down, on an issue of national law, by the Irish Supreme Court: *BUPA Ireland v Health Insurance Authority* [2008] IESC 42 (16 July 2008); see W Sauter, 'Annotation of Case T–289/03 *BUPA v Ireland*' (2009) 46 CML Rev 269.

[181] See above on the Commission's definitions of 'service of general economic interest', 'social service of general interest', and 'service of general interest'.

[182] OJ [2005] C 297/4.

[183] Decision 2005/842/EC, Art 2(1)(b).

[184] Decision 2005/842/EC, Art 3.

[185] The 'service of general economic interest' here covered only part of the population, was 'for profit', was a selective scheme, involved price discrimination, and played the role of topping up a truly universal public provision. See Sauter (2009), n 180 above.

[186] See, eg, rulings of the Italian Antitrust Authority, German Competition Authority, French Competition Council, Latvian Competition Council, Danish Competition Appeals Tribunal, Romanian Competition Council, cited in Lear and Mossialos, 'Balancing economic freedom against services

However, healthcare provided for an entire population as part of a public health system is a 'need in the general interest'/'service of general economic interest'. Public hospitals, financed entirely through state taxation, and similar national healthcare authorities will be subject to public procurement law when purchasing goods and services, but will avoid the application of competition law. Even here, the conclusion that the services provided by such bodies are 'services of general economic interest' is ambiguous. What kind of treatments count? Does plastic surgery? Does gender reassignment? Pain treatment? Spa- or balneo-therapy? Abortion? How quickly should the patient be entitled to receive the treatment for it to count? Does it include receiving treatment in a single room in a public hospital, or only on a ward? Does it include catering or cleaning in a hospital or clinic? Some Member States, such as Belgium, have sought to engage with this issue by adopting specific national legislation to the effect that hospitals perform a task of general interest, and thus are not subject to state aids rules.[187]

The position of hospitals, medical aid organizations, or other healthcare providers that rely heavily on public funds, and form part of the public health system, but are also structured to gain efficiency benefits from operating on a (semi-) commercial basis, for instance where there is choice among competing providers, is more ambiguous. While it is clear that self-employed medical professionals are 'undertakings', even when they are contracted to provide healthcare services by a public healthcare scheme or in a hospital,[188] and it is clear that medical professionals who are public employees are not 'undertakings', the position of other entities within national health systems is much less clear. Challenges to public healthcare structures on the basis that they breach EU competition law have reached national constitutional courts.[189] National competition authorities have shown interest in regulating the practices of public hospitals where they have expanded their activities into private health services, competing with private players.[190] For

of general economic interest; EC competition law and national health systems', available at: <http://www.etk.fi/Binary.aspx?Section=61331&Item=63234>.

[187] See Belgian Hospital Act, December 2006.

[188] Cases C–180 to 184/98 *Pavlov* [2000] ECR I–6451.

[189] Eg the French Constitutional Court upheld a French law requiring bodies providing optical care to be managed by qualified opticians not on the basis that the bodies fell outside the application of competition law, but on the basis that the law was justified on public health grounds; see *Laboratoire de Prothèse Oculaires v Union national de syndicate d'opticiens de France* (1994) European Commercial Cases 457, cited in Lear and Mossialos, 'Balancing economic freedom against services of general economic interest; EC competition law and national health systems', available at <http://www.etk.fi/Binary.aspx?Section=61331&Item=63234>.

[190] Eg the Finnish Competition Authority (FCA) found that the Pirkanmaa Hospital District's Public Laboratory Enterprise was an 'undertaking' with a dominant position in the market. The FCA warned the hospital district that 'when public production is marketized, the authorities should ensure that private players are provided with equal opportunities to compete in the field that used to be completely the responsibility of the public sector'; Finnish Competition Authority 2003 yearbook, available at <http://www.kilpailuvirasto.fi/tiedostot/vuosikirja_2003_englanti.pdf>. Similarly, the German Competition Authority has refused permission for mergers in several cases where private hospitals have sought to acquire public facilities that could achieve excessive dominance in local hospital markets. German Competition Authority (GCA), Press Releases, 17 January 2008, available at <http://www.bundeskartellamt.de/wEnglisch/News/2008_01_17.php>, 29 April 2005, available at

instance, because it is not clear on which product and geographic markets the partially privatized hospitals in the Netherlands operate,[191] we cannot be sure how EU competition law might apply to them. The restructuring of the public healthcare systems in new Member States also raises questions about the application of EU competition law to hospitals, for instance in Estonia,[192] and Lithuania,[193] where the move to public not-for-profit entities, with independent boards, and increasing use of public-private partnerships,[194] means the legal status and public service mandate of many hospitals and other healthcare institutions is unclear. As Lear and Mossialos put it, 'The resulting lack of oversight and coordination in these cases opens questions about whether the provision of care in these quasi-public facilities should be characterized as economic or social activities.'[195]

If a public hospital, or a body such as the English 'Foundation Trusts',[196] has, for instance, an independent board of directors, some control over its own budget, freedom in terms of with whom it contracts for services and goods, and carries out some commercial activities on the side, for instance in provision of single occupancy rooms for a fee, then it may well qualify as an 'undertaking', escape the application of public procurement rules, but be subject to competition law.[197] If such a body is a 'contracting entity' in the sense of public procurement law, then it is probably not an 'undertaking'. If it is, then if it is a hospital, it need not notify receipt of public funds, under the 'block exemption' in the *Altmark* Decision. If it is not a hospital, then if it has been chosen to receive the funds following a public tender procedure, according to the fourth criterion of the *Altmark* judgment, it is probably receiving 'compensation for public service', and need not notify the compensation under the state aids scheme. If it has received funds in a situation where the *BUPA*-type *Altmark de luxe* criteria apply, and the receipt of funds was 'inefficiency neutral', it is also probably receiving 'compensation for public service'.

<http://www.bundeskartellamt.de/wEnglisch/News/Archiv/ArchivNews2005/2005_04_29.php>, 11 September 2006, available at <http://www.bundeskartellamt.de/wEnglisch/News/Archiv/ArchivNews2006/2006_09_11.php> and 8 November 2006, available at <http://www.bundeskartellamt.de/wEnglisch/News/Archiv/ArchivNews2006/2006_11_08.php> (last accessed 24 January 2008). Both examples cited in S Thomson and E Mossialos, 'Private health insurance and the internal market' in E Mossialos, G Permanand, R Baeten, and T Hervey (eds), *Health Systems Governance in Europe: the role of EU law and policy*, (2010).

[191] M Varkevisser et al, 'Defining hospital markets for antitrust enforcement: new approaches and their applicability to the Netherlands' (2008) 3 Health Economics Policy and Law 7.

[192] T Palu and R Kadakmaa, 'Estonian hospital sector in transition' (2001) Eurohealth 7.

[193] Z Logminiene, 'Hospital Sector Reform in Lithuania' (2001) Eurohealth 3.

[194] K Kerschbaumer, 'Public-Private Partnerships in Eastern Europe' (2007) 13 (2) Eurohealth 7–9.

[195] Lear and Mossialos, n 82 above.

[196] Foundation Trusts are hospitals that have been granted special status due to superior performance, placing them outside the National Health Service (NHS) governance structure. Both Foundation Trusts and 'Primary Care Trusts' (which fall within the NHS hierarchy and are managed by NHS employees) contract with either NHS or private providers for services. Foundation Trusts provide services to Primary Care Trusts based on legal contracts, not public-service contracts. They have the discretion to set priorities, to dispose of property, to borrow funds from the private sector and to provide services to private patients. See Lear and Mossialos, n 82 above.

[197] Hatzopoulos, n 149 above, fn 106.

Even if the body is receiving an aid, which must be notified, it could still be granted an individual exemption by the Commission, following the Commission's guidance in its *Altmark* framework.

Finally, the position of social insurance funds that form part of a public health system remains uncertain. The Court has held, following a complaint of collusion from pharmaceutical companies, that German sickness funds do not perform an 'economic activity' when determining maximum amounts (reference prices) for reimbursement of prescription pharmaceuticals.[198] Even though they competed to attract members, the sickness funds were regulated by statute, organized according to the principle of solidarity (with mandatory employee insurance), and hence performed a social function. The Irish Voluntary Health Insurance Board was not in receipt of a state aid when it received resources (essentially from BUPA Ireland) transferred under the national risk equalization scheme. But what about the Dutch mandatory private insurance scheme, which combines restrictions on premium rates and open enrolment with a risk equalization scheme and premium compensation scheme for people with low incomes, and tax deductions for the chronically ill?[199] The Commission held that the scheme constituted an 'aid', but found it justified under what is now Article 106(2) TFEU.[200] The Netherlands Competition Authority considers the private insurers providing social healthcare insurance in the Netherlands to be 'undertakings', subject to competition law.[201] What if a social health insurance fund, alongside its social solidarity function, also competes with private health insurance providers in a related market (by analogy with the *BetterCare* situation), or if membership is voluntary, or if the fund operates according to the principle of capitalization (where an explicit contribution to the budget is allocated to each member of the plan regardless of need)? Following cases involving pension funds,[202] in which the Court refers to a set of criteria that assist in the determination of whether insurance funds are 'undertakings',[203] health insurance funds in these cases might be subject to EU competition law.

It should now be evident that much of the detailed application of the law here to bodies operating as part of the public national healthcare systems of Member States

198 Cases C–264/01, C–306/01, C–355/01 *AOK Bundesverband* [2004] ECR I–2493.

199 See Case T–84/06: Action brought on 13 March 2006 *Azivo* OJ [2006] C 108/27. Withdrawn from the register, October 2008.

200 Commission Decision relating to State aid N 541/2004 and N 542/2004—The Netherlands—Risk equalization scheme and retention of reserves OJ [2005] EC 324/28.

201 See F Paolucci, A Den Exter, and W Van de Ven, 'Solidarity in competitive health insurance markets: analysing the relevant EC legal framework' (2006) 1 Health Economics, Policy and Law 107, 122.

202 Cases C–159 and 160/91 *Poucet and Pistre* [1993] ECR I–637; Case C–244/94 *FFSA* [1995] ECR I–4019; Case C–67/96 *Albany International* [1999] ECR I–5751; Case C–115/97 *Brentjens* [1999] ECR I–6025; Case C–219/97 *Drijvende Bokken* [1999] ECR I–61; Cases C–180/98 to C–184/98 *Pavlov* [2000] ECR I–6451; Cases C–180 to 184/98 *Pavlov* [2000] ECR I–6451; Case C–355/00 *Freskot* [2003] ECR I–5263. See Lear and Mossialos, n 82 above.

203 The criteria are: the objective pursued by the scheme; the compulsory character of the scheme; the way in which the amount of contribution is calculated; the way in which the amount of benefits is calculated; the overall degree of state control; whether the organization operates according to capitalization; cross-subsidization; competitive schemes. See V Hatzopoulos, 'Health Law and Policy: The Impact of the EU' in G de Búrca (ed), n 9 above.

remains untested before the courts. However, we can draw some conclusions about the possible implications.[204]

First, it is not clear when healthcare is provided as a 'service of general interest'. The kinds of treatment provided by Member States under their national health systems vary significantly; the quality of medical treatments also varies, for instance because of qualifications levels of healthcare professionals, quality of infrastructure, and waiting times to access the system or receive a particular treatment; and the quality of non-medical services, such as accommodation, catering and cleaning also varies. Although Member States provide general legislative[205] (and sometimes constitutional[206]) provisions on the levels of healthcare to be provided as a service of general interest, these rules to do not define its precise scope. EU law seems to require a more precise definition, in each Member State, so as to determine which bodies in the healthcare field are 'contracting entities', and how the *Altmark* or *Altmark de luxe* test applies.[207] It is not clear, however, how detailed such a definition should be. There is also the difficulty that legislative definitions of what are the contours of healthcare as a 'service of general economic interest' within a particular Member State are likely to lag behind, or even place a drag on, developments of extent of coverage, quality of care and medical practice within national healthcare systems. Again, the binary structures of EU law do not reflect the practice of public healthcare provision on the ground in the Member States, and hinder its development within the current challenges to healthcare provision.

Second, significant questions remain about whether various mechanisms and practices for financing public healthcare services are consistent with EU law.[208] Third, the question of whether healthcare provision should be subject to public procurement law at all[209] has been inadequately dealt with. Fourth, because it is less

[204] This section draws on Hatzopoulos, n 149 above, in which Hatzopoulos conducts a lengthy exploration and analysis of the possible implications of EU state aids and public procurement law for public healthcare systems, based on hypothetical case studies involving the national health systems of six Member States.

[205] See, eg, Belgian Hospital Act 1987; UK NHS Act 1977.

[206] See, eg, Hungarian Constitution, Art 70(D); Netherlands Constitution, Art 22; Italian Constitution, Art 32; Belgian Constitution, Art 23(2); Greek Constitution, Art 21(3); Finnish Constitution, Chapter 2, s 19(3); Luxembourg Constitution, Art 11(5); Portuguese Constitution, Art 64(1); Spanish Constitution, Art 43(1).

[207] See E Szyszczak, 'Modernising Health Care: Pilgrimage for the Holy Grail' in M Krajewski et al (eds), n 34 above, 213, who argues that an 'inner core' of healthcare activities should be 'protected from the full thrust' of EU competition and free movement rules.

[208] Eg in Germany, the Federal Government recently investigated whether state aid law affected its public financing of in-patient healthcare; see S Boysen, 'Germany' in Krajewski et al (eds), n 34 above, 351–2, citing W Cremer, 'Europäisches Beihilfenrecht und seine Auswirkungen auf das deutsche Krankenhauswesen', (2008) Zeitschrift für ausländisches und internationals Arbeits- und Sozialrecht 198. The investigation concluded that the answer to the question depends on the application of the 'compensation' criterion. For instance, investment assistance for the construction of hospitals providing in-patient care was deemed to be 'compensation', not 'aid'. But the position of hospitals providing out-patient care is less clear cut.

[209] Because the procurement rules lack flexibility, require relationships of partnership to be transformed into competitive relationships, restrict cooperation between local authorities, have a negative effect on setting up long-term relationships with suppliers based on trust, and may result in disruption of public service and increased transaction costs and delays.

constraining to be subject to public procurement law than competition and state aids law, entities involved in healthcare are likely to structure their activities to seek to be classed as 'contracting entities', rather than as 'undertakings'. The obligation to monitor service provision for efficiency (the fourth *Altmark* criterion) will impose a significant administrative burden on the Member States, is likely to increase scrutiny by the European Commission of national provision of health services,[210] and to constrain possible evolution of healthcare systems towards greater efficiencies.[211] This constraint arises because Member States will be reluctant to experiment with service delivery mechanisms that might promote greater efficiency, because if they do, they will have an additional administrative burden—to show *Altmark* efficiency—that would not otherwise apply.

Finally, and perhaps most importantly, the very structure of the reasoning where EU competition law is applied to public health services entails a shift in conceptualization from national healthcare *systems* (the current national logic), to a *set of* national healthcare *services*—albeit offered in the general interest (the logic of EU law). The way that the structure of EU law operates requires that the public healthcare offered by, say, a hospital, be disaggregated into specific services, so that we can identify which are 'services in the general interest' (eg, the service of a clinically mandated surgical operation) and which are not (eg, the service of receiving meals during post-operative recovery time in a single occupancy room within that hospital). Again, the structures of EU law seem to push Member States towards this kind of disaggregation of public health services, even if it is not actually mandated by EU law as it currently stands. The disaggregation of national health systems into their constituent sets of services provides a fundamental challenge to public healthcare as currently provided and conceptualized within the Member States. For instance, some have even suggested[212] that, at least in 'Bismarckian' systems, hospitals do not provide public services at all—only sickness insurance funds provide universal coverage and adequate funding for healthcare of the population. However, this approach is inconsistent with the special treatment for hospitals in the *Altmark* Decision, and in any event does not fit well with the relationship between hospitals and provision of universal healthcare in taxation-based 'Beveridgean' systems.

In general, the structuring of EU competition law, on the basis of binary and mutually exclusive relationships, is not conducive to the development of public health services within the Member States of the EU in ways that continue to serve the solidarity aims of European healthcare systems, but that also capitalize on the potential for efficiency gains through moving away from wholly public systems, which many Member States are currently seeking to achieve. Is this also the case for EU law on free movement? The chapter now turns to consider this question.

[210] Lear and Mossialos, n 82 above.

[211] Hatzopoulos, n 149 above, fn 106.

[212] Eg G Chavrier, 'Etablissment public de santé, logique économique et droit de la concurrence' 2006 Revue du Droit de la Sécurité Sociale 274–87, cited in Hatzopoulos, n 149 above.

4. Free Movement Law

The Treaty on the Functioning of the European Union (TFEU) requires that 'freedom of movement for workers shall be secured' within the EU.[213] To this end, discrimination based on nationality, in terms of employment, as between workers, is prohibited. This principle is extended by secondary legislation to discrimination in 'social advantages',[214] which have been broadly defined,[215] and thus include access to public health systems. Restrictions on the freedom of establishment are also prohibited.[216] These prohibitions are extended to family members of workers,[217] and, in some circumstances, to citizens of the EU,[218] by secondary legislation. To support free movement of natural persons, secondary legislation also coordinates the social security entitlements (including public health insurance—or rather 'sickness insurance') of those who work in different Member States during their active lives.[219] Freedom of establishment is enhanced by secondary legislation concerning mutual recognition of professional qualifications, which of course applies also to healthcare professionals.[220]

The TFEU prohibits 'restrictions' on the freedom to provide services within the EU.[221] Although the general Services Directive[222] explicitly excludes healthcare services, other specific Directives in the services field, for instance the Insurance Directives, have implications for public health systems.[223] Finally, the Treaty prohibits quantitative restrictions and 'measures having equivalent effect' to such restrictions on the free movement of goods.[224] 'Goods' include highly regulated products that are used within public health systems, such as pharmaceuticals and medical devices. The trading conditions for such goods, such as their pricing, who may sell them and under what circumstances, are often fixed within public health

213 Art 45 TFEU (ex Art 39 EC).

214 Regulation 1612/68/EEC, OJ Sp Ed [1968] L 257/2, p 475, Art 7(2).

215 Case 32/75 *Christini* [1975] ECR 1085.

216 Art 49 TFEU (ex Art 43 EC).

217 Directive 2004/38/EC OJ [2004] L 158/77, Art 2(2).

218 Directive 2004/38/EC, Art 3(1); Chapter II (right of exit and entry); Chapter III (right of residence); Chapter IV (right of permanent residence); Art 24 (right of equal treatment, with exceptions as provided elsewhere in EC law, and a derogation for social assistance and student benefits).

219 Regulation 1408/71/EEC (to be amended by Regulation 883/2004/EC, when the implementing legislation is agreed, see COM (2006) 16 final).

220 Directive 2001/19/EC of the European Parliament and of the Council of 14 May 2001 amending Council Directives 89/48/EEC and 92/51/EEC on the general system for the recognition of professional qualifications and Council Directives 77/452/EEC, 77/453/EEC, 78/686/EEC, 78/687/EEC, 78/1026/EEC, 78/1027/EEC, 80/154/EEC, 80/155/EEC, 85/384/EEC, 85/432/EEC, 85/433/EEC, and 93/16/EEC concerning the professions of nurse responsible for general care, dental practitioner, veterinary surgeon, midwife, architect, pharmacist and doctor OJ [2001] L 206/1.

221 Art 56 TFEU (ex Art 49 EC).

222 Directive 2006/123/EC of the European Parliament and of the Council of 12 December 2006 on services in the internal market OJ [2006] L 376/36.

223 Council Directive 92/49/EEC of 18 June 1992 on the coordination of laws, regulations and administrative provisions relating to direct insurance other than life assurance (third non-life insurance Directive), OJ [1992] L 228/1. See Thomson and Mossialos, n 190 above.

224 Art 34 TFEU (ex Art 28 EC).

systems, as part of regulatory controls to protect patients from unsafe or ineffective practices, and to protect public health systems from unlimited burdens on their financial resources. All of these national regulatory measures are subject to EU free movement law.

The provisions of EU free movement law have been significantly developed by the jurisprudence of the Court of Justice of the European Union, in part through its jurisdiction under what is now Article 258 TFEU (ex Article 226 EC), in claims brought by the European Commission against Member States, but mainly through its jurisdiction under what is now Article 267 TFEU (ex Article 234 EC), in claims brought by private litigants, in the first instance to national courts, which refer matters of interpretation of EU law to the Court.[225] Unlike competition law, this area of EU law is thus subject to a strong centralizing enforcement effect, although this effect is tempered by the final application of the relevant law by national courts, and of course the fact that remedies are nationally mandated.

As we have already seen, the solidarity basis of the public health systems of the Member States of the EU stands in stark contrast to the perspective of internal market law.[226] European public health systems are based on the sharing of resources with those in need through taxation and redistribution organized *by the state for those within that state*.[227] There are no general pan-European or extra-national obligations of solidarity in the health field: health systems are organized on a national basis, and the benefits for those within each system are achieved, in part, by exclusion of those outside the nation state concerned. By contrast, internal market law is concerned with abolishing national barriers to the movement of the factors of production. The benefits of internal market law include access to a wider market, and consequent efficiencies and economies of scale, that are implied in removing national laws, administrative practices, and other barriers to cross-border trade. In other words, the logic of public health systems is based on protection through exclusion and closure; the logic of internal market law is based on the benefits of inclusion and openness.

All these different bodies of EU free movement law either already have affected public health services within the Member States, by prohibiting certain national laws or practices, or have the potential to do so. The main focus in this chapter is on three interlinked areas of free movement law, as applied to national measures that affect cross-border provision of public health services: Regulation 1408/71/EEC on social security for migrant workers; Article 56 TFEU on free movement of

[225] For discussion, see C Barnard, *The Substantive Law of the EC: The Four Freedoms* (2007); P Craig and G de Búrca, *European Union Law* (2008); D Chalmers et al, *European Union Law* (2010); V Hatzopoulos and TU Do, 'The case law of the ECJ concerning the free provision of services: 2000–2005' (2006) 43 CML Rev 941.

[226] On the tensions between internal market law and social welfare law generally, see, eg, AP Van der Mei, *Free Movement of Persons within the European Community. Cross-Border Access to Public Benefits* (2003); S Giubboni, 'Free Movement of Persons and European Solidarity' (2007) 13 ELJ 360.

[227] Usually citizens and lawful residents, although there are some minor exceptions to this, such as the granting of emergency public healthcare to unlawful residents.

services;[228] and (emergent) secondary legislation on free movement of health services.

A. Regulation 883/2004/EC and Other Existing Secondary Legislation

The principal aim of Regulation 883/2004/EC[229] is to coordinate national social security schemes in the EU, in order to facilitate the free movement of workers. The Regulation applies to 'nationals of a Member State, stateless persons and refugees residing in a Member State who are or have been subject to the legislation of one or more Member States, as well as to the members of their families and to their survivors' and to resident 'survivors of persons who have been subject to the legislation of one or more Member States, irrespective of the nationality of such persons'.[230]

The material scope of the Regulation covers sickness, invalidity and maternity benefits, and so covers entitlements to public health services of those who fall within its personal scope. The question of whether a benefit falls within the scope of the Regulation is a matter of EU, not national, law. Benefits granted without any individual and discretionary assessment of personal needs, to recipients, on the basis of a legally defined position, to protect against one of the listed contingencies (which include sickness, invalidity and maternity) fall within the scope of the Regulation.[231] Thus the Court concluded with little difficulty that the Flemish social care insurance at issue in *Flemish Social Care*[232] fell within the material scope of the Regulation.[233]

The case concerned a social care insurance scheme for elderly people and others unable to look after themselves, operated by the Flemish Community of Belgium. Each of the three Belgian 'Communities' has exclusive legislative competence for matters within its domain. The other two Communities did not have similar care insurance schemes. The Flemish Community scheme applied to persons resident in

[228] On the interactions between Regulation 1408/71/EEC and Art 56 TFEU (ex Art 49 EC), from the point of view of patients, see T Hervey, 'The Current Legal Framework on the Right to Seek Healthcare Abroad in the European Union' (2007) 9 *Cambridge Yearbook of European Legal Studies* 261.

[229] OJ [2004] L 166/1–123. For a corrected version of the text, see OJ [2004] L 200/1–49. This replaced Regulation 1408/71/EEC OJ Sp Ed 1971 II, 416 and entered into force on 1 May 2010.

[230] Regulation 883/2004/EC, Art 2. The personal scope of the Regulation has been extended to include legally resident third country nationals and members of their families; see Regulation 859/2003/EC OJ [2003] L 124/1.

[231] Case 139/82 *Piscitello v INPS* [1983] ECR 1427; Case C–249/83 *Hoeckx* [1985] ECR 973; Case C–111/91 *Commission v Luxembourg* [1993] ECR I–817. For further discussion, see L Luckhaus, 'European Social Security Law' in A Ogus and N Wikeley (eds), *Wikeley, Ogus and Barendt's The Law of Social Security* (2002); T Hervey, 'Social Security: the European Union Dimension' in N Harris (ed), *Social Security Law in Context* (2000); W Palm and I Glinos, 'Enabling patient mobility in the European Union: between free movement and coordination' in E Mossialos et al (eds) (2010), n 14 above.

[232] Case C–212/06 *Government of the French Community and Walloon Government v Flemish Government* [2008] ECR I–1683.

[233] Paras 15–23.

the Dutch-speaking Region of Belgium (or the Brussels-Capital Region),[234] and to EU citizens employed in that territory and resident in another Member State of the EU. It did not apply to Belgians working in that territory, living elsewhere in Belgium. The question arose whether the scheme fell within Regulation 1408/71/EEC (which Regulation 883/2004/EC replaces), and if so whether it was precluded by Articles 3 and 13 of the Regulation, which provided that residents in a particular Member State (within the personal scope of the Regulation) must be treated the same as nationals of that state, and that a person employed in a particular Member State shall be subject to the legislation of that state, even if she resides in the territory of another Member State. The Court was also asked whether the Flemish scheme was consistent with what are now Article 21 TFEU (ex Article 18 EC) on free movement of citizens of the EU, Article 45 TFEU (ex Article 39 EC) on free movement of workers, and Article 49 TFEU (Article 43 EC) on freedom of establishment.

The Court began its analysis with its oft-stated point that 'although Member States retain the power to organise their social security schemes, they must none the less, when exercising that power, observe Community law'.[235] What are now Articles 45 and 49 TFEU exclude 'any national measure, which, even though applicable without discrimination on grounds of nationality, is capable of hindering or rendering less attractive the exercise by Community nationals of the fundamental freedoms guaranteed by the Treaty'.[236] This definition includes measures which have the effect of causing workers to lose their social security entitlements. Legislation like this, because it is based on residence, is likely to produce such effects, because only those living in the Dutch-speaking Region of Belgium (or the Brussels-Capital Region), or in another Member State could be members of the scheme. Migrant workers thinking about finding employment in the Dutch-speaking Region of Belgium or the Brussels-Capital Region might therefore be deterred from moving. This is because if they moved their residence to one of the other parts of Belgium, they would not be eligible for benefits that they might otherwise have claimed.[237] Of course, many non-Belgian EU citizens work in Belgium.[238]

The *Flemish Social Care* case—although concerning social care rather than healthcare—illustrates how the principles of non-discrimination and free movement found in Treaty provisions such as Article 45 TFEU (free movement of workers) and Article 49 TFEU (freedom of establishment), as well as in Regulation

[234] On the relationships between the (socio-cultural) Belgian 'Communities' and the (socio-economic) Belgian 'Regions', which do not coincide geographically, see T Vandamme, 'Annotation of Case C–212/06' (2009) 46 CML Rev 287, and the sources cited therein.

[235] Para 43.

[236] Para 45.

[237] Para 48.

[238] As Advocate General Sharpston explained, in paras 57–8, and 86, this point is illustrated starkly by considering two workers in the same company located in Hoegaarden in the Dutch-speaking Region. A is a Dutch-speaking Belgian, and decides to live in Hoegaarden itself. B is French, and decides to live in Jodoigne, in the French-speaking part of Belgium. They live 7 km apart. Yet A can (in fact must) be part of the social insurance scheme, whereas B cannot.

883/2004/EEC, might affect public health systems organized at regional or sub-regional levels. Several of the Member States devolve public health service provision to sub-national levels. If such schemes provide public health services based on residence, there is no reason in principle not to apply the reasoning of *Flemish Social Care*. Where public health service provision is devolved to sub-national level, and this devolution results in differences in healthcare entitlements between different regions within a particular Member State, we might envisage similar challenges through litigation to such 'postcode lotteries' as found in *Flemish Social Care*.[239]

Regulation 883/2004/EC essentially provides three types of entitlement to cross-border healthcare. There is an entitlement to *emergency* medical treatment that becomes necessary during a stay in the territory of another Member State.[240] This is administered through the European health insurance card.[241] There is also a system whereby Member States may *authorize* individual treatment in another (host) Member State.[242] The home Member State pays for the treatment, and retains responsibility and control over whether to authorize it. Some Member States use the ability to authorize treatment in other Member States relatively often; others hardly at all.[243]

Originally, the only exception to this principle of home Member State control was 'where the treatment in question cannot be provided' for the patient in the home Member State. However, following the *Pierek* litigation concerning experimental treatment,[244] the EU legislature amended the Regulation, so that it now requires authorization where the treatment (a) is covered by the health (insurance) system in the home Member State; and (b) cannot be given to the patient within 'treatment time limit which is medically justifiable' in the home Member State—taking into account the patient's 'current state of health and the probable course of his/her illness'.[245] This means that, *in exceptional circumstances*, a patient may rely on a third type of entitlement under the Regulation. This right is implicit in Article 20(2) of the Regulation, which provides that a patient is entitled to authorization if the treatment sought is provided for under his or her home legislation *and* the

[239] However, it would be open to a Member State to advance an 'objective public interest' justification for the discriminatory effect of its residence-based policy (see below). No such justification was advanced in *Flemish Social Care*, save a reference to the constitutional arrangements of Belgium. Consistent EU law holds that national constitutional structures cannot justify a failure to comply with EU law; Case 11/70 *Internationale Handelsgesellschaft* [1970] ECR 1125, para 3, so the Court did not accept this justification.

[240] In determining whether the healthcare or medical treatment has become necessary on medical grounds during a stay in another Member State, account must be taken of the nature of the healthcare or medical treatment and the expected length of the stay: Regulation 883/2004/EC, Art 19.

[241] COM (2003) 73 final, Commission Communication of 17 February 2003 concerning the introduction of the European health insurance card. Part of the EU action plan on skills and mobility, COM (2002) 72 final, Commission Communication of 13 February 2002.

[242] Regulation 883/2004/EC, Art 20.

[243] Eg, Luxembourg uses it widely, as does Malta. See Palm and Glinos in Mossialos et al (eds) (2010), n 232 above; N Muscat, K Grech, J Cachia, and D Xuereb, 'Sharing capacities— Malta and the United Kingdom' in M Rosenmoller, M McKee, and R Baeten (eds), *Patient mobility in the European Union—Learning from experience* (2006), 119–36.

[244] Case 117/77 *Pierek (No 1)* [1978] ECR 825; Case 182/78 *Pierek (No 2)* [1979] ECR 1977.

[245] Regulation 883/2004/EC, Art 20(2).

treatment is not available *for that patient—in terms of their current state of health—* within the time regarded as medically justifiable for obtaining that treatment in their home Member State.

Thus, under Regulation 883/2004/EC, although the principle of non-discrimination can have some effects on public health services within the Member States, as they must not be structured to exclude those within the scope of the Regulation from other Member States from access to public health services in accordance with the social security system of the host Member State, essentially Member States retain control over their public health systems. The vast majority of the patients entitled to public health services under the Regulation are economic contributors to the host Member State in any event, and are thus contributing to the public health system on a solidarity basis alongside nationals. There are a few exceptions to this at the margins (emergency care, and exceptional care under Article 20(2) of the Regulation), but these do not constitute a major incursion on the ability of Member States to arrange their public health services as they wish. However, another line of EU free movement law has changed the regulatory landscape here: litigation based on what is now Article 56 TFEU on the free movement of services, which is discussed below.

Before turning to discuss the application of the Treaty provisions on free movement of services, it is worth briefly considering a different body of secondary legislation: EU law on (non-life) insurance services.[246] This body of law, based on the Treaty provisions on free movement, promotes cross-border provision of insurance services within the EU, and encourages competition among insurance providers. The relevant Directive explicitly exempts social health insurance schemes from its scope.[247] However, if an insurance fund operates a social security scheme at its own risk, then this constitutes an 'economic activity' and falls within the Directive.[248] In general, Member States are prohibited from restricting prices or conditions of insurance services that fall under EU law. Nonetheless, Member States may impose such restrictions on 'insurers providing a partial or complete alternative to health cover provided by the statutory social security system' to 'protect the general good'.[249] This category would include open enrolment, community rating, standardized benefits packages and risk equalization schemes. The Directive operates on the basis that healthcare insurers that provide insurance that *substitutes* for public social health insurance are to be exempt from the constraints of EU free movement (and competition) law, whereas *supplementary* health insurance should be subject to the rules of the market. This distinction may have been appropriate at the time the Directive was adopted, but is ill-suited to the current situation where the boundaries between economic activity and social

[246] Council Directive 92/49/EEC on the coordination of laws, regulations and administrative provisions relating to direct insurance other than life assurance, the third 'Non-life Insurance' Directive, OJ [1992] L 228/23.

[247] Directive 92/49/EC, Art 2(1).

[248] Case C–206/98 *Commission v Belgium* [2000] ECR I–3509.

[249] Directive 92/49/EC, Art 54(1). See also Commission Interpretative Communication, 'Freedom to Provide Services and the General Good in the Insurance Sector', COM (1999) 5046.

security have become increasingly blurred.[250] It provides another example of the inflexible nature of EU law as applied to public health services.

The EU secondary legislation on free movement as applicable to public health services has been profoundly affected by a body of case law based on the Treaty provisions on free movement. As 'primary' measures of EU law, these provisions apply in preference to secondary legislation. The practical effect of this relationship is that the driver of legal change in this area of law is the Court of Justice of the European Union, rather than the EU legislature. The most widely reported element of this case law is the case law on free cross-border receipt of public health services.

B. Article 56 TFEU (ex Article 49 EC)

Article 56 TFEU provides that 'restrictions on freedom to provide services within the Union shall be prohibited'. The Court has interpreted this provision to establish a right for individuals to travel to another Member State to *receive* services.[251] In order to determine whether a measure of public health service provision in a Member State is prohibited under Article 56 TFEU, we need to ask whether there is a 'service', whether there is a 'restriction' on that service, and whether the restriction is justified.[252]

1. Is There a Service?

To fall within Article 56 TFEU, a service must be provided for remuneration. The essential characteristic of remuneration is that it constitutes consideration for the service in question. There is a growing market in cross-border private health services, especially in areas of fertility treatment, as well as experimental treatments of various sorts, both within the EU and globally.[253] The Court has explicitly held that privately remunerated health services fall within the Treaty provisions on freedom to provide services.[254] Moreover, the Court held in 1988 that remuneration need not come directly from the recipient of the services.[255] This ruling suggested that healthcare paid for by a sickness insurance fund or a charitable organization could fall within the Treaty concept of services. The Court confirmed this in the *Kohll* case in 1998 (much to the consternation of public health

[250] See Thomson and Mossialos in Mossialos et al (eds), n 190 above.

[251] Case 186/87 *Cowan v Le Trésor Public* [1989] ECR 195.

[252] For general discussion on the internal market in services, see V Hatzopoulos, 'Legal Aspects in Establishing the Internal Market for services', College of Europe, Research Papers in Law 6/2007; C Barnard, *The Substantive Law of the EU: The Four Freedoms* (2007), ch 14.

[253] See N Cortez, 'Patients Without Borders: The Emerging Global Market for Patients and the Evolution of Modern Health Care' (2008) 83 Indiana Law Journal 71.

[254] See Joined Cases 286/82 and 26/83 *Luisi and Carbone* [1984] ECR 377, para 16, Case C–159/90 *Society for the Protection of Unborn Children Ireland v Grogan* [1991] ECR I–4685, para 18.

[255] Case 352/85 *Bond van Adverteerders* [1988] ECR 2124.

authorities in all the Member States) by finding that 'remuneration' is present in the provision of some forms of publicly funded health services.[256]

Initially, the Court's case law applying what is now Article 56 TFEU to cross-border healthcare services concerned medical treatment reimbursed under a national social security scheme, where the treatment is paid for by the patient, but reimbursed by a public sickness insurance fund, and provided extramurally 'outside any hospital [ie public] infrastructure'. However, in 2001,[257] the principle was extended to *intramural* treatment (within a hospital), reimbursed by a national sickness insurance fund, even where such reimbursement is on the basis of regulated pre-set scales of fees. The decisive factor, in terms of whether Article 56 TFEU applies to welfare services, such as public health services, is not the nature of the service, or the nature of its provider (public hospital or private dental clinic), or its position within national welfare systems, but the manner in which the service provision is financed.[258] If there is an element of choice, either for the service recipient, or for the body paying for the service, or for both, then 'remuneration' is present. A monopoly state provider of free-to-recipients healthcare would not fall within EU law. This is probably the case whether the system is funded as a national health service or through insurance. A unitary public insurance system, characterized by subsidization and compulsory membership, probably has insufficient elements of choice. But there is no *general* exclusion for welfare provision, such as public health services, from Article 56 TFEU. Public health services are provided in the Member States through a variety of mechanisms: many of these involve provision of 'services' in the sense of Article 56 TFEU.

The earliest case (*Kohll*) involving cross-border health services concerned a Member State where public healthcare is financed largely through an insurance model, operating on the basis of cash benefits in the form of refunds for healthcare or medical treatment given. However, the Court subsequently confirmed that the principle established in *Kohll* applies also to Member States that operate a benefits-in-kind system.[259] Moreover, the Court has implicitly confirmed that this position applies in principle where the cross-border service of healthcare is received by a patient who is 'insured' (if that is the correct term) under a national health system

[256] Case C–158/96, n 2 above. For discussion see, eg, A-P Van der Mei, 'Cross-Border Access to Medical Care within the European Union—Some Reflections on the Judgments in *Decker* and *Kohll*' (1998) 5 MJ 277; A Bayens, 'Free movement of goods and services in health care: a comment on the Court cases *Decker* and *Kohll* from a Belgian point of view' (1999) 6 European Journal of Health Law 373; Editorial, 'Public Health Insurance and Freedom of Movement within the European Union' (1999) 6 European Journal of Health Law 1; P Cabral, 'Cross-border medical care in the European Union—bringing down a first wall' (1999) 24 ELR 387; J Nickless, 'The internal market and the social nature of health care' in M McKee, E Mossialos, and R Baeten (eds), *The Impact of EU law on health care systems* (2002); W Gekiere, R Baeten, and W Palm, 'Free Movement of Health Services in the EU and Health Care' in Mossialos et al (eds) (2010), n 14 above.

[257] Case C–157/99 *Geraets-Smits and Peerbooms*, n 2 above. For discussion, see A-P Van der Mei, 'Cross-border access to Health Care within the European Union: Some Reflections on *Geraets-Smits and Peerbooms* and *Vanbraekel*' (2002) 9 MJ 1.

[258] Contrast the education Case 263/86 *Belgian State v Humbel* [1988] ECR 5365; see also the Opinion of the Advocate General in Case 293/86 *Gravier* [1985] ECR 593.

[259] Case C–368/98 *Vanbraekel* [2001] ECR I–5363.

financed largely by public taxation,[260] provided of course that the patient has received a cross-border service. It should, however, be noted that, in *Watts*, involving the UK,[261] and in the subsequent *Stamatelaki* case, involving Greece,[262] the Court was not required to answer the specific question whether hospital treatment provided by a national health system funded largely by taxation constitutes a service in the sense of what is now Article 56 TFEU. As the Court noted, in those cases, the patients themselves had directly remunerated a hospital in another Member State which provided the health service at issue, thus bringing the situation within Article 56 TFEU.

Until 2006, all the litigation on freedom to receive healthcare services under what is now Article 56 TFEU[263] involved so-called 'social insurance systems', in terms of the binary model which distinguishes 'social insurance' 'Bismarckian' systems (based on the compulsory insurance of categories of persons, now expanded to include virtually all the population) from taxation-based 'Beveridgean' national health systems (funded by public taxation). Indeed the conclusion that 'remuneration' was present was based on the fact that the sickness fund at issue had paid for the health service. Such a categorization has a limiting effect on the Court's analysis. The categories represent only 'ideal types'. In practice it may be more difficult than the model implies to distinguish between them. All national healthcare systems in the EU rely on a mix of revenue sources, including compulsory or social insurance, user charges and voluntary or private insurance, with taxation playing some role in all systems.[264] Further, as Member States face similar challenges to their national health (insurance) systems, they may 'borrow' solutions from other states, leading to a certain amount of convergence. There is every reason to encourage this kind of policy isomorphism, especially if it leads to the spread of good practice, high quality, and efficiency. Because of this, the Court's implicit finding in *Watts* that, at least in principle, Article 56 TFEU applies to patients receiving cross-border healthcare services belonging to either type of national health system is correct. If public health systems in the Member States all use taxation to some extent, there is no good reason to exempt those that use taxation to a larger extent from the application of EU free movement law. The Court is right to depart from its earlier jurisprudence based on a binary distinction between 'social insurance' (remuneration) and 'national health system' (taxation) models.

[260] Case C–372/04 *Watts* [2006] ECR I–4325; Case C–444/05 *Stamatelaki* [2007] ECR I–3185.

[261] For details on the healthcare system within the UK, see European Observatory on Health Care Systems, *Health Care Systems in Transition: United Kingdom* (1999), available at <http://www.euro.who.int/observatory/Hits/TopPage>.

[262] For details on the Greek healthcare system, see World Health Organization, *Health Care Systems in Transition: Greece* (1996), available at <http://www.euro.who.int/observatory/Hits/TopPage>.

[263] For a review see A Kaczorowska, 'A Review of the Creation by the European Court of Justice of the Right to Effective and Speedy Medical Treatment and its Outcomes' (2006) 12 ELJ 345.

[264] For details see the country reports in WHO Europe's series *Health Care Systems in Transition*, available at <http://www.euro.who.int/observatory/Hits/TopPage>.

2. *Is There a Restriction?*

The term 'restriction' in Article 56 TFEU has been defined as any measure that actually or even potentially inhibits provision of services between Member States.[265] As the Court put it in *Stamatelaki*:[266] 'Article [56 TFEU] precludes the application of any national rules which have the effect of making the provision of services between Member States more difficult than the provision of services purely within a Member State.'[267] The effect of this interpretation is that all kinds of national measures within public health services—given that they are, in general, organized on a national territorial basis—potentially fall foul of Article 56 TFEU.

In particular, national rules on prior authorization for medical treatment in another Member State, envisaged by Regulation 883/2004/EC, may *themselves* constitute 'restrictions' on free movement of services, wherever such a system of prior authorization 'prevents or deters' patients from seeking healthcare from providers in other Member States.[268] This will be the case, for instance, where authorization is subject to the requirements that the treatment be 'normal within the professional circles concerned' in the home Member State, and that the treatment be a 'medical necessity', meaning that adequate treatment cannot be obtained without undue delay in hospitals in the home Member State that have a contractual relationship with the sickness fund.[269] Where the application of the prior authorization rules under Regulation 883/2004/EC results in a lower level of cover where treatment is received in another Member State from that in which the patient is insured, this also constitutes a restriction in the sense of Article 56 TFEU.[270] A restriction is also present where the rules on reimbursement of costs associated with the medical treatment itself (for example, board, lodging, travel) are different where the medical treatment is sought in another Member State.[271] So a rule making reimbursement for travel, board, and lodging conditional on a medical professional finding that the healthcare is 'absolutely necessary owing to the greatly increased prospects of success outside the home State', *applicable only where the healthcare is sought abroad*, is a 'restriction'.[272] Indeed, expenditure on board and lodging can be regarded as forming an integral part of the healthcare

[265] See Case 186/87 *Cowan v Le Trésor Public* [1989] ECR 195, paras 15–17; Case C–76/90 *Säger v Dennemeyer* [1991] ECR I–4221, para 12; Case C–43/93 *Vander Elst* [1994] ECR I–3803, para 14; Case C–272/94 *Guiot and Climatec* [1996] ECR I–1905, para 10.

[266] Para 25.

[267] See also Case C–381/93 *Commission v France* [1984] ECR I–5145, para 17; Case C–158/96 *Kohll*, n 2 above, para 33; Case C–368/86 *Vanbraekel*, n 260 above, para 45; Case C–157/99 *Geraets-Smits and Peerbooms*, n 2 above, para 61; Case C–372/04 *Watts*, n 261 above, para 94.

[268] Case C–8/02 *Leichtle* [2004] ECR I–2641, para 30; Case C–372/04 *Watts*, n 261 above, paras 95–8.

[269] Case C–157/99, *Geraets-Smits/Peerbooms*, n 2 above, paras 60–9; Case C–385/99 *Müller-Fauré/Van Riet* [2003] ECR I–4509, paras 37–44. For discussion see M Flear, 'Annotation of Case C–385/99 *Müller-Fauré*' (2004) 41 CML Rev 209; G Davies, 'Health and Efficiency: Community Law and National Health Systems in the Light of *Müller-Fauré*' (2004) 67 MLR 94.

[270] Case C–368/98 *Vanbraekel*, n 260 above, para 45.

[271] Case C–8/02 *Leichtle*, n 269 above.

[272] *Leichtle*, n 269 above, para 41.

itself.[273] Another example is where there is no need to seek prior authorization to have medical treatment in national health service hospitals, free of charge, in the home Member State, but that receiving treatment from a hospital in another Member State, at the expense of the national health service, is not permitted without prior authorization.[274] Similarly, where a patient need not pay out in advance for emergency medical treatment in a public hospital or a private hospital located in that Member State (whether or not that hospital has an agreement with the national health system); whereas if he is admitted to a private hospital in another Member State, he has to pay the costs of the treatment himself, this is a 'restriction'.[275]

The conclusion that national rules requiring prior authorization, as envisaged by Regulation 883/2004/EC, which gives the home Member State control over whether a patient may seek cross-border health services at the expense of the public health system, are prohibited by EU law may seem surprising. However, Regulations are 'secondary' EU law, subsidiary to the 'primary' or 'constitutional' sources of EU law, that is, in particular, the Treaty on European Union and Treaty on Functioning of the European Union.[276] Where an individual enjoys a right based on a primary source of EU law, this cannot be compromised by secondary EU legislation. Rather, the legislation must either be set aside[277] or interpreted consistently with the Treaty provisions.[278]

The relationship between what is now Article 56 TFEU and Regulation 1408/71/EEC, Article 22, arose in *Inizan*.[279] Ms Inizan, resident in France, was covered by a French sickness insurance fund. She sought multidisciplinary pain treatment at a hospital in Germany. The sickness insurance fund refused to pay for the treatment, on the grounds that Article 22(2) (2) Regulation 1408/71/EEC had not been met, in other words, the treatment sought was not 'among the benefits provided for by the legislation of the Member State on whose territory the person concerned resides and where he cannot be given such treatment within the time normally necessary for obtaining the treatment in question in the Member State of residence, taking account of his current state of health and the probable course of the disease'.

The national court asked whether Article 22(1)(c)(i) of Regulation 1408/71/EEC was valid. In particular, was it consistent with what is now Article 56 TFEU, given that the condition of prior authorization could be a 'restriction' on the free movement of services within the internal market? The Court began its analysis, as it

[273] *Leichtle*, n 269 above, para 43.
[274] Case C–372/04 *Watts*, n 261 above, paras 95–6.
[275] Case C–444/05 *Stamatelaki*, n 261 above, para 27.
[276] Case 294/83 *Parti écologiste 'Les Verts' v European Parliament*, [1986] ECR 1339, para 23.
[277] Under Art 230 EC.
[278] The duty to do so is implicit in Arts 5 and 7 EC, which constrain the powers of the legislative institutions of the EU, and in Art 220 EC, which provides that the ECJ is under a duty to ensure that in the interpretation of the Treaty (and implicitly, acts adopted on the basis of the Treaty), 'the law is observed', and Art 234 EC, which gives the Court jurisdiction in acts concerning interpretation of acts of EU law.
[279] Case C–56/01 [2003] ECR I–12403.

often does in these cases, with the assertion that EU law 'does not detract from the power of the Member States to organise their social security systems'. However, 'when exercising that power, the Member States must comply' with EU law.[280]

The purpose of Article 22 of the Regulation, according to the Court, is 'to confer upon insured persons an entitlement to benefits in kind . . . as though the insured person were in the [host] State'. In other words, implicitly, the purpose of Article 22 is not to protect national public health systems, and give Member States control over whether or not authorization to receive health services in another Member State is granted. Its purpose is to protect free moving persons within the EU. Therefore, the Court was then able to find that Article 22 'helps to facilitate the free movement of persons'[281] and 'to the same extent, the cross-border provision of medical services between Member States'.[282] Thus, the Treaty does not invalidate the provisions of Regulation 1408/71/EEC, Article 22. Rather, the Regulation must be interpreted consistently with the Treaty provisions on free movement within the internal market.

The national rules at issue in *Inizan*, which allow a sickness fund to refuse prior authorization for medical treatment provided in another Member State, where the same or equally effective treatment cannot be provided in the home Member State without undue delay, are 'restrictions' on free movement of services in the sense of Article 56 TFEU. This is because the need to get prior authorization, and to show that no treatment the same or equally effective was available in France, make it more difficult for patients to receive services in another Member State.[283] Because national rules on prior authorization make it more difficult to receive the health service in another Member State than to have the health service provided purely within the home Member State, the rules are 'restrictions' in the sense of Article 56 TFEU.[284] The consequence is that such national rules are prohibited, unless they are justified.

As well as rules that restrict free movement of service recipients, EU free movement law prohibits national measures that restrict free movement of service providers. This is illustrated by *Commission v France (Bio-medical Laboratories)*. France required laboratories providing bio-medical analysis to have the 'seat' of their business in France, so as to be licensed and authorized to work within the French statutory health insurance scheme. The Court found that this constituted a restriction to the freedom to provide services because 'it *de facto* precludes laboratories established in another Member State from being able to provide services to insured persons established in France'.[285] As Gekiere, Baeten, and Palm point out, such restrictive national measures can comprise both those that restrict access to a national market for a health service provider, but also more general regulation that governs the provision of health services. These can be quantitative restrictions, limiting the number of providers of a particular health service within a particular

[280] Para 17. [281] Paras 21 and 25. [282] Para 21.
[283] Para 54.
[284] *Watts*, n 261 above, para 94.
[285] Case C–496/01 *Commission v France*, [2004] ECR I–2352, para 91.

Member State, for example, territorial planning rules restricting the number of pharmacies according to the number of inhabitants and the minimum distance between them, or quota systems limiting the number of health professionals working within the statutory health system.[286] They can also be qualitative measures which limit access to a certain activity. In short, a very wide range of national regulatory measures within public health systems are covered by Article 56 TFEU. For instance, the following measures are included:[287]

- ownership rules for clinics and pharmacies;[288]
- a ban on operating more than one entity;[289]
- a ban for enterprises active in the distribution of medicines (or having links with companies active in this area) on the acquisition of holdings in private pharmaceutical companies or community pharmacies;[290]
- the limitation of the choice of legal form for clinics or pharmacies;[291]
- a ban on opening a pharmacy in areas without a doctor's surgery;[292]
- the refusal under a national social security scheme to reimburse services of clinical biology laboratories whose members, partners, or directors are not all natural persons authorized to carry out medical analyses;[293]
- prohibition on the enrolment in a register of the order of any doctor or dental surgeon who is still enrolled or registered in another Member State;[294]
- national rules reserving the task of carrying out certain medical activities to a category of professionals holding specific qualifications to the exclusion of health providers who are not qualified medical doctors;[295]
- the requirement of an authorization to set up a private outpatient clinic for dental medicine[296] or the requirement to have a place of business on national territory in order to obtain the requisite operation authorization and to work under the statutory health insurance;[297]

[286] Case C–456/05 *Commission v Germany*, [2007] ECR I–10517.
[287] List taken from Gekiere, Baeten, and Palm, n 257 above, updated.
[288] Cases C–171/07 *Apothekerkammer des Saarlandes* and C–172/07 *Neumann-Seiwert* [2009] ECR I–4171 (prohibition of foreign ownership of pharmacies), and Case C–531/06 *Commission v Italy (Pharmacies)* [2009] ECR I–4103 (national rules reserving the ownership of pharmacies for pharmacists or legal entities consisting of pharmacists).
[289] European Commission, 'Internal market: infringement proceedings concerning Italy, Austria and Spain with regard to pharmacies', *Press release*, IP/06/858, Brussels, 28 June 2006.
[290] Case C–531/06 *Commission v Italy (Pharmacies)* 2009] ECR I–4103.
[291] Cases C–171/07 *Apothekerkammer des Saarlandes* and C–172/07 *Neumann-Seiwert* [2009] ECR I–4171.
[292] European Commission, IP/06/858, n 290 above.
[293] Case 221/85 *Commission v Belgium* [1987] ECR 719.
[294] Case 96/85 *Commission v France* [1986] ECR 1475.
[295] Case C–108/96 *Mac Quen* [2001] ECR I–837.
[296] Case C–169/07 *Hartlauer Handelsgesellschaft mbH v Wiener Landesregierung and Oberösterreichische Landsergierung* [2009] ECR I–1721.
[297] Case C–496/01 *Commission v France* [2004] ECR I–2351. The fact that the ECJ recognizes that it is for the Member State in which the patient is affiliated to decide which medical treatments are covered by sickness insurance and to establish the extent to which sickness coverage is made available to

- minimum staff levels or equipment norms for hospitals;[298]
- the requirement to access secondary and tertiary care through a 'gatekeeper' general practitioner.[299]

All such national rules are prohibited under EU free movement law, unless they are justified.

3. *Is the Restriction Justified?*

In a judgment dating back to 1974,[300] the Court held:

[T]aking into account the particular nature of the services to be provided, specific requirements imposed on the person providing the service cannot be considered incompatible with the Treaty where they have as their purpose the application of... rules justified by the general good... which are binding upon any person established in the State in which the service is provided.

Indirectly discriminatory restrictions on free movement of services can thus be justified by an objective public interest,[301] if four conditions are met.[302] The restriction must be applied in an objective, non-discriminatory manner,[303] based on judicially reviewable criteria known in advance.[304] There must be imperative reasons relating to the public interest (mandatory requirements). The public interest must not be already protected by the state of establishment (equivalence).[305] The restriction must not be disproportionate to its ends (proportionality).[306] The test in *Gebhard* was later confirmed in two cases involving health

its insured patients does not change the conclusion that the requirement comes under the scrutiny of free movement rules (Case C–385/99 *Müller-Fauré*, n 270 above, para 98).

[298] Included in the initial proposal for a Services Directive.

[299] COM (2008) 418 final.

[300] Case 33/74 *Van Binsbergen* [1974] ECR 1299.

[301] For similar exemptions from or exceptions to the free movement rules, see Arts 36, 45(3) and (4), 52(1), 62, and 65 TFEU (ex Arts 30, 39(3) and (4), 46(1), 55, 58 EC); and the jurisprudence of the ECJ on 'mandatory requirements' (see, eg, Case 120/78 '*Cassis de Dijon*' [1979] ECR 649) or 'objective public interests' (see, eg, Case 33/74 *Van Binsbergen*, n 301 above; Case 71/76 *Thieffry* [1977] ECR 765; Case C–384/93 *Alpine Investments* [1995] ECR I–1141; Case C–55/94 *Gebhard* [1995] ECR I–4165). For further discussion see J Scott, 'Mandatory or Imperative Requirements in the EU and the WTO' in C Barnard and J Scott (eds), *The Law of the Single European Market: Unpacking the Premises* (2002).

[302] See Case C–55/94 *Gebhard* [1995] ECR I–4165, para 37; Case 220/83 *Commission v France (Insurance Services)* [1986] ECR 3663; Case 252/83 *Commission v Denmark* [1986] ECR 3713; Case 205/84 *Commission v Germany* [1986] ECR 3755; Case 206/84 *Commission v Ireland* [1986] ECR 3817.

[303] If distinctions are made on the basis of nationality, then the measure can be justified only under the grounds set out in Arts 45(3) and 52 TFEU.

[304] Case C–157/99 *Geraets-Smits*, n 2 above, para 90; Case C–385/99 *Müller-Fauré*, n 270 above, para 85; Case C–372/04 *Watts*, n 261 above, paras 116–20.

[305] See, eg, Case C–272/94 *Guiot and Climatec* [1996] ECR I–1905.

[306] See, eg, Case 427/85 *Commission v Germany (Lawyers Services)* [1988] ECR 1123, para 26.

services, *Mac Quen*[307] and *Gräbner*,[308] which concerned national laws that restricted the provision of certain medical services to qualified physicians. In both cases the restrictions were considered justified and necessary to protect public health.

The concept of 'objective public interest' is open. The Court has recognized interests such as the application of professional rules, including those relating to the organization of professions, qualifications or professional ethics, for the public good,[309] the social protection provided by national social security systems,[310] the financial viability of such social security systems,[311] and consumer protection.[312] In the case law on cross-border health services, the most significant of these is the protection of the financial viability of social security systems.

Here, the Court's jurisprudence is based on a distinction between 'extra-mural' and 'hospital' care. So while in the *Kohll* case, the Court found that 'reimbursement of the costs of dental treatment provided in other Member States, in accordance with the tariff of the state of insurance, has no significant effect on the financing of the social security system',[313] a different conclusion was reached in later cases involving hospital care.[314] In these cases, the Court refers to the distinct characteristics of the hospital sector, in particular, the planning of the number of hospitals, their geographical distribution, the mode of their organization, the equipment they are provided with, and the nature of the health services they are able to offer. This kind of planning aims to ensure sufficient and permanent access to a balanced range of high-quality hospital services in the Member State concerned. It is necessary for public health and even the survival of a population. Hospital planning assists with cost control (which the Court explicitly notes is necessary, as financial resources are limited, yet demands are increasing), and fosters efficiency in the deployment of financial, technical, and human resources. Rules requiring prior authorization for hospital treatment may be justified, although the proportionality test must be met.[315]

307 Case C–108/96, *Mac Quen*, n 296 above: Belgian national rules reserving the task of carrying out certain optical examinations to a category of professionals holding specific qualifications, such as ophthalmologists, to the exclusion of opticians who are not qualified medical doctors.

308 Case C–294/00 *Deutsche Paracelsus v Gräbner* [2002] ECR I–6515: prohibition of the exercise of the activity of 'healer' by people not being qualified as doctors.

309 Case 33/74 *Van Binsbergen*, n 301 above, para 14; Case 292/86 *Gulling* [1988] ECR 11, para 29, Case C–106/91 *Ramrath* [1992] ECR I–3351.

310 Case C–272/94 *Guiot and Climatec*, n 306 above.

311 Case 157/99 *Geraets-Smits/Peerbooms*, n 2 above; Case C–368/98 *Vanbraekel*, n 260 above; Case C–385/99 *Müller-Fauré/Van Riet*, n 270 above, Case C–8/01 *Leichtle*, n 269 above; Case C–372/04 *Watts*, n 261 above, para 145; Case C–444/05 *Stamatelaki* n 26 above.

312 Case 205/84 *Commission v Germany*, n 303 above, para 30; Case C–288/89 *Gouda* [1991] ECR I–4007, para 27; Case C–76/90 *Säger* [1991] ECR I–4221, para 15; Case C–275/92 *Schindler* [1994] ECR I–1039, para 58.

313 *Kohll*, n 2 above, para 42.

314 Case C–157/99 *Geraets-Smits/Peerbooms*, n 2 above, paras 76–82; Case C–385/99 *Müller-Fauré/Van Riet*, n 270 above, paras 67–71 and 76–83; Case C–56/01 *Inizan*, n 280 above, para 56; Case C–372/04 *Watts*, n 261 above, paras 102–10; Case C–444/05 *Stamatelaki*, n 26 above, paras 31–2.

315 *Geraets-Smits*, n 2 above, para 82; *Watts*, n 261 above, paras 106, 114, *Stamatelaki*, n 26 above, para 34.

As is the case with the application of Article 106(2) TFEU, the question of proportionality is crucial in terms of the substantive outcome of claims to the effect that measures within public health systems constitute unlawful 'restrictions' on free movement of services. The version of the proportionality test adopted by the Court in the context of what is now Article 56 TFEU is the 'strong' proportionality test: the Member State must show[316] that the measure constitutes the least restrictive means of protecting the objective public interest, and that no other imaginable measure could achieve that objective with a lesser detrimental effect on free movement of services. In the case law to date, the Member States have not been particularly successful in meeting the proportionality test. In part, this is because in several cases, Member States have not really articulated why their policy or practice serves an objective public interest in a manner proportionate to that aim.[317] This silence on the part of the Member States is probably because the Member States were reluctant to accept that Article 56 TFEU could apply to public health services at all. However, it is also because the strong version of the proportionality test is very difficult to meet. Where a particular policy or practice forms part of a public health system, it is not always easy to show that revision of *that specific policy or practice*, to make it easier for cross-border health services to be received, will really jeopardize the financial viability *of the entire system*.[318] So, for instance, in *Kohll*, the Court found that to reimburse the costs of dental treatment provided in other Member States, at the tariff rate for treatment provided in Luxembourg, 'has no significant effect on the financing of the social security system'.[319] In *Vanbraekel*, the Court found that no additional financial burden would be placed on the sickness insurance system of the home state.[320] In *Watts*, although in principle the requirement that the national system will only assume costs of hospital treatment provided in another Member State where prior authorization has been given 'appears to be . . . necessary and reasonable',[321] the lack of a legal framework for oversight of the procedure by which authorization was refused meant that what is now Article 56 TFEU applied.

316 Member States have fallen foul of this requirement in several of the relevant cases. For instance, see Case C–8/02 *Leichtle*, n 269 above, para 47: 'as regards the justification based on the need to avoid a risk of serious harm to the financial equilibrium of the social security system, *no clear argument has been put* before the Court in support of the assertion that [the national law] is necessary for such purposes' (italics added); Case C–386/99 *Muller-Faure*, n 270 above, para 93.

317 Eg, Case C–385/99 *Müller-Fauré*, n 270 above, para 92 '. . . It is not clear from the arguments submitted to the Court that such waiting times are necessary . . .' and para 93 '. . . no specific evidence has been produced to the Court . . .'; Case C–8/02 *Leichtle*, n 269 above, para 47 '. . . no clear argument has been put before the Court . . .'.

318 Gekiere, Baeten, and Palm, n 257 above, show that 'providing good evidence to justify public intervention under the free movement rules is very challenging for health authorities', 'the Court requires examining all the particular circumstances of the individual case. Even if a rule is in general justified, this does not automatically mean that it is justified in each specific situation. This requirement of flexibility is very demanding for regulation'; see also Davies, 'The process and side-effects of harmonisation of European welfare states', n 15 above, 29.

319 Para 42.

320 Para 52.

321 Para 110.

The uncertainty of the application of Article 56 TFEU, and the undesirability of 'law making through litigation' in this field,[322] has prompted the governments of the Member States and others, such as healthcare providers and sickness funds, to call for a legislative response.[323] To date, however, the EU legislative institutions have been unable to agree on a Directive that covers health services in the internal market. There is now, however, a Commission proposal on 'patients' rights in cross border health care'.[324]

C. Proposed Secondary Legislation on 'Patients' Rights in Cross Border Health Care'

The obvious route for secondary legislation on health services in the internal market—through internal market legislation—was not politically acceptable. This is because health is not seen as a 'service' in European societies, and to attach health to the general Directive on services in the internal market would have been politically impossible. As it was, the so-called Bolkestein Directive[325] was watered down from the Commission's original proposal.[326] Directive 2006/123/EC does not apply to '(f) healthcare services whether or not they are provided via healthcare facilities, and regardless of the ways in which they are organised and financed at national level or whether they are public or private'.[327]

Following the European Parliament and Council calling for a specific legal instrument on health services in the internal market, the Commission (DG SANCO) ran a public consultation in 2006–2007 to inform its proposal drafting. Although an unofficial version of a proposal was circulating around Brussels in late 2007, it was never formally promulgated as a proposal—probably because the Council and Commission were concerned not to derail the Lisbon Treaty. The Commission proposal eventually appeared in July 2008.[328]

According to the Commission, the aims of the proposal are threefold:

1. To help patients exercise their rights to reimbursement for health treatment in any EU country (cross-border healthcare);

[322] Further litigation is in the pipeline, eg, Case C–336/08 *Reinke*, involving German rules on access to emergency medical treatment in private hospitals in other Member States.

[323] See Palm and Glinos in Mossialos et al (eds) (2010), n 232 above; T Hervey and L Trubek, 'Freedom to Provide Health Care Services within the EU: An Opportunity for a Transformative Directive' (2007) 13 (3) Columbia Journal of European Law 623. Various other 'non legislative' or 'soft law' responses have also been pursued. For discussion, see T Hervey, 'The European Union and the Governance of Health Care' in G de Búrca and J Scott, *Law and New Governance in the EU and the US* (2006).

[324] COM (2008) 418 final.

[325] Directive 2006/123/EC on services in the internal market OJ [2006] L 376/36.

[326] For discussion of the health services proposals in the original proposal, see W Palm and I Glinos, 'Enabling patient mobility in the EU: between free movement and coordination' in E Mossialos, G Permanand, R Baeten, T Hervey (eds), n 232 above.

[327] Directive 2006/123/EC, Art 2(2)(f). For discussion of the Services Directive, see C Barnard, 'Unravelling the Services Directive' (2008) 45 CML Rev 323.

[328] COM (2008) 414 final.

2. To provide assurance about the safety and quality of cross-border healthcare;
3. To foster cooperation between health systems to improve healthcare for all.

Following some 46 Recitals, the proposed Directive is structured in five Chapters, covering General Provisions; Responsibilities of Member States for compliance with general principles for healthcare; Use of Healthcare in another Member State; Cooperation on Healthcare; and Final Provisions.

Chapter I on General Provisions covers the aim, scope of the provision; its relationship with other measures of EU law; and definitions. A number of existing pieces of EU legislation[329] could potentially come into conflict with the proposed Directive. These include Regulation 883/2004/EC on coordination of social security schemes. The proposal explicitly rebuts the normal *lex posteriori derogate priori* rule.[330] For instance, Article 3(2) of the proposal states that where a patient is entitled to authorization under Article 20 of Regulation 883/2004/EC, the provisions of that Regulation apply, and Articles 6–9 of this Directive 'shall not apply'. As explained above, Regulation 883/2004/EC envisages three situations where authorization must be granted: (i) emergency care is needed in another Member State;[331] (ii) where the treatment in question cannot be provided for the patient in the home Member State within the time normally necessary for obtaining the treatment in the home Member State;[332] and (iii) discretionary authorization.[333] It appears from the wording of Article 3(2) of the proposal that if a Member State grants authorization for cross-border care under the administrative and procedural arrangements it sets up for Regulation 883/2004/EC, this does *not* exclude the potential application of the proposed Directive. This is consistent with Recital 23, which says: 'the patient may choose which mechanism they prefer'. It is not quite the case, however, as Recital 22 claims, that 'the two systems are coherent: either this Directive applies or Regulation 883/2004'. Rather it appears that there could be circumstances where either measure could apply, and the patient may choose.

[329] Such as Directive 95/46/EC on the protection of individuals with regard to the processing of personal data and on the free movement of such data and Directive 2002/58/EC concerning the processing of personal data and the protection of privacy in the electronic communications sector OJ [2002] L 201/37; Regulation (EC) No 726/2004 of the European Parliament and of the Council of 31 March 2004 laying down Community procedures for the authorisation and supervision of medicinal products for human and veterinary use and establishing a European Medicines Agency OJ [2004] L 136/1 and Directive 2001/83/EC on the Community code relating to medicinal products for human use OJ [2001] L 121/34; Directive 2001/20/EC of the European Parliament and of the Council of 4 April 2001 on the approximation of the laws, regulations and administrative provisions of the Member States relating to the implementation of good clinical practice in the conduct of clinical trials on medicinal products for human use OJ [2001] L 121/34; Directive 96/71/EC of the European Parliament and of the Council of 16 December 1996 concerning the posting of workers in the framework of the provision of services OJ [1997] L 18/1; Directive 2000/43/EC of the Council of 29 June 2000 implementing the principle of equal treatment between persons irrespective of racial or ethnic origin OJ [2000] L 180/26.

[330] If two pieces of legislation are irreconcilable, the latter prevails.

[331] Within Art 22(1) of Regulation 1408/71/EEC.

[332] Art 22(2).

[333] The original aim of Art 22 of Regulation 1408/71/EEC—leaving Member States the choice of whether or not to authorize cross-border healthcare.

There are benefits and drawbacks of each route. Article 56 TFEU implies free choice on the part of the patient. However, patients using Regulation 883/2004/EC have assurance that their costs will eventually be covered, they do not need to pay in advance, and may even benefit from some services that are not available at home. The position that patients will continue to have a choice is also consistent with the Court's case law under what is now Article 56 TFEU.[334] It does not significantly clarify the existing legal position or increase certainty.

Chapter II of the proposal contains a single article, providing that the Member State of treatment shall be responsible for the organization and delivery of healthcare. This provision responds to concerns that patients moving across borders might be unsure which public health system is responsible for quality; safety; ensuring that provision meets good medical practice, based on international science; monitoring of quality and safety; providing information to patients; providing complaints mechanisms, remedies, and compensation; a professional liability insurance system or similar arrangement; respecting the right to privacy; and equal treatment on grounds of sex, race, age, disability, and so on. The EU is to play a role in developing guidelines on these matters in the future, 'in so far as it is necessary to facilitate the provision of cross-border healthcare'.[335]

Chapter III covers 'use of healthcare in another Member State', which is defined as healthcare provided in the Member State other than where the patient is insured.[336] The general principle[337] is that patients 'will not be prevented from receiving healthcare provided in another Member State'. Member States 'will reimburse the costs to the insured person'.[338] This obligation is subject to two provisos: the treatment in question must be among the benefits provided by the legislation to which the insured person is affiliated; and the obligation is also subject to the remainder of the proposed Directive.

The first of these responds to a concern that followed some of the case law on free movement of patients. Which Member State was to determine what treatments were available, at the expense of the public purse? Some Member States, for

[334] It is because of the fact that the social security coordination mechanism grants rights and advantages which citizens would not otherwise have, that the Court explicitly upheld the coordination route: Case C–56/01 *Inizan*, n 280 above, para 22; see Palm and Glinos in Mossialos et al (eds) (2010), n 232 above.

[335] Art 5(3).

[336] See Art 4(c).

[337] Art 6.

[338] Art 6(2) provides that the costs of healthcare provided in another Member State shall be reimbursed by the Member State of affiliation up to the level of costs that would have been paid out had the same or similar healthcare been provided in that Member State. However, the Member State must not pay out more than the actual costs of the healthcare received. This provision clarifies the case law. Following the *Vanbraekel* case it appeared that a patient might actually make a profit on healthcare received in another Member State. Art 6(2) will prevent that from arising. It means that, whatever the actual costs of the healthcare, the patient should be neither out of pocket, nor have made a profit at the expense of the home Member State. In theory at least, this provision could encourage greater efficiency in healthcare provision across the EU. However, in practice the numbers of patients actually taking up the opportunity to receive cross-border healthcare is likely to remain low—at less than 1 per cent—and mainly confined to border areas and treatments for rare diseases, with only a few going abroad because of lack of capacity in their home Member State.

instance, recognize spa treatments or balneo-therapy, where others do not. The proposal makes it clear that it is the Member State which will be financially responsible—that is, the home Member State, or the Member State of affiliation—that determines the basket of healthcare that is to be reimbursed under its public health system. Control remains with the Member State which pays for the service.

The second of these makes it clear that later provisions in the proposal, for example the rule in Article 8 that a Member State may have prior authorization systems for hospital care, are not undermined by Article 6. Article 6(3) clarifies that the home Member State may impose conditions of eligibility equivalent to those imposed on patients seeking treatment at home. So, for instance, the requirement to access secondary and tertiary care through a 'gatekeeper' general practitioner (which could potentially be a 'restriction' on free movement of services under Article 56 TFEU) may be relied upon by the Member States. However, such national rules must not be discriminatory, nor an obstacle to the free movement of persons. Many of the national rules tackled by the case law to date were exactly that. For instance, the rule in *Kohll* discriminated directly on grounds of nationality, as it required authorization for treatment outside the Member State, but no authorization was required for treatment within the Member State. Indirectly discriminatory rules include those such as at issue in *Geraets-Smits/Peerbooms*,[339] or *Leichtle*.[340] The proposed Directive does not change the legal position with respect to such rules.

Article 6(4) also clarifies an issue that has arisen in the case law. It requires Member States to have a mechanism by which costs of healthcare received in another Member State are to be calculated. This mechanism must be based on objective, non-discriminatory criteria, known in advance. One of the arguments in cases such as *Watts*, involving the UK—which has a taxation-based free-at-the-point-of-receipt national health system—was that there were no nationally set tariffs for the reimbursement of patients, and so the amount of reimbursement to which Mrs Watts was entitled was not clear. The Advocate General suggested that the rates of reimbursement could be determined by the UK's NHS (Charges to Overseas Visitors) Regulations 1989. Under the proposed Directive, Member States will have to provide clear statements of what tariffs apply for cross-border healthcare—even if they have no system of tariffs for healthcare received within the public healthcare system within the Member State itself.

Articles 7 and 8 draw a distinction between hospital care and non-hospital care. According to Article 7, reimbursement of cross-border non-hospital care may not

[339] n 279 above, where no authorization was needed for contracted hospitals, but authorization was needed for hospitals with which the sickness insurance body did not have a contractual relationship (though the Court held this could be objectively justified).

[340] n 269 above. There authorization for healthcare, and the associated costs of healthcare, were subject to the condition that a medical professional had determined that the healthcare was 'absolutely necessary outside the home State, on account of the greatly increased prospects for success'. Such a condition, by its very nature, has the effect of hindering or inhibiting cross-border receipt of healthcare services.

be subject to prior authorization, where the cost of that care, if it had been provided at home, would have been covered by the social security system.

Article 8 covers hospital care. It begins with a definition of what hospital care is:

(a) healthcare which requires overnight accommodation of the patient concerned for at least one night;

(b) healthcare, included in a specific list,[341] that does not require overnight accommodation. The list is to be limited to:

(i) using highly specialized medical infrastructure or equipment

(ii) involving treatments posing a particular risk for the patient or the population.

The use of the word 'requires' suggests a more stringent standard than, say, 'is conveniently provided by'. Following the Court's case law, the test of whether a particular treatment requires hospital care for the purposes of this Article must be in accordance with international medical science, not with national law, cultural, administrative, or medical practice.

Article 8(3) contains the meat of the provision. According to Article 8(3), Member States may provide for a system of prior authorization for reimbursement of the costs of cross-border hospital care. The Member State may only do so if the primary purpose of the prior authorization system is:

> to address the consequent outflow of patients . . . and to prevent it from undermining, or being likely to seriously undermine:
>
> (i) the financial balance of the Member State's social security system; and/or
>
> (ii) the planning and rationalization carried out in the hospital sector to avoid hospital overcapacity, imbalance in the supply of hospital care and logistical and financial wastage, maintenance of a balanced medical and hospital service open to all, or the maintenance of treatment capacity or medical competence on the territory of the concerned Member State.

The prior authorization system must be limited to what is necessary and proportionate. It may not constitute a means of arbitrary discrimination. These 'objective public interest' justifications come directly from the case law of the Court.

What is the legal significance of this proposed provision? Two elements are of particular interest: the proportionality test and the distinction between hospital and non-hospital care. Article 8(4) states that 'the prior authorisation system shall be

[341] The specific list is to be set up and maintained by the Commission, according to a comitology procedure. This is a system whereby a committee of national civil servants, chaired by the Commission, makes recommendations that the European Parliament and Council have to oppose or adopt, within a particular time frame. It is widely used in EU law, and ensures that detailed technical decisions are not held up by extremely slow political processes or opposition. See, eg, M Andenas and A Turk (eds), *Delegated Legislation and the Role of Committees in the EC* (2000); C Joerges and E Vos (eds), *EU Committees: Social Regulation, Law and Politics* (1999); R Dehousse, 'Comitology? Who watches the watchmen?' (2003) 10 Journal of European Public Policy 798.

limited to what is necessary and proportional to avoid such impact, and shall not constitute a means of arbitrary discrimination'. How should we interpret this provision? Proportionality is a general principle of EU law.[342] But, as already noted, proportionality has a wide range of possible interpretations: ranging from a very strict or high standard and a soft or lower standard. In the context of its internal market jurisprudence, where the Court applies proportionality to test whether national law that impedes free movement of services or goods, is nevertheless objectively justified, it applies a strong test—that the measure must be the least restrictive possible in the circumstances.[343] It seems that the Court has continued this line of jurisprudence when applying the proportionality test to restrictions on free movement of healthcare services under what is now Article 56 TFEU.[344]

Recital 31 of the proposal purports to interpret Articles 8(3) and (4): 'As the assessment of the precise impact of an expected outflow of patients requires complex assumptions and calculations, the Directive allows for a system of prior authorisation if there is sufficient reason to expect that the social security system will be seriously undermined.' This interpretation appears to imply the lower or softer proportionality test. It does not appear to be necessary to show definitively that no other approach would have protected the interests concerned with less intrusion on free movement ('the same result cannot be achieved by less restrictive rules'), what the Member State must show is 'sufficient reason to expect' that the consequence of removing the prior authorization rule will be serious for the national public health system. So, according to the recital, Article 8(4) involves a weaker proportionality test than that adopted by the Court in its jurisprudence to date.

Of course, recitals are non-binding. But, nonetheless, they are to be used in interpretation of the binding text, because they are regarded by the Court as evidence of the intention of the authors.[345] However, in interpreting a Directive, the Court will also assume that the legislature intended the Directive to be consistent with the Treaty, as primary law. Where a Directive is open to two meanings, the one consistent with the Treaty[346] is to be preferred.[347] This suggests

[342] Art 5(4) TFEU (ex Art 5(3) EC).

[343] Case 36/75 *Rutili* [1975] ECR 1219 (workers); Case C33/74 *Van Binsbergen*, n 301 above (services); Case 120/78 *Cassis de Dijon* [1979], n 2 above (goods).

[344] For instance, in Case C–158/96 *Kohll*, n 2 above (though on non-hospital care), the Court stated that none of the parties involved, nor the governments of the MS, had shown 'that the rules were indispensible...' (para 52) to achieve their legitimate public interest objective. In Case C–368/98 *Vanbraekel*, n 260 above, there was no need to get to the level of strictness of the proportionality test, as 'it could not be argued that making the sickness insurance fund [pay for the treatment] would be liable to have a significant effect on the financing of the social security system (para 52). In Case C–157/99 *Geraets-Smits*, n 2 above, the proportionality test was stated to be that national rules 'do not exceed what is objectively necessary for that purpose and that the same result cannot be achieved by less restrictive rules' (para 75). This same point is repeated in para 68 of Case C–385/99 *Müller-Fauré*, n 270 above.

[345] Case 29/69 *Stauder* [1969] ECR 425, para 5; Case 83/78 *Pigs Marketing* [1978] ECR 2371, para 54.

[346] That is, in practice, the one consistent with the jurisprudence of the European Court of Justice on the Treaty.

[347] Case 218/82 *Tariff Quotas* [1983] ECR 4075.

that, unless the Court alters its interpretation or approach, the approach in the case law would still stand, and the Directive on patients' rights in cross-border healthcare must be interpreted as involving the current (strict) proportionality test. In this respect, then, properly interpreted, Article 8(4) does not change the existing legal position—irrespective of what the proposal says in the recital.

The distinction made in the proposal between hospital care and non-hospital care is a distinction that emerges from the fact patterns of the case law on free movement of patients. The proposed Directive appears to imply that national rules involving prior authorization of non-hospital care are never permissible in EU law.[348] This part of the proposal goes beyond what the Court has said about such national law under what is now Article 56 TFEU. *The fact patterns* of the rulings involve situations where rules involving prior authorization for non-hospital care have been found to be unjustified, and therefore unlawful in EU law,[349] and rules involving prior authorization for hospital care have been found (at least potentially) justified.[350] However, the *rationes* of the rulings imply that objective public interest justifications are available, where they are made out and are non-discriminatory and proportionate, in accordance with the Court's general case law on the internal market.

If the proposal becomes law, what will its relationship be with the TFEU, which is the basis for the Court's case law? The Treaty is primary law. The Court has said that it constitutes a 'constitutional charter'.[351] Thus, EU legislation cannot contradict or undermine the Treaty. Rather, the legislation must be interpreted consistently with the Treaty, or can be set aside as invalid under Article 263 TFEU or Article 267 TFEU. The Treaty provision at issue here is Article 56 TFEU on freedom to provide and receive cross-border services, which is subject to a possible exemption for 'objective public interests'. How is the Treaty affected when a Directive is adopted in the field that it covers?

The answer depends upon a distinction between 'field occupation' and 'minimum harmonization' measures. Where a Directive 'occupies a field', that is, the Directive harmonizes an area totally, including ensuring protection of the Treaty-based grounds for exemptions, Member States may not lawfully diverge from the Directive in national rules, even if in so doing they claim a legitimate public interest. The legitimate public interest is (presumed to be) protected by the EU Directive. However, if a Directive imposes only *minimum harmonization* requirements, that is, it sets only a floor of harmonization, then stricter or different national rules, which protect a legitimate public interest, are not pre-empted by it.

The wording, purpose, and context of a Directive determine whether it is a field-occupying or minimum harmonization measure. In this case, consider the wording of Article 1 of the proposal: 'This Directive establishes *a general framework* for the provision of safe, high quality and efficient cross-border healthcare.' This is supported by Recital 8 of the proposal: the Directive aims to 'establish a general

348 Art 7. 349 *Kohll*, n 2 above.
350 *Geraets-Smits*, n 2 above; *Müller-Fauré*, n 270 above.
351 *Les Verts*, n 277 above.

framework' whilst 'fully respecting the responsibilities of the Member States'. It is also supported by the context: Article 168(7) TFEU (ex Article 152(5) EC) provides that 'Union action . . . shall respect the responsibilities of the Member States for the . . . organisation and delivery of health services . . . '. Taking all these into account, the proposal must be a minimum harmonization measure. Therefore, relying on the argument that the proposal is only a 'minimum harmonization' Directive, and not a 'field occupying' Directive, it would still be open to a Member State or public health authority within a Member State to claim, under Article 56 TFEU, that restrictions on access to cross-border non-hospital care were justified, provided that the strict proportionality test of the case law had been met.

Article 11 deals with the applicable rules for when cross-border healthcare is provided. The proposed Directive sets a rule that the healthcare is provided 'in accordance with the legislation of the Member State of treatment'. This provision aims to clarify the legal position, with respect to matters such as non-contractual liability for damage, quality and safety, information management, and all the matters covered in Article 5. It responds to concerns from governments of Member States and healthcare providers, as well as patient-led NGOs, that patients might be receiving health services elsewhere within the EU, paid for by the home state, under the false assumption that, because the national authorities were paying, national law applied. A patient going abroad under the proposed Directive is only entitled to the legal protections given by the Member State where the treatment is given. Article 12 requires Member States to set up 'national contact points' for cross-border healthcare. The contact points must cooperate with each other, and provide information to patients,[352] help patients with dispute settlement involving another Member States, and 'facilitate the development of an international out-of-court settlement scheme for disputes arising from cross-border healthcare'.[353] There will be a network of national contact points, coordinated by the Commission.

Chapter IV on Cooperation on Healthcare is probably the most innovative of the provisions in the proposal.[354] Article 14 concerns recognition of prescriptions issued in another Member State. Lack of cross-border recognition of prescriptions is a major impediment to free movement of goods and services within the EU. Several cases before the Court have concerned national law applying to pharmacies and the supply of pharmaceuticals including prescription pharmaceuticals—for instance, the *DocMorris* case[355] and *Commission v Germany (Pharmacies)*.[356] The *DocMorris* case concerned an internet pharmacy, operating across the German/Dutch border. The Court found that national law prohibiting sale of

[352] As Palm and Glinos, n 232 above, point out, 'there is an opportunity and equity cost related to increasing the level of information about cross-border options while at the same time information about domestic options is also not optimal'.

[353] This last one would seem to be outside the scope of EU law.

[354] For further discussion see T Hervey, 'Co-operation between health care authorities in the Proposed Directive on patients' rights in cross-border health care' in J van de Gronden, M Krajewski, U Neergaard, and E Szyszcak (eds), *Health Care and EU Law* (2011 forthcoming).

[355] Case C–322/01 *Deutscher Apothekerverband eV v 0800 DocMorris NV and Jacques Waterval* [2003] ECR I–4887.

[356] Case C–141/07 [2008] ECR I–6935.

pharmaceuticals by internet and mail order inhibited the free movement of goods. However, the restriction could be justified with respect to prescription-only pharmaceuticals, because of the greater risks posed to consumers and the system of fixed prices applicable to them as part of the German health system.[357] In *Commission v Germany (Pharmacies)*, a German rule making it impossible in practice for German hospitals to be supplied on a regular basis by pharmacies established in other Member States was found to be justified on the ground of protection of public health.

Surveys of whether prescriptions are recognized by pharmacists across European borders, and about the possibility of electronic prescriptions being used, suggest that there are many barriers to prevent a prescription given in one Member State being fulfilled in another.[358] The new proposal will provide that restrictions on recognition of individual prescriptions have to be 'limited to what is necessary and proportionate to safeguard human health', 'non-discriminatory' and 'based on legitimate and justified doubts about the authenticity or content of an individual prescription'. In order to bring this provision into effect, the Commission—or rather a comitology committee—is charged with developing 'measures enabling a pharmacist to verify' whether a prescription is authentic. Verification is to be supported through a 'Community prescription template' and also by interoperability of e-prescriptions. The practical implications of implementation of these measures will be quite far reaching for prescribing practice and the operation of pharmacies across the EU. Whether the Directive will open up the types of markets at issue in the *Commission v Germany* case is less clear.

Article 15 concerns 'European reference networks'. This notion responds to the idea that the EU can 'add value' to public health service provision in individual Member States, in particular in areas of medical expertise where the incidence of the medical problem is very low within a single Member State. If such health services are provided, and resources and expertise pooled, at EU level then patients can benefit from economies of scale. Emergent networks of specialized providers of care for rare diseases have already been supported for some time through EU funding under the public health programmes administered by DG SANCO.[359] These networks share expertise, innovation, and best practice in the specialized

[357] Para 117. However, the Court found that no evidence of the necessity of the national rule had been submitted to the Court; see para 123.

[358] Eg, the Commission has launched enforcement proceedings against Estonia for its national rules prohibiting recognition of medical prescriptions made out by medical practitioners who are qualified to act in their Member State of establishment but are not registered in Estonia; see Commission, 'Free movement of services: infringement proceedings against Estonia and Portugal', IP/08/1033, Brussels, 26 June 2008.

[359] Decision of the Council and Ministers of Health for the Member States 91/317/EEC adopting a plan of action in the framework of the 1991 to 1993 'Europe against AIDS' programme, OJ [1991] L 175/26; European Parliament and Council Decision 1786/2002/EC adopting a programme of Community action in the field of public health (2003–2008)—Commission Statements, OJ [2002] L 271/1; European Parliament and Council Decision 1350/2007/EC establishing a second programme of Community action in the field of health (2008–13), OJ [2007] L 301/3.

areas in which they work. The proposal provides that Member States must facilitate their development.

Article 17 on 'management of new health technologies' is another example of an attempt to promote more efficient use of resources across the EU. At the moment each Member State individually assesses whether a new medical technology, new drug, or new treatment represents 'value for money' in the public health system.[360] The proposal requires the Member State to 'facilitate development of a network connecting the national authorities' that are responsible for this. Within the network, there is expected to be cooperation on health technology assessment. Such a sharing of decisions that are often highly politically charged[361] is likely to present significant challenges in the future.

The Commission's view is that the impact across the board of the proposed Directive—if it is adopted—will be limited, because of the relatively small numbers of cross-border patients.[362] No significant impact on national budgets is predicted. But for individual patients, the impact could be significant.

D. What Are the Relationships between EU Free Movement Law and Public Health Services?

Because some of the elements of public health systems are also goods and services traded within markets, it is not possible for Member States to organize their public health systems entirely to the exclusion of internal market law. This observation, which is trite law from the point of view of EU law,[363] is nevertheless still hotly contested by healthcare practitioners, public healthcare bodies and indeed the governments of the Member States.[364] The implications of the application of internal market law to public health systems are still being discovered through

[360] J Abraham and G Lewis, *Regulating medicines in Europe: competition, expertise, and public health* (2000).

[361] C Newdick, *Who Should We Treat? Rights, Rationing and Resources in the NHS* (2005).

[362] See W Palm and I Glinos, 'Enabling patient mobility in the European Union: between free movement and coordination' in Mossialos et al (eds) (2010), n 232 above: 'Although the available data on the extent of cross-border care is extremely patchy, it is commonly agreed that the current volume of patient mobility is relatively low, estimated at around 1 per cent of overall public expenditure on healthcare' (Commission Communication, 'Consultation regarding Community action on health services', SEC (2006) 1195/4, 26 September 2006, 6). On the available data see also R Busse and E van Ginneken, 'Cross-Border Healthcare data' in *Cross-Border Healthcare: Mapping and Analysing Health Systems Diversity*, European Observatory, 2006, 219–58.

[363] Many cases, dating back to the 1960s, concern the free movement of pharmaceuticals and medical devices. The principle that medical treatment can be a service in the sense of internal market law was established in Case C–159/90 *Society for the Protection of Unborn Children Ireland v Grogan* [1991] ECR I–4685. See S Greer, *Power struggle: the politics and policy consequences of patient mobility in Europe* (2008); S Greer, 'Choosing paths in European Union health services policy: a political analysis of a critical juncture' (2008) 18 Journal of European Social Policy 219, describing the cases as a 'critical juncture', which is a break with the past practice.

[364] See, eg, Art 168(7) TFEU. AG Tesauro described healthcare as 'an island beyond the reach of Community rules'; see Opinion of the Advocate General Tesauro in Cases C–120/95 *Decker*, n 2 above and C–158/96 *Kohll*, n 2 above.

litigation. There are also emergent legislative and 'new governance' responses to this litigation,[365] both at national and EU level.

From the point of view of patients, the parallel routes in EU law, whereby migrant patients are entitled to receive cross-border health services, involve very different bases on which the health services are provided.[366] Under Article 56 TFEU, the basis of the entitlement is free movement of services. Thus migrant patients are treated as if the treatment was provided in the state to which the patient is affiliated. Under the older route of Regulation 1408/71/EEC, now Regulation 883/2004/EC, the basis of the entitlement is free movement of workers (or persons, in the case of their families). Cross-border patients are treated as if they were insured in the state in which they receive the treatment. Consequently, different benefit packages, tariffs, and administrative formalities apply in each case, and the consequences of application of EU free movement law for public health services are different. This distinction will remain even if the proposed Directive on patients' rights in cross-border healthcare is adopted.

The free movement of patients case law on 'undue delay' has prompted policy or legislative changes in some Member States.[367] In those states, patients now have a guarantee of treatment within a particular time within the home state. If this is not met, the patient may seek treatment elsewhere in the EU and be reimbursed by the home state. Other Member States[368] have redefined what constitutes treatment 'abroad', so as to include—at least within certain circumstances—health services received within the EU as part of their national systems. These reforms increase choice for patients, but at the same time have implications for the territorial basis of public health systems.[369]

The distinction within the case law between hospital and non-hospital care, which the Commission seeks to embed within the proposed Directive on patients' rights in cross-border healthcare, is problematic. It is true that the hospital sector enjoys distinctive characteristics, and hospitals are significant institutions within public health systems. This justifies the detailed planning that goes into hospitals' geographical placement; the populations they serve; what services they provide, to whom, through what 'gatekeeping' procedures; and how they are organized: all of which are related to equal access, quality, efficiency, and cost control, and public health in the sense of population health. However, all these matters are important for non-hospital elements of public health systems too. Distinguishing the hospital sector on what is a matter of degree, rather than a difference in substance, is legally indefensible. Moreover, embedding special immunity from EU law for hospitals, and not for other public health service institutions, within EU free movement law, is likely to discourage public health

[365] Hervey in de Búrca and Scott, n 324 above.

[366] Palm and Glinos in Mossialos et al (eds) (2010), n 232 above.

[367] See Palm and Glinos in Mossialos et al (eds), n 232 above, citing changes in Denmark, Ireland, and also Norway. However, effects in other states seem to be minimal (see, eg, E Bergamini, 'Italy', in M Krajewski et al (eds), n 34 above, 302) or designed to restrict free movement as much as permissible (see, eg, T Madell, 'Sweden' in M Krajewski et al (eds), n 34 above, 431).

[368] France, Sweden.

[369] D Sindberg Martinsen, *EU for the Patients: Developments, Impacts, Challenges* (2007).

services from altering the current arrangements with respect to treatments provided within hospitals. The proposed Directive's approach of the 'exempted list' of non-hospital care is likely to prove similarly inflexible. Developments in healthcare practice are encouraging more focused and targeted hospital use, alongside a move to more community-based care, in view of the risks of picking up secondary infections in hospitals, the inefficiencies of hospital care, and so on. Reifying a distinction between hospital and non-hospital care within EU law will introduce unjustified brakes on such developments.

In general, however, although the litigation concerning cross-border patients has received significant attention, on balance this very specific body of EU law is likely to affect public health services only at the margins. Numbers of cross-border patients are small.[370] EU law requires some enhanced entitlements for some patients, in particular in border regions, and pensioners who have retired to another (usually warmer) Member State.[371] Member States have slowly (and reluctantly) adjusted the administration of their public health systems to comply with the requirements of EU law on free movement of patients. The proposed Directive, if adopted, will smooth out some remaining legal questions.

What is likely to prove more significant is the application of EU free movement law, especially that on free movement of services and freedom of establishment, on other regulatory aspects of public health systems, including, for instance, taxation arrangements concerning health insurance contributions.[372] Now that the Court has determined that public health services are services in the sense of Article 56 TFEU, litigation is being brought by health service providers (in particular, 'big business' providers, such as international hospital chains, pharmaceutical manufacturers and wholesalers) seeking to offer their services in other Member States. Also, *internal* domestic competitors are seeking to employ EU law (for instance, by complaining to the Commission of breach of Article 56 TFEU), to challenge regulatory measures of public health systems that limit their freedom to operate on the domestic market. For instance, in a case before the Court at the time of writing,[373] Spanish pharmacists are using EU law on freedom of establishment to challenge Spanish law that restricts the number of pharmacies that may be operated within a particular geographical area, in order to ensure that people living in less populous areas have access to pharmaceuticals. As Gekiere, Baeten, and Palm note, EU internal market law is being used politically, to 'criticise the rigidity of healthcare systems and plead for market-oriented reforms,

[370] For details on different types of cross-border patient activity, see M Rosenmoller, M McKee, and R Baeten (eds), *Patient Mobility in the European Union: Learning from Experience* (2006); I Glinos and R Baeten, *A Literature Review of Cross-Border Patient Mobility in the European Union* (2006).

[371] For further discussion see Palm and Glinos, n 232 above; P Dwyer, 'Retired EU Migrants, healthcare rights and European social citizenship' (2001) 23 Journal of Social Welfare and Family Law 311. For instance, the Commission has commenced infringement proceedings against Spain for failing to allow EU pensioners access to free medication when they stay temporarily in Spain; see Commission, 'Commission warns Spain on EU pensioners' access to necessary healthcare', IP/09/295, 19 February 2009.

[372] See, eg, Case C–544/07 *Rüffler* [2009] ECR I–3389.

[373] Joined Cases C–570 and 571/07 *Pérez and Gómez*, Opinion of AG Maduro, 30 September 2009.

enhancing free choice and opening new markets'. Given changes that are taking place within public health systems, it will be difficult for Member States to avoid these arguments by structuring their public health systems 'in a non-market way'.[374] To the extent that such arguments are successful, the free movement rules affect, or have the potential to affect, the regulatory autonomy of Member States in organizing their national public health systems.[375] Health policy actors are concerned about the deregulatory effects of these processes on the steering instruments of public health systems, in particular that 'inconsiderate liberalisation and deregulation in healthcare could make health systems less effective, more costly and less equitable'.[376] There are particular concerns about the quality of care, where wide variations exist between the ways and extents to which Member States have implemented policies and embedded practices to ensure high quality of care.[377]

Palm and Glinos take the view that the assault by the Court on national prior authorization systems has an important symbolic significance. Prior authorization is only one of several measures used within public health systems to control costs and ensure safe, high-quality, and efficient health services. Seen alongside the potential for application of EU competition law to public health services, the Court's jurisprudence on prior authorization systems can be seen as a harbinger for much more fundamental conflicts between the objectives of public health systems and obligations under EU law. A similar symbolic effect can be seen in the English High Court's ruling in the *Watts* case to the effect that the freedom to seek and provide services in EU law entitles English patients to look for treatment abroad. While this is uncontroversial from the point of view of EU law, existing English law (and indeed human rights law) provided no basis on which national health service patients could claim they have a 'right to treatment'.[378]

As with competition law, then, perhaps the most important effect of EU free movement law on public health services is that the very basis of its reasoning (free movement of services) entails a shift in conceptualization towards a set of (individual) health services and away from national healthcare systems. Legal challenges to public health systems on the basis of free movement law involve identifying specific restrictions on services within the internal market, thus separating out specific services from the system as a whole. In order to defend public health systems, within the constraints of the structures of EU free movement law, Member States must defend each specific policy or practice within their national public health

[374] G Davies, 'Welfare as a Service' (2002) 19 Legal Issues of Economic Integration 27.

[375] Gekiere, Baeten, and Palm, n 257 above, claim that 'progressively almost any regulatory or institutional aspect of healthcare provision can be challenged as a potential obstacle to the free movement'.

[376] Gekiere, Baeten, and Palm, n 257 above, citing, eg, A Maynard, 'European health policy challenges' (2005) 14 S1 Health Economics 256.

[377] There is particularly great diversity on the quality of clinical care. See Gekiere, Baeten, and Palm, n 257 above, citing H Legido-Quigley, M McKee, E Nolte, and I Glinos, 'Assuring the quality of health care in the European Union', European Observatory on Health Systems and Policies, Observatory Studies Series No 12, available at: <http://www.euro.who.int/document/e91397.pdf>.

[378] J Montgomery, 'Impact of EU Law on English Healthcare Law' in M Dougan and E Spaventa, *Social Welfare and EU Law* (2003).

systems, on an individual, case-by-case basis, under the jurisprudence of 'proportionate objective public interest justification'. The logic of the reasoning in the Court's case law on justification cannot be faulted. But it rests on a premise—that elements of what were previously seen as holistic systems, immune to internal market law, should be subjected (on a case-by-case basis) to the rigours of that body of law—the application of which remains highly contested for social services of general interest, such as health services. There are existing moves with European health systems to increase the use of market logics, particularly in reforms from the 1980s onwards. The application of EU law supports the overall direction of these reforms.[379]

Thus the entire structure of EU free movement law involves a move from viewing public health services as part of an integrated system of protection, based on territorial solidarity, towards viewing such services as a system of individually based entitlements or rights. Moreover,[380] these entitlements are constructed as 'negative rights', the right to freedom of choice, without state interference, removing state intervention in individual liberty, and promoting freedom to choose medical treatment in another Member State. The original notion of the 'right to health' in European societies is based on a 'positive right',[381] requiring states to take positive action to ensure the right is respected, protected, and fulfilled. The main emphasis of such positive social rights consists in a *claim on* the public authorities for protection and assistance, rather than the *freedom from* state interference that is said to characterize 'negative' civil and political rights.[382] Thus, positive rights are framed in terms of collective interests, and have strong relationships with equity and solidarity. By contrast, a strong claim of individual 'negative' rights (to freedom of choice) may undermine collective decisions reached through constitutionally mandated political processes about the agreed allocation of collective resources, and may in fact bring about a substantively unjust result in terms of their allocation.[383]

[379] RB Saltman, R Busse, and E Mossialos, *Regulating entrepreneurial behaviour in European health care systems*, European Observatory on Health Care Systems Series (2002).

[380] See Palm and Glinos, n 232 above; C Newdick, 'Citizenship, free movement and health care: cementing individual rights by corroding social solidarity' (2006) 43 CML Rev 1645.

[381] On the nature of such 'positive' social rights, see, eg, H Steiner and P Alston, *International Human Rights in Context: Law, Politics, Morals* (2000); M Craven, 'A View from Elsewhere: Social Rights, International Covenant and the EU Charter of Fundamental Rights' in C Costello (ed), *Fundamental Social Rights: Current European Legal Protection and the Challenge of the EU Charter on Fundamental Rights* (2001); A Eide, C Krause, and A Rosas (eds), *Economic, Cultural and Social Rights* (2001). On 'the right to health' more generally, see V Leary, 'The Right to Health in International Human Rights Law' (1994) 1 Health and Human Rights 3; B Toebes, *The Right to Health as a Human Right in International Law* (1999). On the 'right to health' in EU law, see T Hervey, 'The right to health in EU law' in T Hervey and J Kenner (eds), *Economic and Social Rights under the EU Charter of Fundamental Rights* (2003) 193–222; T Hervey, 'We don't see a connection: the 'right to health' in the EU Charter and European Social Charter', in G de Búrca and B de Witte (eds), *Social Rights in Europe* (2005), 305–35.

[382] See further A Rosas and A Eide, 'Economic, Social and Cultural Rights: A Universal Challenge' and A Eide, 'Economic, Social and Cultural Rights as Human Rights' in A Eide, C Krause, and A Rosas, n 382 above.

[383] See contributions of M Minow, K Anderson, and M Mandler, Human Rights Program, Harvard Law School and François-Xavier Bagnoud Center for Health and Human Rights Workshop, *Economic and Social Rights and the Right to Health*, September 1993, available at: <http://www.law.harvard.edu/programs/HRP/Publications/economic1.html>, 4.

An individual travelling to another Member State to receive healthcare (perhaps more quickly), effectively bypasses policy choices made for the allocation of resources within the national public health system. Moreover, those able to travel to another Member State are often not those most in need of healthcare.[384] Thus applying free movement law to public health services also has equity implications. In short, the structure of EU law on free movement of services, when applied to public health services, has the effect of emphasizing patient choice at the expense of efficiency, solidarity, and equality of access, which are fundamental values of European healthcare systems.[385]

5. Conclusions: The Structures of EU Law and Ways Forward

Where EU internal market and competition law interact with public health services, the basic structures of EU law are based on a series of binary relationships: undertaking/not undertaking; competition/not competition; economic act/exercise of official authority; competitive market/social solidarity; procurement and tendering/state aids; private service/social security entitlement; competitive private service/public service; remuneration/taxation; social insurance/taxation-based; hospital/non-hospital; proportionate/disproportionate; competence/no competence, and so on. These binary relationships are too simple. They are insufficiently flexible as a regulatory framework to respond to the structures that are currently being developed in the Member States for delivery of welfare entitlements such as public health services. Moreover, added together, they create incoherent matrices in which a particular element of a public health service belongs in one category in one set of binary relationships, but in the opposite category in another, related, relationship. The legal inconsistencies that arise are unsatisfactory in themselves. These binary relationships also support the tendency, noted throughout this chapter, of EU law to contribute to a move towards a conceptualization of public health services as comprising *separate services*, rather than as forming a coherent integrated *system*. Public health systems in the EU do partially rely on ideas of services or goods being provided within (regulated) markets—and they may do so increasingly in the future. But European public health systems also rely on values of solidarity, which in practice are achievable only within holistic structures in which individual desires are sometimes secondary to collective determinations of entitlement within the context of what the system can afford. What is needed is a balance between these different conceptions of a public health service. National constitutional settlements provide such a balance. But their equilibrium has been upset by the application of EU law to public health services. The current structure or underlying

[384] As Palm and Glinos, n 232 above, explain: 'These population groups tend to be more articulate, confident and targeted in terms of their health care needs and expectations.' See Z Cooper and J Le Grand, 'Choice, competition and the political left' (2007) 13 (4) Eurohealth 18. They are likely to be more knowledgeable about their rights and more familiar with travelling abroad; and can afford the transport costs as well as the medical expenses before reimbursement.

[385] Hervey and Trubek, n 324 above.

'code' of EU law supports the former conceptualization of public health services, to the detriment of the latter. We cannot go back to a position where public health services are totally outside the scope of EU law. Rather, what we need now is a revised balance within EU law: a new structure or underlying code. This new structure needs to incorporate a better understanding of the roles of markets in welfare provision in Western societies, including the EU's Member States, in the 21st century. We need to rewrite the 'code' of EU law, to enshrine the new values upon which, and contexts within which, public health service provision is based, and to move away from a framing vision that is based on a series of simple, binary relationships, and on too much of a reliance on conceptualizations of healthcare services primarily as individual and separable entitlements. Such a 'rewriting' could take a number of (not mutually exclusive) legal forms.

One possibility is the reformulation of the Treaties, to better reflect the reality of the interactions between public health services and EU law than the current statement in Article 168 TFEU (ex Article 152 EC). However, although Article 168 TFEU has changed in successive Treaty revisions, the Treaty provisions on free movement and competition law have remained the same. Moreover, the difficulties in ratifying the Treaty of Lisbon suggest little political appetite for the almost constant Treaty revisions that characterized the 1990s, so, at least for the foreseeable future, further Treaty reform is unlikely to prove a viable option in practice.

A second possibility is to call on the legislature, and also in some cases other forms of networked governance process,[386] to act as a corrective to the Court's jurisprudence on the application of free movement or competition law to public health services. For instance, the legal position of 'social services of general interest' could be strengthened within the relevant legal instruments.[387] But EU-level legislative solutions look increasingly unlikely to gain the necessary political support. For instance, after a significant number of Member States blocked the Commission's proposed Patients' Rights Directive at Council in early December

[386] For a discussion of how the OMC may be used to encourage reflexive processes, involving social and economic discourses reflecting upon one another's objectives, see M Dawson, 'The ambiguity of social Europe in the open method of coordination' (2009) 34 ELR 55. For discussion of how the tensions between competition and 'social Europe' may be resolved in 'old' and 'new' governance, see I Maher and C Scott (eds), *Regulating Markets and Social Europe: New Governance in the EU*, special issue of the (2009) 15 (2) European Law Journal. There is a significant body of literature on the use of 'new governance' to solve social or welfare problems, both pertaining to the USA and the EU. See, eg, J Zeitlin and D Trubek (eds), *Governing work and welfare in a new economy* (2003); J Zeitlin and P Pochet with L Magnussen (eds), *The OMC in Action: the European Employment and Social Inclusion Strategies* (2005); D Ashiagbor, *The European Employment Strategy: Labour Market Regulation and New Governance* (2005); G de Búrca and J Scott, n 324 above; G de Búrca and J Scott (eds), 'Narrowing the Gap? Law and New Approaches to Governance in the European Union', Special Issue (2007) 13 (3) Columbia Journal of European Law; C Sabel and J Zeitlin, 'Learning from difference: the new architecture of experimentalist governance in the European Union', (2008) 14 ELJ 271. Space precludes a detailed discussion of how the Court could be assisted by 'new governance' activity in this field; but see T Hervey, 'Adjudicating in the Shadow of the Informal Settlement: The European Court of Justice, 'new governance' and social welfare' Current Legal Problems (2010 forthcoming).

[387] Proposed by Gekiere, Baeten, and Palm, in Mossialos et al (eds) (2010), n 257 above. Art 14 TFEU (ex Art 16 EC) gives a new legal basis on which to establish principles and conditions to enable services of general economic interest to fulfil their missions.

2009, the Commission announced that it was considering withdrawing the proposal.[388]

Therefore, although legislative institutions will have a role to play, the principal change in institutional practice will have to come from courts. Both national courts (and competition authorities) and the Court of Justice of the European Union will be involved. The underlying structures of EU law need to be reinterpreted, to achieve a different balance between individual entitlements within a market and solidarity, in the context of public healthcare systems. The Court (which currently decides where, in terms of a binary relationship, a particular fact pattern falls) should now develop a more explicitly value-based approach, which takes account of changes to public health service provision within the Member States. There are changes to the Treaties, adopted at Lisbon, upon which the Court could base such a new approach. For instance, the 'values' of the EU now include both 'freedom' and 'equality', in a 'society in which . . . solidarity . . . prevail[s]'.[389] In defining its policies and activities, the EU is required to take into account requirements linked to 'protection of human health'.[390] The old Articles 2 and 3 EC, on the tasks and activities of the EU, which put the internal market and competition 'up front', and thus implied a duty on the EU institutions to place a strong focus on free movement and free competition, have been repealed. Their nearest replacement is Article 3 TEU on the aims of the EU. These are to promote peace, the EU's values and the well-being of its peoples. No one would disagree that health is a key indicator of well-being. Article 3 TEU includes a more balanced list of activities for the EU than the old Treaty provisions. The list begins with the internal market, but includes the combating of social exclusion (another core activity of public health systems) and promotion of solidarity. It also includes a new obligation on the EU to work for a 'highly competitive *social market economy*'.[391] Given that public health systems are among the mechanisms that Member States use to achieve these aims, following Lisbon, there is an even stronger argument to the effect that there is a duty to interpret EU law in a way that reflects a readjusted balance between markets and solidarity mechanisms. Taken as a whole, the Lisbon amendments do not imply that public health services should be *insulated* from free movement and competition law. Rather, the place of public health services *as systems* must be determined *within* a single European market and indeed regulatory space. Because it posits a binary position, according to which *inter alia* component services are

[388] With Spain instrumental in leading the group of Member States blocking the proposal, and the Spanish health minister on record as being personally in opposition to it, it seems unlikely that the proposal will be adopted under the Spanish Presidency in the first six months of 2010. See M Slegers, 'Health Council: EP Rapporteur regrets failure of talks on cross-border health care' *Europolitics* 2 December 2009; J Rankin, 'Ministers reject proposal on cross-border health care' *European Voice* 1 December 2009. The Commission may be right in an assessment that there is insufficient political momentum behind the proposal.

[389] Art 2 TEU (new).

[390] Art 9 TFEU (new).

[391] Art 3(3) TEU (in part, ex Art 2 TEU), italics added. Widely perceived to be a response to the French referendum rejecting the Treaty establishing a Constitution for Europe, see I Maher, 'Introduction: Regulating Markets and Social Europe: New Governance in the EU' (2009) 15 ELJ 155, 156.

either inside, or outside, the application of 'ordinary' EU law, the current inherent structure of EU law allows the Court to avoid determining where public health *systems* belong, and how they fit, within the contours of the EU's regulatory space. In short, my argument is that it is time that EU law, and especially the Court, stepped up to that task.

How should the Court reinterpret the place of public health services within EU free movement and competition law? Because the 'social' is legitimated at national level in the EU's multilevel constitutional processes, the Court should give greater respect to social settlements reached at national levels.[392] In practice, this means, for instance, adopting a softer version of the proportionality test,[393] to check compliance of national policies with EU competition *and* free movement law. This greater respect for national choices is *not* mandated because of the separation of spheres, with the social belonging to the Member States, and the economic at EU level. Rather it is because *both* spheres (which incidentally are not separable except in theory) are regulated within the EU's multilevel polity. But in European societies, social services of general interest, including public health services, are provided through systems that express solidarity *in themselves*, as part of the systemic (and even symbolic) statements of obligations of redistributive community, which are expressed at national level within the EU. This is the case whether, within these systems, a specific service is provided entirely through state-owned institutions, or through private enterprises, or through a 'third way'[394] mix of markets and the state. It follows that if—and only if—Member States seek to gain efficiencies in their social provision, that is not to be primarily (with their implicit agreement or acceptance, expressed through the Treaty provisions on free movement and competition) through internal market law, driven by litigation. Rather, such a convergence around a 'European social model' that also benefits from efficiencies that some market models can provide, should come either through

[392] See N Boeger, 'Solidarity and EC competition law' (2007) 32 ELR 319. The practical effect of this proposal is similar to Joerges and Rödl's 'conflict of laws approach' or 'deliberative supranationalism'; see Ch Joerges and F Rödl, 'Informal Politics, Formalised Law and the "Social Deficit" of European Integration: Reflections after the Judgments of the ECJ in *Viking* and *Laval*' (2009) 15 ELJ 1; Ch Joerges and F Rödl, 'On the "Social Deficit" of the European Integration Project and its Perpetuation through the ECJ Judgements in *Viking* and *Laval*' RECON Working Paper 2008/06, available at: <http://www.reconproject.eu/projectweb/portalproject.RECONWorkingPapers.html>; Ch Joerges and J Neyer, 'From Intergovernmental Bargaining to Deliberative Political Processes' (1997) 3 ELJ 273. However, Joerges and Rödl's paradigm of 'horizontal constitutionalism' differs from the paradigm proposed here, which remains within the more traditional 'supranational constitutionalism' (JHH Weiler, *The Constitution of Europe* (1999); FG Jacobs, *The Sovereignty of Law: The European Way* (2007)) understanding of relations between EU and national law, and assumes a greater responsibility for courts in general and the European Court of Justice, as the EU's 'constitutional court', in particular.

[393] The Court already recognizes that different versions of proportionality apply in different circumstances, see, eg, Case C–558/07 *SPCM*, judgment 7 July 2009, nyr in ECR, Opinion of AG Kokott, paras 71–7; Case C–553/07 *Rijkeboer* [2009] ECR I–3889, Opinion of AG Ruiz-Jarabo Colomer, para 58, fn 46; Case C–127/07 *Société Arcelor Atlantique et Lorraine* [2008] ECR I–9895, Opinion of AG Poiares Maduro, paras 32–4. Thanks to Niamh Nic Shiubhne for pointing this out.

[394] See A Giddens, *The Third Way* (1998); A Giddens, P Diamond, and R Liddle (eds), *Global Europe, Social Europe* (2006); A Giddens, *Europe in the Global Age* (2007).

new modes of governance, or through EU-level legislation in accordance with the currently agreed constitutional settlement in the Treaties. In other words, ironically, the Court needs to lead by stepping back, so that litigation is no longer the sole driver of the process by which the relationships between EU law and public health services are determined. But the Court also needs to lead by reconceptualizing the place of public health services within EU law.

The implications of this approach are apparently fundamental. They suggest the end of the separation of economic and social competences which is the normative constitutional structure implied by an ordo-liberal approach to the EU, with the strict divisions of competences as a legitimating feature and justification of EU internal market law. Perhaps the separation of economic and social competences never really captured the EU's constitutional processes. Or perhaps it became less and less appropriate following amendments to EU law following the Treaty on European Union in the early 1990s, with its wide-ranging new policy competences in social fields for the EU institutions. Either way, social services of general interest such as public health services are now *both* firmly within the scope of EU free movement and competition law, *and* a matter of national competence.

Therefore what I am proposing involves nothing less than a fundamental shift in the structure of EU free movement and competition law. It involves a recognition that EU law is not (if it ever has been) simply, or even essentially or fundamentally about markets, leaving 'the social' to the Member States and national law.[395] The roles of EU internal market and competition law are no longer (if they ever were) simply a *means* to achieve movement between markets, opening markets, and preventing nationality-based discrimination. Rather, EU free movement and competition law should become (or have become) a *locus* within which we collectively determine the balance of values, between (economic) freedom and (social) security; between competition and solidarity.

Post scriptum

This chapter was completed in December 2009. Since then, three key developments have taken place in the relevant law. First, Regulation 1408/71/EEC has now been repealed and replaced by Regulation 883/2004/EC. The text above has been altered at proof stage to reflect this change. Second, the proposed Directive on patients' rights in cross-border healthcare has successfully completed its first reading

[395] Contrast F Scharpf, 'Legitimacy in the Multilevel European Polity' MPIfG Working Paper 09/1, <http://www.mpifg.de>; Publications, Working Papers, 19: 'European law is not the expression of shared value but an instrument to discipline and transform national policies, institutions and practices'. Joerges and Rödl, n 15 above take the view that the characterization of the EU as a 'market-embedded polity governed by an economic constitution', ostensibly the position up to the TEU, is 'too simplistic by far'. By the time the TEU was establishing new policy competences in labour law and social/welfare fields, the idea that the EU was constituted simply as a system of free movement and free competition was completely out of step with the legal norms constituting the EU. More detail in C Joerges, 'Economic Law, the Nation State and the Maastricht Treaty' in R Dehousse (ed), *Europe After Maastricht: an Ever Closer Union?* (1994), at 29–62.

by the European Parliament (following over 800 amendments to the Commission's text). In spite of Spanish opposition, a compromise version of the Council text was agreed under the Spanish Council Presidency in June 2010. The revised text includes a change to the legal basis, to include Article 168 TFEU, alongside Article 114 TFEU. Greater patient choice has been promoted, at the expense of further complicating the relationship between the proposed Directive and Regulation 883/2004/EC. Where a patient is entitled to authorization under Regulation 883/2004/EC, this is to be granted 'unless otherwise requested by the patient'. Chapter II of the proposal has been revised, to cover only responsibilities of Member States with regards to *cross-border* healthcare, and distinguishes between the responsibilities of the Member State of treatment and the Member State of affiliation. Chapter III concerns reimbursement of the costs of cross-border healthcare. A new provision—at the behest of Spain with its large migrant pensioner population—clarifies the position of pensioners living in another Member State but returning to their country of origin for healthcare. The country of origin will be responsible for paying. The distinction between hospital and non-hospital care remains. However, the category 'hospital care' has been augmented in practice by reference to healthcare that is 'subject to planning' because it involves highly specialized cost-intensive infrastructure or equipment; and 'treatments presenting a particular risk for the patient or the population' or which raise serious concerns about quality or safety of care. An extended list of situations where Member States may refuse prior authorization for cross-border healthcare now includes where there is a reasonable certainty of an abnormal risk to the patient; where there is a reasonable certainty that the general public will be exposed to a substantial safety hazard; and where the proposed healthcare providers raise serious and concrete concerns about standards and guidelines on quality of care and patient safety. The wording of Chapters IV and V has been softened in various respects. For instance, 'measures' (which can include hard law) has been replaced with the softer 'guidelines'; there is a move away from mandatory cooperation supported by comitology, towards a model based on incentives for cooperation; and the powers of the Commission under comitology have been circumscribed by opt-out provisions. Third, Cases C–570 and 571 *Pérez and Gómez* were decided on 1 June 2010. The Court did not decline to hear the case on the basis that the matter raised was 'internal' to one Member State: Spanish pharmacists were challenging Spanish law for breach of EU free movement law. The Court held that a national rule restricting the number of pharmacies on a geographical basis, as part of national healthcare planning, would not, in general, breach Article 56 TFEU. However, the Court held that such a rule would do so, in so far as such rules prevent, in a particular area, the establishment of sufficient pharmacies to ensure adequate pharmaceutical services [para 114].

Index